The Growth of the Mind

The Growth of the Mind

AND THE ENDANGERED
ORIGINS OF INTELLIGENCE

Stanley I. Greenspan, M.D.

WITH BERYL LIEFF BENDERLY

A MERLOYD LAWRENCE BOOK

PERSEUS BOOKS

Reading, Massachusetts

Library of Congress Catalog Card Number: 98-86948

ISBN 0-7382-0026-3

Perseus Books is a member of the Perseus Books Group

Cover design by Sara Eisenman
Text design by Karen Savary
Production editor: Beth Burleigh Fuller
Set in 11-point Minion by Shepard Poorman

1 2 3 4 5 6 7 8 9-DOH-020100999897
First paperback printing, August 1998

Find us on the World Wide Web at http://www.aw.com/gb/

*Dedicated to my wife Nancy, my children
Elizabeth, Jake, and Sarah, my parents Jean and
Phil, and my brother Kenneth*

Contents

Acknowledgments

I WISH TO EXPRESS MY SPECIAL APPRECIATION TO MY WIFE NANCY for her thoughtful and challenging discussion of the ideas in the book and to Serena Wider, Steven Porges, and the late Reginald Lourie for many years of generative collaboration and clinical work, research, and theory-building. My thanks to Jan Tunney for her very helpful assistance with the manuscript and reference preparation and to Sarah Miller for her sensitive support of the office and the families we have worked with. I also wish to express my gratitude to Merloyd Lawrence for her unusual sensitivity and insight in organizing and clarifying this work.

The Growth of the Mind

Questioning a Historical Dichotomy

IN RECENT YEARS, THROUGH OUR RESEARCH AND THAT OF others, we have found unexpected common origins for the mind's highest capacities: intelligence, morality, and sense of self. We have charted critical stages in the mind's early growth, most of which occur even before our first thoughts are registered. At each stage certain critical experiences are necessary. Contrary to traditional notions, however, these experiences are not cognitive but are types of subtle emotional exchanges. In fact, emotions, not cognitive stimulation, serve as the mind's primary architect.

Historically, psychologists and philosophers have tended to separate emotions and cognition. More recently mental capacities have been further divided into different types of intelligence. "Emotional intelligence" is said to be involved in social interactions and empathy while "moral intelligence" is involved in a sense of right and wrong. Various types of cognitive intelligence (e.g.: "multiple intelligences") are said to be involved in verbal, math, music, artistic, and other skills. In our own work, however, we have discovered that these different mental abilities are not separate types of intelligence. Instead, they are an outgrowth of the same early emotional interactions and formative stages.

While charting these earliest stages in the growth of the mind, we have been confronted with mounting evidence that such growth is becoming seriously endangered by modern institutions and social patterns. There exists a growing disregard for the importance of mind-building emotional experiences in almost every aspect of daily life: child care (especially out-of-home care), education, marriage, psychotherapy, conflict resolution, and approaches to violence and to helping at-risk families. The lack of this foundation can even be seen in the processes we use to communicate, govern, and build international cooperation. Ironically, the very mind that created a complex society is now that same society's potential victim.

In the chapters that follow, we will first explore the mind's emotional architecture and map its deepest levels. Then we will discuss the practices, beliefs, and social processes that will determine its future.

The elevation of the cognitive over the emotional aspect of our minds has deep-seated origins. Ever since the ancient Greeks, philosophers have elevated the rational side of the mind above the emotional and seen the two as separate. Intelligence, in this view, is necessary to govern and restrain the base passions. This concept has been profoundly influential in Western thought; indeed, it has shaped some of our most basic institutions and beliefs. Modern psychologists such as Jean Piaget, while advancing our understanding of the dynamic interactions and cognitive strategies that children use to learn from and about their environment, have continued to regard intelligence as relatively independent of affect or emotion.[1] For his part, Freud, even in his pioneering observations on the role of emotions in shaping personality, also viewed them as separate from and even antagonistic to intelligence. He saw the rational "rider," the ego, as guiding and controlling the passionate "horse," the libido.[2] Because of this dichotomy, our culture has an immense, longstanding intellectual and institutional investment in the notion that reason and emotion are separate and irreconcilable and that, in a civilized society, rationality must prevail.

But are these long-held assumptions correct? Striking new results from a variety of disciplines—from research into infant development, neuroscience, and clinical work with infants, children, and adults—are revealing some gaps in these traditional beliefs.

Consider this encounter between a psychologist and the twelve-month-old child I will call Cara. The child sits in her mother's lap at a table, staring defiance at a psychologist who holds out a scarlet peg and motions toward a bright blue board. Won't she put it in a hole, he asks encouragingly. Won't she try, her mother cajoles. Cara, as she's done many times before, grabs the peg and hurls it to the floor.

Is she, as her mother fears, cognitively delayed? Does a one-year-old who habitually throws food and toys but never babbles like other children her age have a significant intellectual deficit? With no better luck at eliciting Cara's interest in hunting for a bead hidden under a cup, the examiner concludes that, yes, cognitive delay is very likely.

For fifty years, experts have asked babies like Cara to sit still in their mothers' laps, pay attention, and perform prescribed tasks so that adults can figure out how smart they are. For fifty years, experts have consigned those tots unable to grasp and comply with these arcane requests to various multisyllablically labeled categories of developmental deficit. Specialists have long insisted that carefully scoring how well a tiny child fits pegs into boards, sorts cards by shape, or hunts beads under cups accurately measures her intelligence and the growth of her competence.

But new results from research and clinical practice now suggest that this entire approach rests on false premises. Consider what happened when a second examiner took a different approach with Cara. He first watched her playing by herself and saw an active, eager explorer. She listened to the sound of toy cars crashing, examined a rubber ball's rough surface, tried to yank on her mother's nose.

At the examiner's suggestion, the mother permitted the pull and responded, "*Toot toot!*" Cara smiled and pulled again. This time "*Oop shoop!*" greeted her effort, bringing a bigger smile. Then Mom gestured for Cara to offer her own nose for pulling. The delighted child thrust out her scrunched, beaming face. Mother gently squeezed and, to her astonishment, heard her joyful daughter utter "*Mo mo.*" These contributions to the game were Cara's very first distinct sound.

Seeing Cara engage in this complex if wordless "conversation" convinced the examiner that her overall cognitive development fell well within the normal range. Further observation revealed an extremely energetic, highly physical toddler who liked to have her own way and control her surroundings. When her mother altered her parenting style to encourage many more such playful exchanges, Cara's energy quickly became more focused, her babbling richer. If a series of such simple, pleasurable "discussions" with her mother could reveal Cara's capacity for language development, then any system of testing or conception of intellect that marked her as cognitively delayed has serious flaws. Clearly, as Cara's thrilling linguistic debut demonstrates, early relationships and emotional experiences—the excitement of reciprocity with her mother, not isolated skills like fitting pegs and finding beads—hold the key to her intelligence and mental development.

Observation and clinical work with older children also amplify this new view by showing how children actually learn to think. For instance, in conversations with school-age children, we posed a simple question: What do you think about people who are bossy or who try to boss you? First to reply was five-year-old Carl. "Well," he said, "let's see. Parents are bosses, and teachers are bosses, and sometimes baby-sitters are bosses." Rather like a living computer, he rattled off a formal classification of different types of bosses, but without tying these categories to his own life or experience of bossiness.

Jimmy, about the same age as Carl, gave a strikingly different response. "Most of the time I don't like being bossed," he said. "Especially when my parents get too bossy and try to tell me when I can watch TV and when I should go to bed, and I'm big enough to decide that myself." He found his answer in his own, apparently generally irritating, brushes with bossy people. Rather than simply cataloguing categories, however, Jimmy abstracted a principle from underlying emotional experience ("Most of the time I don't like it") and then illustrated it with cases in point ("Especially when my parents . . .") that he supported with a possibly controversial but nonetheless reasoned argument ("I'm big enough to decide that myself").

Eight-year-old Josh gave an even more refined answer. "Sometimes I don't like it, especially when there are things I want to do and they don't let me. But sometimes it's okay because adults know best." He next listed examples of unreasonably bossy parents and teachers, then went on to relate the ways he might react to them. When he's in a bad mood, Josh mused, he particularly resents being bossed, but at other times he doesn't mind so much. He even noted different styles of bossiness. Some people are nice about it; those who don't show "dagger eyes" or a "mean tone of voice" don't bother him nearly as much. Asked to sum up, he offered, "I guess I don't have just one answer, but there are times when I don't like it and times when it's okay. It depends on how they do it and what kind of mood I'm in."

Though talking about an apparently simple matter, Josh and Jimmy nonetheless demonstrated the method that all human beings use to solve any problem, to puzzle out any explanation—in short, to think creatively about anything, from recess to relativity. Both boys drew abstract conclusions about bosses, but arrived at them by examining what their own experiences had taught, what their own contacts helped them to understand. The feelings that these lived sensations had engendered led each of them to insights that suggested general conclusions. Lived emotional experiences were thus the source of the boys' ideas. Their capacity for formal logic, in keeping with their ages, helped them organize their thoughts and place them in a sensible arrangement. Abstract thinking requires both components. Carl, by contrast, catalogued different types of bosses almost by rote, as if counting wholly objective entities. His thinking remained concrete, as does all thinking that does not first involve lived emotional experience.

Gleaned from children like Cara, Josh, and Jimmy, such insights into the role of emotion in how we learn to think fly in the face of the traditional understanding of mental development, which separates emotion and reason and emphasizes one or the other. Immanuel Kant, regarded as the father of modern philosophy and psychology, framed the questions that have since guided work on cognition and language. The basis for objective knowledge, he suggested, is the mental process involved in "knowing," the way we figure out how the world works, rather than any set of facts or beliefs.[3] Piaget and other recent cognitive theorists have more or less followed Kant's lead and described in some detail how children learn to think. But the followers of both Kant and Piaget have never fully considered the place of affect or emotion in their views on intelligence and cognition.

Freud, in contrast, revealed complex emotional pathways that profoundly influence behavior. Building on the work of philosophers such as Schopenhauer, he showed that unconscious desires were not the poor, rude stepchildren of the intellect, but powerful challenges to rationality. Freud not only charted the contours of hidden wishes and conflicts; he revealed how people relate, care, and love. New movements in psychology focusing on relationships, the positive and adaptive aspects of emotion, empathy, self-awareness, and family patterns (e.g., ego psychology, interpersonal approaches, object relations theory) have grown from his discoveries. Between the late 1930s and early 1970s, pioneers such as Heinz Hartmann, Silvan Thomkins,

Heinz Kohut, and many others further mapped out the different positive and negative roles of emotions.[4] Child-rearing practices ranging from discipline to scheduling of meals began to reflect these insights. Instead of following the maxim "Children should be seen and not heard," parents started to talk with their children about feelings. Rigid, fixed feeding schedules gave way to demand ones. For a time in the 1960s and early 1970s, recognition of the emotional side of behavior found its way into American education. In many schools discussions about relationships, feelings, motivation, self-image, and individuality entered the classroom.

Clinical interest, however, then turned to new discoveries in neuroscience and psychopharmacology—the use of drugs to treat mental illness. The development of drugs like Prozac stirred researchers' fascination by showing how the brain's chemical environment alters feelings and behavior more quickly than insight or understanding. This biological revolution in the treatment of mental illness so obscured Freud's ideas that two recent popular works reviewing current behavioral science and neurological research on the importance of emotions struck a novel chord in the American public. To differing degrees, these books preserve the traditional division between feeling and cognition. Daniel Goleman, science writer for the *New York Times*, uses the label "emotional intelligence" to draw much-needed attention to the positive aspects of emotions in development earlier described by Freud, Thomkins, and others, including the ability to read and respond to emotions and to empathize and cope with them in relationships.[5] He suggests that these capacities are more important to success in life than traditional IQ-type intelligence. Antonio Damasio, a neurologist, found that patients with injuries in the part of the brain called the prefrontal cortex could have relatively normal IQ scores but be perilously lacking in judgment.[6] He postulates that emotions, such as those involved in evaluating the consequences of taking a certain course of action, are important for judgment, and damage to the prefrontal cortex, which regulates emotions, could seriously impair this faculty. It is interesting to note that this area of the brain is also involved in what we call motor planning, the sequencing of behavior. Children or adults with sequencing problems invariably have difficulty in making judgments because they do not easily construct patterns; they can't see the forest for the trees. This neurological research supports and emphasizes

the findings of many researchers and psychotherapists on the importance of emotions for such complex personality capacities as reality
testing as well as judgment.[7]

However, both these efforts to restore an interest in the role of
emotions in human development maintain the historical dichotomy
between cognition and affect, one setting up a rivalry—emotional
adaptation is more important than cognition—and the other showing
that brain injuries can affect emotions and therefore judgment while
leaving critical aspects of cognition unaffected.

We still find most educators, mental health workers, politicians,
and even parents split on one or another side of this dichotomy. On
the one hand, we see support for emotional development, such as
individually tailored programs in education, understanding and gentle firmness in discipline, talking out emotions in therapy, and improved social support for the poor. On the other are approaches that
rest on an impersonal cognitive view, such as back-to-basics instruction, "tough love" discipline, medication, and harsh welfare reform.

The perennial dichotomy between emotions and intelligence persists because, until recently, there has been little inquiry into the way
emotions and intelligence actually interact during early development.
Historically, emotions have been viewed in a number of ways: as outlets
for extreme passion, as physiologic reactions, as subjective states of
feeling, as interpersonal social cues.[8] Our developmental observations
suggest, however, that perhaps the most critical role for emotions is to
create, organize, and orchestrate many of the mind's most important
functions.[9] In fact, intellect, academic abilities, sense of self, consciousness, and morality have common origins in our earliest and ongoing
emotional experiences. Unlikely as the scenario may seem, the emotions are in fact the architects of a vast array of cognitive operations
throughout the life span. Indeed, they make possible all creative
thought.

Support for the link between affects and intellect comes from a
number of sources including neurological research, which has found
that early experiences influence the very structure of the brain itself.[10]
Interactive experiences can result in brain cells being recruited for particular purposes—extra ones for hearing rather than seeing, for instance.[11] Deprivation or alteration of needed experiences can produce a
range of deficits. When there is early interference with vision, for exam-

ple, difficulties have been observed ranging from functional blindness to problems with depth perception and spatial comprehension.[12] Experience continues to influence brain structure during childhood and adulthood. In brain-imaging studies, practicing a musical instrument has been seen to produce additional neural connections in the cortex for the frequently used fingers. Successful behavioral therapy for people with obsessive-compulsive symptoms brings about changes in both behavior and brain structure.

The importance of emotional experience in particular for high-level intellectual and social capacities is supported by studies showing that areas of the brain having to do with emotional regulation, interaction, and sequencing (the prefrontal cortex) show increased metabolic activity during the second half of the first year of life—at the same time that infants are involved in more reciprocal interactions and evidencing greater intelligence, such as making choices and beginning to search for hidden objects.[13] Recently it has been found that in order for neurons to make connections through the use of a neurotropic factor, they must be activated through experience.[14] Experience can stimulate hormonal changes; for example, soothing touch appears to release growth hormones, and hormones such as oxytocin appear to foster critical emotional processes such as affiliation and closeness.[15] Furthermore, emotional stress is associated with changes in brain physiology.[16] In general, during the formative years there is a sensitive interaction between genetic proclivities and environmental experience. Experience appears to adapt the infant's biology to his or her environment.[17] In this process, however, not all experiences are the same. Children seem to require certain types of emotional interactions geared to their particular developmental needs.

Such research leads to the question of what types of early experience are most helpful to the child's growing intellect. Should a toddler's growing memory, for example, be met with flash cards showing pictures and words, or natural interactions that include words and imaginative play? Should young children be taught geometry as soon as they can appreciate spatial relationships, before they have the capacity for complex causal thinking?[18] Such precocious activities are not the foundations of true learning. Newborns can stick out their tongues after they see someone else do it. These perceptual motor capacities and other tools of the nervous system are remarkable, but they do not in and of themselves constitute reasoning. We will explore these implications for learning in Chapters 4 and 8.

The new and, for many, startling notion—that emotion has an integral, and perhaps the most crucial, role in shaping the intellect—has already begun to change how we assess infants and young children. In the June 1994 *ZERO TO THREE*, published by the National Center for Infants, Toddlers, and Families, we suggest that babies' emotional exchanges with their caregivers, rather than their ability to fit pegs into holes or find beads under cups, should become the primary measuring rod of developmental and intellectual competence.[19]

In my own research, I have found support for this view of mental development from investigations in three areas. One is the work my colleagues and I have done with children at extreme biological risk, including very young children evidencing signs of autism. In these children, it isn't biology alone that gives rise to autistic symptoms. Rather, their physiology makes it difficult for them to engage in the interactive emotional experiences that are required for mental growth. It is the absence of these critical emotional experiences that is mostly responsible for the development of autistic symptoms. Over time, we have figured out ways to work within and around some of these physiological limitations and make the needed emotional experiences possible. Many of these children have since grown to be intelligent and emotionally healthy.[20] By noting the effect of various emotional experiences on intelligence, we begin to understand how each type contributes to intellectual and social growth.

I have also learned more about the role of early emotional experience in working with infants and young children who are developing relatively normally, observing the stages they go through (described in Chapters 2–4) as their cognitive abilities and social skills emerge. These observations make clear that certain kinds of emotional nurturing propel them to intellectual and emotional health, and that affective experience helps them master a variety of cognitive tasks.[21] According to experiments conducted by Stephen Porges of the University of Maryland and myself, parts of the brain and nervous system that deal with emotional regulation play a crucial role in cognition.[22] They react along with the portions of the brain devoted to registering the appropriate sense perceptions when babies are presented with sights or sounds. When the regulatory system is working well, children can attend and comprehend what they see or hear. But in some children the system is impaired. Babies whose brains lack the ability to regulate emotions have trouble paying attention and discriminating among sensations. They have difficulty figuring out what they are looking at or listening to. They often become irritable and their reactions disorganized. In a separate study we found that measurements of this emotional regulatory function taken at eight months of age correlate with children's IQ scores at age four.

A third source of this insight into the relation between intellect and emotion comes from our work with "multirisk" or multiproblem families, which is discussed in Chapter 13. In these families, afflicted with almost every imaginable problem from child neglect and spouse abuse to alcoholism or drug addiction, the degree to which children fail to develop their cognitive and social skills matches the degree to which their families fail to meet their emotional needs at each stage of their growth. We found that children in families with multiple risk factors have over a twentyfold increase in the probability of marginal cognitive performance at age four, and these trends persist into adolescence.[23] We have discovered what such children need at each stage by seeing the effects of its absence.[24] Other early intervention studies have shown the positive effects of providing needed experiences for at-risk infants and their families. These new adaptive capacities often continue into childhood, adolescence, and adulthood.[25]

From these various sources, a new understanding of how the mind develops in the earliest stages of life has emerged, one that integrates the child's experience of emotional interactions with the growth of intellectual capacities and, indeed, the very sense of self. The following pages explore this developmental perspective and its implications for how we bring up our children, function as adults, and participate in our society.

PART ONE

The Processes That Build the Mind

CHAPTER ONE

The Emotional Architecture of the Mind

INSIGHTS FROM AUTISM

Perhaps the most vivid understanding of the fundamental way emotions influence cognitive growth comes from observing autistic children. These children, who suffer some of the most severe biologically based thinking and language problems imaginable, can teach us a great deal by how they learn to think, relate, and communicate.[1] The children my colleagues and I work with have very serious deficits related to clear neurological problems, such as poor ability to process sounds, comprehend words, and plan sequential movements. Diagnosed between eighteen months and four years of age, these youngsters display a variety of bizarre and disturbing behavior—wandering aimlessly, compulsively flapping their arms, continually rubbing a spot on the carpet, repeatedly opening and closing a door, painstakingly marshaling small objects into rigidly straight lines—but almost no ability to respond to even the most basic attempts at communication.

Therapeutic programs for such severely challenged youngsters have traditionally concentrated on trying to teach them language or selected cognitive skills such as making particular sounds, acting out various social conventions, or imitating certain actions—the sort of isolated actions without context that we call "splinter skills." But even when these children learn to construct sentences, tie their shoes, or bang on drums, their actions usually do not show the joyful spontaneity and zest, flexible problem solving, and emotional openness that should come naturally at their age. We have, for example, observed children with autistic symptoms in intensive behavioral programs (twenty to forty hours a week). Many, when they did speak, tended to exhibit a rote and stereotyped quality in their thinking, though we felt they had the potential for more creative, abstract thought, greater imagination, and closer peer relationships.

The results are very different, though, with a program like the one that revealed the true abilities of Cara, the year-old girl whose mother was concerned that she was developmentally delayed (see introduction). Such a program of emotional cuing, which begins at the point when the child turns away from her parents' smiles and overtures, exploits the role of emotion in normal mental development. It appears more effective in fostering healthy intellectual and emotional patterns than are strategies of direct cognitive stimulation.[2] Using this approach, we have helped a number of children work around specific disabilities by wooing them first into relationships and then into countless emotional exchanges with a caregiver, often beginning with simple facial expressions and gestures.

One such child, whom I will call Tony, came into our program when he was eighteen months old. His parents had spotted something amiss almost as soon as he was born. He had arrived about a month prematurely, weighing only four pounds. Moderate cerebral palsy distorted the movements of his legs and, to a lesser extent, of his arms as well. He passed his first year withdrawn and undemonstrative, barely acknowledging the smiles and coos that were showered on him. Only with a great deal of effort did his gentle, indefatigable mother get him to respond a bit to her touch. He offered in return very few of the glances, giggles, and cuddles that make babies of his age so gloriously engaging. In fact, he hardly tried to communicate at all. His parents became deeply worried.

Approaching eighteen months without beginning to speak, Tony also acted a good year younger than his age. He uttered the odd sound now and then and moved about almost randomly. He crawled rather than walked and seemed to grow more vague and remote with each passing month.

With the specter of autism looming in their minds, his parents took him to one of the East Coast's most respected medical centers for evaluation. A child development expert noted serious social and cognitive deficits on top of his physical impairments. Tony would never function intellectually at better than an IQ of 50. This evaluator also diagnosed "severe pervasive developmental disorder"—in lay language, autism. The news horrified Tony's college-educated parents. Their beloved firstborn son appeared to be condemned to live in a dreaded borderland of incapacity and isolation.

Three years on, this prognosis suggested, Tony would have slipped ever further behind his less challenged age-mates. By that time his impairments would have locked him into a lonely, detached realm of repetitive, stereotyped actions, mental delay, and near exclusion of human relationships. He would be closed out of the world of friendships, learning, and hope for a satisfying future.

But Tony's parents looked further for help. Three and a half years into a program of treatment that focused on affective interactions, Tony, by then nearly five, was a different boy. He played happily with a circle of friends, engaged his parents and teachers in animated discussions, contested his bedtime with vigorous arguments, and asked and answered countless lively questions about why the world works the way it does. He fooled around with his baby brother, kicked a soccer ball with buddies, immersed himself in elaborate fantasy games about heroes and bad guys. In one discussion, which we were able to capture on a videotape documenting Tony's growth from eighteen months of age, he talked about wanting "*that* toy that Steven has," a smile lurking beneath his smirk. When asked why, he responded, "Because it's fun to play with." Queried further about how Steven would feel about giving up such a prized plaything, Tony answered with a giggle and a growing sheepish grin, "He wouldn't like it. He would be mad." More recently he has shown both his capacity for abstract thought and his appreciation of nuances of human behavior. When, in response to his father's trying to convince him that another child liked him, he commented, "Oh, he's nice to me, but that doesn't mean he wants to hang out with me." Standard IQ testing puts his verbal and cognitive abilities significantly above age expectations. With each passing year—he's now approaching ten—his mental and physical abilities have continued to grow. Though still somewhat hampered in his bodily coordination, he nonetheless generally enjoys the adventures of any little boy on the road to wholesome development.

Most of the autistic children we have worked with have made progress. Many, like Tony, eventually display real creativity and empathy, ultimately passing through the series of developmental stages described in Chapters 2–4. With our help, these children learn to interact with others first by connecting gestures and feelings, then words and feelings. Tony, for example, initiated his very first interaction when his father tried to turn a wheel the opposite way from the way he had been turning it. His look of protest and his defiant spin in the other direction began his enormous journey. Each of these children progresses at his own slower rate and has to work around severe problems in processing sounds, especially words, and often sights as well as touch and movement, but all of those who have made very good progress travel the same road and arrive at the same destination as other children, with the ability to think creatively and interact flexibly.

Working with these children, we found that the basic unit of intelligence is the connection between a feeling or desire and an action or symbol. When a gesture or bit of language is related in some way to the child's feelings or desires—even something as simple as the wish to go outside or to be given a ball—she can learn to use it appropriately and effectively. Until she makes that connection, however, her behavior and communication remain disturbed; indeed, the difficulty in making such connections constitutes a basic element of the disorder.

In therapy, we therefore use each child's own natural intentions and feelings as his or her personal foundation of learning. A boy trying to get out to the playground, for example, might constantly encounter adults pointing in the wrong direction. He eventually has to point in the right direction, or say something sounding like "Out!" in order to get someone to open the door. A girl who loves crashing one toy car into another might come upon an adult pushing a car that would make a dandy target. The hope of a noisy pileup is used to lure her into a cooperative "game" of hit-and-run. Tony's early use of words was often directed at getting his mother and occupational therapist to turn a chair he loved to spin on "more fast."

In another instance we used a child's rather alarming repetitive motion to communicate with her for the first time. This two-year-old girl neither spoke nor made any response to those around her, but would spend hours staring into space, rubbing persistently at a patch of the carpet. We saw in her abnormal repetition, however, not only a symptom of her autism but also a sign of interest and motivation—at least involving that little spot of pile. Perhaps it could serve as an opening wedge for emotional connection and, later, learning.

We had the girl's mother place her hand next to hers, right on the favorite stretch of floor. The child pushed it away, but her mother gently put it back. Again she pushed, again the hand returned. A cat-and-mouse game ensued, and by the third day of this rudimentary interaction, the little girl was smiling while pushing her mother's hand away. From this tiny beginning grew emotional connection, a relationship, and then thoughts and words. From pushing away an obstructing hand to seeking out that hand and then offering flirtatious grins and giggles, the child progressed to using gestures in a reciprocal nonverbal dialogue. When she began repeatedly flinging herself on her mother, the therapist recognized that this behavior gave her sensory pleasure. He instructed the mother to whinny like a horse each time her daughter lunged at her. Soon she was whinnying too, imitating her mother. Before long, she had started making her own sounds and then her own words. The therapist thus helped the mother stretch this sensation into a richer, more complex interaction. Over time, mother and child pretended to be neighing horses, mooing cows, barking dogs. As their imaginary menagerie became more populous, their social and emotional interchange grew more complex. It wasn't long before stuffed bunnies were fighting and hugging. Symbolic play led all the way to language and thought. Today, at age seven, this girl has a range of age-appropriate emotions, warm friendships, and a lively imagination. She argues as well as her lawyer father, and scores in the low superior IQ range. We have worked with a large number of such children and observed many of them make similar progress. In our recent study of over two hundred youngsters with autistic spectrum diagnoses undergoing this type of therapy, we found that between 58 percent and 73 percent have become warm, loving, and communicative.[3]

LEARNING FROM INFANTS AND CHILDREN

The insights we have drawn from our work with autistic children have led us to understand intellectual development in a new way. We asked ourselves how the abilities these autistic children developed only through hours and hours of therapy and of working with their parents emerge in ordinary circumstances where biological difficulties are not present. How do most children learn to think? From our observations of babies and children, we have pieced together a series of stages that are outlined briefly here and discussed in more detail in the following chapters.

A baby begins the lifelong task of learning about the world through the materials at hand, which at this stage of life are the simplest of sensations, such as touch and sound. How babies learn to attend to, discriminate among, and comprehend these sensations has been well known for many years. Infants' increasingly complex emotions are also well described in other studies. Relatively ignored in these investigations of initial perceptions and cognition, on the one hand, and emotional development on the other is a seemingly obvious observation whose importance cannot be underestimated. In the normal course of events, each sensation, as it is registered by the child, also gives rise to an affect or emotion.[4] That is to say, the infant responds to it in terms of its emotional as well as physical effect on him. Thus a blanket might feel smooth *and* pleasant or itchy *and* irritating; a toy might be brilliantly red *and* intriguing or boring, a voice loud *and* inviting or jarring. Mom's cheek might feel soft and wonderful or rough and uncomfortable. The child might feel secure when Mom gives a hug, or frightened if she jerks away. As a baby's experience grows, sensory impressions become increasingly tied to feelings. It is this *dual coding* of experience that is the key to understanding how emotions organize intellectual capacities and indeed create the sense of self.

Human beings start to couple phenomena and feelings at the very beginning of life. Even infants only days old react to sensations emotionally, preferring the sound or smell of Mother, for example, to all other voices or scents. They suck more vigorously when offered sweet liquids that taste good. Somewhat older babies will joyfully pursue certain favorite people and avoid others. By four months of age children can react to the sight or voice of a particular person with fear.

Another aspect of this new understanding of thought and emotion is a recently discovered fact: a given sensation does not necessarily produce the same response in every individual. Inborn differences in sensory makeup can make a sound of a given frequency and loudness—say, a high-pitched voice—strike one person as exciting and invigorating while it impresses another as piercing and shrill, rather like a siren. A light of a certain brightness might seem cheerful to one person but glaring and irritating to another. A gentle caress may soothe one but painfully startle another, like a touch on sunburned skin. Despite long-held assumptions that we all experience sensations like sounds or touch in more or less the same way, significant variations are now known to exist in the manner that individuals process even very simple sensory information. A given sensation can thus produce quite different emotional effects in different individuals—in one case pleasure, for example, but in another anxiety. We each unwittingly compile our own personal, sometimes quite idiosyncratic, catalogues of affective reactions to sensory experience.

The first sensory experiences an infant has occur within the context of relationships that give them additional emotional meaning. Whether positive or negative, nearly all of children's early affects involve the persons on whom they depend so completely for their very survival, and who discharge their responsibilities in a manner that can range from all-encompassing nurturing to near-total neglect. Having a bottle might mean the bliss of love and satiation with a warm, generous mother or hunger, frustration, and fear with a peremptory attendant who snatches the nipple away on schedule. Playing with Mother's hair may occasion giggles or an angry scolding.

As infants grow and further explore their world, emotions help them comprehend even what appear to be physical and mathematical relationships. Simple notions like *hot* or *cold*, for example, may appear to represent purely physical sensations, but a child learns "too hot," "too cold," and "just right" through pleasant or painful baths, chilly or comforting bottles, too much or too little clothing—in other words, through sensations coded with the child's emotional responses. Rather more complex perceptions like *big* or *little, more* or *less, here* or *there* have a similar foundation. "A lot" is a bit more than makes a child happy. "Too little" is less than expected. "More" is another dose of pleasure or, sometimes, of discomfort. "Near" is being snuggled next to Mother in bed. "Later" means a frustrating stretch of waiting.

Abstract, apparently self-contained concepts, even those forming the basis of the most theoretical scientific speculations, also reflect at bottom a child's felt experience. Mathematicians and physicists may manipulate abstruse symbols representing space, time, and quantity, but they first understood these entities as tiny children toddling toward a toy in the far corner of the playroom, or waiting for Mother to fill the juice cup, or figuring how many cookies they can eat before their tummies hurt. Einstein and other thinkers such as Schrödinger came by their most penetrating insights through "thought experiments." The grown-up genius, like the adventurous child, continues to take imaginary rides on intergalactic elevators or beams of light or capsules hurtling through space. Ideas are formed through playful explorations in the imagination, and only later translated into the rigor of mathematics. Einstein described this process thus:

> The words of language, as they are written or spoken, do not seem to play any role in my mechanism of thought. The physical entities which seem to serve as elements in thought are certain signs and more or less clear images which can be "voluntarily" reproduced and combined.
>
> There is, of course, a certain connection between those elements and relevant logical concepts. It is also clear that the desire to arrive finally at logically connected concepts is the emotional basis of this rather vague play with the above-mentioned elements. But taken from a psychological viewpoint, this combinatory play seems to be the essential feature in productive thought—before there is any connection with logical construction in words or other signs which can be communicated to others.[5]

Although time and space eventually take on objective parameters, the emotional component persists. For a physicist used to measuring nanoseconds with precision, half a minute on hold on the telephone might feel like half an hour. A topology professor late for a plane and lugging a heavy suitcase might see a flight of stairs as a slope steeper than a mountain. For these sophisticated thinkers, as for an infant wriggling toward a toy far out of reach or a toddler enduring the minutes until Mother gets home, a few yards or a few minutes can reflect felt emotional experience.

Indeed, before a child can count, she must possess this kind of emotional grasp of extension and duration. She must be able to express, perhaps with gestures before she can do so with words, whether an object is far away or a snack is coming soon. Numbers eventually objectify the "feel" of quantity, giving it logical parameters, much as Jimmy and Josh, the boys I spoke about in the introduction, put into logical arguments the feel of their contacts with bossy people. For a child without an intuitive sense of *few* (somewhat less than she wants) or of *many* (lots more than she can hold), no matter how precisely she might be able to recite their names, numbers can have no real meaning, and operations like addition and subtraction cannot describe realities in her world. Working with children facing a variety of challenges who could nonetheless count and even calculate, we found that numbers and computations lacked significance for them unless we created an emotional experience of quantity by, for example, arguing with them about how many pennies or candies or raisins they should receive.

THE DUAL CODE

Each sensory perception therefore forms part of a dual code. We label it both by its physical properties (bright, big, loud, smooth, and the like) and by the emotional qualities we connect with it (we might experience it as soothing or jarring, or it might make us feel happy or tense). This double coding allows the child to "cross-reference" each memory or experience in a mental catalogue of phenomena and feelings and to reconstruct it when needed. Filed under both "eating" and "feeling close with Mother," for instance, each feeding eventually joins with other experiences to build up a rich and detailed but inherently subjective description of a child's emotional and sensory worlds. Later on we will see how the emotional organization of experience guides access and, by establishing meaning and relevance, supports the development of logic.

But how can a handful of emotions organize so vast a store of information as is housed in the human brain? To fine-tune our selections, we modulate our emotions to register an almost infinite range of subtle variations and combinations of sadness, joy, curiosity, anger, fear, jealousy, anticipation, and regret. We possess an extraordinarily sensitive "meter" on which to gauge our reactions, and in a certain sense it almost possesses us. Anyone who pays attention to the subjective state of his body will almost always perceive within it an emotional tone, though it may be elusive or hard to describe. One might feel tense or relaxed, hopeful or fatigued, serene or demoralized. This inner emotional tone constantly reconstitutes itself in the innumerable variations that we use to label and organize and store and retrieve and, most important of all, make sense of our experience.

Our entire bodies are involved. Our emotions are created and brought to life through the expressions and gestures we make with the voluntary muscle systems of our faces, arms, and legs—smiles, frowns, slumps, waves, and so forth. The involuntary muscles of our guts and internal organs also play a role; our hearts might thump or our stomachs register the "butterfly" sensation of anxiety. Affects like excitement, delight, and anger are primarily controlled by the voluntary system. Others, including fear, sexual pleasure, longing, and grief, are mostly involuntary. Some responses, like the intense fight-or-flight alertness stimulated by adrenaline, affect us more globally and belong to portions of the nervous system formed early in evolution. Those involved in social reciprocity, the ones that signal reactions and that negotiate acceptance, rejection, approval, annoyance, and the like, belong to more recently evolved parts of the nervous system and rely on the highest capacities of the cortex.

EMOTIONS AND JUDGMENT: LEARNING TO DISCRIMINATE
AND GENERALIZE

This explanation of how affect organizes experience and ultimately thinking solves one of the enigmas that has mystified modern psychology: How does a child know when to take a behavior or skill or fact or idea learned in one situation and apply it in another? How, in other words, does she figure out how and when to generalize? How does she discriminate among situations—at home, church, school, Grandma's house—and select particular behavior—laughing loudly, sitting quietly—for the appropriate situation? How, in short, does she learn to perceive relevance and context?

This question has especially challenged clinicians seeking to help youngsters with developmental disabilities apply what they've learned in one situation to others in which it is also appropriate. How, for example, does a child learn that she must limit her aggressive behavior at home or school just as she has learned to do in a therapeutic setting? Or, conversely, that she should play with the children who live on her block in the same friendly way she does with her therapist? Or that she can run in the yard but not in the schoolroom? Clinicians have tried all kinds of approaches—teaching the desired behavior in multiple contexts, making environments as similar as possible, helping the child understand the reason for the new behavior—but with only limited success.

The key to the puzzle lies in the fact that emotion organizes experience and behavior. Consider, for example, how a child learns when to say hello. This seemingly trivial skill is based on the mastery of subtle, complex cues. A youngster must learn to use the greeting only with those for whom it is appropriate. Teaching him some general principle, such as "Greet everyone who lives within three blocks of our house," won't work; he can't stop to ask people their addresses. Nor will "Greet everyone you see" suffice; he might give a warm smile to a would-be thief or kidnaper. Nor can we count on "Greet only our friends and members of our family"; there are many old chums and distant relatives he hasn't met. Even if he could learn a set of rote rules, by the time he decided whether to say hello, the person would be gone.

Instead, through countless encounters in his early years, the child works out the problem for himself. As he goes about his daily life, he eventually comes to associate saying hello with a particular emotion—the warmth of seeing someone he or his family knows. That friendly feeling, he learns, calls for the most basic unit of social discourse, a smile and greeting. Having learned through experience what is actually a very abstract principle, "Say hello when you feel friendly toward someone," he can apply it appropriately wherever he goes. Strangers don't rate a hello because he doesn't feel friendly toward them; they don't fit the emotional context. Neither do people—even kith and kin—who make him worried, cautious, or uncomfortable. Such folk instead get downcast eyes, a quizzical face, or scrutiny from behind Mommy's or Daddy's legs. But for the rest of his life, whenever the child feels friendly in an unfamiliar situation, he will recognize the familiar emotional context and say or communicate something like "hello."

A child thus discriminates not by learning conscious or unconscious rules or examples but by carrying his own set of emotional cues from situation to situation. Whenever this "discrimination meter" composed of past emotional cues confronts new circumstances that reproduce a familiar feeling, the child will tend to produce the relevant behavior. Without this highly accurate meter, however, reacting appropriately becomes difficult. Some children have a type of developmental problem that hampers the connections between thought and affect. When such a child learns to say hello, for example, she may acquire the skill mechanically, either greeting only the person who first taught her or indiscriminately greeting everyone, even threatening strangers.

The complexity and subtlety of human interactions obviously make it impossible for us to reason out each situation individually before deciding what to do. Instead, in most cases we simply *know* what to do, apparently intuitively. The affects we carry from situation to situation tell us what to think, say, and do. They place a given event within the total emotional context of our lives. We are thus able both to comprehend (to ascertain what sort of situation we find ourselves in: friendly? formal? frightening?) and to discriminate (to determine what kind of action is suitable: a casual "hi"? an elaborate curtsy? a hasty retreat?). When a youngster recognizes in her teacher, for example, the same gentle firmness and warm regard she feels at home, she takes the cue to speak politely and to obey. Should the teacher stir up feelings of humiliation or overexcitement, however, she'll probably behave entirely differently.

A cocktail party forms the archetypal adult setting for this kind of quick sizing up we're talking about. If the stranger reaching for the canapé next to yours seems friendly and engaging, you might smile and offer a conversational opening: "Warm for this time of year, isn't it?" Or does he seem to be scanning the room over your shoulder for a more desirable interlocutor? You take the hint and cut the contact short with a curt nod or by saying something like, "Excuse me. I think I'll go get something to drink." We accomplish all this in microseconds—much too quickly for any logical thinking, but not too quickly for our emotional thinking.

Thus our ability to discriminate and generalize stems from the fact that we carry inside us as we go from one situation to another the emotions that automatically tell us what to say, do, and even think. Long before a baby can speak much, even before she reaches eighteen months of age, she has already developed this capacity to size up a new acquaintance as friendly or threatening, respectful or humiliating, supportive or undermining, so that she can behave accordingly. Before she has words to describe her reaction or can even think consciously, for that matter, this ability to discriminate emotionally begins to operate as a "sixth sense" allowing her to negotiate social situations.

FROM EMOTION TO ABSTRACTION

Not only learning when to say hello, surmising other people's intentions, and maneuvering at cocktail parties, therefore, but any sort of creative thought or problem solving follows an emotional pathway. An individual must first decide which of the myriad physical and emotional sensations that constantly bombard each of us or the innumerable ideas stored in our minds are relevant to the issue at hand. The only way a person can make this decision—the only way he can determine which ideas and features to emphasize and which to ignore—is to consult his own catalogue of physical and emotional experience. The emotions that organize it create categories from which to select from the compiled memories and intuitions the information that bears on a given issue. Different people may make very different judgments about a particular item's relevance, but the essential selection process is the same. Only then can the individual proceed to generate possible solutions. He then tests the possibilities, using whatever faculty of logic his age and developmental stage permit.

Even a very simple question requires the emotional experience to produce a sensible answer. For example, the query "What did you do today?" is almost never intended to elicit a bare chronology of activities. Indeed, reciting a precise list of your doings would strike others as overly concrete, not to say bizarre. Rather, in recounting your day, you go first to the most important happenings, those that give the day its tone, its place in the story of your life. Whether they are exciting, annoying, or disappointing depends on your ability to give events emotional meaning and the degree and texture of that meaning. It also depends on whom you are talking with and the point you are trying to make. The answer "Nothing" doesn't literally mean that the hours passed wholly uneventfully, but rather that nothing occurred that felt significant.

Thinking, therefore, requires two components. We need to have at least partially in place an emotional structure that sorts and organizes events and ideas even before we use words and symbols to represent them. This emotional organization literally allows us to "create" ideas, as it did for Jimmy and Josh in talking about their experience of bossy people. Second, we need a process of testing, refining, or elaborating that then evaluates these thoughts in light of our capacity for logic. Sometimes an idea doesn't make sense; it doesn't fit with our understanding of logical, sequential reason. "I'd better keep quiet about this one," we think. But others do fit because they pass our test of reality and logic.

At any level higher than the most concrete, thinking involves the ability to form abstract concepts. The question of how this ability arises has long challenged educators, psychologists, and child development specialists. We know how to promote memory and how to teach counting. But how do you teach someone to be more abstract, to progress beyond concrete ways of thinking? Must we depend on the child's learning abstract thinking on her own? If she can't, must we assume that it is a fixed limitation?

Viewing intellect as based on emotion gives a new perspective on the process of learning to abstract. From this novel vantage point, the ability to form abstractions is actually the ability to fuse various emotional experiences into a single, integrated concept.

The abstract concept represented by a word like *love*, for example, begins to be formed not from any dictionary definition but, quite literally, in the heart. A baby may well first know it as hugs and kisses and a readily accessible nipple. Over the next few years, she learns that it also has to do with admiration, security, pride, forgiveness, the ability to recover from anger and retain a sense of security. The concept soon widens to include aspects of companionship, a variety of pleasures, and the demands of loyalty. The child learns that disappointment and dissension don't seem to destroy it. In adolescence, sexual longing is added to the mix, along with jealousy, perhaps, and pride. In adulthood the concept broadens further to encompass a sense of commitment and the willingness to work hard to sustain family life. As our emotional experience and the richness and reach of the loves we can feel continue to grow, so does our understanding of love. Where once it was an undifferentiated sense of well-being, it can unfold into a wide spectrum of loves—brotherly, erotic, filial, maternal, altruistic. It encompasses the devotion of a long-married couple, the inseparability of army buddies, the intimacy of best friends, the ecstasy of romance, the poignancy of posthumous memory, the awe and reverence a believer feels toward God. The concept of love can thus become very complex and abstract as we incorporate into it many challenges in many contexts: fulfilling our responsibilities, seeking our happiness, coping with loss and disappointment, coming to terms with other people's vulnerability and fallibility. To the concrete thinker, love is hugs and kisses and happiness. To the abstract thinker, it is far less simple, a many-layered formulation acquired gradually from life's experiences.

Concepts like *justice* and *mercy*, though seemingly more abstract still, also prove to have similarly emotional foundations. How do we come to an understanding of what is fair, what is just, what constitutes suitable retribution and atonement? How do we measure a person's guilt or decide what sort of punishment he merits? Once again, we refer to notions that we have formed through specific emotional experiences.

A child may think justice is hitting back the child who hit him or taking away the toy he grabbed. Through years of fights in the schoolyard, struggles on the playing field, temptations to cheat on tests, promises to shield a friend who has shoplifted or to exact vengeance for a slight, he eventually develops a far more complex picture of what it means to be fair. But always, no matter how long he lives, no matter how learned a philosopher or legal scholar he may become, that sense remains grounded in felt, lived experience of justice and injustice. Our courts may hand down closely argued decisions running to many pages and bolstered with row on row of footnotes and citations. Yet like all thinkers, a judge finally selects the considerations that are relevant to the case—the principles that override, the rights or responsibilities that counterbalance. Does an individual's freedom take precedence over the welfare of the group? Does the weight of established tradition outweigh newly discerned demands? Does a slave become free by entering a free state? Can separate facilities for different categories of people be equal? Resolving such complex questions requires abstract principles and modes of analysis that are at bottom the product of emotional experience. Only the abstraction of lived experience provides the basis for reasoning at this level. As we saw with the concept of love, an abstract notion of justice differs from a concrete one in that it integrates the essence of disparate and even competing experiences of just behavior into a body of principles that will stand up to logical analysis.

The second aspect of thinking is logical analysis of emotionally derived ideas and concepts. Jimmy and Josh generated their ideas about bossy people and being bossed from emotional experience, but organized them into groups based on their ability to construct logical categories (distinguishing between good and bad styles of bossiness). The ability to scrutinize emotionally created ideas and organize them logically is related to the maturation of the brain and central nervous system but also to the accumulation of experiences that challenge and give form to this biological potential.

Many of the experiences that help shape logical capacities are at least in part emotional in nature. As we will discuss in more detail later in this chapter when we explore some of the limitations of Piaget's theory of intelligence and in Chapter 5, the earliest sense of causality, reality, and logic is emotional. It begins with a child's first insight that "My smile leads to Mommy's smile" and continues with the recognition that reaching up results in getting picked up, or saying "I'm mad" makes Mom look sad. Before the child can understand the difference between fantasy and reality, she must experience her own intentions or wishes having an effect on others. It is the emotional bridge between her wish, intent, or affect and another's response that establishes the foundation for logic and reasoning. Thus both the creative, generative aspect of thinking and the logical, analytical aspect derive in part from emotional experience. The most highly intellectual endeavors combine generative and analytical thinking. They are the product of our accumulated wisdom, our level of understanding based on our ability to abstract from lived emotional experience.

HOW EMOTIONS ORGANIZE INFORMATION

Every time we encounter a new person or situation, whether in a dark alley at night or in a receiving line at the White House, the structure of affective categories we have erected from past experience serves as a means of perceiving the social and emotional overtones and meaning of the event. Our ability to make these discriminations tells us whether to say hello or not, whether to pursue a conversation or move on, whether to run from the spot, screaming for the police at the top of our lungs, or whether to extend a hand and a comment on the perspicacity of the administration's current policies. Each of these actions is appropriate and useful in some circumstances and inappropriate, perhaps even disastrous, in others.

In making such discriminations, we depend on these affective categories to function essentially as a sense organ, much as we depend on our eyes to perceive light and our ears to perceive soun' Our eyes tell us first when a pedestrian is standing in front of the moving car we are in, and our ears tell us first when thunder is resounding through the sky. Sorting through the emotionally coded categories under which our minds have stored our previous experiences, this affective sense tells us, long before we could figure it out consciously, that the guy approaching from a dimly lit alley is up to no good. Then our minds instantly retrieve other similarly coded information that might be relevant about menacing situations and how we have handled them before.

We are able to get at our stored experience so rapidly and reliably because our affective capacity organizes information in an especially functional and meaningful manner. Let's say we're in an unfamiliar place and we see someone. Almost simultaneously with registering this sight, as part of our making sense of what we see, there is an immediate emotional reaction, often preceding a purely cognitive one. Prior to figuring out who the person is and whether or where we've met him before, we may react to the person with warmth and attraction or fear and repulsion.

Emotional reactions have often been thought to be secondary to cognitive perceptions, but in fact, in many circumstances they may be primary. You need only reflect on your own day-to-day experience, in the office or at home, to recognize how your emotional system serves as an efficient "sensor." Your perception of other people's kindness or hostility, acceptance or rejection, warmth or aloofness is hardly a logical deduction you make based on the shape of their faces or tone of voice. Subsequently you may reflect on these quick impressions to see if they "make sense." In a threatening situation requiring a fast decision, we usually favor our emotional sensors rather than our slower deductive processes. Children who have trouble using these emotional sensors often have difficulties with judgment. Those who rely on cognition—thinking, for example, "Hmmm—her face is turned down and she looks away every time I look toward her, so maybe she doesn't like me"—are taking so long to make a judgment that they miss the other new cues in their surroundings.

What significance does the fact of this emotional reaction to experience have for how we store, organize, and retrieve information? If, as I am suggesting, information is dual-coded according to its affective and sensory qualities, then we have a structure or circuitry set up in our minds that enables us to retrieve it readily. Picture a massive library with different rooms and aisles for storing various kinds of information. Is the labeling of these areas based on our sensory impressions of the stored information—size, shape, color, smell, or sound? Or are the rooms and aisles labeled according to the emotions that accompanied the intake of these experiences—pleasure, displeasure, annoyance, relief, gratitude? Or are they perhaps categorized according to both affective and physical features, cross-referenced, so to speak? In that case, which card file do we consult first?

When trying to figure out the solution to a problem, do people conjure up all possible logical solutions and then select the best one?

Or do they first feel an emotional tone in their bodies, often somewhere in the chest and abdominal area, which then gives cues to a relevant strategy to deal with the situation? In my view, it's often the latter. After we arrive at what we may call an intuitive (i.e., emotionally mediated) response, we expose the strategy it yields to logical analysis to see if it fits the problem at hand. In other words, the first ideas we have on any particular subject are generated by the affective categories that constitute the organizational architecture of our minds. Only then do we analyze these initial responses logically.

We also categorize ideas and information according to the physical features recorded by our senses. But this is often a slower, more deliberate process. Individuals with organic brain damage resulting from tumors, strokes, certain toxins, or some types of psychosis, often regress and lose their affective organizing ability. They then operate in a very concrete, rote manner, basing their thinking on one or two isolated sensory impressions without any way to assess the significance of a situation. Such a person might make the inference "You are evil because you are wearing black and the devil wears black." Such responses, which are often viewed as a failure of logical thinking, may more precisely be viewed as a failure in the emotional organization of thinking.

The emotional guides to our thinking can also lead us astray during extreme states of anxiety, depression, fear, anger, or the like. At such times our emotions become so overwhelming that we are unable to fine-tune our ideas. Thoughts become polarized, rigid, fixed, while inflexible beliefs dominate the mind. A man who is convinced, for example, that he is a bad person or that everyone hates him or that things are completely hopeless interprets new information through the clouded lens of his extreme emotional state rather than taking any one of a variety of perspectives a sensitive repertory of affects can afford. "That man I just met was only nice to me because he could see I'm bad and wants to fool me." Such extreme states or disorders of processing that distort or interfere with the ability to regulate feelings can thus seriously complicate learning. Nonetheless, we have the potential both to code, store, organize, and retrieve vast amounts of information efficiently by virtue of its emotional meaning for us and to analyze this meaning rationally to make sense of our lives.

LANGUAGE AND EMOTION

These observations on the emotional nature of intelligence impel us to reexamine our assumptions about human intellect. Philosophers have maintained for centuries that intellect and emotion represent two distinct parts of the mind, with logic, reason, and objectivity forming one realm and passion, feeling, and subjectivity another. This polarized view of the mind is not a relic of the past. Two of the most influential modern theories of the mind's distinctly human capacities for language and cognition have adopted this basic dichotomy. Both Noam Chomsky, who formulated a model for the acquisition of the grammatical structure of language, and Jean Piaget, who described the steps children go through in learning to think, treat the emergence of cognitive skills in isolation from emotional development.

Our observations of children suggest that even the capacities generally considered to be innate, such as the ability to learn language, require an emotional base in order to acquire purpose and function. Unless a child masters the capacity for reciprocal emotional and social signaling, her ability to use language (as well as her cognitive and social patterns) develops poorly, often in a fragmented manner. Words lack meaning, pronouns are confused, and scraps of rote learning, such as repeating illogical phrases, dominate her speech. Her social interests remain focused on her own body or inanimate objects.

To illustrate why emotions are so important in the development of language, even if the ability to grasp grammatical structures is innate, consider how children learn to use verbs and connect them with nouns. I have observed in my clinical practice that a child first has to connect a sense of purpose or emotional intent to her behavior, including expressions and gestures, before learning how to connect words properly.[6] Autistic children, for example, often do not relate to other people or express wishes or intents. During the initial phase of our work with them they will not ask for juice, say, or even gesture for it. Without emotional intent, even children who have lots of words and phrases do not use them in a grammatically correct manner. They may senselessly repeat phrases from a television show or utter seemingly random words. As we help them engage in purposeful affective interactions and gesturing, two things happen. First, their behavior becomes intentional. They grab Mom and take her to the door to open it. They point at something they want. They look angry, happy, or needy and use these facial expressions to communicate intent or desire. Second, words that have been in their vocabularies as well as newly acquired ones also gradually get used in an intentional manner. Disjointed utterances like "Car" or "Balloon" become "Want car," "Give balloon" and eventually "I want the car" or "Give me the balloon." Verbs, nouns, and pronouns are used correctly. Over time, expressions of past, present, and future and other grammatical complexities take proper form as well.

Like autistic children, children who have been severely emotionally deprived may also lack language skills. When encouraged to develop emotional relationships they may go through the steps described above to learn first intentional behavior and then grammatically correct language. Often, however, they are able to master language faster than children with autism because they don't have biologically based processing problems.

Grammar aligns the different components of language in a structured way to convey meaning. At its most basic, this involves organizing intent and objects of intent (conveyed through verbs and nouns). Because awareness of a wish or intent is primarily an affective experience, such experience is necessary in order to make this grammatical alignment. The development of grammar may thus be similar to that of other mental functions. Neurological structures may first need to mature for the potential to exist. Then, however, experiences of emotional interaction may be critical for this potential to be realized.

According to this view, only one aspect of the acquisition of grammar is innate, and this component may depend on general features of the environment to unfold properly. The other component is based on emotional experiences, and in the absence of these experiences, language will not develop properly. A child's theoretical potential to use language can become a request for a glass of water or a love sonnet only if she forms emotional ties to other persons and with them engages in a wordless dialogue of interactions.

The importance of emotional experiences as the basis for the development of grammatical language may have eluded Chomsky and other linguists because it is all too easy to take such experiences for granted: the great majority of families, after all, provide them as a matter of course through give-and-take interactions in play, discipline, and countless negotiations. It is only when these experiences are not provided that we see how essential they are. Their usual availability should not obscure their pivotal role in the acquisition of language and other capacities. The necessity of routinely available and therefore easily ignored experiences in directing the growth of brain structures is also being documented in a variety of neurological studies.[7]

THE MISSING PIECE IN PIAGET'S VIEW OF COGNITION

Examining the relationship between affect and intelligence enables us to take a new look at our understanding of cognition. Piaget and many of his followers, who have significantly refined his notions, advanced a comprehensive theory of the stages of development of human intelligence that maintained the ancient split between emotion and cognition. Continuing in the philosophical tradition of Kant, Piaget and most current cognitive theorists studied processes of knowing. Although their observations represented a vast improvement over approaches that simply described the motor, language, or cognitive milestones children achieve at different ages, their model was nonetheless limited insofar as it did not fully integrate the role of affect. For a detailed discussion of this point, as well as Piaget's views of the role of affect in cognition and how his ideas can be fit into an integrated developmental perspective, see my book *Intelligence and Adaptation*.[8]

Piaget viewed cognitive structures as growing primarily from a child's interactions with the outer world. While he believed that affect and intelligence, which he saw as developing in a parallel fashion, were interrelated and influenced one another, he asserted that affect was not the "cause of the progressive structuralization that marks cognitive growth," stating, for example, that "affectivity can be considered as the energetic force of behavior whereas its structure defines cognitive functions."[9]

Piaget and his followers revealed how important aspects of intelligence develop by studying how a child operates on the physical environment to form concepts. In one famous experiment, in which an infant learns to pull a string to ring a bell, Piaget pinpointed the beginning of the child's capacity to appreciate causality at a sensori-motor level. Months before a baby is able to pull a string, however, he can pull his mother's heartstrings with his smile and thereby elicit a hug, a kiss, or a smile.

Piaget's experiments focused on how children comprehend the relationship between physical objects, developing the ability to classify them by such parameters as shape or size. But most children can classify their emotions and emotionally relevant relationships far earlier than they can physical objects. For example, they know members of their families from those who are not members, classifying the family as a unit. Some of Piaget's observations are limited because he depended so heavily on children's perceptual and motor performance to signal cognitive advances, even though motor skills often lag behind other skills.

More important, however, is Piaget's relative lack of focus on the role of emotions. He emphasized learning through doing but did not realize that the "doing" generates formative emotional reactions as well as perceptual, motor, and cognitive ones. Consider how a child learns what an apple is. You can have her handle an apple and determine it is something red and round, bigger than a peanut and smaller than a watermelon. Alternatively, the child can observe the aspects mentioned above, experience the relatively greater satisfaction of eating an apple when she is hungry versus when she's full, and know the pleasure of giving one to her favorite teacher.

She can also imagine how the teacher feels when she gives her the apple. She may catalogue how she herself feels when she throws one at her younger brother and gets him on the shoulder, as well as her disgust when another one rots or she discovers half a worm inside. If you ask creative adults to write an essay on apples, they will probably bring an enormous amount of personal affective experience to their reflections.

Piaget did emphasize how children's thinking comes to incorporate multiple perspectives as they grow older. A classic Piagetian experiment shows how school-age children learn to solve a problem involving weights on a seesaw. Assessing the heaviness of the weights and noticing where they are placed, they are able to figure out how a seesaw works. But what was not appreciated by Piaget was that the children's postulated perspectives incorporated the additional almost infinite numbers of perceptions afforded by affective experiences. To neglect this element is therefore to fail to appreciate the rich array of experiences that contribute to forming abstract concepts.

As we saw earlier, some children who lack certain kinds of experience tend to consider a concept such as bossiness only along a restricted number of dimensions, such as identifying parents, teachers, and so on in bossy roles. When we ask these children to tell us more about bossy people, some of them offer another dimension; for example, "They have loud voices." Some go even further: "They have loud voices and always think they're right." Children without these difficulties, whose responses are more creative and abstract, are able to integrate many other emotionally relevant dimensions into their concepts of bossy people and bossiness. Bossy people included ones who humiliate you, scare you, nag at you, charm you, and so forth. What often emerges is a concept that takes in a wide range of subtle features of bossy people.

In looking at how creative children and adults deal with abstract concepts, we found that they form these concepts out of a huge variety of emotional experiences. If we limit our concept of bossiness or apples, or of love or justice, to just a few cognitively familiar dimensions, we seriously shortchange the conceptual richness that is generated by considering bossiness, apples, love, or justice in the context of the enormous spectrum of affective experiences that relates to each of them.

Certain models in science and math take into account only a limited number of variables. In relatively closed mathematical systems, only a few parameters may be used to describe an object. To determine the area of a rectangle, we need to look only at its length and width. As Piaget pointed out, when a child begins to be able to incorporate both dimensions of the rectangle in his thinking rather than just length alone, he has made a significant cognitive advance.

Nevertheless, to grasp even these variables, prior emotional experiences are needed. To understand the dimensions of a rectangle, a child must have a "feel" for quantity, which originates in earlier countless experiences of having "more" or "less," of something being "too little" or "too big." Children without this sense of quantity have a hard time learning math. Formulas that have no meaningful reference points in experience are learned only by rote and cannot readily be applied from one situation to another. The more complex the phenomenon being studied, from the formation of stars to the components of cells, the more we require the foundations established by our previous emotional experiences.

Most concepts are not part of limited systems. The words we use to express our ideas often have numerous subtle meanings that are enriched with experience. We are continually abstracting more of these experiences into our evolving definitions. Often seemingly simple terms can be fully understood only in the context of growing affective experience. The word *run*, for example, has one of the longest definitions in the dictionary.

The very capacity to grasp causality symbolically, so central to most cognitive abilities, originates in personal affective experience. As described earlier, in order to develop a sense of causality, a child first has to sense her own affect as a want or a feeling or a wish and then to relate this affective intent to a consequence that resides outside of her growing definition of who she is as a person. If, when she feels insecure and her arms fly up and she looks woefully at her mother, she is met by arms that lift and hug her, she experiences this type of affective causality.

Affects enable us to identify phenomena and objects and to comprehend their function and meaning. Over time they allow us to form abstract notions of interrelations. Piaget's formal operative aspects of knowing are a theoretical shell around which we can build an understanding of a richer, more creative process. The dichotomy between emotional and cognitive development falls away when we observe how babies and young children, as well as older children and adults, actually think. Affect, behavior, and thought must be seen as inextricable components of intelligence. For action or thought to have meaning, it must be guided by intent or desire (i.e., affect). Without affect, both behavior and symbols have no meaning.

Our clinical observations of normally developing children and those who develop autistic patterns suggests that the first half of the second year of life may be the time when these important aspects of affect, cognition, and language are joined. This new unit makes more complex communication and thinking possible. For example, this is the time when we may observe a child taking Dad's hand, walking with him, and getting him to open the door to Mom's bedroom, the refrigerator, or the toy chest, depending on the current object of desire.

In our review of over two hundred children, the vast majority of children later diagnosed as autistic did not master this affect-behavior connection, even though many of them could use words to label objects, count, or sing songs. In contrast, almost all nonautistic children we observed began at this time to use affect to give meaning to behavior and words. As we will explore later on when we discuss the mind's growth, making the affect-behavior-language connection may, in part, involve a connection of parts of the brain dealing with affect, motor planning, and symbol formation, including aspects of the left and right sides of the brain.[10] These pathways which connect affect to behavioral sequencing and symbolic elaboration may represent a primary deficit in autism and a critical step in the formation of human intelligence.

A FULLY HUMAN MIND

In addition to new approaches to language acquisition and cognitive development as well as to the treatment of autistic disorders, the conception of emotional experience as the foundation of intelligence offers a better understanding of human nature and relationships. Though this conception runs counter to the prevailing view of the human being as a conglomeration of rationally based skills and capacities on the one hand and emotions on the other—a view that pervades our culture and social institutions—it also suggests new avenues for dealing with such issues as child care, education, conflict resolution, family disintegration, and violence. We will explore these issues in greater detail in Part Two of this book.

The work of computer scientists seeking to synthesize intelligence illustrates especially pointedly the limitations of a view that separates cognition and emotion. To be sure, researchers trying to replicate human thought have had many successes and raised challenging questions. They have, for example, used computers to translate video images into tactile stimuli that, when applied to a blind person's back, enable him to identify objects. They have postulated different types of perceptions and different kinds of consciousness. They have constructed neural loops equipped with feedback circuits in imitation of those in the brain. But though they have programmed computers to exceed humans by far in rote calculations and other tasks, they have not succeeded in making computers that can arrive at the complex perceptions and thoughtful judgments that human beings, even small children, do with apparent effortlessness.

Proponents of the computer's ultimate ability to rival the human mind claim that inadequate capacity alone explains the failings of technology to replicate human consciousness to date. But they do not generally consider the most fundamental limitation of artificial intelligence: the computer's inability to experience emotion, and thus to use it to organize and give meaning to sensation, which remains simply inputs of data. No matter how sophisticated the technology may become, it is unlikely that a machine will ever acquire the emotional software possessed by a small child. Even a pet dog, despite the fact that its nervous system is in some respects quite different from our own, can respond in a more "human" manner than the most brilliantly designed computer because it does feel affect and, to the limits of its ability, can learn from what it feels. No computer is likely ever to have anything like the uniquely human "operating system" composed of feelings and reactions that would enable it to "think" like a person. The basic element of thinking—the true heart of the creativity central to human life—requires lived experience, which is sensation filtered by an emotional structure that allows us to understand both what comes through the senses and what we feel and think about it as well as what we might do about it.

This realization compels us to reconsider our social priorities. If our society were truly to appreciate the significance of children's emotional ties throughout the first years of life, it would no longer tolerate children growing up, or parents having to struggle, in situations that cannot possibly nourish healthy growth. Mastering our current social challenges requires that we discard older views that divide the mind into distinct segments, that see intellect and emotion as separate, even contradictory, elements. These outdated distinctions have too long permitted us to ignore every child's need for a stable, loving setting in the early years, the very environment that well-functioning nuclear and extended families seem tailor-made to provide. The fundamental capacities of mind that develop in the enveloping intimacy of the child's first home are then maintained, reinforced, and brought to full fruition through similarly compelling emotional exchanges that are, ideally, repeated in other places and with other persons throughout the developmental stages. As we shall see in the next chapters, emotion shapes not only human intelligence but also an individual's psychological defenses and coping strategies—indeed, the entire structure of personality.

We can no longer afford to ignore the emotional origins of intelligence. Theories of, say, cognitive versus emotional intelligence, however helpful in emphasizing the importance of emotion, unfortunately leave us with a conception of human nature that separates two of our most important capacities. The common origins of emotions and intellect demand a conception of intelligence that integrates those mental processes that have been traditionally described as cognitive and those qualities that have been described as emotional, including the sense of self or the ego, the awareness of reality, conscience, the capacity for reflection, and the like. The mind's most important faculties are rooted in emotional experiences from very early in life—before even the earliest awareness of symbols, conscious or unconscious.

More than anyone else, Freud focused the attention of Western thought on emotions as motivators of behavior. Any attempt to understand the origins of our most important mental abilities must therefore begin with his revolutionary concepts. In the following three chapters we will see, however, that observations of infants and young children in the process of learning to express emotions through wishes and desires, as well as developing conscious and unconscious thoughts, suggest that emotions contribute to the building of mind and intellect significantly earlier than thought by Freud, many of his followers, or other schools of depth psychology.

CHAPTER TWO
The Deepest Foundations: Security and Engagement

UNTIL FREUD, REASON WAS THOUGHT TO HOLD CENTER STAGE as the main engine of human behavior. Overturning this understanding, Freud and his followers elaborated the shocking notion that everyone harbors unconscious irrational thoughts and wishes and, even more horrifying, that unacknowledged urges underlie the actions of even the most outwardly rational people. Instead of the roots of reason that had entranced earlier investigators, Freud uncovered, to the profound disgust of his contemporaries, a miasma of unspoken desires. Neither the supporters of rationality nor the advocates of subjectivity, however, considered that the two might share an intimate link and common origin.

Despite great resistance, even skeptics finally acknowledged that seemingly incomprehensible irrational wishes emerge in the light of Freudian analysis as the simple and predictable products of the unconscious mind. Freud mapped the anatomy of that unseen entity, revealing a complex but intelligible machinery of desire and control. For four generations Freudian theory has evolved in response to changing times and growing knowledge. For millions of people, Freud's central, liberating idea has continued to offer a deeply satisfying explanation of why people act the way they do.

In explaining how the unconscious mind develops, Freud posited a child who can both formulate wishes and desires and represent them in unconscious form. But he never explained how an infant develops these crucial abilities, how a newborn imposes order on the incoherent mass of her own sensations, how she organizes both her internal and external experience into something as complex, comprehensive, and pointed as a wish or a desire. Occupied in making the first, pioneering outline of the symbolic unconscious and its dynamic role in adult life, he left for future generations the work of investigating the processes that give rise to conscious and unconscious thought.

Freud repeatedly pointed to the importance of early development, hoping that science would one day discover the perhaps biological underpinnings of many of his clinical observations. Working largely with adults, he did not systematically witness at first hand significant numbers of babies growing into young children. He therefore didn't have an opportunity to see how the earliest emotional interactions provide the common origins of intelligence as well as desires.

We now know from our studies of infants and children that the foundations of both thought and emotion lie far deeper than Freud imagined, and that they shape the entire superstructure of intellect and personality built on them. Understanding them, I believe, can aid in solving both some of the psychological puzzles that perplex researchers as well as many of the personal and social problems that beset society.

In this new view, the deepest strata in the development of the mind are laid down by sensations as well as their close cousins affects or emotions, which are the product of the earliest relationships. These early affects emerge through a number of stages, each with its own goals.

THE DEVELOPMENTAL LEVELS OF THE MIND

For the newborn baby flooded with an uncontrollable tide of inchoate sensory data to become a child capable of forming her feelings and experiences into wishes and thoughts, whether conscious or unconscious, obviously requires a good deal of learning very early in life. This process consists of six specific stages that together prepare the baby to translate the raw data of her senses and inner feelings into images that represent them both to herself and others. Mastering the learning tasks at each of these stages forms the mental architecture that eventually creates the basis for conscious and unconscious symbolic thought.

Traditional conceptualizations of the mind, in terms of different types of psychosexual and psychosocial interests (as described by Freud and Erikson), stages of cognition (described by Piaget and his followers), and hypothesized innate structures underlying language (described by Chomsky and other linguists), may be understood as building on these more basic processes. For example, unless a child masters the level we call two-way, intentional communication, normally achieved by an eight-month-old infant, his language, cognitive, and psychosexual and social patterns ultimately develop in an idiosyncratic, piecemeal, disorganized manner. Words, if spoken, lack meaning and are unclear and unpurposeful. Pronouns are confused. Rote learning, such as songs repeated endlessly for no reason, dominates. Emotional and social interactions remain unconnected and focused on the child's own body or inanimate objects.

The levels of the mind described in the next three chapters may be thought of as the mind's deepest structural components, supporting all later development, just as the massive piers and girders at a skyscraper's base allow the top floors to reach the clouds. They require both nature and nurture to form properly. Capacities thought to be basic to human nature, even those hypothesized to be innate, biological ones, such as language, must be grounded in these deeper levels to acquire purpose and function. Without this structure the mind cannot function coherently, but only in a fragmented, jumbled fashion. With these developmental levels firmly in place, however, the mind can operate with intentionality and purpose, finding creative solutions to problems, grasping complex interactions intuitively and empathically, and allowing the growth of the warm intimacy that makes relationships and family life both possible and pleasurable.

This understanding of the early levels of the mind is derived from our studies of different groups of infants and children, including not only those with relatively healthy physiological and family patterns but also those with severe biological or environmental challenges. In this research, and in intensive clinical work with a variety of infants, young children, and adults, we have observed that infants without family problems or physical challenges often progress easily through these levels. In stressed family situations, caregivers often require assistance in providing the experiences that make it possible for the infant to master the expected emotional tasks.

Many infants with marked physiological difficulties such as autistic symptoms also achieve emotional health, but only with the help of intensive, innovative therapeutic strategies. In each and every instance, autistic children who progress to develop the capacity for intimacy, emotional expression, language, creativity, abstract thinking, solving problems, and forming healthy peer relationships have to pass through the same emotional stages as children without this handicap, though they do so at a different pace. While the connection between emotions and intelligence has not been fully explored before, there are numerous studies of early emotional development that are consistent with these clinical observations on the early levels of the mind (see "Further Sources" in the back of the book).

THE FIRST LEVEL: MAKING SENSE OF SENSATIONS

The first developmental level involves learning to organize life's wondrous sensations as well as the body's responses. From a hodgepodge of sounds, sights, smells, and tactile feelings, patterns begin to emerge. Sounds become rhythms; sights become recognizable images. The ability to control movements of the head, arms, and legs makes it possible to cuddle, to follow an object, or to stand up in Mom's lap. Basic security is grounded in the ability to decipher sensations and to plan actions.

This earliest security is the foundation for the next level: establishing relationships. As sensations are exchanged between child and caregiver, the emotion of pleasure or joy often emerges. Out of the experience of joy grows a continuous sense of engagement as the caregiver responds to expressions of curiosity and assertiveness. Mother offers not simply pleasure and excitement but relief from distress as well as a safe haven in which to make bold declarations of anger and rage. The early sense of security and the capacity for relating send the mind on its lifelong journey of growth.

Equipped with an immature nervous system, a baby arrives into a clamorous world of stimuli that come both from within and without her growing body. In the early months of life, a normally developing child begins the task of making order out of the sensations that stream unbidden and unchanneled through her maturing senses. First she must attain control over her body's motions and internal sensations and over her own attention. She must learn to remain calm while simultaneously attending to and sometimes taking action on objects or events outside herself. Eventually these abilities to process sights, sounds, and other sensations and to organize responses in a calm, focused manner support mastery of further basic skills of development. The infant who has attained calm attention has taken a first, gigantic step on the road to fulfillment of her human potential.

Severe emotional problems, even psychoses, may result from a failure to master this most elementary of developmental tasks. The baby I will call Steven was first brought to our practice so severely sensitive to sound and touch (including his mother's voice and caresses) that he either screamed for hours or stared vacantly into space. He had already been diagnosed as having autistic symptoms by a major medical center. When we began working with him at twelve months, he was completely unconnected to his parents, using repetitive rubbing of a soft rug as his only means of calming himself and relating to the outside world. We began our treatment by looking for ways to get around his special sensitivities. We found a narrow band of sound to which he would briefly respond and showed his mother how to use this as an opening to form a relationship. We also found that Steven tolerated firm pressure on his back, which we used as a basis for his learning to enjoy touch. From these humble beginnings, a relationship and then interactions gradually began, and Steven got back on the road to healthy development.

Another example demonstrates the lifelong effects when one of these levels is not achieved. Jeannie, a twenty-two-year-old woman diagnosed with borderline personality disorder, had a history of almost continual difficulties. In sessions with her psychotherapist she either sat squeezed into the corner of the room or sprawled on the floor with her legs in bizarre postures. For long periods she sat silent, refusing to look at the therapist or respond to his comments about her behavior. When he labeled her "passive-aggressive," she stopped coming in for sessions altogether.

Jeannie later came to the attention of a second therapist, who saw a different root to her troubles: the inability to regulate her sensations—in other words, a failure to master the first basic level of psychological organization. All her life, he eventually established, Jeannie had felt an extreme sensitivity to touch. Skin contact that other people find trivial—inadvertently brushing against a stranger, for example—unnerved, even overwhelmed her. Like many others with such sensitivities, only clear physical boundaries between her body and other objects allowed her to feel secure. The pressure of the corner walls or floor on her back, for instance, provided her with this assurance.

Further probing also revealed a similar history of problems with motor control. It was hard for her to carry out acts that most people accomplish with ease, such as balancing on one leg, or planning a series of movements culminating in tying her shoe or drawing a picture. She therefore liked to assume postures that gave her a feeling of comfort, even if others found them strange; thus her contortions on her first therapist's floor. And finally, delving further still, the therapist learned that Jeannie had always been disturbed by noises that left others unfazed. When a companion's voice seemed too loud or animated, she coped by retreating into herself—thus her apparent refusal to respond.

Children or adults with similar difficulties often have problems in comprehending or decoding certain types of sensory information. Some can't easily figure out the sounds or words they hear. Others may have trouble deciphering what they see—how shapes or designs fit together, say. Fortunately, this was not the case with Jeannie.

Though her senses were extremely acute, Jeannie had never mastered the fundamental ability to regulate her attention so that she could respond with calm attention to the people and events around her. Stimuli that most people easily tolerate or take for granted intruded insistently, distracting her and leaving little concentration for dealing with other cues. Learning to cope effectively with her environment, to master a crucial skill that had eluded her since infancy, therefore became the first task of her intensive therapy.

Treatment proceeded on two levels. First, as she explored the physical sensations she found offensive, her therapist helped her identify coping methods that afforded her a feeling of security. "I notice that if I speak more softly, you can understand me better," he observed at one point. At another he said, "I see that the pressure of the wall on your back helps you sense where your body is."

Next, Jeannie probed the feelings, ideas, and behavior—the lived emotional experience—that grew out of her vivid physical sensations. "When I'm in a room with a lot of noise," she said, "it gets to be too much for me. I start thinking that someone is going to hurt me." She came to understand her particular reactions and the emotions they inspired as well as learned various means of controlling them. She could insist on a calm, quiet atmosphere, for example, or sit on a hard-backed chair that gave her the physical pressure she found reassuring. By such simple methods, she vastly increased her ability to focus her attention while remaining calm.

Mastering the early tasks that lead to thought and feeling must proceed in a certain order, with more basic (though not simpler) ones preceding those that are more advanced; the advanced work, as with all learning, depends on the skills gained earlier on. Children normally learn particular skills and move on to more advanced tasks within certain age ranges. But those who, like Jeannie, fail to master a given ability either remain stymied at that stage, unable to move on to the ever more complex tasks that lie ahead, or move ahead only partially and with great difficulty.

Of course, different individuals reach different levels of achievement at each stage. Some children become virtuosos—whizzes at math or expository prose, standouts at the lay-up or the line drive, prodigies at the keyboard or on the steel drum. Most people achieve more modestly, becoming reasonably competent but not truly expert. And some struggle simply to get by. Students may pass a course with an A+ or a D–, but clearly, the better students become away with a stronger foundation for later work. The same holds true for each stage of psychological development.

Not infrequently, the early tasks are not mastered at all. Some children simply fail, either because of inborn defects or inappropriate nurturing, or a combination of both. Variations in a baby's nervous system, musculature, or sense organs may keep him from developing a given ability, as they did Jeannie. A child with a well-endowed nervous system may still fail to achieve mastery because his caretakers don't provide the nurturing he needs. A drug-addicted mother, for example, may leave her baby alone in a filthy crib in a bare room, without the sights and sounds, the holding and rocking, required to entice his attention away from himself and direct it to the thrilling world around him.

Either of these deficits—neurological or emotional, in the individual or in the environment—can produce a child unprepared for further progress, hampered in the tasks of establishing self-regulation, forming relationships, and making sense of the world. Sometimes when the problem is an inborn deficit, an insightful caregiver, whether through exceptional empathy or professional intervention, can provide the support needed to make growth possible. For example, a parent can offer just the right amount of pleasurable stimulation to the oversensitive child, a soothing combination of touches, coos, and smiles that engages her attention without overwhelming her. The child then has a good chance of learning to attend, of moving toward mastery of this task and on to the others that lie before her.

Thus during the first stage of learning, usually in the first three or four months of life, a child developing normally acquires a powerful tool for dealing with the world: the ability to regulate her state of mind. For each child, however, her sensory universe and ability to plan actions, based on her native endowment modulated by the care she has received, are entirely and uniquely her own. Most people assume—and for many years clinicians and scientists believed—that the experiences of hearing, seeing, touching, and moving are pretty much the same for everyone, except perhaps the rare individual with a difference in color perception. A noise is a noise, or so it seems; a red dot is a red dot.

But now we know quite definitely that the functioning of the senses varies from individual to individual, and therefore so does sensory experience. Every individual has a personal version of the world of sensations, and that version is the one that counts. If loud noises or bright lights or soft touches irritate a child, it makes no difference that you find them pleasurable. If an infant cannot organize what she sees well enough to make out her mother's smile, it makes no difference that another child can. Every child comprehends and reacts to each type of sensation in a particular and characteristic way. But whether born with normal or compromised nervous systems, when children develop the ability to regulate and begin to organize their sensations, they can use that skill to gain the experiences on which they will build their individual identities.

THE EARLIEST SELF: GLOBAL ALIVENESS

As an infant takes in sensations, we have to wonder how he experiences his emerging sense of self. What type of consciousness does he have? His world is an array of sights, sounds, textures, tastes, and smells that strike his notice fairly randomly. We may see him gradually begin to turn toward a noise, then try to get together a smile, then cast his gaze in the general direction of a colorful toy. Though he can't quite manage yet to focus on his sensory impressions or to complete motor actions, he nonetheless seems full of an affective aliveness, a sense of the wonders around him. He seems to take pleasure in his involvement with the world without yet being able to interact with it in any purposeful way. He has no active self that engages with others or wills action. Rather, he responds to the features of his environment globally or wholly. If things overwhelm him, he screeches in distress; if they please or soothe him, he beams with delight. He feels lung-wrenching anger, limb-flapping joy. His affects are primary in the sense that simple and undiluted colors are primary. There is nothing nuanced or complex about his relationship to the world. Indeed, he seems not so much to relate to the world as to belong to it through a sense of oneness with his surroundings, an encompassing excitement or anguish in all he experiences.

Speculations abound about an infant's fantasies and even intra-uterine experiences. Freud, for example, wondered about a baby's hallucinations of Mother's breast. We have no evidence, however, that a child at this stage can differentiate himself from either the physical or the emotional world at large. He shows a synchrony of reaction in both the physical and the personal spheres; Mother's laugh and a tinkling bell both produce a sense of eager curiosity. Cognitive tests show that he can already distinguish Mother's voice from those of others, but as yet he shows no initiative in seeking her out. He can also discriminate other auditory as well as visual patterns but does not use this cognitive capacity purposefully. For the moment his ability to organize sights and sounds is more advanced than his ability to organize the desires and intentions that will eventually help him define who he is. The self is at this stage an undifferentiated consciousness consisting primarily of that wondrous sense of alert, affective aliveness and reactivity.

When we observe both older children and adults, it is difficult not to notice the range of differences in how people experience sensory aliveness. Some adults bristle with interest in colors, shapes, or sounds, while others seem dulled to the potential excitement their senses can bring them. Some easily attend to what they sense, while others become overloaded or so underreactive that they hardly notice their outer surroundings.

THE SECOND LEVEL: INTIMACY AND RELATING

Once a baby has acquired the ability to maintain a level of calm that permits her to attend to her surroundings, she is ready for the next stage. With this powerful new resource, the possibility of engaging with another person, emotionally registering her awareness of a fellow being's presence, now arises. Using her capacity for calm attention, she increasingly notices the tones, expressions, and actions of the people close to her. Before long she reacts to them with pleasure and starts building intimate relationships with those who love her.

At this second stage, when caregiver and child mutually fall in love, adults actively and intentionally signal their feelings, but the baby is not yet fully intentional. The parent-child duo behave synchronously rather than in a true give-and-take. They create a matched pair of radiant grins, one on an infant face, the other on an adult's; a chorus of purrs or coos or giggles; smiles at rocking or being rocked; whoops of delight at swinging or being swung. This exchange begins with the rapturous attention of an infatuated caregiver, which the baby glowingly returns. Out of this first immersion in delirious relating sprouts a sense of shared humanity that can later blossom into the capacity to feel empathy and love. As the baby experiences varying opportunities for closeness with others, varying levels of intimacy become possible.

Without some degree of this ecstatic wooing by at least one adult who adores her, a child may never know the powerful intoxication of human closeness, never abandon herself to the magnetic pull of human relationships, never see other people as full human beings like herself, capable of feeling what she feels. Whether because her nervous system is unable to sustain the sensations of early love or her caregiver is unable to convey them, such a child is at risk of becoming self-absorbed or an unfeeling, self-centered, aggressive individual who can inflict injury without qualm or remorse.

Consider Tom, a young man given to angry outbursts. His repeated tantrums, though less extreme than the gang violence so prominent in today's headlines, nearly cost him his job. He came into therapy as a last resort to stave off dismissal. Early on, the therapist noticed that Tom's descriptions of other persons utterly lacked emotion. People seemed to exist solely to meet his needs for interesting conversation, challenging tennis games, or tasty home-cooked meals. Nor did he show much more flair for identifying his own feelings, whether anger, sadness, loss, or jealousy. Superficially charming and outgoing, he had a long history of broken relationships and only the most rudimentary capacity to form ties with others.

As the therapist probed his past, Tom recalled how his detached, distant mother's emotions had always gone flat at the slightest sign of his childish anger, assertiveness, or excitement. She withdrew so completely at the sound of a raised voice or the sight of flailing arms or any other normal sign of intense feeling that she almost never responded to the emotions her young son was trying to convey. In effect, she appeared to reject Tom whenever he began to express any strong emotion. Her habit or retreating taught baby Tom two hard lessons: the pain of rejection, and an effective means of avoiding it. He could save himself anguish, he learned quite early, if he stopped trying to engage deeply with the person closest to him. Tom's emotional growth suffered a second, disastrous blow when his father died during Tom's infancy, ending the baby's only other chance to form a deep bond with a loving adult.

Over the years Tom never made the kind of profound human connection that would have given him the experience of oneness with others. As a young man, he responded to frustrations at work with an elemental, uncontrollable rage toward other people, whom he perceived as mere agents of his own needs. Either good luck or a sharp eye to his ultimate advantage kept his anger from flaring into actual physical violence.

Many people blocked, like Tom, at the stage of learning to love and feel a sense of shared humanity inflict grievous, even fatal, harm on others, quite unaware that their victims have feelings every bit as strong and valid as their own. As we will see in Chapter 13, the remorseless young criminals who plague our society today were often deeply deprived children who never experienced enough warmth and pleasure to become full members of the human race.

THE RELATED SELF: A SENSE OF SHARED HUMANITY

As a baby begins showing his preference for the people who regularly care for him, smiling directly at Mommy or Daddy, the global sense of self, which had just awakened to the panoply of sensations the world has to offer, now seems more focused on the human world, especially the primary caregiver. His emotions demarcate a difference between the human and inanimate spheres and strengthen his unity with the human. His sense of self reflects the same emerging differentiation as he and Mommy grin and gurgle and coo together. He smiles at bright colors or objects, too, but not with the special joyful excitement that greets his favorite people. He still does not differentiate between himself and what is not himself. Attaining a sense of union with his mother or other close adult, he is nonetheless beginning to distinguish the inanimate world from the living vibrancy of relationships. His affects show more differentiation as well. Happiness and anger now have degrees of intensity as his pleasure in human company focuses on particular individuals.

This first hint of emotional selectivity ushers in the second stage of the development of the self. A pleasurable unity with the human world, a sense of shared humanity, suffuses the baby's consciousness. His affects become steadily more distinct and discriminating as he begins to protest rather than simply erupt, to show anger rather than undirected distress, glee rather than generalized happiness, surprise rather than a startle. He takes delight in Mommy's attention and knows when the source of that delight is missing. If Mom becomes preoccupied or distracted while playing with baby, sadness or dismay settles on the little face. Even fear, which doesn't ordinarily appear until some months later, can now show up, prematurely but unmistakably, in a baby who has been traumatized or seriously frightened.

The self now exists in relation to others. It is aware of shared pleasures and joys and even of loss or despair, as when the caregiver doesn't return the infant's overtures. It will, barring unforeseen traumas, now and forever define itself by the sense of relatedness to at least one other person. The earlier stage of coming into vivid awareness of the sensations stimulated by the surroundings has given birth to the capacity for intimacy with another. To be sure, an adult or older child may try to escape from this interpersonal self of relationships, but this wish to be entirely independent of others is often an expression of anger, frustration, or despair about the very relationships that define the self.

The consciousness that embraces the human world—the sense of shared personhood so critical to the development of an individual's feeling part of the human community—flowers out of these early and enduring interchanges. The sense of aliveness that infused the consciousness of the newborn baby flooded with sensations now becomes a sense of affective harmony. Though not yet symbolic or reflective, a distinct consciousness is beginning to define itself.

CHAPTER THREE
From Intent to Dialogue

DURING THE FIRST YEAR OF LIFE THE CAPACITY TO BE purposeful leads to unspoken interchanges between infants and parents—"dialogues" conducted in expressions and gestures rather than words. These dialogues give rise to what we will later recognize as wishes and desires. Before a child learns to say "I," his sense of purpose as expressed in these interchanges begins to distinguish between the initiator and the receiver of particular actions.

As a baby becomes able to reach out to be picked up, knock food he doesn't like off the table, and make facial expressions for a variety of emotions, such willful behavior gradually demarcates the boundary between "who I am" and "this other I wish to influence." In order for an intent to flower into purposeful action, one or a number of caregivers must read and respond to it. When a child extends his arms to be picked up, scowls in disgust, or smiles fetchingly and loving adults then respond, a nonverbal dialogue is begun. Made up of expressions and gestures, it can grow from simple two- to three-sequence interactions to fifty or sixty in a row. As these purposeful interactions multiply, the first fragments of the child's emerging sense of self begin to fit together. Thus an organized sense of self starts to form even before a child can use symbols.

THE THIRD LEVEL: BUDS OF INTENTIONALITY

The ability to connect with at least one other person leads to the next developmental level, a willed exchange of signals and responses. Children who have successfully completed the passage to deep engagement gradually come to perceive that the actions passing between themselves and others are part of a two-way exchange. There is *intent* in the world—a smile leads to a smile; a frown leads to something else. Though symbols and language still lie far in the future, in the second half of their first year babies begin actively using gestures and expressions to participate in a preverbal dialogue.

A subtle change comes over the simplest of gestures—smiles, frowns, nods, shifts in body posture, blinks of the eyes, gruff or tender murmurs. From being merely synchronous, as in the previous developmental stage, the baby's and caregiver's actions now become truly interactive. Mother talks enthusiastically and baby nods in reply. Baby looks at a toy, Dad reaches for it, and baby gurgles with delight. The lifelong habit of communication begins with these simple interactive sequences, which we call circles of communication. At this stage, these interactions involve physical or somatic learning; behavior and emotions are closely tied to physical consequences such as getting a hug or hearing an answering coo.

At the same time, a fundamental psychological ability essential to all future mental development is unfolding: the child's capacity to define the boundary that separates "me" and "you," to appreciate that she occupies only a portion of the universe, while other people occupy other portions that lie beyond. From these very basic interactions children begin to understand that their own actions can elicit responses from beings who are separate from them, that an outer reality, distinct from themselves and not always subject to their will, lies beyond their own feelings and desires. For the rest of our lives, the seemingly trivial gestures first understood in late infancy serve to anchor both our human relationships and our thought processes. They also delineate the borders of the individual person. By the way people nod when we approach or catch our eyes across a room or mumble "uh-huh" as they listen to us on the phone, we know where we end and they begin. With the same simple yet subtle gestural signals that defined our very earliest interactions, we will negotiate all our relationships as long as we live. Does the person we're eagerly speaking with make an apt comment at the right moment or smile as we make a point? If so, we sense engagement, and our talk flows easily. Should someone stare at us blankly, gaze off into space, or remain mute, however, we begin to feel confused, rejected, perhaps even unloved. Very sensitive individuals may even find their thinking becoming disorganized, their sense of purpose gradually dissolving.

This pattern can be seen vividly in infancy. In a well-known study of infants at four months of age, mothers of healthy babies were asked to forgo their customary smiles, nods, and affectionate coos and show only blank, expressionless stares. The babies followed a predictable pattern in response, first smiling, cooing, and reaching with more and more intensity, as if to say, "Hey, pay attention! I'm talking to you!" When that failed, they paused momentarily, then tried again, more frantically. In a few minutes they had become irritable and frenetic, their gestures disorganized and increasingly purposeless. At last apathy and disinterest set in and they gave up.[1]

In a small way, anyone who has tried chatting with someone who maintains a poker face or giving a speech to an unresponsive audience has felt this confusion and disorientation. But the effect on babies raised by unresponsive caregivers is infinitely greater, depriving them of the chance to establish effective boundaries for their emerging selves. Unlike the babies in the study, whose mothers soon scooped them up in affectionate hugs, infants consistently deprived of appropriate responses become permanently disorganized. They lose interest in communicating, ultimately growing apathetic and even despondent.

Such early deprivation has recognizable repercussions in adulthood. One patient, though in his early twenties, nonetheless lacked the clear sense of boundaries between himself and others that makes normal relationships possible. A brilliant mathematician and inventor, when Bill began psychotherapy, he seemed to ignore the gestural level of communication—the eye contact, facial expressions, and body postures that people intuitively use to signal their intentions and guide their interactions with others. At the start of his sessions he would briefly fix his gaze on the therapist before shifting it to a nearby window. Then would begin a long, rather toneless soliloquy about his recent activities. He rarely mentioned emotions and never responded to the therapist's raised eyebrows, nods, hand motions, or changes in body position. Indeed, Bill barely acknowledged the therapist at all. Needless to say, outside of therapy as well he was oblivious to the most basic cues of others, thus getting into all sorts of difficulties in both his work and his social life. Whether people were tired, bored, annoyed, happy, or sad, Bill went on with his self-absorbed monologues. He finally came to treatment because of increasing feelings of numbness, of having "nothing inside," from a lack of relationships outside of the perfunctory ones at work.

As his story unfolded, it turned out that at the age of nine months he had lost both parents in an auto accident. A much older aunt and uncle took him in and throughout his childhood indulged his every whim. Though extremely devoted to him, they never imposed any limits or requirements, never objected to his incessant talking, never overtly disapproved of his behavior or signaled that disapproval with a stern look or a shaking finger or a clicking tongue. Rather, they hung on his every word through hours-long monologues like those the therapist now endured. During all his years performing for this adoring audience, Bill never had to wait his turn in a conversation, figure out if some prank had gotten him into hot water, guess his guardians' mood, or mold his behavior to their wishes. The toddler had never learned, and the grown man still did not know, how to send and receive the nonverbal messages that define both the boundaries that separate individuals and the common ground that lies between them. Bill's long treatment began to succeed when the therapist adopted the traffic cop's simple stop-and-go hand gestures to "direct" the conversation so that both got a chance to speak. Through practice, Bill became increasingly aware of a range of gestural communication and thus began to experience other people as emotional beings who have desires and intentions of their own.

THE WILLFUL SELF

As emotions become expressed in purposeful actions, they usher in the third level of self and consciousness. The baby no longer simply basks in the mirroring smiles of the prior period. Now she interacts reciprocally and contingently; that is, she wants something back for what she gives, and her actions answer other people's. In recent research done with Stephen Porges, my coworkers and I found that this new organization of self is matched by an important neurological shift. Willful reciprocity heralds a higher level of the central nervous system coming into operation as new pathways in the brain are recruited for social cuing and response.[2]

As indicated earlier, these willful acts form a child's first circles of communication: baby gurgles, Dad raises his eyebrows, baby smiles, Dad picks up baby, baby pats Dad. Now she aims a smile to get one back; a frown, a smirk, a gurgle, a glance, a giggle each get the recognition of a gesture in return. Over time, motor gestures gradually become smoother and more polished as she begins reaching and taking and handing back as well as making a variety of sounds. Emotions and sensations lead to richer and more differentiated dialogues as the baby learns ever more expressive and inventive ways of engaging with the world. Twenty, thirty, even forty circles of communication routinely link up now, as pats, waves, smiles, winks, laughs, squeaks, jiggles, and frowns multiply into long gestural conversations that tie the baby to those around her.

It is at this time that the baby begins to have a discrete sense of herself as a separate being—not, to be sure, a whole, integrated, or organized self, but one no longer incapable of distinguishing itself from others. First the infant experiences little pieces of herself—happiness, anger, fearfulness. She senses different feeling tones in her body as her hand reaches out to get a ball or to snatch the cookie from Mom's mouth and put it in her own. Her first sense of intention and desire coincides with, and starts to define, what we call the intentional or willful self. Now there is not only a wish to do something but a "me"—or at least a piece of a "me"—doing it. Through the combination of intending and doing, the baby begins to experience these rudimentary bits of herself.

This sense of self does not, and as yet cannot, exist in the abstract or in isolation from other people. However, the nervous system has now matured sufficiently that the child can show emotion as well as perceive and respond to emotion, and she can turn these experiences into an exchange. Through the caregiver's initiatives and responses, the baby comes to experience initiative and response within herself—in other words, a sense of "me" that is interactive. What she does and what she responds to define the pieces, which are inseparable from this new intentionality.

At the start there was no intentional or willful self, only a sense of unity with the caregiver. D. W. Winnicott put this dramatically: "A baby alone does not exist." From this amorphous core, the first tiny shoots of a sense of self begin to grow if—and only if—the child, who now has the physical ability to interact, lives in an environment that responds to her overtures and encourages her to make use of this new power. The first psychological boundaries between the baby and the outside world, the first delineation of a contained self, are drawn between the impulsive actions of an infant and the reactions of an adult. The response to these early purposeful interactions begins to draw a boundary between the subjective and the objective. In this way the sense of a reality outside ourselves is born. Our sense of reality is a product of both subjective and objective processes. It begins, however, with the establishment of this earliest boundary.

From signs of intentional behavior, such as touching Dad's nose or throwing food off the table, we read desires, wishes, motives. At this point motor behavior is our evidence of desire or motivation. Interestingly, without the growing ability to coordinate his muscles due to the development of his nervous system, the child might not be able to construct something as organized as a desire or wish. In other words, the desire or wish most likely cannot yet exist as an idea in its own right. It must be tied to an action that defines it. An action defines a desire in the same way that a verbal symbol will later define an idea; it provides the necessary form or structure to move the intent from the baby's inner world of subjectivity to the outer one of interpersonal objectivity. Without such defining actions, the potential wish may not become an independent wish or desire.

The child does not yet have the ability to create symbols or ideas to represent wishes or desires. His main way of knowing and communicating is through his motor system. For this reason we encourage children with severe motor problems or developmental delays to use any part of their functioning motor system, such as their tongues or neck muscles, to convey intent. If a child is unable to express early intentionality, intellectual and emotional development can be arrested.

Children with severe motor delays who have done well, even when intervention has been late, often develop ways to communicate with looks, sounds, or limited motor movements.

While the motor system provides a means of defining and expressing wishes or desires, it is the combination of affect and purposeful motor behavior that defines intent. Earlier on, the baby had needs—to be fed, to be changed, to be held—but did not express them in any intentional form. His hunger or discomfort or glee led to changes in facial expression, sounds, body posture, and the like. But these changes were purely reactive to the sensations and emotions that he was experiencing. Now the ability to use his arms to reach, grab, pull; his ability to yell in annoyance, rather than because of physiological distress (or to giggle to get a giggle back, rather than because of a gas bubble), heralds the child's will. A curious "me," a fearful "me," an angry "me"—all buds of the self—are still not unified. Initially they exist as separate little islands; only later do they coalesce. The self that was no more than a global alertness first became a self related to and engaged with the world. Now a new, willful self sprouts. Consciousness at this point consists of a budding sense of intentionality, of being an agent of willful action.[3]

THE FOURTH LEVEL: PURPOSE AND INTERACTION

Once a child connects sensation and emotion to intentional action, he can proceed to the fourth level of development, when increasingly complex, presymbolic communication equips him to find his way in the world of social interaction.

This step, too, is taken gradually. When a mother smiles at her baby because he smiled at her, or when she shakes her head and says "No, don't do that" because he pushes away his plate while she tries to feed him his puréed carrots, the baby begins to learn things about her and about himself. He is someone who can inspire affection and warmth in others. She is someone likely to insist that he do as she says. And so, having earlier blocked out the boundaries between himself and those around him, at twelve to eighteen months the child, by now a toddler, begins to fill in the rough outlines with some detail.

The process proceeds haltingly. A child's earliest sense of who he is is very incomplete, a map with large areas left blank. While he may already have laid out the stretch involving the responses that his own smile or sense of pleasure elicits from Mom, may have tried out reactions to frowns and screeches, there are still vast uncharted territories in his relationship with her.

The picture gains greater resolution as reciprocal gesturing becomes more complex. A toddler glances questioningly toward his mother. She returns the inquisitive look and asks, "What?" He takes her hand and pulls her toward the refrigerator, babbling with excitement. Fifty circles of communication later, all wordless on his part—fifty sets of pointing and questioning, leading and laughing, raising eyebrows and nodding happily—he gurgles in delight as he helps her uncap a cup of the very flavor of yogurt he wanted all along.

As a toddler's gestural repertoire grows in richness, he begins to discern patterns in his own and others' behavior. Mom usually responds when he makes friendly requests but not when she's cranky. Dad loves to roughhouse but not to sing lullabies. Grandma is a good deal less strict than either Dad or Mom. He gradually draws these items on the map delineating himself as a person and, when others impinge on him, adding to his expanding notion of how his actions, intentions, and expectations fit in with those of the people around him. Which actions get him affection and approval? Which yield only rejection or anger? Is he worthy of care, attention, and respect? Are those around him also worthy? In a similar way he is discovering how the physical world works—turning this little plastic thing causes a funny animal to pop up, or pushing this big, smooth-feeling, see-through object makes a big noise and maybe even produces a splatter of little pieces and yelling from Mom.

Surveying this unknown terrain and placing himself in relation to it is the pressing task of the early toddler stage, a monumental project that begins well before a child can talk in phrases or hop on one foot. At this crucial time the individual either meets or fails to meet perhaps this most basic emotional challenge of the human lifetime and in so doing forms crucial elements of character. Indeed, long before an infant can speak, personality is already being molded by the countless interactions between caregiver and child.

Twelve-month-old Jason, for example, reaches repeatedly for closeness with his mother, but each time his demands make her feel tense and overwhelmed, and she withdraws from him. The active, energetic child soon learns to seek in stimulation the satisfaction he cannot find in intimacy. He becomes more aggressive, more and more impulsive. As he grows older he responds belligerently whenever he feels the loss, sadness, and vulnerability first experienced at his mother's rejection. When a friend moves away, a favorite teacher misses several days of school, or his parents ignore him, Jason gives no thought to his sadness or loneliness. Rather, he applies the solution he learned as a baby: aggression, counter-rejection, and the attitude that is later expressed as "I don't need anyone."

At the same time, baby Emma embarks on her own cautious explorations. Extremely sensitive to sound, she nonetheless begins experimenting with her own voice, and one day, babbling excitedly, she also boldly tries to explore Mom's nose with her fingers. But her mother becomes tense when Emma grows inquisitive and fears that the childish overtures are a sign of inappropriate aggression rather than simply assertiveness. She pokes back at Emma's nose and drowns out the infant's protests with admonitions that "touching people's faces isn't nice." This pattern is repeated in numerous ways every time Emma is assertive. Before Emma has reached ten months, she has learned the risks of expressing herself. She gradually abandons exploration in favor of whining, displaying increased passivity in the face of her fear. Later on, when bolder children pick on her, this bright and dutiful child may well blame herself, remaining all the while passive, insecure, and easily frightened. She may even choose domineering friends who can lead her around.

Jason and Emma each drew these powerful conclusions about themselves not from any rational deliberation but from their emotional experience of how other people act. They based their conclusions about how their own actions fit in with those of others mainly on their caregivers' reactions. Both children, unfortunately, learned lessons that will serve them ill in later years. Over time, the reactions a child elicits combine with her own desires and expectations to form a characteristic pattern of attitude and response.

As each developing human being works on the map of her own and others' natures, she naturally fills in certain areas in far more detail than others. No child's family or daily life affords equal exposure to all areas of experience. No child can give the same attention to every possible theme. Just as each child learns only one, or at most two, native tongues and each family eats only a certain range of foods or practices a certain religion or spends time with certain friends at certain hobbies, so the individual's early emotional repertoire emphasizes some areas but not others. One child's environment may offer Mexican Spanish, tortillas, and Roman Catholicism, that of another American English, fried chicken, and Christian Science. In the same way, one child's family life may be infused with humor and joking and the child herself become readily able to laugh off problems and join in the fun, whereas another may learn to respond to challenges with aggression or anxiety or passivity. Each individual develops areas of emotional strength and weakness, flexibility and constriction.

In areas of constriction, as we have seen, the groundwork may be laid for problems in coping later on. A person may fail to learn flexibility of response in a particular emotional realm. Anger or anxiety or intimacy or separation thus doesn't elicit a response appropriate to the circumstances or one that can lead toward a resolution. Rather, it calls up a narrow, stereotyped, ritualized response, a sort of one-size-fits-all reaction that fits no situation well: intimacy always engenders flight, anxiety always builds up to hysteria, separation always culminates in panic. Emotional constriction can also produce extreme and polarized reactions. An individual might alternate between moods and attitudes of jollity and moroseness, passivity and antagonism, admiration and contempt.

Such constrictions occur in even the best-endowed child raised by the most loving, conscientious parents. If the essence of humanity is to be emotional, then the fate of humanity is to be imperfect. Authentic, spontaneous emotion is unpredictable, sometimes even uncontrollable. The more emotionally sensitive and subtle a person is, in fact, the less governable his feelings and emotional reactions will be. No one, no matter how well balanced and flexible, can maintain constant equanimity. At one time or another everyone gives in to feelings that are out of proportion to the situation. More important, because of these patterns established as each of us grew up, we are more comfortable with some emotions than with others. We may have five thousand different responses to love and pleasure and only two to anger, or vice versa. We may completely avoid certain emotions. There is no interaction and therefore no sense of give-and-take in these avoided areas. No child's environment is perfect, and parents who try too hard to provide one often quash the emotional spontaneity that is so critical to the entire process of development.

Even so, the developments of this formative period, though influential, are not definitive. Many elements of personality form early in life, but daily interactions continually redefine it. As older children or even adults, the aggressive Jason and scared, passive Emma may be able to rework these patterns. They may, of course, seek out friends and spouses who maintain the status quo, but they may also have the luck to engage with someone in the area they originally had to abandon—vulnerability in Jason's case, assertiveness in Emma's.

As a toddler advances at this fourth developmental level and becomes able to distinguish facial expressions and body postures, she can now discriminate among basic emotions, distinguishing those meaning safety and comfort from those meaning danger. She can tell approval from disapproval, acceptance from rejection. Life's most essential emotional themes are identified and patterns of dealing with them formed. The child also begins to use this new ability in increasingly complicated situations. Rather than simply registering the actions of those around her, she begins to size up situations on the basis of subtle behavioral cues. Were the two people who fell silent when she entered the room hugging or arguing? Does her mother fear the man who has just come up to her? The child starts to use this awareness to respond differently to people depending on their demeanor, to distrust someone who strikes her as untrustworthy, to withdraw from a situation that seems threatening.

For the rest of her life, this ability will serve as a kind of radar she can use to navigate through her social universe, allowing her to form the unspoken impressions that provide our first and often most reliable assessment of others' feelings and intentions, that let us see beyond words into the emotional meaning of an encounter. The intuitive ability to figure out human exchanges, to pick up affective cues before any words have been exchanged and understand their significance, eventually comes to function as a kind of sense organ.

Indeed, it becomes a sort of "supersense" that subsumes elements of all the others and lets us make instantaneous assessments and adjustments in our own reactions. It is in fact what make social life possible.

Well before she acquires symbolic language, then, the typical child has developed the basic skill that will enable her to learn the values, norms, and attitudes of the culture to which her parents or caregivers belong. Using this supersense as she watches those around her live their daily lives, she deciphers the subtext of their emotional reactions to routine events. Their behavior provides an unspoken but utterly frank running commentary along a scale of approval, disapproval, anger, excitement, happiness, and fear. Picking up cues from this subtext, the child learns more vividly and precisely than through any language what is good and bad, what is done and not done, what is acceptable and unacceptable in the social world she inhabits.

Once more our work with autistic children elucidates a critical aspect of development in healthy children. Our observations suggest that autism results from a primary deficit more fundamental than the language, cognitive, or social deficits usually described, one that lies at precisely the level of development we have been discussing. In reviewing more than two hundred cases, we found that at the time of diagnosis 68 percent of children with various types of autistic spectrum disorder had not reached the level of complex purposeful behavior, in comparison with only 4 percent of children who did not have autistic symptoms, even though many had some rote or repetitive language skills.[4] As we have seen, most children acquire the capacity to discern emotional cues naturally during their development. It is this capacity that enables them to behave purposefully. The ability to connect motor behavior to desires or interests later leads to the emergence of symbolic proficiency during the course of ordinary interaction. Autistic children, however, are unable to connect affect to either behavior or thoughts. But when we have been able to help them overcome this inability, such children can progress.

The connection between affects, behavior, and the use of symbols may explain the puzzling observation that many children who are somewhat engaged and purposeful in their earliest development begin to exhibit obvious autistic symptoms only between eighteen and thirty months of age, with perseveration and self-stimulatory behavior such as spinning, lining up toys, and opening and closing doors. In his second year, a child learns to go beyond simple peek-a-boo interactions to sequences in which, say, he takes his father by the hand and walks him to the cupboard, to the front door, to the television. Such complex, goal-directed interactions require a sense of purpose and direction, a sense imparted by the child's emotional response to others. Moreover, as the nervous system develops, the use of symbols (e.g., the ability to match a picture to an object or to repeat words) becomes possible. Affect again provides purpose and direction to this new capacity. It is affect that makes "juice" something that tastes good and gives "more" the meaning of getting additional experiences of the type you want. Without affect, however, the emerging behavior and thinking become idiosyncratic and disorganized, like members of an orchestra playing without a conductor. Directed and purposeful behavior and thinking, in contrast, are organized by affect and operate in harmonious concert.

Trouble in connecting affect to behavior and thinking may arise from difficulties in neuronal connections among functions ordinarily carried out in separate parts of the brain. In most right-handed persons, the right side of the brain deals more with affect and intent than the left side, which is largely concerned with sequencing language, symbols, and behavior. It is interesting that many children with autistic spectrum disorders often prefer to look at objects out of the corners of their eyes and also avoid direct eye contact, even when being affectionate.[5] They may hug and even kiss their parents, but their eyes do not convey any loving look. Parents are understandably perplexed by this behavior. "She'll hug me but not look at me," explained one frustrated father. By looking askance, such children are using only one side of the brain alone, whereas when we look directly in front of us, we have to use both sides of the brain in an integrated fashion.

Perhaps behavior learned earlier in life, such as calming, attending to sensory impressions, being affectionate, and even performing simple gestural interactions, can be carried out by parts of the brain that are not fully integrated, including one or the other side of the brain alone, and it is only when areas must work more fully together that autistic symptoms may first be exhibited because of specific nervous system difficulties. The developments that take place during the second year of life, allowing elaborate planning of behavior and, over time, meaningful use of words, may thus require the coordination of different areas of the brain, including functions associated with the left and right hemispheres. Consistent with this thesis is a body of research with both animals and humans looking at what happens when one side of the brain functions alone.[6] Complex affect-directed action appears to require both sides working in tandem.

It therefore seems that the primary deficit in autism has to do with the relationship between affect and the planning or sequencing of behavior and between affect and the emerging ability to use symbols. Problems in developing empathy or in constructing a theory of the mind (i.e., the ability to grasp the attitudes and intentions of others), which some researchers pinpoint as involved in autistic disorder, are in all likelihood secondary difficulties that derive from this more primary deficit.

Neurological findings in regard to autism are at present inconclusive. While affected children evidence many physiological differences, we have not yet identified any single underlying deficit or group of deficits.[7] Developmental observations about the link between affect and behavior may help us identify the most critical biological patterns. Meanwhile, the treatment approaches that we have found most successful first and foremost involve helping children with autistic spectrum symptoms make these affective connections. When they have been able to forge these links, their use of language, cognitive skills, and social behavior take on a more spontaneous quality. When we have been unsuccessful in helping children form such links, or when more mechanistic behavioral approaches have been used, we have sometimes seen progress, but it is not of the same caliber. Language and cognition tend to remain stereotyped, rigid, and repetitive. Even children with excellent reading and math skills have difficulty when abstract thinking is required. Friendships and the capacity for creativity are problematic.

For all children, including those facing unusual physiological challenges, emotional interaction plays a vital role in learning. Although it is too early to know for certain whether therapy can correct the original neurological handicap or build compensatory strengths, it appears that both are happening. The improvement seen in autistic children who have gradually passed through the stages of affective development underlines the importance of understanding the emotionally based mental architecture supporting intelligence.

THE PREVERBAL SENSE OF SELF

As the child's interactive world grows more complex and he engages in presymbolic bargaining, his sense of self permits more organization, so that he can play an active role in his world through directed plans and objectives. His neurological hardwiring now supports much larger units: for the child, the happy "me" and the "me" that wants the apple and the "me" that gets a kiss can all combine into the "me" that is happy when he gets an apple or a kiss. Happiness is no longer a series of fragmented sensations, but one connected experience that may include going for a walk with Mommy and visiting Grandma and playing with the dog. This presymbolic but coherent sense of self emerges as the islands of emotion, intention, and motivation that defined the earlier, fragmented "me" now coalesce into a larger, more unified "me." The toddler can take Mommy by the hand with the intention of getting the treat he wants, and when she demurs, can charm or cajole. Out of these long chains of affective cuing, he develops a sense of self that can get its needs met through various means.

At twelve or thirteen months, this self is still in disparate though rather large parts. The happy "me" has subsumed the curious and exploratory and assertive "me," but it lies quite far from the angry or sad "me." When a twelve- to fourteen-month-old gets angry at someone, he may have no sense that just moments ago he was playing happily with that person. If he had a gun, one suspects, he'd shoot without remorse. By fifteen months or so, however, a dawning awareness that a relationship of trust and security can coexist with anger has often begun to moderate his temper. The sense of self now consists of larger and larger unified parts, although significant splits still remain. Indeed, in some adults, the happy side doesn't know the angry one; Dr. Jekyll and Mr. Hyde live in the same skin but never meet.

By eighteen or twenty months, a child angry at a loved one would use a gun to threaten but would not shoot. His rage now has a different quality; it seems more qualified, more complex, like the anger of a long-married couple who know that no quarrel, no matter how bitter, can sever the ties that bind them. The child has managed to merge two quite different "me"s, an angry one and a loving one, into a single overriding self.

As a child unifies distinct and even conflicting affects into his sense of self, he also forges emotional bonds across space and eventually across time. Earlier he felt only Mom's warmth when lying in her arms or Dad's playfulness when sitting in his lap. Now, however, he can look up from his blocks, glance at Mom across the room, see her smile, and feel the security of having her near. Or he can gurgle to Dad, hear an answering sound from the next room, and feel reassured by this communication. By the middle of his second year he can communicate across space, which frees him to explore in ever wider circles away from his caregivers but still affords him the comfort of knowing they're close.

When they talk on the phone with a person on the other side of the continent or even read a letter from someone overseas, most adults can achieve this sense of connection across space. Some, however, cannot. Developing this knack is a major step for the small child, as Margaret Mahler has pointed out. Moving away from Mother, she observed, can seem to a frightened baby like losing her. The desire for independence and dependence at the same time constitutes a dilemma of "separation and individuation."[8]

But a child who can figuratively carry Mommy across space can resolve this dilemma. He can explore in the playroom while she works in the kitchen and yet keep close by looking at her from a distance. An occasional approving nod from her can feel like a nice cuddle. If he is out of sight, calling out and hearing her voice may convey the same sense of security and warmth. The child's ability to decode his mother's gestures and vocal patterns gives him psychological security, though if she ignores his looks or calls he may have to run back and cling to her for a time. Later he will be able to carry a mental image of Mom across time as well as space. He can picture her now as she was a few minutes ago. By developing the ability to communicate with those he loves even when he can't touch them, the toddler incorporates a powerful sense of emotional security.

The solid achievement of the fourth stage is the coalescence of larger and larger parts of the self through the bringing together of many intentions and affects. This organization arises in action. The child can connect his anger with his happiness if he experiences both within a single episode. Playing with Mommy, for example, he becomes frustrated because she won't let him pull off her glasses. She tells him no, and when he tries again to grab them, she tells him no again. Perhaps she holds him at arm's length and gives him her "Stop it, I mean business" look. When he scowls, she playfully scowls back. "I know you're angry," she says, "but I can't let you play with my glasses. I need them." Then with a few more grumpy protests he goes back to their earlier game. He has gone from happiness to anger and back to happiness again. He senses that the anger and the happiness both belong to him, and his sense of self begins to integrate a "me" that can be angry and one that can be happy at almost the same time. The integration happens because he experiences, and his caregivers tolerate, a wide range of feelings.

This integration happens over time. When I play with toddlers of different ages and manage to get them mad at me, I see different reactions. The anger of a twelve-month-old seems unbuffered by any awareness that I'm the person he liked or even loved a few minutes ago. This child, I feel, would definitely pull the trigger. By eighteen months, however, his anger is quite different. It can be intense, but underlying it is the recognition that I'm the same person whom he was enjoying playing with a few minutes earlier.

This integration might not occur, however, if, for example, each time a child showed frustration a caregiver imposed a "time out" and disappeared. He would not have the chance to experience the sequence of emotions from annoyance and anger back to content. In this situation anger remains separate from, and indeed threatening to, happiness: it becomes something that makes Mom disappear. Happiness thus becomes a feeling that can exist only in the absence of anger. It is not surprising, therefore, that children of very depressed caregivers who can tolerate little stress often learn to couple their anger with feelings of abandonment, emptiness, even despair. Rather than the possibility of returning to happiness, it is the threat of being left alone that becomes linked to anger.

The child's sense of self now also grows through imitating the motions, gestures, expressions, and tones of voice of the people he loves. This is the time of putting on Daddy's hat and mimicking his walk, of scolding a doll with a perfect replica of Mommy's irritated expression, and of more elaborate bouts of monkey see, monkey do. Wearing Daddy's hat and walking to the door as if on his way to work, he *is* Daddy. Stirring a pot on his toy stove while Mommy stirs a bigger pot in which she is making dinner, he *is* Mommy. No longer learning about Mommy and Daddy only in bits, he can imitate whole patterns. He takes it all in at once, the way a skilled athlete who watches a pro play tennis can go out and hit the ball with improved strokes. Becoming like other people by trying out their actions also serves a second important purpose beyond building up a sense of self. Experiencing himself as another, the toddler prepares for the development of empathy when he reaches a more advanced stage of consciousness.

Although at this stage imitation is motivated by feelings, it is based on the emergence of the hardwired ability of the brain to see, listen to, and reproduce whole patterns rather than only bits and pieces.[9] With this new ability toddlers learn social behavior, language, cognitive skills, and the like very rapidly. To the child who suffers the trauma of serious frustration or fear, however, imitation becomes not a means of expanding consciousness and selfhood but of trying to hold on to what has been lost. Replaying the traumatic situation, he attempts to recapture what was once his. Used in this way as a defense against terror, imitation loses its emotional flexibility. Instead of integrating the roles and traits of others into the growing self, he begins taking in chunks that he cannot digest. Smiling at Daddy while donning his hat, the child can get a smile in return; the imitation and the smile become one, and his own. But if the child is walking like Daddy to exorcise fear of being attacked by Daddy, the imitation remains isolated, a foreign body in the psyche. Children who acquire a false maturity through trauma and lack of interactive nurturing often grow into adults unsure of which parts of themselves are truly their own, which of their actions really express their own selves.

Rigid rituals are also characteristic of a constricted sense of self. Rituals that take on symbolic meaning can eventually be elaborated on, for example in drama. These are very different from rituals used solely to gain a sense of security and for self-stimulation. The latter are often a poor substitute for the human interaction and soothing that are lacking.

For the child who is moving ahead, the new neurologically based capacities for pattern recognition and imitation permit larger and larger interactive patterns. She now learns how to deal with the deepest and most fundamental human feelings. Anger, love, closeness, assertiveness, curiosity, dependency become integrated into the child's experience as she tries out her parents' emotional reactions and makes them her own. Through imitation, Dad's scowl of annoyance and impatient pacing, Mom's look of surprise and anxious finger-tapping take on emotional meaning for the child and become part of herself. If smiling like Mom is tied to a feeling of warmth and love and results in intimacy with Mom or Dad, it becomes a real part of the emerging person. Similarly, if growling like Dad is tied to anger and serves to scare a sibling away, it too might be integrated into the growing self. If the pattern is not tied to affect or serves no purpose, however, it remains aimless. If tied to certain negative emotions, it can become rigidly repetitive.

When the ability to recognize larger patterns appears at around eighteen months, the toddler is better able to read the feelings of others and learns to deal with them in a more effective way. Now the child can tell, from the set of Daddy's head or the tension in his shoulders as he comes into the room, that this evening he feels grouchy and is in no mood to play. It's best not to show him a new ball right now or try to engage him in a game. Such a level of perception comes into being only through interaction—through untold opportunities to read the shape of Mommy's mouth, the wrinkles in Daddy's brow. For the toddler who lacks sufficient interaction, making these readings can become problematic. Lack of practice in complex preverbal communication may lead her to misread a teacher's silent signal that this time she means business, or get too close to another child without paving the way for nearness.

All these abilities have by now combined in something greater than behavioral patterns. At this point we can begin talking about the child's self as her character structure or personality, her particular way of dealing with the world. Built up of her expectations and usual responses, of the links she has made with her feelings, it is still independent of the use of symbols. Does the child expect others to love her or reject her, to tolerate her anger or abandon her when she shows it, to encourage her curiosity or demand that she remain passive, to allow her to explore in security or condemn her to loneliness when she ventures out on her own? These earliest behavioral and emotional presuppositions do not depend, as Freud thought, on conflicts dealing with some symbolic fear of anger, but on the lessons learned directly in innumerable interchanges with others. These interchanges form a significant part of character before even unconscious symbols are formed to any significant degree. A small child knows how others will react to her not because she can think about it logically but because her emotions, linked into extensive patterns based on experience, tell her about closeness, about assertiveness, about sexuality, about frustration, about what leads to acceptance and what leads to fear or pain.

Values and attitudes begin here, well before they are represented by symbols. The child's emotions, now attached to patterns of response, provide a constant, running commentary on her behavior. Desire, expectation, and intention are being transformed into patterns of meaning, with emotion as a guide through the increasingly complicated challenges of life. Consciousness at this stage consists of a greater awareness of feelings, behavior, and actions—the patterns that are the foundations of the sense of self. Equally important is the awareness of others as interactive beings with purpose and even some predictability. The world of discrete units of interaction is now one of patterns. And the awareness of self and others for the first time involves complex emotional and social expectations.

CHAPTER FOUR

Creating an Internal World

DURING THE NEXT TWO STAGES OF DEVELOPMENT, OUR MINDS make the essential transition to grasping symbolic meaning. The emotional relationships and expectations formed in the earlier stages now find additional expression.

Wishes and intents are now represented internally by multisensory images. We become able to play out behavior in our minds before we carry it out. We learn to solve problems through thought experiments. We "picture" relationships, dialogues, and feelings, gradually creating new images to express our growing range of emotions. Together these images begin to create an inner world.

Initially, the images emerge in a free-floating manner, like unconnected balloons. Over time logical bridges are formed that connect these images to one another. Bridges also begin to connect various emotions, like anger and loss, to the awareness of time, such as an understanding of "now" and "later," and experiences with space, such as the knowledge that "Mommy is not here—she is around the corner." As this happens, the inner world develops a cohesive organization that permits what we call thinking.

During these stages, consciousness and self go through momentous changes. For the first time we experience ourselves in terms of images, not simply affects, physical sensations, and behavior. Also for the first time we create categories—anger versus love, make-believe versus reality, what we want to do versus what we do do.

Symbolic expression becomes a shorthand in which the mind expresses its desires and goals. Instead of taking Mother by the hand, walking her to the refrigerator, and banging on the door for juice, a child can say "Juice now." Instead of scratching or biting, he can say "Mad!" or "Want hit you!"

At first this emerging world of images makes it easier for the child simply to communicate what he already wants. We have seen the ability to know what one wants develop in the earlier stages of learning how to attend, engage, and communicate with simple and then more complex affects and gestures. Without the mastery of these stages, the images and symbols that are now formed will remain hollow, lacking intent and feeling and ultimately meaning. Children who have not mastered the earlier tasks will operate only in a concrete, rote manner, such as rigidly playing out scenes they saw on television or listing a series of nouns.

Symbols and images are an economical way not only to organize experiences but to create new ones. The ability to manipulate them thus creates a foundation for self-elaboration and understanding as well as for the vast developmental strides ahead. The symbolic capacity is the principal gateway between the submerged world of emotion and intent and the ever-expanding intellectual and social world in which each individual participates. We enter this gateway not just once, in childhood, but again and again throughout our lives.

THE FIFTH LEVEL: IMAGES, IDEAS, AND SYMBOLS

The child who has mastered the ability to create patterns of intent, behavior, emotion, and expectation can move ahead, through countless small exchanges, to the stage of true symbolic expression. In the second or third year, she begins to deal not only with behavior but with ideas. She begins to grasp that one thing can stand for another, that an image of something can represent the thing itself. This realization allows her to create an inner picture of her world. Moreover, these symbols can represent not only for her own intentions, wishes, and feelings but those of other people as well. We first see this ability in a child's pretend play, when dolls can hug and teddy bears wave "bye-bye." We see it when a child who has lost a favorite toy can say "I feel sad." The ability to abstract a feeling and give it a name—to know that tightness in the chest is fear, the desire to throw a punch is anger, or a lift of the heart is joy—allows her to bring emotions to a new level of awareness and express them symbolically rather than by acting on them physically. She can tell Dad she feels scared rather than shrieking in fear. She can tell Mom she wants a cookie rather than dragging her to the kitchen.

The child who does not attain this level can experience her feelings only at the level of behavior or visceral reaction. Rather than knowing that she feels lonely or disappointed or apprehensive or scared, she feels an emptiness in her belly, or she cries, or her stomach tightens or her hands sweat. She can't give a particular state of being an abstract name that will allow her to identify and understand it.

How does a child go from the action mode of being, in which satisfaction lies in behavior, in meeting bodily goals and desires, to the symbolic mode of being, in which satisfaction can lie in the picture or idea of an action rather than in the action itself? The way this happens has been an unsolved psychological problem. Piaget and others have described aspects of the process, but they did not explain the child's motivation for making this crucial transition.[1] With developmental understanding, however, we can approach the question in a new way. A child makes this transition, like the previous transformations, through the maturing possibilities of her neurology combined with the richness of her affective experiences. Both the nervous system and the child's emotional development must be ready for this next step.

In the action mode, when a child wants love, he demands a hug; when he feels frustrated, he bangs his spoon on the high chair tray; when he feels hungry, he grabs a cookie. In the symbolic mode, he must take at least some satisfaction in the idea that Mom and Dad love him, or in the knowledge that Mom said she'll let him go outside in a moment, or in the image of dinner coming soon. The initial images are those of actions—vivid pictures of hugging Mom or climbing down from the high chair or biting into a favorite food. Later on, symbols will represent feelings as well, along with other aspects of the self: an image will express affection rather than just hugging, freedom rather than just climbing, satiation rather than just eating.

For this to happen, the child must learn to take pleasure in contemplating the patterns in his own mind. What motivates him to want to make this switch? Clinical work with children between eighteen and twenty-four months suggests that, not surprisingly, many find it difficult, and do not succeed until later in childhood or even in adulthood. The key, once again, is a warm, close relationship with an adult, one in which communication becomes important enough to provide satisfaction in itself. Eventually the thoughts or images that arise from such communication themselves become imbued with pleasure.

This shift in modes therefore requires the long-term participation of someone who promotes interaction, who supports ever greater use of signals, who joins in the child's pretend play, who helps him link the pleasure of relating to the skills of communicating symbolically. The sheer enjoyment of being listened to, the satisfaction of gaining attention through the use of images, motivates the first step in this epochal move. The child delights not only in getting what he wants or having his expectations confirmed but in letting others know what they are. At first, when he wants a tickle, he tickles Daddy; later he points to his own armpit and giggles. He tells Daddy what he wants to do without actually doing it. He takes pleasure and delight in the successful communication of his wish, much as adults take pleasure in the warmth of swapping experiences and feelings with a friend.

At the end of the second year of life, as communication for communication's sake begins to overtake communication merely to meet a need, the child embarks on a course he will continue throughout life. His love for his caregivers and the pleasure they bring him leads him to enjoy communicating in its own right. He never completely loses his need for action and direct satisfaction, of course, but the pleasures of symbolic expression deepen with the years, and gradually conversation, reading, writing, poetry, mathematics, music, drama, painting, sculpture, and all the arts and sciences can become sources of profound gratification. Even before a child has words, his pleasure in relationships becomes pleasure in communicating within relationships. This pleasure then gradually attaches to communication itself, to the idea in addition to the act. The idea becomes more than a way of relating; it comes desirable in itself.

The caring adult encourages the child to translate his immediate, concrete aims into words and images. Caregivers who themselves take pleasure in communicating foster this new ability. They can encourage symbolic interaction by not being intimidated by the child's fierce desires and by helping the child reflect. Something as simple as a child saying "I want to go outside" can be responded to with a yes or no on the one hand or, on the other, "What do you want to do outside?" The latter response helps the child reflect on his wish, while the former only gives in to it or inhibits it. Reflection fosters the use of symbols and, more broadly, the ability to think, while inhibition or immediate giving in both foster only a tendency toward action. From satisfying exchanges of this kind comes the motivation to communicate more, producing more pleasure in the process of communication and finally pleasure in the words or images themselves. At this point contemplating his intentions and emotions and clothing them in symbols becomes one of the child's chief joys. Pretend play, acting out (as opposed to merely imitating), and acquiring new words all result from the child's excitement in his new powers.

Children whose caregivers tend to be more literal may only partially develop the ability to use words and symbols. If, when a child wants to go out in the rain, the parent asks why and helps the child to see—in his mind's eye—the possible outcome of his plan, the youngster gets practice in creating ideas and substituting them for actions. But the parent who simply bellows no affords no such opportunity. With such responses, the child may not learn to create symbolic representations of his emotions, desires, and wishes. Those pictures he does create tend to be concrete and oriented toward action.

Meanwhile, the child's concomitant neurological growth helps his repertoire of symbols multiply rapidly. The nervous system allows for quicker learning now, and he accumulates words and ideas with growing ease. He can imitate almost any sound or word and does so regularly. This is still not automatic, however. New words take on meaning and become part of the child's vocabulary only when attached to emotion or intent. Talking like Daddy means being like and being close to

Daddy. Saying "juice" means the pleasure of tasting juice. It is these feelings and intentions that give meaning and purpose to the otherwise neutral new words and symbols that are accumulating.

The neural hardwiring continues to grow in complexity, allowing a child not only to create images but to recreate complex scenes and events he has observed and to combine them in new ways. Memories are formed that involve not only images of patterns of action but also emotions, intentions, and desires. Without these affective components, memory would be a mere computer screen that showed pictures by rote, without meaning or structure. Because of them, however, memory becomes part of the expression of an individual self. Meaning and purpose, in other words, together with remembered sensations, form the dual code that is essential to our humanity.

When a child lacks nuanced relationships or cannot for neurological reasons learn from them, the images he develops contain less detail and complexity, his personality is less differentiated, and his later ability to form relationships is much reduced. Many adults have never sufficiently mastered the ability to form images. One such person, Susan, came into therapy in the hope of saving her deteriorating marriage. Her husband was spending increasingly long hours at the office, and their relationship was becoming more and more acrimonious. Whenever Jim's work hours lengthened, she would complain and criticize, which naturally made him spend even more time working—which in turn only stepped up her complaints. Try as she might, she lamented to the therapist, she could not get him to pay her the attention that she needed and deserved.

Susan couldn't connect the couple's problems to her own feelings. She knew only that she felt generally "bad" but couldn't find words to describe her state of mind or the root of her trouble. Nothing she tried seemed to break the pattern that was driving Jim away.

Her intense orientation toward changing Jim's behavior alerted the therapist to the fact that Susan had great difficulty representing many of her feelings symbolically rather than simply acting on them. When he asked her for more details about her feelings, she said that Jim's refusal to come home made her behave coldly toward him. She could describe her actions or tendency to act a certain way, but not how she felt. The therapist, hoping to help her focus on her feelings, asked her first to attend to her physical sensations. She began by describing her muscles as tight and tense. Over time her descriptions hinted at emotions: for example, her body felt as though it were "getting ready for an attack." Only gradually did feelings like anger and fury emerge clearly.

Eventually Susan learned to identify the bodily manifestations of fear and loneliness as well as anger. She came to realize that she felt vulnerable, helpless, and lost. Never before had she discussed her anger or feelings of loss; she had only sensed a vaguely defined, overly inclusive state of panic. Once she learned to talk about her sense of loss, she was able to connect her anxiety at Jim's absence to similar terrors she had felt as a child. Whenever Susan had become needy, her stubborn, domineering mother responded by rejecting her emotionally. Distant and controlling, her mother had refused to brook any communication around issues of vulnerability, helplessness, or loss. Anger was completely taboo. Thus she had prevented the little girl, and the woman she became, from learning to represent to herself the feelings that surround rejection and abandonment. Unable to abstract and understand the painful feelings Jim's angry absences evoked, Susan could only act them out and experience a global state of distress.

I see many cases of depression among people who cannot make a mental picture to substitute for a palpable presence.[2] People who are able to represent their feelings can use the image of a loved one or of a favorable outcome to comfort themselves in pain and cheer themselves in discouragement. They can tell themselves, "My mother loves me, even though she isn't here with me," or even "though she is no longer living"; even better, they experience the nurturing person in their lives as an image that stands in and actually holds and comforts them in their time of loneliness, fear, or emptiness. They carry within themselves soothing, nurturing images that give them a sense of security. They can assure themselves that all will be well, that their efforts will be crowned with success and their fears will not come true. Those unable to form such positive images thus lack a useful emotional resource. In times of need there is no inner sense of security, no soothing inner voice or image, only an empty space or negative, recriminating images. For such individuals the lack of this inner nurturing presence may make them more susceptible to depression when things go wrong.

Mike Tyson, the prizefighter imprisoned for rape, pondered his own transition from action to reflection in a radio interview. Before he went to prison, he explained, he had been a person who simply behaved on instinct, without reflection or foresight. As a large, active child raised in a poorly nurturing home, and then as a millionaire celebrity athlete, he had all his life simply done and gotten whatever he wanted. He acted out every wish. During his incarceration he perceived for the first time that he had consciousness, that he could know and evaluate what he wanted to do. Once he became a prisoner, the man who had always found satisfaction in action alone had to learn to take pleasure in contemplating and communicating about action.

In a far less painful and more constructive way, the parent who encourages symbolic interaction and communication provides a child with the necessary experience that prison provided Tyson. By gently but firmly helping the child to translate her impulses into images and then to transmit these images to the consciousness of another person, the parent teaches the child the attitude of reflection. The images need not be verbal to fulfill this function. Sign language or complex gestures may serve just as well. A visually oriented youngster who is also very good with her hands might explain her wish to hit her sister in a series of connected drawings: panel one might show the impulse, panel two the act, panel three the punishment. Just as one can say "I love you" in many languages, the specific grammar and vocabulary of a child's symbolic interactions matter infinitely less than whether or not they take place.

With the ability to create ideas, the child has arrived at the threshold of awareness and consciousness. Here she has crossed into the world of human culture, the world that includes *Hamlet*, the World Series, and quadratic equations. The basis of this fuller consciousness is a sense of self that has become symbolic, that functions in a universe of thought and meaning. Its deepest roots, however, lie in the infant's first experience of sensory arousal. Through relationships and their emotional connections, consciousness has grown from the appearance of the first tiny islets of intentional "me" to the increasingly detailed world of symbolic "me."

The images now informing the individual's inner world are multi-sensory in nature. They are not simply pictures like those one sees on a television screen or in a movie, but rather full images of life itself, with sound, smell, and feeling-tone all mixed together. The rich inner life that is forming evolves in several directions at once. We can glimpse this evolution through the window pretend play provides on children's inner lives. From set pieces like tea parties or putting dolly to bed, such play develops into dramas in which a tea party, an argument, making up, and going to sleep follow in rapid succession and then, as the characters awaken, a whole new adventure begins. With increasing complexity, play gradually comes to embrace more and more of life's basic themes: nurturance and dependency, assertiveness and aggression, curiosity and intrigue, empathy and loving, limits and boundaries, fears and anxieties. Ideally, all become part of the rich fabric of the child's internal life. Some children, however, do not develop their own complex dramas rich in emotional themes. Instead their inner lives remain narrow, and satisfaction or vicious aggression replay themselves over and over. Rather than a rainbow, there are only one or two colors.

THE SYMBOLIC SELF

As the child learns to use symbols to create an internal sense of security as well as to think about the world inside and around him, he first begins to experience himself in the way that Freud observed, through conscious and unconscious representations of desires and emotions. He begins to experience himself in part as adults do, in inner images of himself. Other people and his relationships with them take on symbolic form as well. The child can sense through these images how he operates, how he feels, what he wants. The sum of images in the mind's eye constitutes what people commonly mean by a sense of self. The degree to which they have definition, organization, and purpose determines how clear the sense of self is. Aspects of this emerging self will be conscious and others unconscious or outside of daily awareness. Later we speak of the individual's "identity," a closely related concept that includes the place this symbolic self occupies in the human world, in the past and future, in the larger purposes of life.

The sense of self organizes the internal worlds of individuals in different ways. For some, this organization gives a detailed, balanced, and flexible panorama of feelings and intentions, while for others the sense of self is more polarized or rigid.

At one level are individuals who do not develop the ability to use inner images and ideas to deal with emotions, and who remain in the mode of acting out their feelings. At another level are those who can use images, but these images are recapitulations and variations of their actions. Such persons think not about feeling angry, sad, or happy but instead mentally play out actions such as hitting, kicking, spitting, yelling, hugging, or kissing. The content of their inner lives, while one step removed from action, remains very close to it. When asked how she feels, such a person will answer, "I want to hit her," or "I want to hug her," rather than simply stating her feelings.

At a third level of organization, internal images are tied to physical sensations. "How do you feel?" elicits a response like, "My muscles are exploding" rather than "I'm furious," or "My blood is pounding in my temples" rather than "I'm horribly upset."

At the next level, some people become locked into very polarized ways of looking at the world; things are either wonderful or terrible, all good or all bad. We see this pattern in rationalizations of prejudice and discrimination against any group that is characterized as having extremely negative attributes. Subtlety, balance, and appreciation of individual differences play no role in evaluating others.

Such polarized images are also frequently seen in adults during extreme moods. Not infrequently, children have polarized views that vacillate from one extreme to another, particularly in the preschool years. Adults too get caught up in extreme views of their own feelings or of other people's motives. A person's spouse is always wrong, or people are always picking on him, or he can't do anything right.

At yet another level, although attitudes are not so extremely polarized, the individual still seems rigidly locked into just a few patterns of viewing the world. A handful of repetitive themes characterize the dramas enacted in the inner life: rivalry, success, anger toward others. Relatively little attention is given to themes such as tenderness, dependency, or joy. Sexuality, when it does arise, is played out in scenes of competition and victory rather than intimacy and pleasure.

Why some people play out only a limited number of dramas while others have access to a rich variety is not difficult to understand. As we have seen, adults participate in varying degrees in the dramas that occupy a child's inner life. Some parents become detached whenever the child's words, pretend play, or other symbolic acts touch on themes of aggression or even assertiveness. Others become anxious, change the subject, or withdraw when the theme turns to body parts and sexuality. Still others have a hard time when the scene involves fears of separation. Some families avoid certain scenes down through a number of generations.

The child can develop a rich inner life only if she has experiences from which she can derive and refine inner images. While the child's own physical makeup will strongly influence how her caregivers respond to her and thus certainly contribute to her experiences, the personalities, preferences, and limitations of the adults around her inevitably put their stamp on her character as well. An individual fortunate enough not to be locked into a few rigid themes may be able to advance to a level that involves a range of human dramas. These will enable her to experience images of warmth and dependency, pleasure and sexuality, assertiveness and curiosity, anger and protest, love and empathy as well as the expected fears and worries characteristic of her age. With a wide variety of themes at her disposal, she can embark on relationships that combine intimacy with assertions of will as well as allow the expression of anger.

As an individual builds an internal life, the sense of self attains one or another of these different levels of organization. Although the level we may reach depends heavily on the kind of experiences available during early childhood, as adults we are not entirely limited by the developments of these formative years. Patterns of feelings, perceptions, and expectations can perpetuate certain types of interactions and relationships, as when a person repeatedly becomes involved with people who reject or abuse her. Yet the good fortune of a special friendship or therapeutic experience may provide the chance for relationships not determined by earlier patterns. Such relationships can help to enlarge and refine the sense of self. Though often difficult and even painful, significant emotional growth in adulthood thus remains, in the proper circumstances, a genuine possibility for many.

THE SIXTH LEVEL: EMOTIONAL THINKING

A child's first ideas emerge as discrete islands of thought with little relation between them. A two-year-old may say, "Juice," "Want book," "You GI Joe" (meaning "I"), and so forth. As caregivers respond to symbolic expressions in both pretend play and the interchanges of daily life, in the third and fourth years the child begins to form bridges among his ideas and between his own thoughts and those of others. "What" or "why" questions begin to be answered rather than ignored. Dolls hit or hug because someone was mean or nice. "No go sleep, not tired" staves off bedtime a bit longer. As ideas broaden to involve such varied emotions as love and competition, so do the connections between ideas. But here too, the connections a child makes depend on the caregiver's ability to read and respond to ideas, allowing the child to respond without stress or anxiety to a variety of emotional themes.

Once a child learns to build bridges among symbols, he has attained a skill so formidable that he can begin to construct a cohesive internal world of his own. This effort ideally continues throughout life as the individual uses his ability to perceive connections to refine, enrich, correct, elaborate, and enlarge his map of reality as new experiences unfold.

Even before he has mastered whole sentences, a child is able to tie together different parts of his experiences. Ideas can be linked into sequences of inner images that allow him to consider actions before carrying them out. Reason can supplant fear, inhibitions, or obedience. Ideas can link up to emotions: "I am sad because I can't see Grandma." Time becomes comprehensible, separated into past, present, and future. Space too becomes orderly, perceived as here, there, somewhere else. Categories of fantasy and reality arise. The comic strip "Calvin and Hobbes" cleverly portrays a child's dual realization that, although in reality his stuffed tiger is a mere toy, in imagination he is a loyal and exciting companion. The ability to understand how present acts relate to the future makes consequences rather than fear the basis for controlling impulses. It also contributes to the development of the abilities to concentrate, plan, and work toward goals that are essential for success in school.

Along with the power to assess oneself accurately, these abilities together make up what we sometimes call basic personality or ego functions. They include reality testing, impulse control, and concentration and constitute the bedrock of mental health and cognitive achievement. All thought and endeavor thus ultimately grow out of the ability to create symbols and to forge connections among them.

Truly effective symbolic representation requires the capacity to see connections among many different feelings and ideas. "The doll is happy" becomes "The doll is happy because I love her"; "The teddy bear is waving bye-bye" becomes "The teddy bear is waving bye-bye because I'm leaving"; "I feel sad" becomes "I feel sad because I miss Grandpa." The child no longer simply asks "What?" but is now fascinated with "Why?"

Both in pretend play and real life, ever more elaborate plots and motivations arise. The action figures fight because they're mad at one another. Mom is disappointed because Johnnie got his good pants dirty after she asked him to keep them clean. Clare feels jealous because her sister is having a birthday party.

The ability to make connections among affects and ideas grows with maturity into the capacity to step back from and reflect on one's own emotions, to deal with them at the level of their meaning rather than of the behavior that embodies them. "He banged into my car and I wanted to hit him" can become "I was extremely angry when he banged into my car. I told him that I held him responsible for the damage." "I am a failure as a parent because my child isn't doing well in school" can become "I am very disappointed and concerned that my child isn't doing as well in school as I had hoped." Concrete reactions involving only the behavioral level of experience, which attempt to explain or even change circumstances, are transformed into symbolic representations, which explore the roots of a situation and connect it to outer reality. Such representations thus provide a check on the logic and validity of our mental constructions. Does the child's inability to perform up to a parent's standards necessarily imply poor parenting, as if good nurturing necessarily guarantees academic success? Or are parental hopes for scholastic achievement unrealistic in light of the child's talents and interests? Is the problem the youngster's attainments or the parent's expectations? Only a symbolic formulation allows us to untangle the true emotional connections.

Failure to develop this representational ability can lock people into rigid, unproductive patterns. Rather than being able to use ideas to get to the emotional roots of a problem, they repeatedly and futilely try to force others to behave in the way they desire.[3]

Joan, for example, regarded her marriage as satisfactory from every rational standpoint. Her husband was caring, affectionate, a good father and lover. His only fault, she noted, was that he was a trifle dull. Though she didn't want to jeopardize her family, she was toying with the idea of having an affair with a man she considered more exciting and romantic. When her therapist commented that she quite illogically wanted both the stability of marriage and the thrill of an affair, she responded with hurt and rage so acute that she thought about leaving therapy.

The therapist's probing soon revealed her distress that he was not acting like a good therapist. After a great deal more talk, she discovered a "deep wound" within herself, inflicted by an angry, depressed mother who would abruptly withdraw from the young Joan whenever their relationship produced intense exasperation. To dull this pain, Joan began to fantasize about the perfect person, a knight in shining armor who would protect her from both her mother's anger and depression and her own inner anguish. Even in adulthood she couldn't tolerate a feeling of disappointment either in herself or the person currently cast in the role of her perfect knight.

Both her father and the nondepressed side of her mother had played the role of knight, but she could not connect the two parts of her mother into a single image. A good person, she inferred, could not also be imperfect; when a good person acted imperfectly, Joan therefore felt herself somehow to blame. Whenever anyone close to her failed to behave in a "knightly" fashion, she felt she had to flee because her badness must be contaminating the person's perfection.

For some months the therapist tried to help Joan to connect her feelings of rage and disappointment to the self-defeating and repetitive script she acted out with everyone close to her. She rarely spoke about these emotions, however, preferring to dwell on how people ought to behave and what she would do if they didn't. Finally the therapist decided to discuss the script itself, and she responded immediately and at a deep emotional level. She began to wonder aloud what her true feelings were, the feelings that drove her to repeat her script endlessly. But she couldn't say, she told him, because she felt only numbness in her body. She then described many variations of numbness that went along with her desire to escape.

Only gradually, and over a considerable time, did she come to realize that, as she put it, she couldn't stand it when people didn't act the way she needed them to. Eventually she managed to excavate the layers of emotion behind her numbness: first physical feelings that suggested anger, then an anger she could symbolize, and then disappointment and hurt and sadness. In making these connections, she began to understand that she could tolerate her feelings even if people didn't act the way she wanted, and that their inability to measure up to her standards was largely the result of her own need for them to be perfect so that they could protect her. Finally, able at last to represent and then reflect on her feelings, she was able to stop acting them out.

THE THINKING SELF

At the level at which we can connect inner symbols, the self is increasingly articulated and defined. Previously unrelated regions form an ever denser network of consciousness. The child knows that she can't take her friend's ball because the friend will be angry, or that she doesn't want to go to bed because she isn't tired, or that she doesn't want to wait until her birthday to open her presents. Asking "Why?" and "How?" and "What?" she consciously creates connections among the different parts of the symbolic self that have emerged. An inner sense of causality provides the impetus; the action and satisfaction take place entirely internally. "Mommy will be here later," she can say, or "I saw Grandma yesterday."

Even dialogue becomes internal as the habit of interaction with others continues even in their absence. People exist both in real life and within the child's consciousness, both as external presences and as internal representations. The child's inner and outer worlds increasingly connect, and her sense of reality becomes stronger. The limits on behavior become more self-motivated. Her moods become more stable. The basic elements of a differentiated sense of self have all taken shape.

For this to happen, of course, the child must be nurtured through years of intimacy, through countless conversations, debates, negotiations, responses, remonstrances, and games. She must have learned to argue, negotiate, discuss, and propose in order to build internal bridges among her ideas. Children who lack dynamic inter-action at this stage, whose parents leave them to their own imagina-tion or pretend play, tend to devise rich and creative symbolic images but may not learn to test them against a stable inner sense of reality. In the face of an emotional challenge, they often retreat into fantasy or remain fragmented, living in a piecemeal world of changing images rather than one of stable, coherent meaning.

This ability to build bridges among different ideas or images develops only gradually. In working with children who are having difficulties with this task, we have learned much about how the pro-cess takes place. When it is more strung out than usual, we gain a more detailed view of how it happens and how, when necessary, it can be helped along.

For example, Linda, a nine-year-old girl, could become enthusi-astically involved in various make-believe dramas with complex dia-logues. However, she would abruptly go from one scene to another, one drama to another, just as if she were switching a television dial without letting others know that she was changing the channel. She might start off by announcing to her mother or father, "I'm going to be Cinderella," but after a few lines of talking to the fairy Godmother she would suddenly flip to an episode from "Snow White." Instead of hearing about the exploits of the Fairy Godmother in getting Cinder-ella to the ball, the listener would inexplicably get skillful imitations of the seven dwarfs, including their repertoires of sneezes, moans, and giggles. The baffled audience initially had no way of knowing where apparently irrelevant lines were coming from.

With these shifts a change would come over Linda's vocal tone, emotional expression, and responses. The knowing look would fade from her eyes; the reciprocity of her performance, in tune with her listener's nods and comments, would cease and her vocal rhythms would grow monotonous. At these times Linda seemed to have got-ten lost in her own internal landscape. What had started off as a mutual experience, full of emotional connection through shared gestures and common ideas, would become a self-absorbed, dis-jointed monologue.

In essence, the emotional bridges that held the elements of Linda's personality together seemed to fall away, taking with them the ties that connected her to others. It was as though she operated with chunks of partially organized images and ideas that had not aggregated into a coherent self. Certain groups of symbols and images remained lashed together, but they floated around quite independently from any others. Those that retained an emotional charge had the feel of the real Linda, while others seemed just to be indifferently, mindlessly repeated.

Often in cases like Linda's an auditory processing problem, alone or in combination with motor and verbal sequencing problems, vastly complicates the task of establishing a network of logical connections among images. To assist such children in mastering this ability, we attempt to accentuate a process that goes on in ordinary development but can easily be overlooked.

Linda's parents had fallen into the trap of filling in the links among her jumbled thoughts rather than helping her learn to supply them herself. When Linda suddenly jumped from "Cinderella" to "Snow White," her parents didn't express their confusion about the switch. Instead they'd join in making dwarf sounds or ask Linda how many dwarfs she could name. She would give a disjointed answer and then again turn her internal dial to play out, say, a GI Joe commercial. Her parents would jump in either with choruses of the jingle or questions about Joe's uniform, equipment, and the like.

What these concerned and loving parents weren't doing was helping Linda find herself. They faced a challenge on two levels. Linda was getting lost within her own ideas, but at the same time she was losing her emotional ties with her parents. The reciprocal gesturing, smiling, and head nodding—that is, the affective cuing between individuals that signifies their relationship—quickly evaporated.

Before we could help her parents recapture Linda's stream of ideas, they had to realize that it was this emotional connection that was lost whenever Linda's voice became monotone and her look flattened in affect. We then helped them learn to reestablish emotional contact with her by making their own faces and voices more expectant and conveying their confusion when Linda shifted story lines through their expressions and posture. By acting more animated and intense, in other words, they worked to maintain the emotional give-and-take with their daughter. These tactics can often pull a child back toward the outer world of other people.

Linda's parents also learned to use dolls to intrude into her incoherent reveries. Her father might make a doll he was holding sit on the Cinderella doll in Linda's hand and say forcefully, "Hold on! I have a question!" or "Wait! I don't get what's going on!" until Linda looked up and reengaged. Then he would announce that he had lost the thread of the story. Instead of joining in the new scene or asking questions about it, her parents would insist on knowing what had happened: "Where did Cinderella go?" "How did the dwarfs get into the act?" Or they might point out that Linda had gone from "Cinderella" to "Snow White" with no explanation of how the two stories were connected. If Linda didn't respond, they might offer her some possibilities to choose from. Was this puzzling shift something she saw on television, or in a movie? If that didn't work, they'd try a simpler yes-or-no question. Was Cinderella coming back, or had she gone for good? The point was to work with Linda to "find" her and keep her in touch with them. It was less important that she return to the original story or explain where the new scene was headed than that she respond to their concerns. This would reconnect her emotionally with them and, in the process, with herself.

Such methods have helped children like Linda move from piecemeal ideas and scripts to a pattern of thought and therefore sense of self that is cohesive. Through sharing and discussing images and symbols, and by constantly searching for the real Linda, her parents were helping her connect the pieces of her emerging self. The more we let children like Linda wander off on tangents, the more we structure their language for them, or the more we use rote learning to keep them organized, the more fragmented and concrete their sense of self remains.

In children without processing difficulties, progress toward integration of the self occurs more easily and quickly. Parents generally indicate their confusion about a child's meaning or ask what his purpose is or why he's doing something, especially when they feel relaxed and talk to the child just as they would to each other or a good friend. In ordinary development, an enormous number of symbolic interactions occur simultaneously. The emotions attached to these exchanges give the symbols substance and ultimately cohesiveness. As caregivers engage in opening and closing symbolic circles in different emotional realms—love and dependency, assertiveness and aggression—the child organizes his inner world of ideas and meaning. When this process does not occur, either because of severe processing problems or extreme anxiety or trauma, a child may grow into an adult who functions in a scattered way, with a fragmented inner sense of self.

While difficulties in brain processing obviously make it hard for a child to make connections among ideas, family relationships that confuse meanings can also pose an obstacle. If, for example, the child says "I feel sad" and Dad simply ignores him, then comments a moment later, "The grass needs to be cut and I'm tired," what ideas will the child form? Will he connect sadness with cutting grass or with being ignored or with an empty or angry feeling? Will his thoughts simply remain discrete and unconnected? What if he says "I'm sad" and Dad says "No, you aren't. You have everything to be happy about"? What if expressing his feeling of sadness leads to recriminations between his parents, with each blaming the other for neglecting him? We have found that processing problems and distorted relationships can each lead to confused or disorganized thinking. When both occur, as they do not infrequently, severe problems in thinking are likely to emerge.

In extreme form, such splintered thinking can be seen in a number of clinical problems with thinking. In my clinical work I see varying degrees of such thought disorders. The same principles outlined for Linda's treatment apply also to adults who have a tendency to fragmentation. The emotional core that shapes intentions and desires must become the reference point for images and symbols that have, for a variety of reasons, never merged in a whole, unified sense of self. Often a single secure and stable emotional relationship within which a person can realize intentions can make this development possible. With adults it's not always easy to find the core affects to build on, but occasionally themes will run through the disjointed aspects of the self, or certain components will appear more emotionally grounded.

Even when her thoughts are quite disconnected, a patient may communicate in bits and pieces different sides of her dilemma with, for example, dependency. Loneliness, rage, denial of the need for others, grandiose images of power or sexual conquest that make her invulnerable to loss—all are pieces of the same puzzle. Traditional insight about "dependency needs" is not enough to pull the pieces together. Such a person may have to form an emotional tie to her therapist and, by his emotional availability and refusal to let her words or feelings "get lost," let him help her build bridges among her disconnected thoughts.

If all goes well, however, growing boys and girls will be able to create in childhood a strong self-image consisting of pictures, words, feelings, and other sensations (e.g., "I'm nice, pretty, sweet, and bright"; "I'm skinny, stubborn, and like to get my way"). This pictorially or verbally accessible image of one's self is possible because the mind is able to connect ideas in both time and space. It can, for example, synthesize the different piecemeal images we may have of ourselves in the immediate past, present, and future as well as in different settings (with Mother, with friends, with grandparents, etc.).

This integrated image, what is sometimes called a "personal narrative," doesn't suddenly appear from nowhere. It is merely the surface representation of deep behavioral, emotional, and symbolic patters that have been forming for some time. Nor is it fixed. It continues to evolve through subsequent life experiences.

What is particularly interesting is its retrospective aspect. Not only does it reflect the preverbal and presymbolic patterns that came before it, but it serves to interpret and explain them. The content of one's self-image need not accurately mirror prior patterns. It is constructed so as to help us give meaning to our wishes and feelings as well as our thoughts and behavior. For example, a person might very early abandon overt expressions of anger and assertiveness because they evoke frightening reactions from her mother. Long before she can think it out, she adopts passive, avoidant behavior as a safe solution to many of life's conflicts. Once she comes to the point of creating a self-image, she might persuade herself that she is a calm, sweet person who abhors competition, violence, and all forms of aggression. She might adopt values and even political beliefs to support this self-image. The initial source of this approach to life—avoiding anger at nearly all cost—never surfaces. The anger cannot even be called part of what we call the unconscious, because the passive pattern was adopted before unconscious symbols were formed.

The images each of us has of ourselves explain both who we are and who we are not. Without intensive self-reflection or therapy, it is impossible initially for us to know what we are missing. Suppose, for example, that someone who lacked early nurturing—whose parents failed to dole out emotional chicken soup—adopts a view of himself that insists, "I like to make people feel good. I have a talent for making people happy. It makes me happy to make them happy. I'll say any-thing to them—even make up things—because then we'll both feel good, and that's what's important. I do this with new people I hardly even know, because it's important for people to connect." He may see this approach as an asset, as a desirable way to be, rather than as a reaction to deprivation.

However transparent a person's underlying needs may be to a therapist or even a friend, it's difficult for him to know what's buried in his personal history, below even his deepest unconscious symbols. We form an initial definition of who we are in terms of what we want and desire. Just as it would be impossible to know about television if all we've ever heard was the radio, similarly it's impossible to guess what we could be when we have not had the experiences that would show us.

A clear example is the person whose prior experiences failed to establish a grasp of the difference between what is and is not real. He may believe that others are out to get him, and that he must be constantly cautious and vigilant. Helping such a person realize that the sense of threat is only a feeling is nearly impossible. A huge gap separates this blindly suspicious person from the one who says, "I don't know why I suddenly feel like I can't trust people. I wonder why I'm in this mood." This person not only appreciates the distinction between what is real and what is not but can also observe himself making it and ponder whether his feelings make sense.

Lost opportunities and unmastered challenges thus underlie and set certain boundaries on the images, story lines, and values that feed into our constructions of who we are. If we can create a capacity for self-observation, we can begin to explore the limits of our consciously constructed images of ourselves and even of the symbols that prevail in our unconscious minds. As we will see in Chapter 9, therapy with patients who have missed out on attaining these levels of emotional experience must focus on assisting them in developing such skills as reality testing and the capacity for self-observation before they can seek out the limits of their own personal stories.

HOW THE MIND DIVIDES CONSCIOUS AND UNCONSCIOUS EXPERIENCE

One of the more interesting mysteries of intrapsychic life is the way some experiences and memories remain conscious and others are relatively inaccessible to consciousness. Freud originally postulated that certain experiences and memories are actively repressed because of conflicts with other aspects of the personality. So, for example, many features of what was originally termed infantile sexuality are kept out of consciousness because they are in conflict with the emerging superego or conscience. Anna Freud appended to this understanding of the unconscious an explanation of experiences that are never conscious in the first place but are a part of the early formation of the mind. These fundamental theories are still generally accepted within the field of psychoanalysis. They don't, however, fully account for our varying degrees of access to past experience.

Our observations of infants and children as they develop images and symbols and organize them in different ways have afforded us some additional insight into how this division between conscious and unconscious experience may occur. Children appear to have access to the memories and experiences of the stage of development they're currently going through, but they often lose this access as they enter the next stage. The degree to which they lose access appears to be determined in part by the modes of thinking characteristic of the former stage and the new stage. For example, when children are just learning to make connections between different experiences, their memories of these are quite sharp. They will frequently talk about an exciting toy or something that happened while playing with another child. Once their thinking becomes more elaborately logical, how-ever—say at the level characteristic of an eight- or nine-year-old, in which new ideas can be classified in many different categories—access to earlier, more loosely organized experiences is significantly lessened. In general, the time that has elapsed does not appear to be the principle factor in whether a person can remember experiences. We are all familiar, of course, with how a 65-year-old woman might vividly remember experiences of her adolescence, while adolescents themselves may have a hard time remembering elementary school experiences that are only seven to twelve years in the past. They find it even harder to remember experiences from their preschool years.

How is it that a person can easily remember experiences that happened fifty years before and yet another has a hard time remembering much more recent events? Our observations suggest that it may have to do with the way in which experience is organized. There is greater similarity in the organization of the mind at seventeen and sixty-five than there is at seventeen and, say, three or four years of age.

These observations are consistent with what a number of years ago was described as "state-dependent" learning.[4] It was noted that individuals who learn something while under the influence of certain drugs are more apt to remember those experiences while in the drugged state than when not drugged. In other words, experiences are best remembered in the same state of mind as when they occurred.

As children grow, their state of mind changes because of the way in which it is developing. In the early stages of symbol formation, not many bridges between different ideas have yet been formed. In the stage of emotional thinking, logical bridges begin to connect ideas. Subsequently these ideas become organized differently, in part because of the child's ability to further classify images and ideas and grasp their relation to one another. During adolescence and adulthood, still other kinds of organization can arise as we learn to anticipate hypothetical possibilities and broaden the range of application of our ideas.

The division between unconscious and conscious symbols may therefore reflect the structure of the mind that prevails when these symbols are formed. Those that are formed when the mind is nearing its mature level of organization would likely be incorporated into adult consciousness, whereas those formed during earlier stages of organization would be less conscious.

A similar division may occur with what are called repressed memories, or avoidance of certain recollections associated with trauma. When people become anxious, their thinking often regresses to an earlier level. In a state of extreme anxiety, individuals are rarely able to be as abstract or differentiated in their thinking as they are when calm. Such disruptive anxiety often leads to a state of mind functioning one or two notches lower than it ordinarily would. A child just learning to make bridges between his ideas and to answer questions about his motivations and feelings may lose this ability when anxious and talk in a seemingly unconnected manner. Adults who are ordinarily able to see shades of gray in any issue may become overly concrete or disorganized in their thinking.

Severe trauma, which produces disruptive anxiety, would tend to be experienced in such a regressive state of mind. The traumatic experience would therefore be sorted with these that occurred during that earlier phase of mental organization. It is interesting to note the two techniques used in psychotherapy to recover traumatic memories. One technique aims to help the individual reexperience the disruptive anxiety and, in this way, the state of mind in which the experience was registered. The other is the use of free association, in which patients are aided in relaxing some of the logical bridges that organize information and enter into states of mind characteristic of earlier stages of development. Both of these tactics help people recover very early experiences or frightening, traumatic, or anxious feelings lost to conscious access by recreating the mental states in which these experiences or emotions occurred. Once access is gained, the experiences can be evaluated and put in perspective in the therapeutic setting using the analytical skills of the individual's most mature or reflective state of mind.

In addition to the concept of repression, Freud introduced a theory of defenses through which both the conscious mind and the superego keep certain ideas and wishes at an unconscious level, describing many of these mechanisms at work in dreams. His daughter Anna later delineated such defenses especially clearly in the lives of growing children. In one, *reaction formation*, a person who unconsciously harbors anger and aggressive wishes may adopt the opposite affects in his conscious mind and express only pleasant thoughts in order to keep the forbidden angry thoughts hidden. Another defense, known as *displacement*, involves transferring thoughts directed at one person to someone else: instead of being aware that you're angry at your father, you take out your wrath on your little brother. Freud postulated that these defenses are affected through a kind of inner energy flow from one image to another that may also transform more instinctive to less instinctive or neutralized forms.

Our developmental perspective on inner life suggests another way of understanding these common ways of dealing with unwelcome thoughts and wishes.

In this chapter we have discussed how children learn to form bridges among various feelings and ideas. Parents sometimes respond accurately and empathically to these thoughts, but at other times, because of their own anxieties or character structure, they may misread or condemn or try to change them. Let's say, for example, that in both pretend play and the subtle interchanges that take place between parents and children, a father responds to a child's expression of anger or "badness" as though it never happened or as though everything the child did was sweet and adorable. Let's also say that he either temporarily disengages or gets an angry glare in his eyes, or in some other way communicates that the expression of anger or badness is dangerous. In many instances, these two countercommunications will over a period of time lead the child to form a bridge between the two reactions. A child in a more flexible and empathic family might link the thought "I'm angry" or "I'm bad because I feel like knocking someone's head off" with the thought "I will get punished if I act it out, but I can say it." The first child, however, might connect "I'm mad" or "I'm bad" with "I'm good and sweet." The child has formed a reaction, denying that he has any bad feelings and acknowledging only "nice" ones.

We now have two conditions existing at once. We have the anxiety associated with the bad feelings, which leads them to be registered at a somewhat lower level of organization and thus less accessible. At the same time, we have an associated idea about the desirability of being good. Every time there are stirrings of potentially angry or bad feelings, the child has only one set of connected ideas that he can play out without experiencing the terror of his father's disengagement or angry look.

Remember, the child is dependent on others (usually his parents or caregivers) to help him elaborate a rich world of connections between ideas and wishes. To the degree that caregivers accurately understand the child's communications and elaborate on them in the direction the child is moving, the child's internal world keeps expanding, forming an ever more logical and refined network of thoughts and images that gives structure and meaning to his inner life. It should be noted as a caveat that helping the child elaborate his ideas and wishes does not mean giving in or not setting limits. Say a child is about to hit his brother and Mother says, "As mad as you are, if you hit him you're going to get punished." If she later takes the child aside and helps him talk about his anger she has not only set a limit but engaged the child is his own territory. Aggression, limits, punishment, and encouragement are all part of a single complex drama. In contrast, if she changes the meaning of the drama and greets aggression with a look that says, "You'd better not tell me about it," or "I only want to hear nice thoughts," the child cannot explore or expand his own emotional space.

Sometimes there are no defenses operating to keep ideas out of consciousness. There is only a lack of connection between one level where ideas are felt and experienced and the next level where ideas are connected with other ideas. If a number of emotional themes are splintered in this way, the person will appear very constricted in what he can discuss with any emotional depth and will seem out of touch with himself. His conversation often sounds like the script of a shallow soap opera overlying a deeper drama.

The existence of this drama is frequently more apparent to others than to the individual himself. Such persons may experience fleeting images or impulses to do things completely inconsistent with their view of themselves. If they yield to such impulses they may quickly dissociate themselves from their actions, almost believing they didn't happen.

As we will discuss in greater detail in Chapter 6, the individual's own disposition—for example, the tendency to be easily overloaded by sensations or to be seemingly thick-skinned and crave lots of input—may also determine in part what stays conscious and what becomes unconscious. A very tuned-in person who gets overloaded easily will tend to blame himself if something goes wrong, whereas an underreactive, action-craving individual may, in a situation of conflict or anxiety, blame others instead. Both thus create conscious, interconnected meanings to deal with a sense of inner overload or fragmentation. Such distortions arise in part because of the way their nervous systems work, but they are also owing to the degree to which the ability to make connections is mastered. Those who have not mastered the ability to create connections between ideas may be more prone to projecting their wishes onto others or internalizing the thoughts and desires of others.

Therefore, when we talk about the role of repression or defenses in the division between conscious and unconscious experience, we can look at these phenomena in terms of how the mind grows and develops. This perspective provides additional ways of understanding as well as an alternative to some of the hypothetical constructs we have used to explain events.

Looking at the ways in which the mind separates conscious and unconscious ideas helps us appreciate more fully the importance of the stage at which connections between ideas are formed. Our first memories are from this period when the eventual adult organization of the mind is being established, since connected ideas are easier to retrieve than free-floating ones or than the intentions and somatic sensations that precede the formation of ideas. At this stage the sense of self goes beyond mere symbols to experience the reality of the world, the pleasure of fantasy, and the connections between different intents and feelings. While only at their budding levels, these developments nonetheless constitute dramatic progress in the formation of a human being.

THE UNFOLDING OF DESIRE

At this point we should take a look at a most critical aspect of conscious and unconscious experience. What is the essence of human motivation? Freud saw unconscious sexual desires as the primary motivator of human behavior. He viewed sadism and aggression as having sexual components as well as independent aspects. In psycho-analytic thought, love and compassion are seen as deriving from sexuality. Various theories account for this transformation. While sexuality is indeed an important motivator, playing a significant part in emotional growth as well as in certain mental disorders, it may not have the universal explanatory value Freud and other practitioners of classical psychoanalysis attributed to it. At the very least, the concept of sexual desire needs to be expanded.

In order to understand more fully the desires that are most char-acteristic of human beings, it is useful to watch these desires emerge during the course of development. The capacity for intimacy and the interest and pleasure derived from the company of others are the earliest phenomena that indicate real desire. The infant or young child seeks out intimate contact. Curiosity, assertiveness, and even anger follow quickly thereafter. Experiences close to later sensual pleasure (rubbing the genitals, taking pleasure in skin-to-skin contact with others) also occur in the first and second years. One can observe a range of desires and feelings that lead the infant or young child to seek out certain experiences. Although there are many ways of categorizing them, the most fruitful approach is to observe these desires unfolding in development and not assume that they are all necessarily subservi-ent to any single, fixed drive.

One desire, with its related set of feelings, emerges early, persists throughout the lives of human beings, and seems responsible for the mental structures that make much of human functioning possible. This desire, for close relations with others, leads to the formation of families, communities, and societies. Although it has sexual compo-nents in the growing child and adult, it is chiefly fueled by the inher-ent pleasure of relationships themselves.

The relationships that nurture the mind of a well-developing child eventually open the way to self-reflection, a new level of con-sciousness. From this stage, depending on the detail and depth of inner mapping and the complexity of the internal connections formed in the mind, arises the possibility of a Shakespeare, a Picasso, or a Newton as well as the capacity to appreciate the work of any of these. The source of the exquisite possibilities that lie open to all human beings lies not in biochemistry or the supernatural, but in a natural process compounded of physical maturation and human interaction.

The more varied and reciprocal these interactions, the richer will be the individual's self-image and the more comprehensive her consciousness. Of course, no one enjoys uniform, exemplary development in all areas of mental life. No parent can provide perfect nurturing or interaction unaffected by his own emotional makeup and personality. Still, at the source of our humanity—its creations and accomplishments as well as its imperfections—are our emotions, desires, and the relationships in which they are refined.

CULTURAL AND FAMILY DIFFERENCES

In viewing the types of experiences that foster the growth of each level of mental organization, it is important to keep in mind different cultural and family patterns. There are many paths to attainment of the different levels, and each culture has its characteristic way of fostering growth. In one culture, for example, a parent might respond to a child's nonverbal signal of reaching for a block with a quiet look of recognition and a soft nod of the head, whereas in another the child's reaching for a block might elicit extravagant praise and the offering of sixteen more blocks. In both instances the child is learning to be intentional and is forming a mental organization in which emotions and desires are integrated into a willful sense of self. Similarly, the very different dramas exhibited by children of different cultures in pretend play and daily conversation will all assist their development of the use of ideas and symbols. It is important not to confuse healthy cultural patterns with obstacles to the advancing process of mental organization.

In general, most cultures support both the development of the different organizational levels and certain basic emotional themes, such as dependency, sexuality, and assertiveness, that are typically dealt with at each level. What tends to differ across cultures as well as from one family to another are the ways these levels are supported and the content of the interaction or drama that gives each person's experiences an individual signature. While love letters differ from culture to culture, what individuals of most traditions share is the ability to experience love through gestures and ideas or symbols.

MIND IN PROCESS

After many months of monumental attainment, somewhere in the third or fourth year if all goes well, the six levels that constitute the foundation of an individual's mind should be solidly in place. Some efforts of depth psychology to understand the origins of the inner world begin at this point. Clearly, though, this is not the beginning of development but the culmination of immense mental growth.

On the way to maturity, however, the child passes through a number of additional developmental stages, all of them built on the foundations laid by the first six. Meeting the challenges of each life stage requires an ever more complex mental organization. As the individual grows older she moves into new social situations and responsibilities, each involving its own typical set of relationships and feelings. By meeting challenges and integrating ideas and feelings as they arise, she constructs a new mental level. Caring for children while earning a living, for example, obviously requires a more complex mental organization than does maneuvering through the social shoals of junior high.

Though the issues faced in the later stages are different from those of the earliest years, emotional ties and relationships remain at the core of mental development. At about the time a child goes to kindergarten or first grade she can relate, communicate, imagine, and think—all capacities developed in the earlier stages. She now enters a stage of boldness, expressiveness, and expansiveness whose slogan might be "the world is my oyster."[5] She is dazzled by the wondrous possibilities of the world and of her own powers. Children at this age explore these possibilities in play, in imagined adventures, and in more complex personal relationships. Now a child begins to perceive three-sided relationships, not only between Mommy and herself or Daddy and herself but among all three of them.

Curious and cocky though at times fearful, the child is acquiring the foundations of creativity as she sees life more and more from multiple perspectives. Now before her is the expanse of the world's

myriad phenomena, her appetite and the fears of her worst nightmares, and the vast number of possible solutions she can generate to
life's inevitable conflicts and paradoxes. There is a danger at this
stage that she will become overwhelmed by all the possibilities and
lose her grasp of reality. Alternatively, she can prematurely narrow
the range of her curiousity and creativity and become overly focused
and rigid. She can also find a balance allowing her to be curious and
creative, to view things from multiple perspectives and to understand context, and to develop responsibility and an appropriate degree of caution that will give her the sense of security necessary for
undertaking the adventures to come. Ideally, a child emerges from
this stage with a firmer grasp of reality, a lively sense of her potential, a rich fantasy life, and a more varied repertoire of social perceptions and responses.

These abilities come into play at seven or eight, when the politics of the playground and the pecking order of the classroom dominate both social life and children's maturing conception of
themselves. In the rough-and-tumble of the social group they learn
to hone their perception of other children's reactions. For a time, in
fact, these reactions become the child's self-image. Every second or
third grader knows precisely where she ranks in popularity, attrac-
tiveness, desirability as a member of a sports team, ability to spell or
add or read, fashionableness, musical talent, and any of a hundred
other criteria on which children of this age constantly rank themselves and others.

While learning about the complexity of peer relations, children
are also learning about group processes in their own microcosmic
society. The child is now partially defined by her membership in this
society. With one foot still in the family, she has put the other forward
into a more complex, challenging group and through her social identity achieves an appreciation of herself as a new type of person. As a
member of a group, she learns that the whole is more than the sum of
the parts; it is in fact a defining part of who she is. Her peer group is
an important foundation not only for understanding social patterns
and social reality, but also for establishing her membership in and
identification with various groups: her family and friends, and eventually her community and society.

By ages ten to twelve, many children start to develop an internal self-image that reflects more of their own needs, desires, aspirations, and values rather than simply the reactions of others. Their growing cognitive abilities also allow them to begin responding more to conscience and less to the fear of punishment. The growing child has by now constructed two worlds, a daily, changing world of peer relations and a more stable world of self-perceptions and emerging inner values. These two worlds provide the groundwork for meeting the challenges that characterize adolescence and adulthood. New relationship patterns will keep modifying the emerging sense of self that provides a core sense of security and stability during this period of growth.

When youngsters move into adolescence their world continues to grow, now including a larger community beyond the immediate peer group. During this period they are presented with such complexities as the differing values of peers and parents while at the same time they begin to develop larger interests, such as in politics, moral and religious issues, social movements, and the like. Growth of the brain also enables them to consider future possibilities and to imagine hypothetical worlds: "What would happen if Jane agreed to be my girlfriend?" "Should I go to the state university or try for a more prestigious school?" "What would it be like to be a doctor/a pilot/a teacher when I grow up?"

Immense bodily changes are now taking place. The child's body is vanishing, an unfamiliar man's or woman's body taking its place. The child's voice is going, too, along with the child's outlook. Along with the new size, shape, muscles, breasts, and hair come new and disquieting feelings and new peer group realities. Friendships are now deeper, those with the opposite sex more problematic. For the teenager, possible identities become more diverse and the need to define himself more pressing: is he a geek, a jock, a punk, a nerd? Is he popular, attractive, smart? What does he want to be? Who is he *really?*

As the massive demolition and reconstruction of adolescence proceeds, only a strong foundation allows a youngster to maintain a centered sense of who he is. But if the scores of bridges set up at this stage are built on shaky footings, the child will not be able to cope with the powerful feelings—sexuality, loss of childhood, new kinds of humiliation—that must be faced.

Early adulthood layers on new experiences: leaving home for college or the military, probably more intimate and sustained romantic relationships, perhaps the need to earn money to pay at least part of one's expenses. The world expands beyond the network of high school groups to include the campus or base community or a body of co-workers. In later early adulthood comes the need to choose a career and the added complications of marriage and the new kind of intimacy it brings. Now the individual moves away from home emotionally as well as physically, seeking to meet basic needs formerly met by parents in other relationships. All the old themes of dependency, desire for intimacy, need for security, and the like persist, but the individual must find new patterns for dealing with them.

Becoming a parent brings a sudden flood of unfamiliar emotions and a tricky challenge in dealing with them. To be a good mother or father, a person must learn to satisfy many of his or her own emotional needs through satisfying the needs of someone else. This calls on a much more subtle empathy and a greater selflessness than most people have known up to this point. To succeed, a person needs both a strong self-definition and the ability to tolerate a range of intense feelings as dozens of interpersonal constellations form. In the face of competition, resentment, fatigue, frustration, uncertainty, anger, responsibility, mother or father love, anxiety, and the rest, parents must maintain a position as leaders of their families and also see to the financial and work realities of paying the bills.

Middle age brings broader responsibilities while at the same time the loss of youth and its grandiose dreams and ambitions becomes real. The individual probably doesn't have the ideal marriage, perfect children, and brilliant career that once seemed inevitable. Nor does she have the great stretches of time that were once available to pursue them. Now, from the mountaintop, we see the way down, and time becomes finite. As a person faces the first intimations of mortality, her children are passing through the stages of her own early life. This period requires a fine balance between the empathy that allows understanding of their situation and the kind of overidentification that uses them to satisfy her own unmet needs.

In later middle age, many people find their perspective shifting again, to a broader, more altruistic consideration of the world as a whole, of all children as the world's children, of the legacy they will leave behind. Issues that occupy the individual are related to a collective sense of adult responsibility—for instance, concern about how the trade balance with Japan will affect the standard of living of the next generation. However, many people do not manage this transition because their own immediate problems with children, work, marriage, infirm parents, or whatever overwhelm and exhaust them.

The central nervous system continues to grow up to age forty-five or fifty. For example, neuronal tracks having to do with judgment and reflection continue to myelinate into the middle of life.[6] Although memory and athletic ability are beyond their peaks, the capacity for judgment and wisdom may well increase. Obviously, experience is critical to seasoned judgment and wisdom, but it's reassuring to know that it can find a home in a growing central nervous system.

Aging brings bodily processes like those of adolescence, but in reverse. Yet at the very time of the individual's decline, his children are rising to adult strength and beauty. Mother goes through menopause while daughter becomes sexually active. Father has a prostate operation while son pursues an active love life. The eyes go, the waistline, much of the physical beauty of youth: the lovely hair that used to make one proud, the smooth skin, the strong muscles. Feelings of rivalry, loss, disappointment, and awareness of the shortening of time become more pressing.

For many people there is a growing realization of their place in the parade of the generations as part of the cycle of nature and of life. As the time, and perhaps the space, at one's disposal shrinks, the sense of time and space on a cosmic level can expand, bringing with it a feeling of unity with nature or God.

Each stage of life is thus an outgrowth of the ones before, while presenting new emotional themes. If, however, a person cannot integrate the challenges of a new stage, he may become emotionally rigid or constricted. These possibilities are discussed in Chapters 9 and 10 in exploring the developmental model's ramifications for mental health. If all goes well, however, the trend is toward a broader, more integrated, and more subtle performance.

We have now seen how the mind's highest capacities, from consciousness to intelligence, form from certain fundamental building blocks. *Each of these blocks, in turn, is based on the human being's capacity to experience emotions.* The ability to *attend*, first of all, is the ability to show emotional interest in various sights, sounds, and other features of the environment. The ability to *engage* is the ability to experience joy, pleasure, and emotional warmth in the presence of another. Over time it also includes the ability to incorporate additional feelings in relationships, including assertiveness, anger, disappointment, compassion, and the like.

The ability to *be intentional* is the ability to create and direct desire, which by its very nature is experienced as an affective or emotional sense of purpose. The ability to *form complex interactive intentional patterns* is the ability to connect one's own emotional signals with those of others in interactions. Negotiations over security, acceptance, approval, pride, and other essential issues are emotional interchanges toward emotional ends. The ability to *create images, symbols, and ideas*, the basis of reasoning and emotional coping, hinges on the ability to invest these mental constructs with emotional meaning. Without such investment, they remain discrete, fragmented islands of mental activity. The ability to *connect images and symbols*, to form what may be viewed as the infrastructure of the mind, entails the ability not only to picture one's own feelings and desires but also to intuitively grasp the feelings and desires of another, all the while comprehending the emotional signals the other person is sending. This ability makes possible reality testing and other forms of logical thinking.

The scheme of mental development that we have presented here leads to some very particular and rather novel conclusions about how children grow. For example, only caregivers who have themselves negotiated the stages of their own emotional growth to adulthood can guide a child successfully through these levels. By the time a child emerges from the stage of presymbolic and early symbolic learning and enters the world of unconscious symbols, he has already mastered a long and complex process of classifying, weighing, judging, and discerning. Immense quantities of adult time and attention have already gone into responding to his smiles, frowns, words, and gestures, helping him to gain control of his attention, to know the warmth of reciprocity, to feel the communicative power of gestures, and to give a symbolic form to his bodily and emotional sensations. It is these processes, and the mutuality that makes them possible, that bring a child from the sensory chaos of the first hours outside the womb to full human consciousness.

This view of the mind reveals its deep unity, the unbreakable bonds between thought and feeling. It lays bare the mechanism long sought by social scientists that permits families and societies to transmit personality structures, values, and cultural meaning across generations. If, as we have argued, the most valuable qualities of the human spirit can grow only in the soil of genuinely personal bonds, then only a society that encourages such bonds to flourish can reap the full harvest of humane, creative citizenry.

CHAPTER FIVE

The Origins of Consciousness, Morality, and Intelligence

THE LAST THREE CHAPTERS DESCRIBED HOW THE SELF AND consciousness emerge in stages during development. This chapter applies this developmental perspective in explaining the origins of consciousness, morality, and the higher levels of intelligence. Here the term *consciousness* is obviously more broad than the sense used in the emergency room, implying a complex combination of perception, intentionality, and selfhood that permits reflection and understanding.

We are concerned here with how children and adults actually grow. The transition from a newborn organism that is simply a biological entity to a person functioning intelligently and self-consciously occurs in observable developmental stages. What appears in the abstract as an inexplicable metamorphosis in fact follows naturally from inherent human characteristics when an individual is placed in a rich, nurturing environment.

THE GROWTH OF CONSCIOUSNESS

Consciousness, a subject at the interface of psychology and philosophy, brings together the perspectives and traditions of each discipline. It has been an enigma to both for good reason. It involves the physical structure of the brain and such subjective experiences as self-awareness and contemplation of specific emotions and ideas. No wonder early theories involved suggestions of both a physical or objective as well as a spiritual or subjective aspect of human consciousness and mental phenomena. The philosopher Bertrand Russell suggested that the dualism between materialistic objective and individualistic subjective views of human nature is a continuing, unresolved theme in the history of Western thought, one that has important social and political implications.[1]

Recent philosophers such as Daniel Dennett as well as many reasonable people would like to believe that all mental phenomena, including consciousness, must be explained by the physical activity of the brain.[2] As we have seen, however, the brain grows through constant interaction with affective experience. Impairments in these experiential interactions lead to impairments in consciousness. For example, children who do not have certain types of interactive experiences, such as children in multiproblem or dysfunctional families, even when their brains function normally, may lack the capacity for self-reflection. Similarly, children with physical problems affecting the functioning of the nervous system also evidence impairments in consciousness. Children with autistic patterns rarely display any degree of self-awareness and self-reflection until later in the course of therapy.

As discussed earlier, when interactions are planned to get around the deficits of impaired children, whether experiential or physical, they go through a series of stages of increasing levels of consciousness and self-reflection. Normally developing children master these same levels, ranging from the earliest awareness of sensory and emotional aliveness to becoming intentional to the capacity to reflect symbolically on their own feelings and desires, albeit with far less effort. But the question remains: How does experience become integrated into the physical activity of the brain to create these levels of consciousness? Part of the answer to this question, I believe, lies in the brain's ability to experience and organize emotion.

Observing infants and children suggests that the growth of consciousness relates to the evolving awareness of our own affects or emotions. Affects that arise from physical processes and gradually take on subjective meaning are unique in that they bridge what we view as the objective aspects of the brain and subjective experience. They produce observable, measurable physiological patterns. For example, many different processes of the sympathetic and parasympathetic nervous systems are associated with different states of affect.[3] Most individuals readily experience these physical states in, say, the tightening of the chest muscles, the pounding of the heart, and the hollow sensation in the gut that accompany fear. Yet emotions also come to have subjective qualities and eventually meaning. Happiness, sadness, hatred, love—all denote a state of mood or mind, a quality of conscious experience. The awareness of these states has traditionally been attributed to the subjective or spiritual side of mental life.

How do physiological processes acquire subjective tone and meaning? What role do they play in the formation of consciousness? As we have discussed, the infant initially experiences global states such as calmness, excitement, and distress that appear to be largely physical in nature. As the nervous system grows, infants are able to experience and express their state of mind more subtly—a special smile for Mom, an annoyed glance at Dad, a delighted look of surprise at a welcome but unexpected sight or sound. For these more refined mental states to emerge, however, an infant must have interactive experiences with caregivers; deprived infants tend to continue to evidence more global expressions. In this way, experience continually refines physiologic expression and growing physiologic regulation serves as an organizer and expressor of more complex interactive emotional experiences. If the muscles tense up, associated with a feeling of discomfort or tension, and experience further shapes this state, a distinct feeling of anger may emerge. This feeling may then serve to organize and give meaning to a variety of interactive experiences accompanied by frustration or discomfort.

In the second half of the first year of life, babies routinely evidence discrete expressions of different affects, such as anger, fear, surprise, despair, happiness, and so on, which then serve to categorize, and in this way give meaning to, subsequent interactive experiences.[4] Over time, as experiences are organized in a continuous cycle by a growing range of affects, a subjective inner world is formed. As all this is happening, a category of experience that gets labeled "outer reality" is also being created. Both the inner subjective world and the awareness of outer reality emerge gradually from the feedback loop of interactions between affect and experience.

Emotions therefore not only become the complex mediators of experience but also serve an internal organizing and differentiating role. What starts off as a physiological system receiving the input of the senses becomes, through the results of developmental experience, both a complex social tool and the vehicle for structuring internal mental life.

The evolving cycle of experiencing and categorizing appears to affect the physiology of the brain, rather than just vice versa, in an intimate dance between nature and nurture.[5] It is misleading to attempt to separate the contributions of each because one can be defined only in the context of the other. Consciousness develops from this continuous interaction in which biology organizes experience and experience organizes biology.

The processes that make affective experience and expression possible take place in living cells, which in turn involve physical processes that are still only partially understood but yet appear to differ from nonliving systems such as those that operate computers. Nonetheless, certain parallels provide a useful clue as to how a physically derived phenomenon might come to acquire subjective tone and meaning and in that way contribute to consciousness.

Our word for emotions indicates their dual nature: what we call "feelings" are not only psychological states but also concrete, visceral sensations. Anxiety may announce itself as a pounding pulse, disappointment as a sharp pain in the gut, sadness as a tightness in the throat, stress as a throbbing in the temples. Many who have suffered deep grief know a broken heart not as a metaphor for desolation but as a palpable ache in the upper chest. Many who have experienced intense fear have physically shivered through a cold sweat.

The tie between emotional and physical feeling is thus neither accidental nor symbolic. Indeed, it is wired into our neurology and musculature. Merely acting out the external form of an emotion can produce something of the genuine affect. If you deliberately arrange your features into a happy smile, chances are you'll feel a fleeting ripple of good cheer. If you clench your face into an angry scowl, you'll feel a flicker of irritation. Crumpling it into a mask of anguish will call up a slight wave of sorrow. We literally feel our emotions in our bodies and, conversely, our faces and bodies express what we feel. What's more, each facial or bodily expression of emotion—each smile or grimace or scowl, each rigid back or slouched shoulder or flailing arm—carries its own subtle gradation in feeling and interior emotional tone.

Emotions alone do not build consciousness, however, any more than sensory experience by itself builds the mind. Rather, an increasing range of emotions gradually becomes abstracted by the nervous system's ability to construct patterns. The affective aspect of the dual code produces a sense of aliveness in a most basic way from an infant's experiences. Sensation, reactivity, the very properties of certain neurons continue to provide the physiological basis for affects or emotions. As these emotional experiences increase in range and complexity, they are abstracted into patterns. The growing brain, with appropriate nurturing, becomes a better and better pattern detective. These patterns become more intentional and complex, organizing into the six levels discussed in Chapters 3 and 4. As described, at levels five and six they are translated into images and a representational sense of self, or consciousness, arises.

Consciousness can thus be conceptualized as having two components. One is generative in nature and involves the reactivity of neuronal cells and their related physiologic and affective activity (for instance, a pleasurable sense of touch). The other is organizing in nature. The hardwiring of the nervous system, as it interacts with certain types of experiences, allows us to abstract and organize sensory and affective patterns. These two components work together to produce consciousness.

What we typically mean by "consciousness" is self-reflection, which represents a fairly late stage of development. At this stage the mind is able to be aware of its own feelings and desires—"I'm happy," "I'm angry," "I'm sad," "I want to hit you," "I want to love you." This capacity for reflective awareness, as indicated in the previous chapter, goes through many stages. In the four- to five-year-old, expressing a wish—"I want to go out now"—replaces the demands of the three-year-old—"Out" or "Open door." As the child progresses in the school-age years, we see an even higher level of reflection: an increasingly stable sense of self through day-to-day experience. The adolescent shows still higher levels. She is able to reflect not only on what is happening in the present but on what may happen in the future. The young adult can comprehend her own past, anticipate her future, and reflect with some perspective on the events around her. In the subsequent stages of life, yet higher levels of consciousness are related to greater awareness of the individual's own personhood in relation to the family she creates, her community, and ultimately the world as a whole and the cycles of nature.

We generally think of conscious awareness as a phenomenon of the later stages of self-reflection, but this capacity is actually the legacy of the long developmental process outlined in Chapters 2–4. The first sign of consciousness is simply a baby's sense of aliveness: the bubbling of his feelings in response to sensations at a time when he cannot yet distinguish himself from the world around him. This early sense of affective aliveness is not attached to any symbols or purposeful behavior. While it may be called "arousal," it might be more appropriately called a sense of affective aliveness. When the infant begins showing his preference for his primary caregivers and taking a delightful, joyful interest in the human world, a second stage of consciousness arises. While there are still no symbols or intentional behaviors attached to his feelings, his consciousness now embraces another human being as part of an undifferentiated sense of shared bliss. Soon consciousness expands to include additional feelings and desires, including dependency, pleasure, and anger.

At the next milestone, as the child develops purposeful patterns of behavior (reaching out to be picked up and the like), a new type of consciousness emerges, which differentiates emerging bits of "me" defined by these intents from other people. Next comes a consciousness of complex patterns involving many of one's own and others' intentions. A more integrated "me" made up of many desires replaces the earlier islands of "me," embracing an awareness of negotiating with others around security, safety, dependency, approval, disapproval, acceptance, rejection, assertiveness, anger, and other daily emotional themes. Even prior to the formation of symbols, there is cohesion, purpose, and a type of meaning. Once our emotions can be abstracted symbolically, in word and images, we begin the journey of symbolic consciousness described earlier.

It is hard for the adult to imagine how an infant or toddler experiences himself during the stages of this process. As mightily as we may try to recreate them through various techniques—deep relaxation, hypnosis, religious practices—these stages of imminent consciousness remain elusive. Even if we could truly connect with these earlier mental states, we wouldn't be able to remember what they were like once we returned to our normal symbolic state. Perhaps only in certain forms of artistic expression can earlier forms of consciousness be tapped. The psychoanalyst Marion Milner suggests this in *On Not Being Able to Paint*: "The experience of outer and inner coinciding, which we blindly undergo when we fall in love, is consciously brought about in the arts."[6]

In addition to its developmental level, consciousness clearly varies from individual to individual in the content of the emotional drama embraced by it. A broad-based, reflective consciousness embraces a range of feelings such as joy and pleasure, dependency, assertiveness, and anger. It enables us to appreciate the feelings of others and join with others in providing leadership, whether in politics, religion, philanthropy, or conservation. More limited degrees of conscious awareness and reflection are associated with only experiencing a few repetitive emotional dramas (for example, always angry or suspicious) and self-centered and rigid attitudes. When we talk about a developed consciousness, we don't mean, say, some ethereal ability to project ourselves across space or time. What we mean is the ability to experience the most basic human emotions in ourselves and others and to reflect on these in the context of our families, society, culture, and environment.

The emotions central to the sense of self may be the nexus or bridge between mind and body, the polarity of which has mystified philosophers and behavioral scientists for millennia. From all the organs of the body, the nervous system carries sensations to the parts of the brain that organize and abstract patterns, connecting physiological systems to emotional ones. The bridge carries traffic in both directions.[7] An injury or illness, especially if painful, can at least temporarily shrink the sense of self down to the mere desire to get out of bed and go to the bathroom, or simply for the pain to stop. Intense, all-encompassing affects dealing with basic needs can redefine who we are, what we want, and what we think, reducing our ability to reflect and putting us back into an action mode in which meeting these needs entirely absorbs consciousness.

Maintaining higher levels of awareness depends on essential physical needs being met and emotions being regulated so that intense affects do not obscure the subtle patterns and variations that support higher mental abilities. A frightened or hungry or ill person finds it difficult to be philosophical. "I must study politics and war that my sons may have liberty to study mathematics and philosophy," John Adams wrote to his wife, Abigail, during the Revolutionary War. "My sons ought to study mathematics and philosophy, geography, natural history, naval architecture, navigation, commerce, and agriculture, in order to give their children a right to study painting, poetry, music, architecture, statuary, tapestry, and porcelain." The highest levels of consciousness only are possible when material requirements and the need for security are met.

The developmental conception of the relationship between mind and body assumes that emotions are not confined to lower parts of the nervous system, such as the limbic system; on the contrary, the highest levels of the cerebral cortex involve affective and not purely cognitive experience.

In recent research with Stephen Porges, we have shown how the mind and body work together in problem solving. Porges has shown that complex problem solving involving two-way affective communication depends in part on an evolutionarily advanced aspect of the parasympathetic nervous system which has pathways into the cerebral cortex.[8] This is the ability to make rapid physiologic shifts in response to affective problem-solving interactions with things and people. We have found that children at risk for learning and behavioral problems had vulnerabilities in this capacity and are currently exploring this capacity in children with severe communication and relationship problems. Porges has further suggested that there are two earlier levels in the neurological organization of the central nervous system, one based on the fight-or-flight reactions described decades ago by Cannon and another, more primitive one based on a component of the parasympathetic nervous system associated with massive shutdown and inhibition in the face of fear or anxiety.[9] These levels of organization parallel our observations of the early levels of affective organization. One type of maladaptive expression at the levels of self-regulation and engagement is massive shutdown of critical perceptual and life support functions. At the level of intentional affective communication, rigid fight-or-flight reactions can take the place of subtly responsive, reciprocal affective cuing. Physiological studies and observations of early emotional organization converge to some degree in explaining the role of affective regulation and interaction in intelligent functioning. Both in terms of the mind's observed developmental levels (described in Chapters 3 and 4) and the levels of neural regulation, primitive, somatically based and global polarized affective patterns are related to more advanced social and symbolic patterns.

The most crucial of human capacities, then, is the immeasurable power to register the world through affects, integrate these into an emerging consciousness, and express with the body as well as words and symbols a vast range of feelings. This capacity, straddling the border of the mental and the physical, the psyche and the nervous system, the mind and the brain, is a function of both realms, binding them into an indissoluble whole.

These speculations about the relationship between mind and body are not merely academic. What has driven the search for the answers to these questions over the centuries is the enormous influence that they have had on human life. The origins that we ascribe to our fundamental qualities help to determine how we treat one another and what solutions we entertain to solve social problems. If the mind is seen to be shaped by purely biological processes, then biological solutions to human problems must prevail. But as we shall explore in more detail in Part Two, if affective development is essential in shaping the mind, solutions to the ills of both the individual and society must take it into consideration.

THE ROOTS OF MORALITY

An apparent decline in the sense of individual responsibility is of wide concern today in both public and private life. Attempted remedies vary. Recently the emphasis has been on parents being firmer, institutions such as schools demanding more from children, and government programs such as welfare giving less and expecting more. Behind this hard-nosed "get tough" approach to strengthening the ethics and values of both youth and adults lies the implicit assumption that just as parents spoil children by giving too much with too few expectations, our nation may be spoiling its citizens, particularly its poorer ones, in the same way.

In order to begin to understand how to enhance the sense of responsibility in individuals and instill empathy and concern for others, we need to understand how, under ordinary circumstances, these desirable traits are learned. Regard for others develops from a sense of shared humanity. This capacity develops only in a baby who has the chance to interact routinely and consistently with an admiring, supportive caregiver in a relationship that provides security and intimacy. Children shuffled from one foster home to another; children who have been abused or neglected; children whose parents are so caught up in meeting their own needs that they are unable to feel for their child; even children whose parents are devoted and protective but are so busy that they have no time left for exchanges of feelings—all are at grave risk for not fully realizing their humanity.

Whereas initially a child feels joy, warmth, and security passively in herself being loved and cared for, she is soon able to extend these feelings to a beloved caregiver and, gradually, to others in her family, then teachers and peers. The feeling of being cared for and caring for others eventually becomes the basis for empathy. Although the beginnings of concern for others can be seen in the fleeting behavior of children at the end of the second year of life, when for example they pat Mommy's sore arm or Daddy's injured nose, true empathy—the ability to put yourself in someone else's shoes and feel concern for that person based on how you would feel in his circumstances—requires more advanced levels of psychological organization. We see early signs of this in the later preschool years and more prominently during the school-age years, when children reach the stage of being able to create two distinct inner worlds, one that reacts to the daily ups and downs of peer relations and another that begins to hold a stable inner sense of identity.

At school age, children are able to be empathic in the true sense of the word because they feel secure enough about who they are to lend a piece of themselves to experiencing what another person might feel. The adolescent and adult can imagine the many possible ways another person might feel to a far greater extent than a ten- or twelve-year-old can, although to be sure, during these years this ability will be further developed and tested. At base, however, the ability to consider the feelings of others in a caring, compassionate way derives from the child's sense of having been loved and cared for herself. Without this, no effort to put herself in someone else's situation will necessarily result in empathy. An individual might, for example, envisage herself in another's situation in order to figure out how to trick or manipulate the person, but she won't feel compassion unless she has had the experience of compassion. We learn about empathy and compassion not from what we're told but from how we're treated. We can be told a hundred times a day to be kind and compassionate. Parents may see themselves as role models and point out their compassion toward others, but their words will be empty unless their children have experienced their caring and concern.

Another important developmental root of morality derives from the child's participation in preverbal interaction. Her awareness of her own and others' intentions, which take in such basic issues as safety versus danger, acceptance versus rejection, approval versus disapproval, pride and respect versus humiliation, are all initially understood through such exchanges between caregiver and child. Attitudes toward aggression are learned before the child can say her first angry word. When the sixteen-month-old raises her voice, points her finger, glares angrily, or pushes over an unwanted cup of broccoli, there is usually a response from a watchful, not unopinionated caregiver. These early communications reflect many of the family's personal and cultural patterns. In one family, annoyance or anger might be welcomed as assertiveness—with a chuckle or proud smile, a parent might fantasize about the politician, CEO, or athlete her child might become. In another family this same expression of feeling might be greeted with silence, withdrawal, intrusiveness, or punishment, accompanied by more fearful thoughts: "Oh my God, I'm creating a monster!" "I don't know what I'll do when he gets bigger!"

To the degree that there are different reactions in different families to a child's expression of emotions, explorations of her body, or first altruistic leanings, varying expectations begin to form regarding what's good and what's bad, what's right and what's wrong. These expectations shape the deepest level of the growing mind, below that of words or even visual images. We may feel them in the pits of our stomachs, at the core of who we are. Yet they may elude any verbal or symbolic expression, except for some creative individuals through art or poetry. Subsequent experience may strengthen or challenge these primary beliefs. Early experiences can give birth on the one hand to prejudice, to self-righteous arrogance, or to the rationalization of polarized opinions. On the other hand, they may be the first step toward developing compassion and a system of morality based on empathy and respect.

In understanding the development of morality, it is important to distinguish compassion and empathy for others from the acquisition of complex social skills that involve comprehending the intentions of others, understanding their feelings, and even behaving in prosocial or altruistic ways. Robert Emde has written about the early roots of morality in certain procedural knowledge such as the rules of give-and-take or reciprocity.[10] Lawrence Kohlberg has discussed reasoning strategies such as the ability to look at all sides of a problem, a sophisticated skill necessary in making moral judgments.[11] But the reading of social signals and the more advanced capacity for cognitive abstraction are not the essence of moral development; after all, the snake oil salesman, the sociopath, the devious demagogue all use superior social skills and logic to trick and manipulate. These abilities, which underlie general intellectual and social development, are requisite before many higher-level social and cognitive skills, including certain aspects of moral reasoning, can be acquired. The critical ingredient that determines how an individual uses these skills, however, is the quality of compassion and caring. Morality is defined by this quality, which rests on emotional experience.

Both developmentally healthy toddlers and those in various states of emotional or physical distress exhibit preverbal patterns relating to the later development of compassion. Optimal interaction patterns between caregiver and child, in which parents read and react to the child's cues and gestures, allow the child to experience a full range of feelings and form expectations based on an assortment of possibilities. In contrast, children who are neglected, punitively intruded on, or overwhelmed, or whose parents selectively ignore their expressions of aggression, competitiveness, curiosity, and so on, form polarized expectations. The child's perceptions are couched in all-or-nothing terms: "They hate me"; "I'm bad."[12]

As the child moves from the preverbal stage into that of using ideas, his view of his own intentions and his expectations of others are vastly enriched. He can now represent others to himself mentally, making distinctions among them, and explore his own as well as others' feelings. Coupled with compassion, the ability to grasp a range of one's own and others' feelings makes possible the gradual maturing of the moral sense. Painful experience, however, can heighten polarized patterns. Projecting one's own inner desires on others can result in a fixed attitude about how the world operates, one that can become self-fulfilling. Regarding other people with suspicion, for example, may lead them to act angrily, which only confirms the individual in believing they are not to be trusted. Fixed beliefs derive from rigid personal needs that do not allow an empathic grasp of the complexities of other people's lives.

Mature empathy and morality are possible only after an individual develops the ability to connect emotions and ideas, to reflect on himself and his actions, and finally to construct an inner world of stable values alongside that of changing experiences. In the best of circumstances, the capacity for creating this inner world blossoms as puberty approaches and continues to grow throughout adolescence and into adulthood.

As indicated earlier, moral capacity has sometimes been assessed along mostly cognitive lines. Can an individual consider many alternatives rather than just one? Can he deal with ambiguity and gray areas, or does he see things only in black and white? What is often not sufficiently understood is the importance of a person's emotional range and flexibility to the growth of moral sensibility. People are not equally reflective in such different areas as dependency, sexuality, and aggression, anger, fear, and passion. In areas in which we feel anxiety and conflict, we often tend to have overly concrete rigid, or polarized views. Most of us are therefore more empathic and morally discerning in some emotional areas than in others. The diversity of opinion among the nine Supreme Court justices in any one hotly contended decision illustrates this point.

Like many faculties that are rooted in our emotional experience, our sense of morality continues to develop throughout our lifetimes. The more experience we have of both the joys and pleasures and the hardships of life, the broader our basis for empathy, morality, and the wisdom that underlies them. A seasoned ethical perspective cannot arise when personal experience does not allow abstracting principles of human behavior. Wisdom and morality are close cousins, both the outcome of a long developmental process cultivated by affective experience.

But what about people who reach a high level of ethical development despite crippling obstacles? How is it that individuals who were deprived as children sometimes go on to become moral leaders, perhaps founding institutions that help thousands of others? Certain people seem to put their traumas behind them by trying to prevent others from suffering as they did. Still, looking at the early lives of such individuals closely, we see that as children they usually had at least one adult who treated them with compassion or love. This love may not have been routine, given within the home by a mother or father; possibly the caring person was only a distant relative or teacher. In a well-known study done on one of the Hawaiian islands, some children growing up under conditions of extreme poverty and adversity seemed to display a natural resilience, and some of these developed qualities of compassion and caring.[13] These "invulnerable" children, however, were in fact by nature no less susceptible to hardship than were the others. Most were fortunate or skillful enough to have had one or more relationships during their formative years that provided them with love, concerned caring, and guidance. These relationships were not always obvious to an outsider. The kindness of an aunt or neighbor, for example, might be found to be the critical factor separating a child who did well in spite of adversity from one who did poorly. In my clinical experience, individuals who lacked any such positive relationship in their early lives are often unable to use their own challenges as a motivation for improving the plight of others. Although some mental health professionals maintain that denying problems can lead to deeds of kindness and caring, it is rare indeed that this is true of anyone not fortunate enough to have had some experience of warmth and compassion in childhood.

Even so, the reader may be thinking, surely loving nurturing alone can't instill the ethical standards and sense of responsibility we want our youth to acquire. What about children who are given everything but who wind up as self-centered, spoiled teenagers and adults with numerous problems such as alcohol and substance abuse and depression?

First, it's important to distinguish between children who are indulged with material things and opportunities and children who are given real warmth and compassion. While most parents provide loving, compassionate care, not all are able to do so. Perhaps their own upbringing hampered their capacity to nurture others. Strong or weak coping skills can be passed on within a family for generations.

Even when this sort of care is provided, however, it is only half of what is required for developing a moral sense. The other has to do with structure and limits. All children need some degree of help in controlling greed and anger, which are as basic to human nature as love and compassion. A child who is not given an appropriate structure and limits often develops a negative self-image because she doesn't feel confident about handling her own feelings. The key to establishing structure and limits is to build them into the child's everyday experience. They must be firm but gentle, consistent but flexible. The child needs to be helped to anticipate her own feelings of anger or greed so that, as she becomes more verbal, she can collaborate in the limit-setting process.

Children who require especially strict limits because of either early challenges or their own physical makeup also need extra warmth and compassion. The more difficult the child, the greater the tendency in parents or other caregivers to increase the limits reflexively, perhaps punitively, without simultaneously increasing their emotional support. Punitive limits alone often lead either to fear or to aggression and rebellion. Firm, gentle limits coupled with a sense of security contribute to an internal sense of responsibility.

Responsibility is further enhanced by appropriately guided challenges in school and after-school activities, challenges that have meaning in the growing child's cultural context: doing chores at home, or, for a teenager, holding a job or perhaps helping out at a day-care center, a sports program for children, or a home for the elderly. A mentor who establishes an ongoing relationship with the child will contribute to the development of not only a sense of responsibility but also a regard for the rights of others.

Moral values are highly personal, shaped by a distinct blend of each individual's religious and cultural background, beliefs, and experiences. Principled people of good will may differ on issues like abortion or euthanasia or the proper role of government in our lives. Even so, they share certain characteristics. They struggle with upholding their views while maintaining an attitude of respect, compassion, and responsibility toward others. While good people can have different views on many complex issues, they agree on the fundamental need for empathy toward their fellow human beings.

A NEW VIEW OF INTELLIGENCE

We have observed how new capacities emerge at each stage of a child's early development, a progression of abilities, such as attention and self-regulation, engagement, intentionality, and complex pattern making, that underlie the sense of self, consciousness, and moral awareness. We have seen how, starting at the very beginning of life, emotional interactions establish the foundations for these abilities.

We now come to a most important issue: that of refining what we mean by intelligence in light of this understanding of development. Intellectual capacity is more than mastery of impersonal cognitive tasks—puzzles, math problems, memory or motor exercises—or analytical thinking. Nor does it seem helpful to regard each separate talent or ability as a special type of intelligence. Our definition of intelligence, while it may include many such skills, should focus on the general process whereby individuals reason, reflect, and understand the world.

Intelligence represents two interrelated capacities: the ability to generate intentions and ideas, and the ability to put these creations into a logical or analytical framework. These two abilities emerge from the successful mastery of the developmental stages we have outlined. The extent to which these abilities can be applied in different areas of life determines the breadth of a person's intelligence. Through literature, scientific observations, and art, lived experience is extended beyond our immediate personal surroundings. No medium can convey the totality of an experience, but it can expand our emotional range to encompass experiences we have "lived" only in our minds.

Intelligence—the ability to create ideas from lived emotional experience, to reflect on them, and to understand them in the context of other information—can probably never be reproduced artificially. Computers may be able to perform certain cognitive operations, sometimes even more effectively, and certainly faster, than humans. But unless they acquire the ability to experience and react to emotion, silicon chips will be unable to exercise intelligent discrimination. If you have ever struggled to convince a computer it has made a ridiculous mistake, you know how essentially moronic, how incapable of judgment and understanding, an electronic "brain" can be. Though it rifles through facts at the speed of light, it can't make the simplest intuitive deduction or abstraction, or even the sort of alteration of categories very small children are capable of.

It is interesting that two different approaches to "educating" computers that to some extent parallel different learning philosophies are both experiencing limited success. One approach, that of Douglas Lenat of the University of Texas at Austin, attempts to program into a huge computer all the factual knowledge and rules of human behavior and conduct in the hope of producing a superior intellect. Rodney Brooks at MIT, taking a bottom-up approach that is closer to the humanistic tradition but is nonetheless materialistic, designs computers that are able to learn from experience. Thus far, both approaches have failed to reach the levels projected for them, and in creative reasoning they can be outdistanced by a young child.

What separates human intelligence from that of computers, robots, androids, and any other cyber-creatures we can imagine, is the fact that we possess a nervous system capable of—indeed, specifically designed for—generating and evaluating affect. Thus, even though machines may "see" in the sense of responding to visual stimuli or "hear" auditory ones or "think" in the sense of manipulating symbols, they do not have the capacity for reflective consciousness, as opposed to simple physical registering of light or sound waves or other signals. Consciousness and all the powers it entails grow out of the reactivity of our cells, the myriad affects this reactivity generates, and the integration of these by the nervous system. Unless and until we solve the problem of creating living cellular reactivity and affects, as well as the capacity to abstract patterns of affects, in an artificial form, no machine will think in a truly human way.

In both theory and practice we have tended to underemphasize the generative aspect of intelligence, the creation of intentions and ideas, instead focusing more on how intentions and ideas are put into a frame of reference. As we discussed in Chapter 1, following Piaget, most modern cognitive theorists have dwelled primarily on the analytical rather than the generative aspects of intelligence. In most schools, likewise, there is enormous stress on teaching children to organize and order their ideas. Children are assumed somehow to come up intuitively with the ideas they are then taught to put into a frame of reference. I was first alerted to the importance of the generative aspects of intelligence in observing children both with and without developmental challenges. In children with autistic symptoms or environmental disadvantages, my colleagues and I saw that unless we mobilized these generative capacities and helped the children learn to form intentions and ideas, their thinking remained overly concrete, stereotyped, and repetitive. When we create natural situations of strong affect, children were able to generate desires and images and to be creative as well as logical and reflective.[14] Children without challenges found it easier to generate intentions and ideas and therefore to learn, but we observed that more emotionally interactive styles tended to produce thinking that was both more creative and more abstract. Among adults, those who combine generative and analytical thinking make more seminal contributions to their fields.

Perhaps we have paid less attention to the generative aspects of intelligence because we haven't understood the processes involved in their production. Because ideas emerge from affects and intentions, it is quite possible that the dichotomy between reason and emotion is partly responsible for our oversight. In the model presented here I am attempting to redress this oversight and give proper weight to the generative component of intelligence.

The finely differentiated ability to create ideas from experience and to reflect on those ideas in a broader context or scrutinize them logically of course operates best in areas where an individual's actual experience is extensive. People often contrast intelligence, by which they mean a high level of cognitive ability, with talent, which is usually defined as outstanding facility in an expressive field. To a certain extent, however, they overlap. An accomplished musician, writer, or visual artist can be every bit as intelligent in her field of expertise—that is to say, as capable of understanding and reflecting on music or poetry or painting—as a brilliant mathematician is in mathematics. Fine differentiation and a grasp of relationships are the essence of intelligence, regardless of the field. Both intelligence and talent imply that an individual is skillful in certain areas of endeavor. But intelligence requires something more. It goes beyond talent in that it involves a systematic understanding of why and how things work—of why a certain color is right, or why a particular equation describes a phenomenon, or why a given note produces the desired emotional effect.

Intelligence also requires the ability to express that understanding symbolically. Thus, not only can the person perform well; she can explain how and why she does what she does. She can see elements and their relationships, rearrange them in novel combinations to meet unprecedented problems, envisage unaccustomed possibilities, and reduce them to terms that others can understand. The surgeon who can explain why a new operation will work, or the plumber who can explain why an architect's plan won't, shows intelligence.

An intelligent explanation, however, needn't be given in words. Imagine a basketball player, for example, explaining to fellow players the qualities of a truly great slam-dunk. Stored in his memory, we might suppose, are the thousands he has smashed through the hoop. Over the years he may well have analyzed these plays, sorting them by various criteria into categories of effectiveness. Trying to explain these observations would take a lot of words and provide aspiring hoopsters a lot less information than a real-life demonstration by the master himself of a series of lunges toward a basket. If organized by an intelligent, analytical scheme, such a demonstration—like a chance to watch a brilliant surgeon—would make a brilliant lesson.

Standard IQ tests measure intellectual aptitude through limited linguistic, mathematical, and spatial tasks. Many areas of intelligent activity are not represented. A gifted designer, negotiator, musician— a high achiever in any number of fields not taken into account by those who quantify intellect—may still possess and display the twin hallmarks of high intelligence: the ability to create ideas and perceive relationships, and the capacity to reflect on them systematically.

Nearly every field of human endeavor thus offers some scope to the exercise of intelligence, though not all in the same way. Some, like higher mathematics, law, and philosophy, afford tremendous possibilities for symbolic abstraction. Others, such as engineering and science, permit the exploration of extremely complex relationships. Some, like literature, music, and the visual and performing arts, allow exquisite subtlety of emotional expression. Even many fields not normally considered intellectual or creative—everyday endeavors like carpentry or child care or gardening—are nonetheless the focus of considerable levels of intelligence by expert practitioners. True intelligence in any field requires deep and extensive knowledge and experience. Although creative ideas may arise at the early stages of learning, when a person is only beginning to understand the vocabulary of the field and feel her way among the concepts, they cannot be refined until later. Fields differ in the kind of demands they make. Some permit mastery early in life; others demand decades of apprenticeship. Adolescent prodigies are far from rare in chess; mathematical brilliance often peaks in relative youth. True expertise as a medical diagnostician, however, requires a breadth of experience possible only in a person of more mature years.

Some fields, to be sure, may afford intelligence only minimal scope. If someone were to resolve to run a saw in the most intelligent way imaginable, try as he might to develop or reflect on systematic knowledge of this effort, he'd soon discover a dearth of possibilities. To exercise high intelligence in such a limited domain, he'd probably have to transcend it altogether, passing into a more promising field like inventing or engineering, where he could devise a superior cutting edge.

Intelligence testers generally concentrate on cognitive skills in certain symbolic fields. Conventional testing thus equates high intelligence with the ability to do well at manipulating words, numbers, or shapes. Over the years, testers have built up a huge body of data about certain skills. It is the usefulness of this data base for making comparisons, rather than any theoretical consistency behind the skills measured, that keeps the traditional tests in favor. Experts rely on them not because they reflect the latest thinking on intelligence but because they're there. But since intelligence arises from affect and not merely from cognition, no true definition can limit it to so narrow a range of abilities.

The genuinely intelligent person has breadth as well as depth: she is intelligent across a range of activities and interests. The popular stereotypes of the mad scientist, the person of great intellect who is devoid of moral sense, and the computer nerd, the whiz who lacks elementary interpersonal skills, reveal an intuitive grasp of this fact. An individual with prodigious skill in a narrow, often extremely symbolic field but great ineptitude in areas involving judgment, personal relationships, aesthetics, or the like, may score very well on standard intelligence tests. But such a person does not embody either the full range or the highest levels of intelligence, nor the array of abilities that a civilized society should encourage.

The prevailing definition of intelligence, and all the life-determining decisions based on this understanding, cry out for radical revision. Theorists like Howard Gardner and Robert Sternberg have in recent years suggested the notion that people possess multiple forms of intelligence—musical, kinesthetic, social, and so forth, in addition to the cognitive skills traditionally measured in IQ tests.[15] Though promising, this suggestion fails to get at the essence of intelligence in whatever field it is exercised.

Rather than measuring intelligence with a single cognitive yardstick, we must find ways to evaluate it in terms of its depth and breadth. Some people evidence creative analytical ability across a wide range of intellectual endeavors. One thinks of J. Robert Oppenheimer, head of the Manhattan Project, which developed the atomic bomb, who pursued a brilliant career in science, and mastered the intricacies of running a complex and secret bureaucracy while maintaining a scholarly interest in Oriental languages and ancient philosophy. Other people excel only in a single field like math or music.

A full description of intellect would also consider the depth of an individual's creative and reflective capacities. The ability to generate or create ideas, then to reflect on them and organize them into a logical framework is, we believe, an essential part of a definition of intelligence. A person breaking new ground in a complex field—

someone who can explain, evaluate, and critically analyze her own contributions and those of others—shows a sort of intelligence different from that of a person only beginning to learn the field. Mastering the content of a field, along with a great deal of experience using it, gives one the opportunity to attain far greater intellectual depth in a discipline than is possible for someone just starting out.

According to our definition, therefore, a "gifted" dilettante cannot, no matter how high his IQ, achieve a high level of intelligence in a given discipline. Only deep and extensive knowledge of a field permits abstracting at the highest levels. In *Creative Experience*, M. P. Follett writes, "Concepts can never be presented to me merely, they must be knitted into the structure of my being, and this can only be done through my own activity."

Intelligence also includes reality testing. We have already alluded to the paradox that a process based on emotion serves the purpose of helping us separate what is relatively objective from what is relatively subjective. This is not so surprising when we consider that most human beings have similar central nervous systems. Although there are enormous variations influenced by personality, family, environment, and culture, they also share many similar experiences in negotiating the early stages of development. A sense of shared reality emerges from these experiences, which are not similar choices of food or toys or types of games, but critical processes of interaction. Such common processes provide the building blocks for separating what is inside oneself from what is outside and, eventually, fantasy from reality. The formation of a sense of reality and the ability to reason logically is in this way fundamentally an emotional rather than a cognitive process.

Piaget identified the child's earliest awareness of causality in his using his motor system toward a specific end (e.g., pulling a string to ring a bell)—apparently without focusing on an even more basic example of the early sense of causality: the smile begetting the smile, or the frown begetting the puzzled look. It is the sense that inner affects and intents can produce affects and intents in others that establishes the psychological boundary necessary for the sense of causality and, later, reality testing.

When individuals have significant dysfunction in the physical makeup of their nervous systems or in their family and interaction patterns, there is a higher likelihood of problems in testing reality. We often observe, for example, psychotic children, those who suffer from delusions and hallucinations, with severe deficits in reality testing who yet have a well-developed sense of motor causality (e.g., hitting a drum to make a sound or even solving a complicated mechanical game).

Our appraisal of reality is in part, therefore, a subjective emotional operation in which we call on our common biology and set of experiences to elucidate a shared sense of reality. This sense, supported by certain critical experiences, such as being part of various groups, in turn supports our social and political institutions. If too many individuals grow up with neurological dysfunctions or extremely disturbed family and interaction patterns, the social consensus on what constitutes reality could easily slip away as our ability to reason loses its stabilizing foundations.

Intelligence in its most general sense is based on our ability to connect affect or intent to our growing ability to sequence behavior and symbols, both verbal and spatial. We see it in its early forms in the programmed (prewired) reactions of infants and certain animals. We observe it progress through global patterns of response into interactive exchanges involving affect signals. As our affects connect with more complex abilities to sequence symbols in dynamic, problem-solving situations, we observe intelligence in its higher forms. Using this general definition, we may be able to see varying levels of intelligence more clearly in other members of the animal kingdom as well as in humans.

Intelligence reflects the mind doing its most important work. Together with reflective consciousness and the sense of morality, it develops through the process of creating and abstracting from emotional experience. As we will see in Part Two, understanding the common origins of basic mental abilities provides a new way of viewing many of the challenges facing our society.

CHAPTER SIX

Fitting Nurture to Nature: The Lock and Key

THE SERIES OF EVENTS THAT LEADS TO THE TRANSFORMATION of a helpless, incoherent newborn into a fully functional person possessed of the emotional, social, and intellectual capacities that distinguish *Homo sapiens* is perhaps the most remarkable metamorphosis in nature. Examining these steps, we have traced the growth of the human mind through the interplay between the child's inborn faculties, which emerge as her nervous system develops, and her early emotional experience. From the very beginning of life, there is thus a robust interaction between nature and nurture. Indeed, we might even say that optimal mental growth *requires* cooperation between them. There is mounting evidence that environmental influences can alter the physical structure of the brain, determining in part how genes express themselves in both biology and behavior. Even when a genetic influence has been well established, subtle environmental factors may still operate.

FROM POLE TO POLE: A CONTINUING DEBATE

No controversy about the predominance of nature or nurture in human development should exist. A child's constitutional makeup interacts with his emotional experience in a reciprocal manner so complex that there is no point in debating which factor contributes more. Nevertheless, scientists and nonscientists alike persist in trying to square away their respective roles, concluding that, for example, environment accounts for 40 to 70 percent of intelligence.

The most challenging current questions, however, focus less on quantifying the relative importance of nature and nurture than on the way the relationship between the two works. How does the environment actually influence biology? Perhaps the most important continuing controversy concerns limits. Do inborn variations prevent individuals from attaining certain skills or intellectual levels? Are biological differences strong enough to restrict a person's potential, regardless of the many possible environments to which he might be exposed? Can a woman become a competent fighter pilot? Can a man become an adequate baby nurse? On the nurture side, how strict are the limits imposed by environmental factors? Can a child born to a family in the urban underclass become a doctor or lawyer or university professor? In other words, the real issue with which the nature-nurture debate must grapple is whether any individual man or woman or child can, given the proper environment, succeed in a chosen endeavor.

Drastically different social policies, each with the power to shape the lives of millions of people, follow from how we answer these questions. In recent discussions of government spending, for example, some legislators suggested that, if heredity is indeed decisive in shaping who we are, the national interest would be better served by devoting less money to special education for those with learning disabilities and other educational challenges and more to the academically gifted, who are likely to make important contributions to society. An opposing approach argues for programs to better the nurturing environment of disadvantaged children through support of families, improved schools, and incentives to improve the economics of poor communities. A purely genetic outlook would dismiss such efforts as essentially futile attempts to change inalterable biology. The question then becomes: Do we invest in classrooms or jail cells, in social workers or prison guards? Do we view large segments of our population as untapped potential or write them off as biologically inferior? Do we, in short, try to develop the hidden abilities of our poorest children or merely try to contain their aberrant behavior?

The pendulum of intellectual fashion swings from pole to pole and back again as first one view and then the other gains political and cultural ascendancy. In highly stratified societies like those of pre-Enlightenment Europe, an individual's qualities were regarded as inextricably linked to his inherited social station. Nobles thus seems innately "noble," gentlefolk "gentle," and traits like intellectual subtlety or artistic sensitivity simply beyond the ken of the "vulgar" peasantry. In the modern period, however, with the emergence of the middle class as a powerful social and political force, the idea that people were restricted to their place in a divinely ordered society gave way to more democratic, individualistic notions. Paralleling this transformation was John Locke's view of the mind as a *tabula rasa,* a blank slate that is essentially malleable and thus perfectible. The "self-evident" truth that all men are created equal emphasized that anyone, given the right opportunities, can aspire to great things. Then, during the nineteenth and early twentieth centuries, scientists dazzled by the insights of Darwin and Mendel, as well as Caucasians bent on justifying colonialism and racial preferences, argued with increasing sophistication that it was heredity that largely determined individual human destiny. Adherents of these views promoted eugenic health schemes and restrictive immigration policies as public policy.

A few decades later, as the insights of Freud and the full horror of Nazi genocide—based on a perverted "science" of eugenics—sunk in, prominent experts just as fervently insisted on the power of environment to shape the individual, once again arguing that the neurology, musculature, and biochemistry an infant brings into the world constitute blank slates on which experience can write what it will. Educational experts maintained that improving children's early environment would raise their intellectual abilities and better prepare them to survive, even thrive, in the complex world they would inherit. This attitude held particular sway for a generation after World War II, as behaviorism and a strict Freudianism dominated educational theory and psychology.

Since that time, stunning revelations based on DNA research have revolutionized biology. The discovery of psychoactive drugs and advances in neuroscience did the same for psychiatry and psychology. While agreeing that both nature and nurture are important, experts began to claim that genetics and physiology set limits on intellectual capacities and personality traits regardless of how a child's environment is enriched. Today the prevailing biological bias of much current thinking goes a good deal further. Perhaps not coincidentally, conservative political views advocating immigration reform and cuts in aid to the needy are once more on the rise.

Apart from these swings in intellectual fashion, also supporting continued controversy is the fact that many researchers do not fully understand how nature and nurture actually work. Though most accept the interdependence of the two factors, studies that quantify individual influences rather than examining how they interact nudge the discussion in the direction of polarities rather than interrelationships.

Genes, however, operate within a larger context. Just as D. W. Winnicott suggested years ago that a baby can be understood only as part of a relationship, most genetic proclivities can also be understood only in the context of complex intracellular and hormonal environments. Furthermore, research strategies sometimes overlook important mediating factors, wrongly ascribing genetic origins to specific behavior.

A recent study of identical twins has shown that schizophrenia, which was assumed to have a genetic basis, is six times more likely to appear when the twins share a placenta than when they do not, suggesting that some intrauterine environmental process can affect the development of this trait.[1]

In another study, Michael McGuire of UCLA found that dominant male monkeys have relatively lower levels of serotonin than do less dominant monkeys (who are also more impulsive). The more interesting discovery, however, was that a monkey evidences average levels of this neurotransmitter prior to his rise to dominance; only afterward does the level drop.[2] This finding undermines the long-held assumption that biologically based levels of serotonin determine aspects of status in nonhuman primates. High levels have been thought to be a factor in violence and impulsivity. This example of the influence of environment on physiology illustrates the complexity of the relationship between genetic tendencies and ongoing experience.

Recently, thrill-seeking behavior has been associated with a particular DNA sequence on the gene D4DR that influences the way dopamine is used in the body.[3,4] It would be easy to assume from this finding that impulsive behavior is genetically based. However, though children who crave sensory input and tend to be daredevils can in certain environments become aggressive and destructive, in others they are thoughtful, reflective, and empathic.[5] Indeed, the many ways in which behavior is learned from one generation to another lead to a healthy respect for the intricate multiplicity of the processes that determine our individual characteristics.[6]

THE DANCE OF DEVELOPMENT

With the birth of each child, a unique set of inborn characteristics begins its lifelong dance with an equally distinctive sequence of experiences. Each side introduces many variables. In the early months and years, environmental influences are transmitted largely through the baby's relationship with her main caregiver. Mom may like to tickle and stimulate her, or just quietly gaze at her. She may be uncertain and retiring or overwhelming and self-assured. Each tendency elicits a difference response from the infant. Occasionally factors in the larger environment also have a direct effect, as when lead poisoning damages the nervous system or malnutrition caused by poverty or wartime scarcity stunts growth.

The traits of the caregiver are often thought to be positive or negative in their own right, but in our developmental model their influence depends on the particular stage the child has reached. A child needs one sort of nurturing in the first stage, when she is learning to achieve calm attention, and quite another as she moves toward complex gestural communication or symbolism. An interactive style that teaches attention or encourages falling in love may fail to teach a capacity to think or imagine, and vice versa.

A mother who has a very low-key and retiring temperament but a highly creative fantasy life may not foster her baby's need to engage deeply with another person during the second formative stage. This would be especially true for a baby who also tends toward reticence and reserve. Neither mother nor child is likely to strike the emotional spark needed to woo the other into a rapturous relationship. If, however, the baby can form such a bond with a jovial, outgoing father or grandmother, she can successfully progress to the stages in which her mother's vivid inner life and openness to imagination make her an ideal companion for pretend play and exploration. Each developmental stage influences the outcome of the interactions between nature and nurture. The child's mastery of the task at each stage depends on how well her human and physical surroundings mesh with her own physical characteristics. The nature of her needs are also affected by how well her development went at earlier stages. Neither nature nor nurture, therefore, is a fixed entity.

PATTERNS OF REACTION

Though children's genetic inheritance varies widely, it does not do so randomly. Like the range of variation in nature as a whole, the range of human traits is enormous but not infinite. The spectrum of human hair color, for example, stretches from albino white through blonds, reds, and browns to the darkest jet black. It does not, however, include green or purple. Thousands of different species of birds inhabit our planet, but none has fur. Variation occurs within patterns. That is true not only of physical traits like skin color and eye shape but also for the behavioral and psychosocial characteristics that make up personality.

Whether children's temperaments are innate has inspired a great deal of research over the years. Parents often insist that, from the very first, each of their children was a distinct individual. Some seem to arrive with sunny dispositions, whereas others are gloomy; some are tense, some relaxed; some responsive, some withdrawn. Many researchers argue that a person's basic temperament or approach to the world remains strikingly consistent throughout the life span. Drawing heavily on parents' reports of youngsters outgoingness or introversion, irritability or calmness, boldness or caution, capacity to focus or distractibility, the work on temperament by the pioneers Stella Chess and Alexander Thomas and their followers has helped both families and child development experts appreciate that no method of caregiving, discipline, or education suits all or even most children.[7]

Some researchers have taken this approach further. Jerome Kagan suggests that tendencies toward inhibition, shyness, and caution on the one hand and gregariousness and flamboyance on the other arise from the genes.[8] The patterns of interaction a child shows in early infancy are, in his view, inborn. Whether an infant seeks out or shuns company, asserts himself or withdraws, is an inherited trait that will, like eye color or blood type, endure for life. Parents or therapists can at best soften this tendency. But though they might, say, help a shrinking violet gain confidence by arranging home or school environments that don't overwhelm him, the child's essential timidity will persist, regardless of intervention. In one form or another, this view represents a large body of opinion that sees temperament as a relatively fixed quality defining an individual's entire personality structure.

However, the work that my colleagues and I have done with both healthy children and those with problems such as autism strongly supports the idea that a person's initial inclinations toward boldness or timidity derives not from any single, overriding genetic characteristic but from the complex interplay of multiple factors. Newborn babies do not exhibit innate traits of temperament such as introversion or extroversion. Building on the observations of professionals in various disciplines relating to children's developmental problems— occupational and physical therapists and speech pathologists as well as developmental psychologists and pediatricians—we have found that both babies developing normally as well as those with challenges show a great variety in physiological traits such as sensitivity to sound or touch or ability to plan or sequence movements.[9] Can an infant easily get his hand to his mouth when he wants to suck? When he is older, can he copy shapes such as triangles and diamonds? Does he pull away from even a gentle touch, hold his ears when the vacuum cleaner is turned on, or shut his eyes when Mom switches on the lights? These patterns of reaction may differ from one sense to another; some children overreact to touch but underreact to sound. Others crave strong sensations.

Children also differ in how they comprehend their world. One might have a tin ear that confuses sounds but an architect's eye for figuring out how things relate to each other spatially. Another could be just the opposite, an acute and perceptive listener who tends to find spatial relationships bewildering. Some children have low muscle tone, so that even holding up their heads or turning to look in one or another direction requires extraordinary energy, whereas others may poke Dad in the nose when they intend only to touch him gently.

These physiological patterns appear to be influenced by heredity as well as by factors in the prenatal environment, such as when a mother uses drugs while pregnant. Though they may contribute to temperament or personality or to tendencies toward illness, they are intermediary influences that can become expressed in different ways. Some children with a genetic tendency toward depression, we have observed, are more reactive to touch and sound, for instance, but these patterns of reactivity are often exhibited by children without any such a tendency as well. Children at risk for autism often seem self-absorbed and underreactive to sensation, but the same traits can be seen in many healthy children.

It is easy to confound underlying physical characteristics with temperament or personality. A number of different research and professional groups have been working to understand these foundations of behavior. Personality research stemming from the work of Chess and Thomas has assumed young children do have general tendencies, such as toward cautiousness or boldness, and that parents should adjust their care to these patterns. In this view, these patterns will more or less persist but can be kept from becoming problems.

Those working with children with developmental difficulties, including occupational and physical therapists and speech pathologists, have focused on developing specific physical capacities: for example, building muscle tone or fostering the ability to plan motor actions, process sounds and words, or react to various sensations. These capacities, though they overlap with a child's temperamental tendencies, go beyond what is normally meant by temperament. The fields of neonatal assessment, neuropsychology, and neurology also look at these physical capacities and their role in registering, comprehending, storing, recalling, and using sensations for solving problems.[10]

All these disciplines seek to understand the foundations of how we think, feel, and learn as well as how personality and behavioral patterns are formed. In work with infants, children, and families, I have aimed to build on this interdisciplinary tradition by examining the different ways auditory and visual information is registered and processed and behavior planned in the first stages of life.[11] Normal children—not just those with difficulties or delays—vary considerably in how they react to sensations and plan behavior. Furthermore, infants who at birth are very competent in their physiological ability to process sensations become, after just one month in chaotic environments, indistinguishable from those born with motor problems or too much or too little reactivity to sights and sounds. One of our most interesting observations is that children with certain physical traits often need not be limited by them. How caregivers respond to children's physical differences may have greater impact than previously thought. Oversensitive children, for example, can become outgoing and confident with the proper encouragement from parents. Children with weak auditory processing and delayed language can become verbally gifted. Parents can go beyond simply finding a "fit" with their children. They can use special methods of care to help their children change the way their nervous systems work and thus their personalities. While there are general personality tendencies that are in part determined by physiological characteristics, these can fall anywhere on a continuum from disturbance to health depending on how caregivers interact with the child.

In a continual interplay, a child's way of processing sensations and organizing motor responses helps fashion the caregiver's reactions, which in turn begin a new round of processing and response in the child. A well-coordinated, vigorous infant might try to grab a toy from her father's hand, initiating a game of tug-of-war, while the parents of a floppy, flaccid baby may give up when she scarcely touches a proffered ball or teddy bear. A child who perks up at her mother's voice may encourage her to sing and coo, unlike a child who pays little attention to sound but lots to colors and shapes. Each child thus stimulates those around her to respond in certain ways. Since the caregiver, through innumerable small actions, serves as the chief mediator between a baby's developing mind and the environment around her, the baby's own behavior therefore helps shape the world she comes to know.

At the same time, parental responses to particular kinds of behavior can vary. Some mothers and fathers tend to reach out toward their children, while others wait for the children to act. Some talk a great deal, while others use facial expressions to convey meaning.

Some are cheerful, others more serious. Some are laid back, others intrusive; some woo their children energetically, while others are more passive and easily become discouraged. These parental patterns, of course, exert their own influence on babies. A very persistent, engaging father can bring his underreactive daughter to love exchanges and seek them out. An exceedingly firm but soothing mother can help her overreactive, daredevil son become organized, disciplined, and thoughtful. In contrast, a mother who feels insecure about being loved may have trouble with a child who has low muscle tone and low reactivity to sound. Assuming that he doesn't like her and that she must not be a good mother, she may leave him alone in his crib, not realizing that a child with his characteristics needs to be enticed into a relationship before he can show love. Such a child might then become more and more self-absorbed. Another parent might overprotect a cautious and sensitive but quite reactive child, leading the child to become needy, clinging, and fearful.

The point is that while a child who is oversensitive may tend toward caution or one who is underreactive and has low muscle tone may tend toward self-absorption, the patterns established by the caregiver can alter these tendencies enormously. Self-absorbed infants can become outgoing charmers by age two and cautious infants bold leaders as toddlers. There are several steps on the way: genetic and intrauterine influences express themselves through the child's physiological patterns, such as reactivity, processing, and sequencing. Through the interactions between these physiological traits and the caregiver's behaviors there emerges personality characteristics. Also exhibited in these early interactions are tendencies toward healthy adjustment or mental illness.

The analogy of a lock and key helps us to understand the relationship between nature and nurture. A baby's characteristic strengths and weaknesses are like a lock that will open only if fitted with the right key. A number of keys will work, but an even larger number won't. To help the infant progress through the stages of development, the caregiver must find keys—that is to say, patterns of interaction and response—that will help the child use her biological gifts to master the tasks of the stage she has reached. Every child, of course, complicates the challenges of parenthood by periodically changing the tumblers in the lock each time she reaches a new developmental stage. Whether and when her parents can repeatedly find the keys that will release her potential vastly influences the child's emerging personality.

Together with that of others, my research has identified a number of personality characteristics and conditions as well as the methods that will and will not work in opening up individual children's talents and strengths.[12] This work shows that physiological traits in themselves do not necessarily limit or define a child's potential. Moreover, the more compromised a child's endowment, short of massive and incapacitating damage, the more powerful and decisive the influence of the nurturing he receives. A child who is physiologically well equipped to master a given developmental task will probably succeed at it despite mediocre nurturing, whereas one with fragile abilities may not attain mastery unless his surroundings provide exactly the help he needs. As noted in Chapter 1, with caregiving geared to their individual differences, many youngsters born with even serious weaknesses can and do achieve healthy mental development. As indicated earlier, in a recent review of over two hundred children diagnosed as autistic with whom our group has worked in recent years, most have enjoyed some improvement in their mental and emotional functioning when their parents and a therapeutic team were able to provide suitable "keys." Between 58 percent and 78 percent made substantial improvements. So few children grow up in truly optimal environments that we have no idea of what the parameters of development really are.

In clinical practice and research over the last five years, we have pinpointed styles of caregiving that can support or counteract particular physiological patterns. We have tried to go beyond general concepts such as nurturing or flexibility in order to describe in some detail the elements that each physiological type requires. Approaches to problems such as antisocial behavior, depression, anxiety, thought disorders, and attention deficit disorder illustrate this new specificity. The same combination of biological traits can embody such valuable gifts as empathy, courage, leadership, curiosity, creativity, determination, self-discipline, self-confidence, perseverance, and originality; alternatively, they can serve as the basis for the development of self-indulgence, recklessness, cruelty, hostility, rigidity, detachment, irrationality, and fearfulness. Whether these features become talents or problems depends, in short, on how the child's nature is nurtured.

In both *The Challenging Child* and *Infancy and Early Childhood*, I discussed five patterns of reactivity, processing, and sequencing and the ways they can be exacerbated or turned into strengths by different styles of interaction between caregiver and child.[13] Here I will offer just a few examples of how these patterns and the nurturing they encounter affect the development of the mind.

Of growing concern to society are violent *antisocial children*, adolescents, and adults who treat others as objects rather than as fellow human beings. Poverty, abuse, and emotional deprivation have largely taken the blame for this dangerous and troubling pattern. John Bowlby's classic paper "Forty-four Juvenile Thieves" described children neglected in early life who became highly antisocial.[14] The intuitively obvious connection between a lack of warmth bestowed on a child and his subsequent inability to feel it toward others convinced many at the time the paper was published in 1944 that environmental influences were all-important in contributing to or preventing delinquency.

Of course, the issue is more complex than that. Among children deprived of nurturing affection in the early years of life, including those in institutional care, two tendencies have been observed. One group of children became withdrawn, depressed, or apathetic. Some stopped developing physically, failed to gain weight, and even became quite ill and did not survive. Those in the other group sought out sensation, becoming aggressive, promiscuous, and indifferent to others, relating to them only to fill their own concrete needs.[15] Other researchers found a higher than expected degree of subtle difficulties in the functioning of the nervous system among antisocial children and adults, with problems in perception, information processing, and motor functioning resulting from these difficulties.[16]

Neither the deprivation model of antisocial behavior, which looks to social causes such as poverty, family breakdown, trauma, decaying morality, and lack of authority, nor the physiological model, which cites inborn differences in the functioning of the nervous system, fully explains this disturbing issue. Rather, it is the interaction of neurological deficits with environmental stresses, which in turn combine with certain types of early parent-child relationships, that increases the likelihood of antisocial behavior. For example, some children crave sensations because they are underreactive to touch and sound and insensitive to pain. If they also have relatively good physical coordination and balance as well as a propensity for movement and action, they will seek stimulation in risk taking and adventure. Whether these thrills take positive forms, such as exploring the Arctic or pioneering new surgical methods, or negative ones, such as joining a gang or taking part in an armed robbery, depends in large measure on the family and community environment the child encounters.

If the immediate environment doesn't provide firm, consistent limits, or if limits are imposed abusively, the tendency toward seeking sensation can take on an enraged quality, with indiscriminate, violent acting out. Even at a very young age, such a child may set fires, destroy property, or torture animals. Later on he may hurt and even kill others with little remorse.

These violently antisocial children need the same kind of nurturing as a more common type, the *active, aggressive child.* Both need extra warmth to woo them into the shared sense of humanity that comes more easily to other children. Ongoing relationships help the aggressive child develop empathy and a desire to use his abilities for good. Very firm limits, lovingly applied, are also crucial in teaching him to control his assertiveness. Practice in labeling feelings and pretend play help him develop a richer inner life. Parents must help him find ways to moderate his energy as well. Games in which the child must learn to change speeds while running, for example, teach modulated control. Parents can encourage safe and constructive physical activities such as very intense sports. They can also involve him in intimate communication that enables him to ponder, give names to his feelings, consider their consequences, and most important, develop compassion for others. A child with these kinds of supportive early relations has a chance of becoming a bold, imaginative leader.

Antisocial behavior appears to arise from a sequence of influences. Neither a "bad gene," or biology, nor a lack of authority or nurturing alone is the cause, though the latter may cause any child severe problems. Rather, the chief factors contributing to antisocial behavior are a specific mode of physiological reactivity coupled with a family environment that fails the child at a number of developmental levels (including those of forming caring relationships, learning to moderate behavior, learning to represent intentions and feelings, and learning to limit oneself out of regard to others) as well as social stresses such as poverty that further deprive the child of nurturing. Other influences may also be at work—trauma, family dysfunction, genetic or biochemical factors—but the combination outlined above is both the most frequent and most preventable.

The *highly sensitive child* presents another common pattern. This person comes into the world with some or all of her senses set at a higher level of responsiveness than are those of the average person. Noises that seem moderate to others blare at her; a cat's meow, say, may sound like a frightening roar. Lighting that seems pleasant to others is glaring to her; touches that soothe others startle her; a toss in the air that would delight most children disorients her. The world may seem a scary place, full of upsetting events that she cannot control and often can barely cope with. As she grows, she feels her own emotions exceptionally deeply and often has great empathy for the feelings of others as well. Psychologically she is sensitive in both connotations of the word, at once very prone to hurt feelings and very tuned in to the subtle cues of others. She has the potential to become an exceedingly aware and observant person, with the qualities needed by a writer, an art critic, a teacher, or a psychotherapist, but if her nurturing doesn't give her the opportunity to build on these strengths and instead accentuates her weaknesses, she can become a fearful, timid, avoidant child and an adult prone to anxiety, phobias, mood swings, and depression.

Some parents react to the clinginess and timidity of the oversensitive child by vacillating between overprotection and anger, which only worsens the problem. Those who react concretely rather than helping the child reflect on her feelings also have a negative effect. A sensitive child needs relationships that are soothing and nurturing and that encourage her to label her feelings in order to prevent her from becoming overwhelmed by them. As a child moves into the stage of symbols and emotional thinking she can benefit from gaining perspective on her affects and reactions. She also needs very gradual and steady support in developing her assertiveness and initiative. Limits need to be set very gently.

From observing the development of highly sensitive children, it appears that a genetic or physiological component manifests itself in the heightened reactions to sensation and affect, not in later problems that may or may not result from this proclivity. Depression, for instance, can be a result of how these sensitivities are dealt with. A person highly sensitive to sound, touch, and her own emotions and who is easily upset is particularly vulnerable to mood swings. If raised by parents who lack empathy and who fail to foster assertiveness, who shift back and forth between anger and overprotectiveness, she may well grow up anxious, unsure of herself, and prone to sadness and depression. If parents combine sensitive soothing with lots of empathy as well as support in gaining assertiveness and the ability to picture feelings, they can help someone with these tendencies grow into a mentally stable person whose sensitive reactions are the basis of her acute intuition and compassion.

In the *inner-focused or self-absorbed child,* problems in processing information, especially sounds and words, coupled with underreactivity to certain sensations can create a less firm hold on reality than others possess. Such a child may tend to get lost in imaginary worlds, maintaining idiosyncratic beliefs, for example, or being confused about whether a voice comes from inside or outside himself.

In extreme form, some of these problems have been labeled schizophrenia. For many years the delusional thinking that characterizes this illness was ascribed to irrationally skewed communication patterns within the family. Beginning more than a generation ago, research by pioneers in family dynamics such as Lyman Wynne, Don Jackson, and Ted Lidz suggested that these disordered communication patterns held the key to understanding schizophrenia.[17] The environmental approach fell out of favor, however, as studies of twins revealed genetic factors at work. But biological factors alone do not fully account for this complex illness either. Wynne has found that individuals at genetic risk for schizophrenia develop the illness only when they live in families that have certain kinds of disordered interaction patterns.[18] Other studies confirm that genetic factors are inadequate in explaining major mental illnesses and that emotional factors must also be involved.[19]

How do genetic and environmental factors interact in the development of schizophrenia? It may be that the genetic aspect expresses itself through a combination of auditory registration, processing, and motor planning problems that make communication difficult. We have observed that children with these physical differences are especially sensitive to disordered family communication patterns.[20]

The inner-focused individual is in many ways the reverse of the oversensitive person. The outside world, rather than intruding jarringly on his consciousness, seems distant and indistinct. He may hear and see normally, but he needs to have his attention "grabbed" before he can respond. Though his senses function normally, they are less acute and emotionally nuanced than most people's.

Creativity and imagination can be very rich in a person who lives in such an inner world. With nurturing that keeps him in touch with others, an individual with these tendencies who is also strong in spatial perception might become, say, an architect or designer of computer games or mathematical models, or he might develop verbal talents. But in other circumstances, this same person can become so self-absorbed that he fails to gain a sense of reality or learn social skills. He can become increasingly idiosyncratic and isolated in his own fantasies.

An adult patient I worked with, George, had the characteristics of the inner-focused child. However, the fact that he was born as the fifth and last child of a boisterous, lively, fun-loving family kept him from drifting very far into his own private world. One or another of his older siblings was constantly holding, bouncing, swinging, tickling, or tossing "the baby"; later his brothers and sisters continued to push him into activity: riding a bike, skating, skiing, joining them on roller coasters and Ferris wheels. While gentle and supportive, his parents were gregarious people who held others' attention with their animated voices and mobile, friendly faces. It took more effort to keep George actively engaged than had been required for any of their other children, but in their family there was no such thing as total self-absorption.

Now a husband and father himself, George retains to this day his reputation as the dreamer of the family. When the whole crowd gets together he is the last to be drawn into the jollity. He is content to listen when friends recount their adventures, while he enjoys his own flights of fancy in Walter Mitty fashion. In his teenage years he excelled at fantasy games in which players construct and manipulate mental worlds. Since on-line computer networks developed, they have played a significant role in his social life. At the university where he teaches he stands out as something of an absent-minded professor, but colleagues in his field recognize him as an original thinker who is able to develop in his mind and at his computer models that have solved several significant theoretical questions.

Parents of a child with this pattern of inwardness who speak to him in low voices, leave him to play on his own a great deal, or generally allow him to avoid the degree of interaction that would help him to engage with others risk letting him fail to develop either the skills or the motivation to read outside signals and test his own creations against them. A concerted effort to lure him out into the wider world, through energetic talk, exciting activity, bright surroundings, and stimulating interaction, will allow him to develop socially and intellectually and thus use his rich inner life to advantage.

Children who are exceedingly stubborn and defiant constitute another type that may share certain reactive patterns. The *strong-willed child* often feels flooded with unwanted and disconcerting sensations. Instead of becoming passive or clingy like the highly sensitive child, however, relatively good motor coordination and planning capacities allow her to try to control the world around her instead of merely retreating from it. Rather than becoming frazzled or overemotional, she attempts to impose her own sense of order on her surroundings. Parents who insist that she do things their way, or who intrude on her efforts to get things done, only encourage her defiance and need for control. Even well-meaning assistance may turn an interchange into a power struggle. In time, the habit of arguing and resisting may become so entrenched that such a child responds negatively to any overtures and comes to see others as hostile to her.

With patience and encouragement toward collaboration, strong-willed children can grow into thinkers who easily grasp the big picture, individuals with a penchant for leading and a talent for planning. Politicians, generals, litigators, founders of movements and organizations tend to come from the ranks of these determined, persistent children. But relentless power struggles from early childhood on can turn them into stubborn, narrow, bossy, argumentative adults unable to deal with authority or maintain relationships. When efforts at control fail, they have a greater than average tendency to become compulsive, avoidant, passive, and depressed. Under extreme stress, they can be dangerously suicidal.

The last set of reactive patterns I will describe in this by no means exhaustive list involves common *difficulties with attention*. Increasing numbers of children and adults are being diagnosed with attention deficit disorder (ADD), to which physiological approaches now largely hold center stage. Studies have in fact revealed anomalies in how glucose is metabolized in the brains of those with this disorder. However, a growing chorus of critics is questioning whether biochemical remedies, such as medications like Ritalin, are being overused. The controversy over whether poor schoolwork and disruptive behavior necessarily indicate ADD is endlessly aired in newspapers, on talk shows, and at PTA meetings.

While clearly there are neurological elements at work in ADD, the experience of the individual child strongly influences whether or not a physiological predisposition develops into a severe problem that interferes with attaining important goals such as getting an education or pursuing a career. Given appropriate nurturing, many affected children may not require medication.

In our work with children diagnosed with attention deficit disorder, we have observed that many such children are in fact surprisingly able to attend to challenging tasks for long periods of time: for instance, they may hold extended conversations or work hard on a jigsaw puzzle or sing a number of songs by heart. For many the problem is not a weakness in general attention but difficulty in some important specific and often related capacity—processing or reacting to certain kinds of sensory stimuli, say, or acting on a series of instructions.[21] Sometimes a child can't sequence her movements. The very act of putting on her shoes distracts her from the real task at hand: getting ready for school. She then becomes sidetracked into considering the possible knots she might tie.

Difficulties with attention arise from any of a large number of different characteristics, each of which needs a carefully chosen type of intervention to help the child take advantage of his strengths. Besides sequencing problems, oversensitivity to sounds or sights, under-regulation of sensation, and problems with processing sounds or sights can all cause inattention. Many adults with these difficulties become anxious or depressed because of problems at work or in their marriages and don't realize why they find so many things hard to do.

People with shifting attention are often at the same time very strong in the senses and capacities in which they do not face challenges. The child who can't keep print from dancing on the page may instantly pick up the beat of a song. The child who can't make sense of a maze may zero in on the point of a story. If caregivers urge the child to focus on difficult tasks, the problem may become self-reinforcing because he has little motivation to work hard at assignments that are unpleasant or lacking in intrinsic interest—imagine having to write with your nondominant hand, for example. In contrast, working with the strengths of such a child can create motivation. A child who has trouble in school because he cannot quickly grasp what he reads may have a strong visual imagination and enjoy drawing, building things, and making pictures in his mind. With the help of an understanding teacher, he can learn the skill of visualizing what he reads. Rather than attempting to grasp concepts in abstract verbal form, he might envisage history as a time line studded with action pictures, novels as films rolling before his inner eye, physics problems as the movement of objects through space.

Such tailoring of nurturing or teaching to a child's individual strengths can also help children ordinarily considered autistic or mentally retarded. Retardation is usually thought to result from pervasive biological damage so severe that children will necessarily be rated in the bottom percentiles on all their mental abilities, motor capacities, verbal and spatial abilities, and the like. A closer look, however, reveals that these children too show a range of individual differences, with some weaker and some stronger in verbal versus spatial abilities or motor capacities and so forth. Working with these differences, playing to children's personal strengths while slowly remediating their weaknesses, has helped many do much better than ever expected.

As mentioned earlier, a number of children diagnosed with autistic disorders with whom we have worked have ultimately developed cognitive emotional and social skills in the normal or even superior range. The fact that even some have responded so well reveals a prognosis far more hopeful than ever thought possible.

FLOURISHING IN THE DESERT,
STARVING IN THE GARDEN

One of the surprising aspects of the nature-nurture debate is the fact that both sides are able to marshal compelling evidence. How can genes possibly account for 40 to 70 percent of intelligence—a figure often cited by respected authorities—while at the same time experience exercises a decisive effect? A closer look at the twin studies so favored of behavioral geneticists offers an interesting explanation for this paradox. Much research attempting to tease nature and nurture apart contrasts pairs of identical twins with fraternal ones. As everyone learned in high school biology, identical or monozygotic twins result when a single fertilized egg (*zygote*) splits to form two embryos, which then share exactly the same genetic endowment. Fraternal or dizygotic twins result when two zygotes happen to be released from the mother's ovaries, fertilized, and born at the same time. Dizygotic twins have genetic endowments no more similar than any other pairs of siblings.

The facial features, hair and eye color, and all other characteristics determined by genes are the same in identical twins. Fraternal twins, who have only some genes in common, will obviously resemble each other rather less. However, since both kinds of twins are born at the same time—and are therefore more apt to have common experiences—and live in the same family, they will share many environmentally based traits. Researchers assume that if the difference between fraternal twins in any characteristic exceeds that between identical ones, the excess indicates the degree of hereditary influence for that particular characteristic. Thus, if identical twins differ by an average of three IQ points and fraternal twins by eleven, the eight point excess represents the genetic contribution.

Identical twins, for example, always have the same eye color, fraternal twins only some of the time. Clearly, then, this trait is entirely under genetic control. But now let's suppose that one member of a set of identical twin brothers has taken clarinet lessons for two years, as has one member of a pair of fraternal twin sisters. Neither of their siblings, however, has spent any time at all learning to play this instrument. Each pair, therefore, consists of one person who has some ability on the clarinet and another who has none at all. The difference between the brothers is just the same as the difference between the sisters. It is plain that knowledge of the clarinet derives from experience.

Most traits, however, are not either-or propositions like these. Rather, height, weight, intelligence, and any number of other qualities vary on a continuum from very short to very tall, from very light to very heavy, from very dull to very bright, and so forth. Furthermore, each trait involves some aspects that are obviously genetic and some that are just as obviously not. A person from a family whose members are all tall might still be relatively short if he grew up during a period of famine. A person with neurological capacity to be bright might still test as dull if she never experienced adequate care.

The question that comparisons of twins seek to answer is how much of these variable characteristics can be ascribed statistically to which factor. For example, we might measure the height of a large number of twins. Calculating the difference in height between the members of each pair, we will probably find that the identical sets are, on average, closer in height than the fraternal ones. We then conclude, according to the methodology of behavioral genetics, that height is predominantly, though not exclusively, a genetic trait.

This procedure of comparing mono- and dizygotic twins provides the database for the study of genetic differences in intelligence and other traits such as assertiveness or shyness. On the surface it makes sense. A closer look, however, reveals significant complexities.

Recently, for instance, a gene has been identified that appears to cause obesity by upsetting the mechanism that signals to the brain how much fat an individual's body has. For argument's sake, let's define this gene as one that produces an excessive appetite. (How much this formulation oversimplifies the actual operation of this and other yet unknown genes I leave to those far more expert than myself.) Babies with the hypothetical appetite gene then, eat a great deal more than those who do not have it. To investigate its contribution to obesity, we decide to study children in Israel and Italy, whose cultures, incidentally, place great stress on the pleasure of eating foods rich in fats and refined carbohydrates. Both Israeli and Italian families would presumably welcome pairs of identical twins with big appetites, pleased to have such good eaters. By age twenty these babies might well grow into young adults much heavier than average.

Now let us expand our study to include a number of fraternal twins in which one sibling has the so-called appetite gene and the other does not. In each pair, one twin always eats heartily while the other only picks at food. By age twenty the weights of the twins diverge widely. We therefore conclude that obesity has a large genetic component, perhaps as high as 70 or 80 percent.

But now let's move our study from the shores of the Mediterranean to the mountains of central Asia, where diets are largely vegetarian and amounts are sparse. Here the available carbohydrates are mostly unprocessed and high in fiber, and whole families work long, hard days in the fields and then hike steep trails to get home. In this society, almost nobody is even mildly overweight, let alone obese, at twenty or any other age. Though identical twins in this culture might share the gene for large appetite and fraternal twins might not, in this rigorous environment, no one's appetite gene gets the chance to be expressed. The postulated genetic tendency, in other words, never gets translated into extra pounds because diet and work habits don't give it the opportunity. Mono- and dizygotic twins show relatively little difference in weight because here almost no one ends up obese. Our results demonstrate insignificant genetic influence on weight.

But how can there be huge differences in how we assess the influence of heredity versus environment when we simply change the setting? I once pressed a leading behavioral geneticist to explain such results. Doesn't genetic influence imply a relatively fixed biological pathway? No, he said; conclusions about genetic influence are relevant only for the population from which they are drawn. The field of behavioral genetics uses statistical models that do not reveal a biological mechanism, only a statistical relationship. Biological pathways must be studied in other ways.

An elegant example posed by R. C. Lewontin, Steven Rose, and Leon Kamin illustrates this point.[22] Suppose we take two handfuls of seed from a bag of seed corn and plant each in a plot of its own. We give one plot abundant fertilizer and water, but the other receives only the barest minimum needed to stay alive. After a while the corn sprouts. We continue to water and fertilize the one plot amply but keep the other on marginal rations. When our seedlings finally grow to maturity, we notice that both patches contain plants of different heights, some much taller than others, some much shorter. Since the plants in each of the two plots got the same quantity of water, fertilizer, and sunshine as all the others in that plot, can't we conclude that height is a primarily genetic trait?

Not if we compare the two plots. A single glance tells us that the stalks in the well-tended patch stand much taller *on average* than those in its dried-out, underfed neighbor. The difference between the average heights of the two plots is clearly environmental. Based on this comparison, we have to conclude that height has a large environmental component. Only when we hold environment constant, by comparing plants from the same plot, can we see the genetic effect. It is therefore completely consistent that a hypothetical appetite or obesity gene could explain 80 percent of variation in weight in a population stuffed with rich, fatty foods and refined carbohydrates, yet exert close to zero influence on people barely getting by on vegetables and high-fiber grains.

Most people assume that a characteristic said to be genetically transmitted is fixed. As we have seen, however, the manifestation of many genetic traits differs over a wide range according to environmental influences. As another example, let's suppose that we have a bag of seed corn containing some grains that have a gene for height that allows the plant to grow tall only under optimal growing conditions, while the rest have a gene for height that can express itself even in mediocre conditions. The grains look identical and are randomly distributed throughout the bag, so we can't tell how many of each kind there are in any handful.

Now we plant three apparently identical handfuls of seed in three plots: one that we keep well watered and nourished, another that we neglect, and the third that we give middling care. In the middling plot, some plants—those with the gene that needs optimal conditions to develop—are stunted, while others—those with the gene that can thrive in average circumstances—stand tall. In the worst-kept plot, no seed grows well, regardless of which gene it carries. In the best-kept plot, all the stalks of both strains are tall because excellent conditions let every seed grow well.

Clearly, then, even when a characteristic has a genetic component, environment may not only modify but actually determine the

outcome. Geneticists have isolated traits whose differential development dramatizes even more sharply the sometimes decisive effect of
environment. Phenylketonuria, for instance, a disease caused by a
single genetic defect in protein metabolism, can result in severe mental retardation under certain circumstances. The fate of a child born
with this defective gene, however, depends entirely on her diet. Given
foods she can't metabolize, her nervous system suffers damage that
leads to retardation. But fed only what her body can handle, both
nervous system and intelligence develop normally.

Behavioral geneticists thus warn against the common fallacy of
confusing genetic influence with immutability. The fact that a trait
has a genetic component doesn't mean that the environment has no
part to play. While we do not know of an environmental influence that
would alter eye color, for example, many other traits, especially those
relating to our mental capacities and behavior, fall somewhere in
between, subject to a subtle interaction of genes and environment,
whether biochemical or interpersonal.

As a general rule, behavioral geneticists observe, a uniform environment magnifies the apparent influence of heredity. Imagine, for
example, a bag of seed corn containing grains with a wide variety of
genetic endowments for height. If we plant a handful of these seeds in
a plot that is evenly watered and nourished, then a great deal of the
variation among the plants must owe to genetic differences. But if we
vary the environment within the plot—say, if we plant a handful of
corn and then give some parts of the plot excellent nurture and treat
others with varying degrees of neglect—the apparent genetic influence is reduced and the apparent environmental influence increased.
When environment modifies genetic influence to an extreme degree,
its apparent effect increases.

Another methodological flaw of twin studies is the unprovable
assumption that the similarities between identical twins reflect their
genetic endowment but the differences between fraternal ones reflect
environment. This assumption disregards the possibility that identical
twins attain similar IQ scores not because they share genes but because they grow up in far more similar environments than do any
other sets of siblings, including fraternal twins. Why would identical
twins experience parenting patterns that are more similar than would

fraternal ones? Because they themselves call forth similar responses from those around them. It's not hard to imagine, in light of what we know about how babies influence their caregivers, that a pair of infants who are alike in every inborn aspect would encourage a very similar style of nurturing. Two very responsive children or two very withdrawn ones, two very active children or two very passive ones, might well inspire in their parents—and even in adoptive parents raising them in separate households—quite similar amounts of cuddling, cooing, and roughhousing or of disappointment and mild rejection. This is true especially if the caregivers are reasonably responsive and not extreme in their behavior. In contrast, fraternal twins, with their different physiological and temperamental characteristics, would call forth different adult reactions. The similarity of IQ in identical twins might therefore in part reflect their more similar experiences.

We have observed that parents tend to react similarly to certain temperamental features—for example, delighting in the charming, outgoing baby and giving more space to the self-absorbed one. Though the trigger for the adult's reactions might lie in the baby's physiological responses and thus, ultimately, in his genes, the results, strictly speaking, would reflect environmental influences. Similar upbringing, not identical "intelligence genes," would thus account for part of the similarity in IQ scores between identical twins. If these children were reared differently from one another, they might well attain more divergent scores.

Clinical observation supports these hypothetical possibilities and reveals some of the subtle psychological mechanisms underlying the nature-nurture relationship. A pair of outgoing and eager identical twins may engage well-educated, enthusiastic, devoted parents in an active, responsive, energetic relationship that accentuates the babies highly social tendencies and develops in them skills of language, judgment, and reasoning. Another monozygotic pair living with intelligent, conscientious parents may appear aloof, even apathetic. After months of animated, even frantic, smiles, coos, and gestures, the parents must reconcile themselves to a more distant, less intense relationship with their twins than they wished. In both these families, genetic and environmental factors respond to and reinforce each other.

Whereas one fraternal twin, by contrast, might be jolly, alert, and sociable, a plump little magnet for his parent's tickling, giggling, and burbling, the other, shy and sober, may inspire less warmth and stimulation. The parents respond to each child according to her nature: one constantly gets encouragement to interact, while the other is left alone. Can these twins accurately be said to live in the same environment? Can the divergent personalities they will eventually display accurately be called the result of genetics alone?

While exploring this point, it is important also to be mindful that many monozygotic (identical) twins do not share early temperamental and/or other sensory processing, modulation, motor tone, or planning characteristics. This is most likely due to different experience in the uterus, during the birth process, or in the first days after birth. As a group, however, monozygotic twins are more likely to share important physical and temperamental characteristics than are dizygotic (fraternal) twins and, therefore, are likely to set in motion more similar environmental responses, and interactions patterns.

A number of years ago I helped to conduct a study exploring the effects of parental perceptions on identical and nonidentical twins.[23] Often parents project their own feelings onto their children—for example, seeing one twin as weak and the other as strong. Two factors contribute to such projections: a parent's own personality and conflicts, and the twins' physiological reactions, which serve as a stimulus to the parent's perceptions. Once parents perceive each twin in a fixed way, they tend to create interactions that support their projection (e.g., overprotecting the "weak" twin).

From intuition or experience, or because of outside help, some parents don't simply go along with their initial reactions. They may begin to notice that one twin is underreactive to sound and touch and has a hard time sequencing body movements. Since ordinary signs of affection seem barely to reach her, they may try talking to her in lively, jolly tones and to jiggle, bounce, toss, and tickle her. With this sort of active, involving treatment, the baby may be gradually drawn into the color and excitement of the outside world. She begins to associate interactions with stimulation and warmth. The parents can then draw her out of her emotional shell and into low-key but gratifying relationships.

Is this just vague theorizing? Are low muscle tone and under-reactivity simply symptoms of a fixed low IQ? I think not. I have seen parents and therapists bring children with very low muscle tone and a pattern of self-absorption not only to intellectual and social competency, but to the realization of outstanding gifts. If large numbers of children who showed such severe physiological symptoms that they were diagnosed as autistic or retarded could be brought into interaction patterns that allowed them enormous growth, what of lesser challenges?

At the crux of the nature-nurture issue, then, as we saw earlier, is whether we can find environmental keys that will fit the genetic lock. As a child grows and matures, experience constantly interacts with endowment to refine his mental and physical capacities. "Environment" isn't a broad abstraction. Rather, from a child's viewpoint it consists of countless seemingly inconsequential experiences with the adults who mediate between him and the larger world. Must he endure repeated episodes that he (unlike most other people) finds unpleasant? Does he constantly encounter stimuli that distract him (but probably wouldn't distract another child)? Do people approach him in a manner too restrained for him (but not for most other people) to notice? Or do those around him interact with him in ways that help him master each of the developmental tasks leading to a flexible and healthy personality?

Our model makes it difficult—and indeed, needless—to state what proportion of a person's characteristics arises from nature or from nurture.[24] The important point is that nature and nurture interact in specific qualitative ways. As we learn more about these interactions, we are beginning to understand how to forge the keys that will open even difficult biological locks.

The goal for research in behavioral genetics is to move beyond statistical correlations and explore more fully the patterns that research on infant-caregiver interactions has begun to reveal. In addition, more attention should be given to studying the connections between inheritance and environment in settings across the entire spectrum of possibilities, including the most brutal and deprived conditions and the most enriched and nurturing. Sometimes the connections will prove very subtle; the most "favorable" environment for a given trait may not be completely obvious. Genes can be responsible for a characteristic that causes an organism to flourish in a desert and wither in a lush tropical garden. To date, few genetic studies that take into account extreme environmental variations have been done. Often they have taken place in the middling sorts of environments that, as we have seen, make genetic factors loom especially large. This lack of knowledge about what happens at the extremes represents far more than a mere methodological oversight. At issue are the implications for society of the conventional wisdom about the origin of complex traits like intelligence.

The belief that inherited traits impose fixed constraints on development is a formidable barrier to many promising attempts to alter destructive environments. Experience with children who suffer from conditions thought to be physiologically determined, such as autism, makes me skeptical of such assumptions. Many such youngsters can, in an individually tailored environment, grow up bright, creative, and compassionate and do well in school, sports, and hobbies. If a tailored early environment can help such children, the dangers of neglecting its influence on the growth of the mind cannot be overemphasized.

PART TWO

The Endangered Mind

CHAPTER SEVEN

The Danger and the Promise

THE FIRST PART OF THIS BOOK OUTLINED THE PROCESSES THAT lead from the "blooming, buzzing confusion" of the newborn, as William James described it, to the flexible, adaptive mentality of the mature adult. In this part we expand our scope to see what light the developmental perspective sheds on some of the problems facing individuals, groups, and communities today. This understanding of the origins of intelligence and morality offers both insight into dangerous trends and promising new approaches to education, psychotherapy, conflict resolution, and prevention of violence.

LEVELS OF IMPERFECTION

The developmental lens does not bring into focus any easy solutions. The very ability to feel and react, without which we could not attain the capacity for nuanced responses and self-reflection that is the glory of human sensibility, places the ideal of mental development at the highest level forever beyond the grasp of any human being. To be emotional is to be feeling, imaginative, open to the possibilities of learning, experience, even wisdom. It is also to be stubborn, irrational, volatile; to be, in other words, inherently imperfect.

Because the formative emotional experiences through which our minds develop vary so much from person to person, individuals differ considerably in the levels of the mind they master and maintain. Some have difficulty with forming relationships and modulating feelings and behavior. Some master only the mind's early levels. They interact and communicate predominantly through behavior (hitting when angry, grabbing when lusty, stealing when greedy). Others progress to using symbols, including ideas and words, to communicate their wishes, feelings, or intentions but still tend to function in polarized, rigid ways. Others who progress further are capable of reflecting on feelings, dealing with gray-area ambiguities, collaborating and negotiating with their own and other's wishes, and formulating values and ideals. Also, as we saw earlier, the depth and breadth of each individual's mental development varies. The inner world of some people encompasses many of the emotional themes of life—closeness, dependency, sexual pleasure, assertiveness, anger, passion, empathy, jealousy, competition. Others experience only a shallow, repetitive drama.

None of us operates at or even near the highest levels of the mind's potential in all circumstances and in every emotional area. Some of us may be capable of reflecting on our own or others' fear or anger or jealousy, but not to neediness or dependency. For others, exactly the reverse may be true. The question thus becomes not what human beings may ideally attain, but what each of us has in fact managed to create out of the emotional experiences that make up our lives.

The mind of every human being thus stands at some particular level of imperfection, as is attested by each individual's personal experience as well as the recorded history of all human societies. Violence and mayhem follow the migrations of our species over this planet. No one even passingly acquainted with the kinds of stories that are covered daily on the news believes unbridled emotionality rare among adults. It is also obvious that these too-common cases of crime and bloodshed almost always involve individuals who, far from being guided by rationality, acted rather than reflected on their feelings. But apart from such extreme instances, all human beings are to some extent in the sway of their emotions.

When religion shaped Western thought, people generally phrased this insight in the vocabulary of sin and evil. Whether we consult a theologian or a psychotherapist, however, a single conclusion seems inevitable: a substantial proportion of individuals do not exercise the ability to reflect on their emotions and instead act them out viscerally. Even those who do have this capacity often fail to use it when in the grip of intense feeling or severe stress.

One barrier to our recognition of this human limitation is the fact that most of us presume that other minds mirror our own. Grown-ups, for example, either habitually or in moments of irritation ascribe quite sophisticated motives to young children who are incapable of such subtlety. "My son always tries to manipulate me," a parent might say, or "He's causing this problem on purpose." In reality, though, only very rarely does a preschooler or even a school-age child have the detachment necessary to engineer his parents' behavior or even, indeed, to perceive them as possessing consciousness distinct from his own. Most probably, what the adult sees as connivance is only the youngster's reacting in the far simpler terms of his own self-centered understanding.

I noted earlier the phenomenon of projection, in which one person ascribes his own feelings to another. An even more powerful though less recognized tendency, I believe, is the projection not simply of emotions or attitudes but of one's own mental structure and level of awareness onto other people. A person able to reflect in at least some emotional areas may assume that everyone else can do the same. This phenomenon is especially apparent in literary characters whose capacities for self-reflection are more similar to the author's than to that of a typical person in the situation in question. Hamlet's soliloquy about the value of existence surely reflects Shakespeare's own matchless ability to translate feelings into words. In the voice of Huck Finn we hear Mark Twain's moral reasoning about the fate of Jim. Outside of literature we might expect a boy like Huck to act at the decisive moment for reasons he does not understand and a despondent man to sink wordlessly into a morass of despair.

Many adults probably cannot reflect on their feelings to a significant degree, and many who can do so only in certain areas. No human being, as I have said, is equally reflective across the entire range of experience. No one possesses the ability to step back and examine with uniform subtlety and flexibility feelings of love, loss, lust, aggression, fear, anger, dependency, intimacy, and the rest. The ideal of the perfectly reflective human is about as illusory as the ideal of the perfectly fit or healthy one—the person whose weight, blood pressure, cholesterol level, blood count, eyesight, and the rest—match the medical textbook model of the human body. Each of us has some physical flaws and weaknesses. Ideals of good health, or perfect weight and lipid levels, of good vision and a vigorous heart remain, however, goals that we can all keep in mind as we live our daily lives.

Where exactly do we stand on the ladder of the developmental stage? Clinical experience suggests that most of us operate in a less than optimal way. I would estimate that only a minority of adults, probably no more than 20 to 30 percent, function at the higher levels discussed in Chapter 5 some or most of the time. The rest range from those who can label feelings but can't easily see connections among them through those who react to life with polarized affects to those who live mostly in a world of behavioral discharge in which feelings are coterminous with actions or physical states. Finally, there are those who live at a level in which thinking, behavior, or both are quite disorganized.

People who have attained fairly high levels of functioning of course do not take advantage of them at all times or in all areas of life. Who has not found herself locked in some apparently insoluble dispute because both sides dug in behind polarized, black-on-white positions? Who has not responded to fear with the certainty that calamity had to follow? Achieving the ability to think reflectively in a certain area of life is no guarantee that one will do so consistently in the future. The measure of a person's mental functioning is how she responds to a wide range of challenges and how stable her responses remain in stress or crisis. Is she able to maintain reflectiveness when she is hurt, scared, insulted, disappointed, rejected, worried, exhausted, or rushed? Or does she slip back into rigid forms of responding, polarized thinking, or concrete action modes? In other words, does she consider alternatives and weigh values, possibilities, and points of view, or does she lash out, dissolve in tears, blame others, and mouth stereotypes? We also need to ask in which emotional areas individuals react in a reflective and integrated manner and in which in a more polarized or disorganized manner. Does anger, assertiveness, or intimacy bring out the best or the worst in a person?

The answers to these questions identify the level of a person's mental abilities. As we shall see, the same goes for groups of individuals, whether couples, families, companies, organizations, communities, and even whole societies.

A PERILOUS EXPERIMENT

From the story of Adam and Eve through the legend of Faust to the modern parables *Doctor Strangelove* and *Jurassic Park*, the theme of the loss of crucial values in humanity's attempt to gain knowledge and power has haunted Western thought. Whether in resigning themselves to banishment from the Garden of Eden, selling their souls to the devil, setting in motion the Doomsday Machine, or combating revived prehistoric monsters, human beings have felt compelled to choose between following the lead of intellect and upholding their central values and beliefs.

The ancient conflict has an ironic new twist, for we may now be in danger of losing both intellect and these precious human values at the same time, and through the same process. As shown in Part One, the dilemma we face is not a trade-off between soul and intellect, emotions and reason. Instead, modern social institutions and much of the technology that supports them have come to threaten the conditions that nurture intelligence, compassion, morality, and creativity.

The intellectual and emotional features of the human mind both arise from a single source, namely, complex emotional interaction. By fostering rapidly increasing impersonality in every aspect of life, however, the structure of modern society undermines the foundations of the mind. Advanced societies thus risk destroying the basis of their own achievements. If certain trends continue, society stands to lose not only its soul but also the prize for which Faust traded his own soul, the ability to acquire and use knowledge.

There is, of course, a centuries-old mistrust of social and technological change. The Dr. Frankenstein image of intellect run amok, of ingenuity become peril, still shapes many people's vision of science and technology. Nuclear and biological weapons, computer technology, the human genome project—all have raised the specter of knowledge turned suicidal, of intellect actively attacking the integrity, even the continuity, of life. But the danger that we have been discussing strikes at a more fundamental level. Beyond threatening humanity's physical survival, the impersonality of our lives produced by social and technological changes menaces the very abilities that have made progress possible, abilities that arise from the earliest intimate interactions between children and the adults who care most deeply for them. The qualities most closely identified with our humanity—reason, compassion, love, intuition, intelligence, creativity, courage, morality, spirituality—develop from the interplay between the individual nervous system and the emotional experience of daily interactions. These common origins must be recognized before we can grasp the particular gravity of the threat of our society now faces.

Over two hundred years ago Thomas Jefferson argued against the fledgling American nation's beginning the process of industrialization, believing that it would weaken the life of communities. Pointing out the dangers of industrialization, he highlighted not its economic consequences but its social and personal consequences, according to Michael Sandel, author of *Democracy's Discontent*. In a remarkable way, he anticipated many of the issues we are confronting today as economic patterns influence such basic issues as the way a family raises its children.

For the great bulk of the human past, the rounds of everyday life permitted children to grow up amid a network of close interactions with adults. Whether in tribes, villages, or small country towns; whether following game, moving with their herds, farming, or pursuing trades, children and their parents lived surrounded by people who knew them, and whom they knew, intimately. More recently, even in cities, families spent their days mostly within the compass of neighborhoods one could easily traverse on foot. Not until the nineteenth century, when the railroad arrived, did the average Englishman, whose country was then the richest on earth, have much opportunity of traveling more than a few miles from the place where he was born.

Through the early modern period, then, children learned their adult roles either from their parents and other close relatives or as apprentices living in the households of their masters. Families frequently remained settled in one area for many generations, so that kin were also often neighbors. In such a world, intimate relationships were not only commonplace but unavoidable. Ordinary life thus naturally and routinely provided the conditions that the complex human nervous system needs to fulfill its potential, a close fit no doubt the result of millennia of social evolution.

Very often, of course, disease or poverty or bad luck deprived people of the intimate family interactions necessary to reach a high developmental level. Since they generally lived in communities bound by profound social consensus and organized by clear and specific behavioral rules, however, even persons functioning at concrete levels were for the most part kept out of trouble.

As the means of producing the necessities of life became increasingly efficient, substantial quantities of time and talent were liberated for other pursuits. The creative advances that were thus encouraged in turn permitted social adaptations, which promoted further economic innovations. Each of these factors—the patterns by which people relate to one another, the ways they obtain their sustenance, and the development of their creative capacities—obviously bears heavily on individual consciousness. Human life cannot develop satisfactorily if any one of these is missing, and whatever threatens the ability of these three factors to work together must therefore necessarily subvert them all.

In the social changes of recent decades, patterns have emerged that alter the relationships on which developmental patterns rest. In both our family and our work lives—realms that have become almost completely separate for most people—intimate personal interaction is declining and impersonality is increasing. First radio, then movies, then television, and finally computer games replaced ancient domestic recreations such as conversation, storytelling, reading aloud, singing, and playing musical instruments. Evenings before the set have been substituted for promenades around the square and visits on the front porch. "Interactive" computer games have supplanted parlor games, homemade dramatics, and elaborate make-believe.

The structure of our families now impedes intimate interaction. With both parents away from home at jobs, or single parents attempting to fulfill all adult roles in the household, more and more babies and children spend significant chunks of their time in group day care, which affords far less opportunity for one-to-one relationships with adults. More and more youngsters return from school not only to empty houses but to neighborhoods that, serving only as bedrooms for people who earn their living elsewhere, have little adult presence. With high divorce rates, rising rates of illegitimacy, fewer extended-family households, and parents with more than one job, children have continuous access to fewer and fewer adults. These trends also affect later opportunities for intimacy that aid mastery of the developmental stages of adulthood.

Even parents with relatively high incomes often find it difficult to provide their children with the kind of intense, intimate interaction that best supports progress in the higher developmental levels. Among those not encumbered by extreme poverty and stress, the middle classes that traditionally carry out much of society's essential work and transmit from one generation to another many of the values and coping skills that sustain communities, parents' ability to nurture their children is becoming compromised. The increasing need of both parents to work for pay away from home reduces, sometimes severely, the time they can spend with their children. Despite the trend to "out-source" work to freelance workers in their homes, the quality of the interactions between parent and child may still be thin.

Our nation has, in fact, launched willy-nilly on a vast social experiment. While the outcome is unknown, the early data are not encouraging. The modern form of mass commercial day care differs in crucial ways from both the upper-class tradition of relying on servants to perform many of the tasks of early child rearing and such alternatives as raising children in groups, as in the Israeli kibbutz. In both these cases, youngsters grow up cared for by adults who remain in their lives for a long period and have a personal investment in their fate. In the first, nannies and nursemaids were generally long-standing family retainers tied by sentiment, pride, and even personal identity to employers who accepted them both as permanent fixtures of daily life and as lifelong responsibilities. In the second, the adults charged with supervising the "children's houses" are permanent, willing members of an egalitarian, voluntary community based on shared goals and values. Furthermore, the children spend significant amounts of time each day with their parents.

By contrast, in American day-care centers and many family day-care arrangements, caregivers change frequently, are often highly stressed by their own financial and family concerns, and frequently come from cultural backgrounds quite different from those of their charges. Workers who are most successful at developing close, intimate relationships with children in their care are often promoted to management or directorial posts where they use these skills less often.

There have been numerous studies of the effects of out-of-home day care on the development of children.[1] The most comprehensive of these raises serious questions about the appropriateness of day care as it is currently practiced in most places. Some of its findings are as follows:

- "Child care at most centers in the United States is poor to mediocre, with almost half of the infants and toddlers in rooms having less than minimal quality."

- "Across all levels of maternal education and child gender and ethnicity, children's cognitive and social development are positively related to the quality of their child care experience."

- "Good-quality services cost more than mediocre quality, but not a lot more."

- "There is evidence of inadequate consumer knowledge, which creates market imperfections and reduces incentives for some centers to provide good-quality care."

The study concluded that "only one in seven centers provides a level of child care quality that promotes healthy development and learning," and that "quality of child care affects children across all levels of maternal education."[2] Another study found that care by a parent or other relative was clearly superior to the different forms of day care.[3]

A major collaborative investigation in progress, sponsored by the National Institute of Child Health and Human Development, is finding that infants spending most of their day in day-care centers preliminarily tend to have compromised attachments to their parents unless the parents have a high degree of emotional sensitivity to their children's affective cues.[4] This study suggests that out-of-home care for most of each day may be a risk factor in children's ability to master early social and emotional patterns. It should be noted that only the results of assessments of children at fifteen months of age have been reported thus far. The initial report is difficult to interpret: presence in day care alone does not produce abnormal attachments to parents, but when it is combined with any degree of parental insensitivity, it puts the child at risk. Moreover, when the quality of day care, the rate of turnover among caregivers in the day-care setting, and the extremely young age of the child are combined with even slight insensitivity to the child's emotional needs, there are negative effects on the child.

Some interpret the fact that day care alone doesn't produce negative effects on children's development as a sign that day care for infants and toddlers is not a risk factor. Perhaps an example will clarify this issue. Say children in day care are prone to getting infections if their nutrition at home is less than optimal—though if they have very good nutrition, their incidence of infection is no different from that of children who are not in day care. Would we then conclude that day care posed no risk at all? Most people, I believe, would agree that it had some risk but that certain strengths could compensate for the risk. The fact that it takes two factors to produce the difficulty should not lead us to ignore the inference that attendance in day care for most of the day appears to be a risk factor when combined with less than optimal caregiving sensitivity to the infant's cues at home.

In the United States in 1990, 23 percent of infants under age one, 33 percent of one-year-olds, 38 percent of two-year-olds, and 50 percent of three-year-olds were cared for in one or another type of day care.[5] A 1994 Carnegie Corporation study reports that over 53 percent of mothers return to work within the first year of a baby's life, and that many infants spend over thirty-five hours a week in substandard care.[6] According to Ronald Lally, this pattern represents a dramatic change since the 1950s and 1960s, when most children were cared for during their infancy by family members, and the figures continue to increase. "Never in history have so many very young children spent so much time" in the presence of others who are not members of their family.[7]

Observing practices in a number of excellent day-care centers, I found that most caregivers try to relate deeply with all their charges. But with the care of three or four infants, a ratio typical of many centers, they find that their attention must go to solving the immediate problem of the one who is crying. What often happens is that another child, perhaps endowed with a less sensitive, more placid temperament, may be lying quietly in his crib and, as the caregiver walks past, catches her eye and smiles, ready for a little playful interaction—a gestural interchange, for example. The caregiver often stops for an instant, looks over at the child on the verge of extending a hand or emitting a coo, and but then determines that he is in no need of a diaper change or a bottle and moves on to a more pressing concern in another part of the room.

The quiet baby thus misses the chance for a moment of relating that would nurture his emotional and thus mental growth. Such a lapse hardly constitutes neglect or abuse and in itself has little lasting effect. Repeated dozens or hundreds of times over the first months or years of life, however, these subtle deprivations of the needed longer sequences of emotional and gestural cuing could slow a child's progress toward the rich, nuanced emotional experience that is the foundation of our higher mental abilities.

Conscientious day-care workers, furthermore, frequently assume that children enjoy a good deal of real intimacy with their parents before and after their hours in the center. Harried by job schedules, commutes, meal preparation, and household chores, however, the most loving parents often find themselves unable to give their children the kind of close attention they would ideally wish on workday mornings and evenings, consoling themselves with a similar assumption about what happens during the child's day at the center. Through inadvertence, the child may thus lose out all around.

I do not mean to imply that institutional care completely lacks merit or offers no benefits. Group day-care settings have been shown to enhance the development of certain motor and cognitive skills. Important though they are, these skills should not be confused with the emotional experience that grows from close interactions and forms the basis of mental growth during the early years.

Also, I should emphasize again that the centers I observed were outstanding facilities whose problems are inherent in the structure of institutional care itself as it is currently organized—unlike centers that are also plagued with difficulties resulting from poor management, staffing, or training. Observations of residents in a number of highly rated nursing homes reveal the same pattern in the impersonal "institutional love" provided by workers on the front lines of personal care.

When members of today's day-care generation grow up and eventually check into nursing homes themselves, an acute critic has noted, they will know exactly what to expect.

Another manifestation of the increasingly impersonal quality that suffuses the experience of more and more American children is the abandonment of genuine interaction in the teaching methods practiced in many schools. Ostensibly emphasizing "basics" through rote learning, drilling, and standardized testing, these methods disregard individual differences. Moreover, in many classrooms there is even greater reliance on so-called interactive, computer-based instruction that does not provide true interaction but merely a mechanical response to the student's efforts.

If the child care and schooling furnished by middle-class families most able to afford them have declined in nurturing quality in recent years, the problems faced by our nation's poor in raising their children have reached crisis proportions. Our cities now harbor sizable populations who lack the material or personal resources to do a decent job of child rearing. In this age of shrinking government commitment to maintaining living standards, public policy seems unlikely to halt the deterioration. In addition, economic and social stresses pose a psychological threat, impeding reflective consciousness and inhibiting compassion. Despite good intentions, therefore, parents themselves may go into a "survival" mode of dealing with the concrete here-and-now that makes them unable to form sustaining emotional relationships with their children. If these trends continue, our society may face a truly ominous situation. As children from all social strata grow up with less personal nurturing—as the sons and daughters of both the rich and the poor become more unreflective and alienated from the lives of others—we can expect to see increasing levels of violence and extremism and less collaboration and empathy.

Even the mental health profession, long a champion of interpersonal communication and intimacy, is moving away from its traditional commitment to the therapeutic power of relationships. Medications are now able to control more and more symptoms of mental illness; at the same time, the issues of cost control through managed care have become more salient in clinical approaches. Many practitioners are as a consequence moving to psychopharmacological and behavioral methods of treatment. Thus, one of the few areas of life in which lonely, disturbed, or distressed people can experience the intimate, nurturing attention they need to move toward greater mental health is leaning toward impersonal strategies that hold cost effectiveness, not health, as paramount. Therapists, clinics, and hospitals across the country, forced to take greater account of simplistic short-term statistics, are finding it more and more difficult to justify treatment plans tailored to individual needs.

In contrast, our new knowledge about the mind's origins calls for a broader, not a narrower, conception of mental health and mental illness and more emotion-centered rather than biologically reductionist approaches to treatment. Modern medications do, of course, ease a great deal of suffering and allow many people to function far more effectively than would be possible without them. But psychopharmacology alone cannot repair the developmental deficits that underlie disorders. Individuals who need to take part in continuing therapeutic relationships in order to rework particular developmental patterns thus have fewer chances of doing so. In the long run this will probably prove far more costly to society than providing extended individual care in the first place.

In the work place, too, there is a trend toward greater impersonality. Working at computer screens, communicating through conference calls or other electronic devices, people increasingly lack face-to-face interaction at their jobs. The opportunity for the emotional growth afforded by genuine human interchange is much reduced. The issue is not that computers, fax machines, and so forth are inherently depersonalizing. E-mail, for example, has revived the almost lost art of letter writing, but with the added feature that delivery and reply can be instantaneous. Many people who would not get out stationery, hunt up a stamp, and then wait a week or two for an answer now keep in close touch with others. Those widely separated by distance converse much more intimately than is possible on pieces of paper traveling from one city or country to another. On-line services and the Internet permit people to meet others who share their interests, regardless of location.

However, technology is increasingly being used in ways that reduce personal contacts in the interest of efficiency or cost cutting.

Automatic teller machines replace familiar faces; "voice mail" obviates the need to speak with a telephone operator or receptionist, or even the person to whom you wish to impart information. Ordering goods by phone, fax, or e-mail cuts down on trips to the store and impromptu encounters that nurture relationships with neighbors. Faxes and e-mail are even substituted for chats with the person at the next desk. Entertainment delivered by television, electronic "home theaters," and personal computers means fewer ventures out into public places crowded with others. In thousands of small ways, people's opportunities to spend time interacting individually with those who know them well are evaporating.

How far along this path have we come? How well are interactive processes that support our mental development able to function? What effects does the level of development achieved by individuals have on society? We explore these questions in the chapters that follow. We first look at the concepts that frame mental health, illness, and treatment, which help to determine our view of who we are and what we want to become. We then examine approaches to education, which sets goals for our intellect and character. Through a look at marriage, families, and the ways we deal with conflict, we can assess the stability of our most basic social unit. The problem of violence and the challenge of the inner cities, however we try to ignore them, reveal much about where society is heading. Finally, we will see that nations as well as individuals can coexist only in a world where people know each other well and understand one another's particular needs, motives, and intentions. Lack of such understanding brings needless peril. In the chapters that follow, I hope to show that the developmental perspective can offer ways to mitigate such danger—everywhere from the nursery to the summit meeting.

CHAPTER EIGHT

Mental Health:
A Developmental View

AN UNDERSTANDING OF THE ROLE OF EMOTIONS AT THE ROOT of all mental development helps us define the elusive concept of mental health. Mental health is more than the absence of symptoms of psychological distress. The developmental perspective encompasses and elucidates Freud's famous formulation: "the ability to love and to work."

It is especially important that we clarify what we mean by mental health in light of our growing ability to tinker with the functioning of the brain. Medications are now available that affect the way the brain works in increasingly subtle ways. Prozac not only alleviates depression but appears to alter personality traits, making some people less shy and cautious, for example. A group of antidepressants called MAO inhibitors can increase narcissism and grandiosity. Ritalin and Dexedrine enhance concentration, but for some they reduce flexibility, sense of humor, and creativity. With new medications being put on the market each year, refashioning personality itself becomes more and more possible. Whether such medications are reserved strictly for treating severe depression and disturbed thinking or whether they are used to produce cosmetic personality changes, however, depends on our definition of what constitutes an emotionally healthy person.

DEFINING MENTAL HEALTH

If we view a person as a collection of traits driven by biological mechanisms, we may be content simply to use neurological research to engineer better adjusted human machines. If, however, mental health is defined by a person's mastery of a series of developmental tasks—the acquisition of the capacity to reflect, to relate deeply to others, and to regard others with empathy in the face of stress or change—we will insist on the importance of intimate interpersonal experiences and emotional growth. In this view, behavioral or biochemical approaches need to be integrated into the overall process of emotional and intellectual development.

Much of what we have learned about mental health has come from observations of individuals whose patterns of thought and behavior fall outside the bounds of the ordinary. What societies make of their aberrant members varies over a vast range, however. Deviant or extreme behavior can be attributed to causes ranging from the divine to the diabolical, from the cosmic to the biochemical. For well over a century, society has alternated in its emphasis between physiological and experiential factors in assessing mental health.

There are three contending definitions of physical health. The most basic entails freedom from symptoms of disease. Another is the state of optimal well-being of a fit, energetic person blessed with a low cholesterol level, excellent heart function, and so forth. The third falls between these two, equating health with the state of the person with average energy levels, blood pressure, blood counts, and so forth. These definitions of physical health are vague enough; when applied to mental health, such standards become downright nebulous. Few experts deny that extreme symptoms are not those of a mentally healthy person—hearing voices, wild, unprovoked fluctuations in mood, inability to control destructive impulses, compulsions, and delusions. But the exact nature of other symptoms is often controversial and subject to change. Premenstrual syndrome and certain reactions to trauma, for example, have occasioned great debate.

Except for the most obvious and acute cases, then, the traditional ways of distinguishing health and illness are completely inadequate in determining mental soundness or disturbance. Most people would agree that not everyone lacking severe symptoms is truly mentally healthy. We all know someone who, though not precisely "crazy," still has significant emotional difficulties. The statistical definition of mental health as the average person's condition fares no better. Thoreau long ago remarked on the "quiet desperation" of the lives of the mass of humanity. More quantitative though less poetic, the Mid-Town Manhattan Study some years past found identifiable neuroses in 70 percent of New York City residents.

Psychodynamically oriented therapists have traditionally seen mental health as a positive state, not a default condition, viewing it as the ability to participate in life in certain optimal ways. Abraham Maslow's concept of self-actualization, Mihaly Czikszentmihalyi's notion of "flow," and Erik Erikson's idea of evolving identity all exemplify this approach. Such prescriptions, however, run a serious risk of describing a state that only a small percentage of the population may be capable of attaining. They may also put too much emphasis on outcomes or goals rather than processes.

The complexity of assessing mental health is best illustrated by examining actual lives. Consider the cases of Paul and Sylvia.

Now entering his fifties, Paul has had a successful life. Born to parents of modest means, he discovered early on his own considerable gifts for making a good impression, good friends, and good grades. In high school he capitalized on his looks and a moderate athletic ability honed by conscientious practice, establishing himself in the popular clique, whose members were mostly children from families much wealthier than his own. A combination of scholarships and part-time and summer jobs supported him while he worked toward his degree from a prestigious college, which in turn landed him a promising position with a *Fortune* 500 company. Early in his scramble up the corporate ladder he married an ambitious and attractive woman, Anne, who became his ally in maintaining an elegant home and raising three bright, handsome, capable children. In middle age he divided his time among high-level business meetings, his large suburban house, the family's beach house, stylish social gatherings with his and Anne's equally fortunate friends, and the children's many matches, tournaments, performances, and prize days.

During his forties, both his parents died after long illnesses. Though always a dutiful son, Paul had gradually lost any sense of closeness with them and his brothers over the years when first college and then his career took him far from his childhood home, both geographically and socially. The emotionally taxing work of caring for the two old people had fallen to his brothers, who still lived in their hometown. Paul did offer advice in dealing with his parents' financial affairs, but he kept in touch mainly by phone. When his brothers would suggest he join them in visiting the nursing home where their parents then lived, Paul usually found himself called away on a business trip or tied up in an important meeting. After his parents died, Anne tried to help him deal with the grief and loss she was sure he was feeling, but Paul would quickly change the subject to his latest success at work, adding that dwelling on sad things held a person back.

During this same period, Anne underwent surgery for breast cancer. Though the cancer had been detected early, the experience shook her deeply. She tried to share her feelings with her husband, but Paul would only emphasize her very positive prognosis and her good luck in not needing reconstructive surgery after the lumpectomy. They were lucky, he said, that once she recuperated from her operation and radiation treatment, everything would be "as if it had never happened."

Other than these trials, during neither of which Paul allowed himself to recognize feelings such as anguish, fear, sorrow, or loss, adulthood has presented him no serious adversity. Affable, assertive, and accomplished, Paul faces life with the cheerful, well-organized, prudent attitude that has accompanied him through so many successes. But he carries the superficiality of his approach to loss and sorrow over into his intimate relationships. Though he loves Anne, he rejoices mainly in her beauty, her skill as a hostess, and her ability to enhance his image. Though he loves his children, he takes pleasure mainly in their impressive attainments rather than in their inner selves. He has difficulty helping them deal with the lost game, the college rejection, the broken romance. They, like their father, are largely strangers to the darker emotions.

Let us turn now to Sylvia, whose life does not present the picture of equanimity coupled with emotional inaccessibility Paul's does. Twice she has faced long periods of sadness bordering on depression. Now entering the ninth decade of an eventful life, she views her world with a wry wariness born of her experience that fate is not fair.

She spent her early years smack in the middle of a large family as the fourth of seven children and the only girl. Through unremitting effort, her poor immigrant parents managed to provide a home that was scanty in material comforts but amply furnished with proud expectation, understanding, and love. She always got good grades, but the need to work full-time after high school foreclosed any chance at college.

Both her parents died before Sylvia reached twenty-five, leaving their only daughter with a strong sense of responsibility for her brothers. She shared a home with the three who were still single until her own marriage in her early thirties. Today, nearly six decades after her parents' deaths, she remains the emotional center around which her family of siblings still rotates.

A whirlwind romance during World War II bloomed into a marriage that lasted half a century and produced three children. At the end of the war, the couple moved to her husband's hometown across the continent, where Sylvia, who had never lived anywhere but in her native city, had to build a life and find friends in a region quite different from the one where she grew up. For many years her middle-class suburban life flowed smoothly, unmarred except for the usual annoyances and setbacks.

Then when Sylvia was in her sixties, she and her husband witnessed, five years apart, the deaths from long, lingering illnesses of their two happy, bright, promising, previously healthy daughters. The first of these tragedies plunged Sylvia into despair. Gradually she regained some of her emotional equilibrium, but then, suddenly, her other daughter fell ill. Again Sylvia thought her loss heavier than she could bear. Again grief threatened to consume her life. Again she struggled back from the darkness, finding the strength to go on living each day.

Through her seventies, bereft of her beloved daughters, she kept their memory alive in her heart but turned her mind not toward the past but to the present and the future. She continued to be an emotional anchor for her brothers. She rallied her husband and son. She returned to old interests like reading, traveling, and sailing and even took on new volunteer activities. She also made a quiet but concerted effort to extend herself to others who were suffering, including ailing or bereaved relatives, friends with a chronically ill adult child—anyone she happened to see in need of comfort and care. Neither maudlin nor morose, she managed to turn her own acquaintance with sorrow into a levelheaded, practical compassion, a knack for giving people the concrete help they need.

Sylvia does not deny the bitterness of her losses and the injustice of her lot. She speaks frankly and not infrequently gives way to temper. She has, however, richly experienced the peaks and valleys of her life, fought her way back from despondency, and regained her balance and her sense of proportion. She has used her life's opportunities and challenges to grow in strength, wisdom, insight, and understanding.

The stories of Paul and Sylvia illustrate the complexity of comparing human lives. In the developmental view, however, Sylvia comes closer to exemplifying the stable yet expanding sense of self, born and fashioned from intensely felt personal experience, that is the essence of mental health. From this experience she built an outlook on life that combines understanding and discerning action. Her bouts with wrenching grief ultimately led not to illness but to growth.

Sylvia's life embodies features that reflect the high level of emotional development that psychotherapy should strive to make possible for all who seek it. She has not always been free of pathological behavior. Her thinking and feelings have not always been reality-based and rational. She has suffered episodes in which her mental and emotional state was far from normal. Her mental health has not, in short, always satisfied the standards of the three common definitions. But she has achieved something that these formulations overlook and that, I believe, constitutes the core of highly differentiated mental development. She has repeatedly exercised the ability to reflect on her life experience and to forge from it a coherent, effective, nuanced, responsive, and age-appropriate consciousness.

This combination of qualities, I suggest, comes close to defining healthy mental development. A mentally healthy person thrives not only in an environment free of pain and tribulation, as Paul has, but like Sylvia, is capable of responding positively in the very teeth of potentially life-destroying trouble. A mentally healthy person not only maintains her well-being but, far more important, regains it after it has been seriously threatened.

It is uncertain how Paul would fare if life were to test him as severely as it has Sylvia. Having built his identity around the contest for prestigious prizes, he has finely honed his competitive skills but neglected to develop the powers of introspection and relating intimately to others that can carry a person through a major crisis. The life goals he has embraced are finally shallow. Losing his prominent and lucrative job, for example, could shatter a brittle identity founded on possession of wealth and power. He seems incapable of openly acknowledging any negative emotions such as sadness, loss, or disappointment. If one of his children were to suffer a serious illness, such a dominant and competitive individual might tolerate the resulting feelings of powerlessness and pain very poorly. A grief that made Paul emotionally dependent on Anne might demolish their marriage, which is built around her willingness to bolster and protect his sense of mastery. It is unclear what strengths he might call on or develop through experience with pain; what is certain is that the qualities we define as constituting mental health are thus far undeveloped in Paul.

When severely tried, Sylvia revealed her ability to experience a broad emotional range—to tolerate anger, disappointment, sorrow, loss, and discouragement, as well as compassion, pleasure, and pride—and to keep functioning well enough to recover her mental balance. Any standard of mental health that emphasizes externals like achievement, equanimity, or a stable life course misses the true foundation of emotional well-being, which is a highly differentiated inner world that allows the individual both to enjoy life fully and to confront and rebound from loss and grief.

This notion of mental health expands and enriches existing definitions. A person who is emotionally healthy by this standard meets Freud's criteria of being able both to love and to work, as well as other criteria, such as the ability to adhere to society's norms, to maintain intimate relationships in a stable family, and to reflect with insight on one's feelings and inner wishes.

MENTAL HEALTH AS PROCESS

As the lives of Paul and Sylvia show, we need a description of mental health that places less emphasis on static mechanical definitions and more on the process of developing and refining critical abilities. Such a view can be applied to a full spectrum of social and cultural circumstances. It looks for ongoing development rather than unchanging states or past accomplishments and recognizes a vast variety of endowments and experiences. From the developmental perspective, healthy growth results in a sense of personhood that is broad, flexible, and differentiated enough to allow individuals to sustain the relationships appropriate to their stages in life, to experience emotions across a wide and nuanced range, and to reflect on this experience to broaden and deepen their thinking and consciousness throughout the life span. There can be no single model of mental health. Examples include a child with lively curiosity and a growing sense of relatedness and efficacy; a youth with the confidence, sensitivity, and sense of purpose to grow beyond the affective support of parents; an adult with the self-knowledge, emotional capacity, and resilience to accomplish worthwhile goals, maintain intimate relationships, fulfill serious responsibilities, accept loss and disappointment, and nourish a rich inner life. A healthy three-year-old doesn't show the empathy expected in a twenty-three-year-old, nor does a young adult ordinarily take on the complex family and work obligations suited to the mid-forties. Each age and situation makes its own demands; building on earlier growth, each requires a new set of adaptive responses.

Healthy development also involves acquiring skills of reasoning, reality testing, and problem solving appropriate to the individual's age. But these cognitive capacities do not imply any particular level of IQ. A high scorer on the Stanford-Binet doesn't necessarily enjoy better mental health than someone with more ordinary results. What matters is not a specific level of cognitive skills but an overall capacity to reflect on and meet the demands of a given stage of life. A professor of theoretical physics may be able to apply abstract reasoning to physical phenomena but at the same time be naive in her personal relationships or political judgments. Someone who never went beyond high school, by contrast, may have a much surer grasp of politics as well as of how to deal with her boss, spring back from a dark mood, inspire trust in her friends, solve family conflicts, or relate to her children. The issue is the ability to solve, survive, and continue to grow through real-life problems.

Furthermore, mental health should not be confused with having any set of fixed emotional or social skills. Recently the notion of "emotional intelligence" has been put forward to describe, for example, the kind of perceptiveness involved in the ability to read other people's emotional cues.[1] How this capacity is used, however—whether to empathize with a distraught friend, motivate a research group, or sell someone the Brooklyn Bridge—is not taken into account. Emotional health at its foundation rests on the integration of such skills into the purposes, goals, intimate relationships, and sense of larger meaning in a person's life. A socially inept person who is loving and caring can experience both happiness and sorrow, and can preserve a sense of moral purpose through loss and crises may have more robust mental health than a socially adept but unreflective person driven to manipulate others.

Emotional health is thus the continual unfolding of various capacities, beginning with the mastery of the basic levels of mental development outlined in Part One. Mastery of these levels may occur on different timetables and with considerable variation. Human beings can differ over a vast range of talents, abilities, outlooks, temperaments, tendencies, and inclinations and still fall within the bounds of healthy development. Whether reserved or outgoing, athletic or artistic, spiritual or practical, adventurous or cautious, visionary or conservative—whatever combination of these and countless other characteristics a person possesses, he may still be following a healthy emotional course.

Constrictions or distortions of emotional growth that disable or even cripple a person's capacity to behave and relate to others in ways appropriate to his age may put his personality outside the bounds of healthy development. This definition leaves out an intellectually brilliant man with an uncontrollable temper or a deeply empathic woman imprisoned in her house by irrational fears. A teenager with the emotional reactions of a grade-schooler or a young adult with those of a senior citizen likewise shows signs of problematic development.

Emotional health is necessarily a matter of degree. In real life, no one epitomizes perfection, no one's emotional range is ideal, no one exhibits flawless insight or invincible fortitude. The same emotions that give rise to intellect and creativity result in enormous variability and at times even seemingly unhealthy reactions.

Healthy development produces individuals stronger and more flexible in some areas than in others. Some may react to sexuality along a broad spectrum—for example, a nursing mother may distinguish feelings relating to her suckling infant, her sexual partner, and her own inner fantasies. She is able to deal reflectively with the emotions surrounding her sexuality, knowing how they relate to herself and to others in her life. Yet this same woman may react much more crudely to angry feelings, seeing them as wrong, forbidden, or unwomanly, and responding by suppressing them. By contrast, another person may have difficulty dealing with sexuality, sensing all or most sexual feelings as evil or forbidden and reacting on a crude behavioral spectrum that includes nothing between complete repression and abandon. But this same individual might deal reflectively with anger, recognizing many degrees, from mild annoyance to rage, assessing whether these feelings fit various situations, and handling conflicts and confrontations sensitively, judiciously, and with self-control.

Looking at mental development as an ongoing process, we can discern the qualities of a mentally healthy individual and observe the levels of the mind from which they emerge. From the very earliest developmental level in the months just after birth arises the ability to organize attention and remain calm, along with the resulting deep sense of security. From the second level comes the capacity for warmth and intimacy with others that endures even when a person is angry, disappointed, or sad. From the third and fourth levels arises the ability to read simple and, later, complex nonverbal cues. This allows the individual to respond both to his own and other people's intentions and to size up situations for safety or danger, acceptance or rejection, and other crucial features without major distortions. The fifth developmental level provides symbolic expressions for a panoply of ideas and feelings. From the sixth comes the capacity for organizing these thoughts, feelings, and ideas logically, reflecting on them, and using them to solve problems in the real world. This skill, which also makes possible the development of morality and ethics, becomes richer, more subtle, and more expansive as a person matures and is eventually applied to additional developmental issues such as love relationships, raising a family, career choices, and responsibility toward a larger community.

Each of these developmental levels can be mastered over a long time span. The exact age at which a child utters his first word or first "Why?" or first sounded-out phrase is in itself not critical. Whether a child first asks "Why?" at four or at six, whether he writes script at eight or at ten matters far less than getting a start that will support these and future attainments. Once he grasps that by asking "Why?" he can gain new ideas through interactions with others, he has decades to puzzle and ponder. Once he divines that letters equal sounds, he has a lifetime to express thoughts and feelings through the written word. Forty years later, it makes no difference exactly when he made these connections. But it matters forever and immensely if he never develops the capacity for abundant inner experience, for emotional richness, for relating to the world beyond himself, for a sound sense of personhood. Without these far more basic abilities, that first "Why?" may never come, those first words never decoded.

When I work with children with severe emotional, physical, or cognitive difficulties, I am always delighted when I sense that they are traveling on a normative trajectory. They may be years behind age expectation, but the steps they have taken fall into a configuration that means continuing growth. For example, it is reassuring to see emotions guiding thoughts, imagination bubbling forth, relationships becoming more intimate and balanced with different feelings, and thinking growing more logical and involving more symbols.

The developmental conception of mental health has four advantages. First, it averts misunderstandings arising from placing too much emphasis on particular behavior, which may differ across cultures. Second, it explains why symptoms do not in and of themselves indicate a person's state. Third, it establishes the importance of an aspect of mental health that is often overlooked: the ability to tolerate the frightening, painful, bitter emotions of life. Finally, it highlights the inadequacy of more superficial views that merely rate social adjustment skills, achievement in various endeavors, or lack of conflict and turmoil. Instead, it makes the process of continuing growth, deepening intimate relationships, and developing more meaningful inner reflection the hallmark of mental health.

STUNTED GROWTH

In exploring definitions of mental health, we have begun to discern the outlines of the developmental approach to mental disorders. The presence of symptoms—fear of elevators, say—is not in itself enough to define illness. One person might have an elevator phobia but otherwise enjoy intimate relationships, be capable of empathy and reflection, and experience a range of age-appropriate feelings, whereas another person who is free of symptoms might have a shallow inner life and self-centered concerns. The developmental understanding affords us a broader perspective in assessing serious disorders.

Disorders arise when one or more levels of the mind do not function properly. This may happen because a level has never fully developed or because something interfered with it after it had been well established. On the one hand, problems may begin very early: a deficient neurological endowment or inadequate nurturing may stunt a child's mental growth, as when an autistic child has difficulty learning to communicate or a baby with a tendency toward emotional sensitivity reacts to her mother's withdrawal with loneliness or despair. On the other hand, difficulties may arise from experiences later in life if physical or emotional factors derail a previously well-functioning individual. A terrible traffic accident might overthrow an eight-year-old's ability to separate reality, now a grim, desolate landscape, from less painful fantasies. Physical causes of deterioration in the functioning of different mental levels include overuse of steroids and biochemical changes brought on by maturational shifts such as puberty or menopause. Drugs, injuries, even the effects of acute stress can sometimes trigger reactions that overwhelm the abilities characteristic of the various levels of mental development.

Whatever the disorder in question, we may usefully ask which levels of the mind are affected. Can the individual attend and feel secure? Can she relate and engage? Can she maintain boundaries and grasp nonverbal patterns of communication to figure out her own intentions and interpret those of others? Can she create ideas and images out of her feelings? Can she form connections between images and use them to reason emotionally and solve problems? Can she extend her ability to reason about her emotions into new realms of experience, new tasks and challenges?[2]

Many people who function well at the higher mental levels can nonetheless harbor areas of constriction that are apparent only in particular situations or when certain themes are invoked. Such a person might fear taking tests, say, or have problems with authority. But emotional constriction can be more pervasive. For example, an individual may be unaware of certain emotions because of problems at the level of forming emotional symbols. She can feel anger and act angry but not recognize her anger for what it is or be able to say "I am angry." In a very real sense, she does not know she *is* angry—she only knows that she is experiencing sensations that prompt her to yell or throw crockery. Perhaps she had a parent who was so uncomfortable with angry feelings that any suggestion of them, even mild irritation or protest, resulted in her being rejected and ignored.

Even more profound difficulties result when disruption occurs at the level of reading nonverbal gestures, which can lead to distorted expectations and a tendency to adopt fixed and rigid beliefs. "No one is trustworthy," an individual may believe, or "Everyone wants to hurt me." Such perceptions can freeze a person's attitudes and inhibit intimate relationships.

Problems may also involve the ability to remain logical and centered in reality. When disruption occurs at the level of ideas, thinking and reasoning become confused but behavior may remain fairly rational. Fantasies infiltrate the mind; thoughts and feelings float free. A more severe disturbance of reality testing occurs when a person does not function well at the deeper level of organizing intentional behavior and defining where his own boundaries begin and end. Ordinarily established in the first or early in the second year of life, this ability allows us to distinguish our own actions and behavior from those of others. Without this rudimentary awareness of the world outside the self, a person may live in a private universe unconnected with reality. For those in the grip of such a disorder, regardless of its cause, no cohesive sense of self separates the experiences of other people from those that originate within themselves. Thoughts may be perceived as voices coming from outside, or one's own perceptions or intentions may be attributed to other people. This confusion is not the same as projecting one's feelings on others, which everyone does to some degree; rather, it is a genuine inability to perceive a distinction between what originates from inside and from outside the self.

At another level of the mind are disruptions of the ability to organize and regulate sensations, perceptions, and emotions. In severe mood disorders, emotions rather than thoughts and ideas fail to cohere into comprehensible patterns. Intense storms of feeling rage across the mind, whipping up huge waves of affect that capsize and wreck thought, logic, and the sense of reality. Buoyed by elation, the individual believes anything possible; swamped by despondency, he fears he can achieve nothing. A person may believe himself a millionaire and make gifts he cannot afford, or try to kill himself in despair over some objectively trivial setback. Because emotion neither reflects reality nor responds proportionally to it, the intellect cannot function clearly either. A healthy person who happens to be optimistic measures objective possibilities of success in his endeavors against his rosy outlook; the normal pessimist does the same with his darker expectations. But in a mind suffering a serious disorder at this level, the ability to structure feelings breaks down, destroying the dike that contains ravaging emotional floods. Disturbances of thinking and severe mood disorders both disrupt mental functioning so completely that the line between self and others or the rest of the outside world blurs.

The ways people react to stress and trauma reflect disruptions at particular levels of the mind. Depending on the severity of the stress, these can vary from relatively mild disturbances to total collapse. Someone who has been mugged, for example, might form a small encapsulation, becoming anxious in situations that remind him of the event. Or he might completely avoid any possibility of reexperiencing anything remotely like the trauma, perhaps refusing to leave his house.

A person who is more severely affected might partially lose her ability to separate her own thoughts from other people's, becoming unrealistically suspicious or unnecessarily depressed. Even deeper fragmentation may occur, in which different parts of the self no longer connect to one another. Depression may alternate with elation, aggression with dependency. The structure that organized these areas of the mind seems no longer to exist. In yet more severe dysfunctions, individuals may withdraw entirely from relationships, becoming absorbed in worlds of their own.

These various reactions to trauma or stress betray which levels of the mind have become disrupted as well as the extent of the disruption, serving not only to indicate the nature of the problem but also suggesting what needs to be done to help the person regain developmental momentum. Often the most important therapeutic work with persons affected by stress or trauma is helping them rebuild from the bottom up the early experiences that originally built the mind. Patients must first reestablish the sense of safety and security through the types of nurturing relationships that formed much earlier in life. Next, they need to slowly reconstruct the ability to communicate intentions and feelings, first nonverbally and then verbally. In this gradual approach, security and relationships take the lead and ideas and communication come second, unlike therapies for stress and trauma in which individuals are encouraged to talk about upsetting matters or relive the traumatic event too soon. Thinking may remain fragmented, and the ability to relate may not yet have returned or may be present only in very immature forms. Building from the bottom up allows a traumatized individual to regroup and then eventually to take on the challenge of reordering the disrupted level of the mind. We will see examples of this in the next chapter.

The chart on pages 192–94 outlines the developmental approach to mental health and illness.[3] For each fundamental capacity there is a range of possible development, from very adaptive and healthy to maladaptive and disordered. Progress occurs from both level to level—from self-regulation to emotional thinking—and toward greater complexity and breadth within each level.

MENTAL HEALTH, MENTAL ILLNESS, AND RESPONSIBILITY

In some well-publicized trials, defendants accused of violent crimes have been acquitted, deemed "not guilty by reason of insanity." In such cases, critics have claimed that a diagnosis of mental illness is used to excuse people from moral responsibility. This argument has turned many with strong moral commitments against much psychiatric and psychological thinking.

SELF-REGULATION

Attention is fleeting (a few seconds here and there) and/or very active or agitated *or* Mostly self-absorbed and lethargic or passive	Can attend and be calm for short periods (i.e., 30 to 60 seconds) when very interested or motivated	Focused, organized, and calm except when over-stimulated (e.g., in a noisy, active setting) or understimulated (in a very dull set-ting), challenged to use a vulnerable skill (e.g., a child with weak fine motor skills is asked to write rap-idly), ill, anxious, or under stress	Focused, organized, and calm most of the time, even under stress

ENGAGEMENT

Aloof, withdrawn, or indifferent to others	Superficial and need-oriented, lacking intimacy	Intimacy and car-ing are present but can be disrupted by strong emotions such as anger or anxiety at separa-tion (e.g., the per-son withdraws or acts out)	Deep, emotionally rich capacity for intimacy, caring, and empathy, even when under stress or feelings are strong

Attempts to relax ordinary standards for those from abusive, impoverished, or neglectful backgrounds—such as the youths from the "depraved on account of we're deprived" school satirized in *West Side Story*—are seen by many to rob individuals of their human dig-nity and society of the ability to ensure safety and tranquillity. The opposite view holds that disregarding the effects of abuse, poverty, and neglect on an individual's development and life chances subjects already disadvantaged individuals to further abuse when society could provide needed support.

INTENTIONALITY

Mostly aimless, fragmented, unpurposeful behavior and emotional expressions (e.g., no smiles or reaching out with body posture for warmth or closeness)	Some need-oriented, purposeful islands of behavior and emotional expressions; no larger cohesive social goals	Often purposeful and organized, but without a full range of emotional expressions (e.g., seeks out others for closeness and warmth with glances, body posture, and the like, but becomes chaotic, frag-mented, or aimless when very angry)	Behaves in a purposeful and organized way and able to express a wide range of subtle emotions most of the time, even when there are strong feelings and stress

THE PREVERBAL SENSE OF SELF:
Comprehending Intentions and Expectations

Distorts the intentions of others (i.e., misreads cues and therefore feels suspicious, mistreated, unloved, angry, etc.)	Can read basic intentions of others (such as acceptance or rejection) in selected relationships but unable to read subtle cues (such as respect, pride, or annoyance)	Often accurately reads and responds to a range of emotional signals except in circumstances involving difficult or very strong emotions or stress, or due to problems with processing sensations such as sights or sounds (i.e., certain signals are confusing)	Reads and responds to most emotional signals flexibly and accurately even when under stress (e.g., comprehends safety vs. danger, approval vs. disapproval, acceptance vs. rejection, respect vs. humiliation, levels of anger, etc.)

The developmental model suggests that both sides are right and both wrong. Optimal mental development—what we have called mental health—requires a feeling of connectedness with humanity, a well-developed sense of empathy, the ability to express and evaluate abstract concepts (including values such as justice, fairness, etc.), the individual's sense of her place in relation to the larger community, an

CREATING AND ELABORATING EMOTIONAL IDEAS

Puts wishes and feelings into action, but unable to use ideas to elaborate wishes and feeling (e.g., hits when mad, hugs or demands physical intimacy when needy rather than experiencing idea of anger or expressing wish for closeness)	Uses ideas in a concrete way to convey desire for action or get basic needs met, but does not elaborate idea of feeling in its own right (e.g., wants to hit when mad but may not because someone is watching rather than feeling anger as though wanting to hit)	Often uses ideas imaginatively and creatively and to express a range of emotions, except when experiencing problematic emotions or when under stress (e.g., cannot bring anger or despondency into verbal discussion or pretend play)	Uses ideas to express a full range of emotions; is imaginative and creative most of the time, even under stress

EMOTIONAL THINKING

Ideas are experienced in a piecemeal or fragmented manner (e.g., one phrase is followed by another with no logical bridges)	Thinking is polarized, ideas are stated in an all-or-nothing manner (e.g., things are all good or all bad; there are no shades of gray)	Thinking is constricted (i.e., tends to focus mostly on certain themes like anger and competition); it is often logical, but strong emotions, problematic emotions, or stress can lead to polarized or fragmented thinking	Thinking is logical, abstract, and flexible across the full range of age-appropriate emotions and interactions; it is also relatively reflective for age level and in regard to endeavors (e.g., peer, spouse, or family relationships) and supports movement into the next stages in the course of life

understanding of consequences, a capacity to weigh alternative values and to place her own wishes in the context of others' wishes and needs, and an ability to recognize legitimate authority and limits. The capabilities necessary for reasoned, considerate, moral thinking and behavior are part of mental health. To develop these capabilities, a child needs the kind of nurturing that permits a warm, intimate relationship with at least one flexible, responsible, engaged, wholly committed adult.

The morally responsible person whom conservatives admire can only grow out of the affectionate and secure family that liberals demand. The two basic features of families that work—empathic, sensitive nurturing combined with clear, firm limits—can flourish in an array of social, cultural, religious, and economic settings. But no child can become a morally responsible adult without experiencing both. Limit setting without nurturing breeds fear and an amoral desire to beat the system. Nurturing without limits breeds self-absorption and irresponsibility.

Holding people to account for their actions while raising children capable of accountability is the central task both of parents and of society. In communities and families that provide every child the opportunity to grow up in a good home with plenty of loving emotional interaction as well as well-defined limits, we can hold every person responsible for using his or her powers at the highest developmental level of which he or she is capable.

In thinking about moral and legal responsibility, we would do well to separate more clearly the procedures for determining whether an individual has committed a crime from those deciding punishment or rehabilitation. The latter judgment would then weigh such circumstances as the person's mental abilities and state of mind. Both determinations might be made by a jury of peers, but this jury, or a judge, would require sentencing options—including appropriate treatment—that acknowledge the developmental levels of the mind and allow for possible remediation in cases in which growth has been blocked. Only through such considerations can we integrate responsibility with compassion and caring.

CHAPTER NINE

Pep Pills, Pep Talks, and Real Therapeutic Experiences

PERSONAL EMOTIONAL GROWTH, SO SOUGHT AFTER, IS nonetheless often thwarted by a paradoxical fact: the therapy chosen can be a symptom of the problem rather than its solution. For instance, many troubled people have escaped from problems with dependency and closeness through dependence on a charismatic therapist or weekend group leader. From this relationship they derive a grandiose sense of omnipotence while ignoring the true nature of the problem. Psychotherapy can often be an unrecognized way of maintaining one's current mental level rather than a real opportunity for progress. Arrested at one of the stages of emotional growth, people are most resourceful at finding ways of remaining stuck at that stage.

Further complicating attempts at emotional growth is the fact that there are so many different kinds of problems that lead people to seek help. The following examples give a sense of the diverse issues people face.

- Tom, though bright, capable, and generally personable, has had repeated run-ins with his supervisors at work. Try as he might, he can't keep minor disagreements from escalating into major confrontations that as often as not have cost him his job.

- Melissa repeatedly fails at romance. She is vastly successful in her career and admired for her community work, adored as an aunt and cherished as a friend. But though she is eager to marry and have a family of her own, she regularly torpedoes promising love affairs just as they show the slightest sign of becoming serious.

- Mark lives with the pervasive sense that he's missing out on something important. He can't say what it is, however, and doesn't know how to go about finding it. Like a child on Christmas morning sitting grumpily amid a mountain of discarded wrapping paper, he only knows that he never experiences the happiness and satisfaction he hopes for, that the dreary succession of days he lives through cannot possibly be all there is.

- Derek likes to think of himself as a man of action, a he-man with a touchy sense of honor who forcefully safeguards his interests and asks questions later, if at all. He has no patience with high-flown talk and prides himself on his decisiveness and the respect, even fear, he inspires in everyone around him. Family, associates, and his few friends, however, regard Derek as a bully with a short fuse, a violent man with a history of blowing up at the slightest affront. Among those concurring in this appraisal are officers at several local police departments.

- Henry careens between elation and despair, exalted optimism and abject gloom. He has repeatedly concocted imaginative but improbable business schemes, financed them by borrowing heavily against expert advice, and then worked around-the-clock to launch his extravagant plans. When each scheme fails, as all invariably do, his previously prodigious energy suddenly deserts him. He then struggles just to get out of bed, unable even to go to a routine and undemanding job that would help him pay off his massive debts.

- Lisa lives in dread of the evil forces that surround her. Demons are constantly plotting to lure her into joining them in satanic acts. She is acutely aware of the threat they pose both to herself and to humanity because she overhears their secret messages to one another on a receiver implanted in her dental bridgework. Much of her time goes into writing urgent letters to government officials, warning them of the impending dangers detailed in these transmissions. To her dismay, however, she hardly ever gets any response.

THE SEARCH FOR HELP

To varying degrees, each of these six people counts among the millions whose problems probably warrant their seeking professional help. But what exactly constitutes appropriate mental health treatment? Which methods work best to promote true growth? What sort of "help" really helps? Because of such confusion, some of the counseling people get not only doesn't help them but can actually do them harm.

Every year millions of Americans undergo treatment by mental health professionals, and countless more would benefit from the opportunity. But even so, many would-be clients are at a loss in knowing just which services they need and which experts have the skills best suited to helping them solve their particular problems or simply increase their life satisfaction and happiness. For the average person, the world of psychological therapy is a baffling maze, with its practitioners bearing dozens of titles and credentials and advocating even more theories and techniques, all shrouded in obscure terminology.

Confusion first arises as the prospective client considers the several apparently competing professions, including psychiatrists, psychologists, clinical social workers, psychotherapists, and counselors, that offer a perplexing array of apparently similar services. Next he encounters a crazy quilt of approaches that cut across these professional divisions. Many members of the same profession differ from one another in their treatment approaches, while some members of divergent professions agree with one another. Assorted spiritual, emotional, and philosophical systems, each propounded by its own charismatic guru or guide, also claim to be able to enhance people's mental well-being. Furthermore, technical areas such as psychoanalysis, various kinds of individual and group psychotherapy, family therapy, psychopharmacology, behavioral therapy, and cognitive therapy all differ from each other in goals, theories, and methods. A person seeking professional guidance must thus divine whether he would most benefit from, among other possibilities, talking out a problem face-to-face for a small number of individual sessions; lying on a couch free-associating many times a week over a period of years; taking medication; learning behavioral or cognitive techniques for changing thoughts, feelings, or actions; or joining one of the many available intense weekend or week-long "workshop" or "seminar" programs that focus on some core component of participants' personalities.

How does an individual make this choice? Does Mark's vague and inchoate unease merit professional attention at all, for example? Do Tom's and Melissa's difficulties with everyday life—which many of their friends and relations believe they could work out with the help of some inspirational reading and a stiff upper lip—need ongoing therapy? How many of Derek's violent outbursts are necessary before professional attention becomes unavoidable? In cases in which some attempt at remedy is clearly in order, as with very troubled individuals like Henry and Lisa, how realistically can we hope to correct disorders that seem to run so deep? Finally, what are the criteria for judging if the chosen treatment is actually helping, and whether it is helping enough?

WHY TRUE HELP IS ELUSIVE

Though many people undergo therapy, for far too few are their experiences truly therapeutic. To be effective, therapy must encourage advances within and through the emotional stages outlined in Part One, with the goal of developing the capacities that constitute optimal mental functioning. Clearly, each of the individuals introduced at the outset of this chapter has failed to master some of the tasks required by this standard of mental health. In some cases, constrictions impede functioning in certain areas, whereas in others, essential foundations seem to be lacking. All of these individuals, however, share a common therapeutic need. To improve their mental health, they all require relationships that will provide the emotional experiences necessary to attain mastery of the particular abilities that are missing. Genuine mental growth can result only from experiences, whether through skilled therapy or life circumstances, that meet each individual's developmental needs.

Many of the failures of mental health treatment thus derive from mismatches between patients and practitioners. In the hope of gaining benefits from therapy, patients often choose not the type of treatment that holds the best chance of improvement but the one that feels least threatening at the outset. Rather than picking a therapy that would work to repair problematic reactions, patients are inclined to choose the one most compatible with their existing personality structures—though that mental architecture, as we have seen, is more often than not at the root of the individual's problem in the first place.

Derek, for example, seems to be stuck in the fourth stage of emotional development, operating on the behavioral action level. Acting out his emotions without reflecting on them, he moves from behavior to behavior essentially without awareness, finding it impossible to speak about or otherwise symbolize even the simplest feelings. Psychoanalysis, therefore—or any other treatment that depends on talking about emotion—would not make sense to him. He would neither comprehend its goals nor comply with the therapist's demands. He can grasp the problem of his violence only as a tendency to do things that get him into trouble. He sees his challenge simply as a need to correct his bad habits—specifically, to learn techniques that will prevent him from slugging people. At his current stage of mental development, he is no more able to understand his feelings or the motives that underlie them than a color-blind man can describe a sunset. He can barely perceive that he has feelings apart from the sensations in his body that spur him to violence.

Faced with trouble, Derek acts. Asking him to delve into his inner life would be to call on abilities he has yet to develop, as futile as asking a toddler to ride a bicycle. Inner exploration involves a realm of experience beyond Derek's ken, a vocabulary that is completely alien to his thought. From his point of view, he needs a solution like counting to ten before swinging. He sees his problem as simply one of learning how to put the brakes on some of his more unfortunate responses.

The developmental perspective, in contrast, gives us a far more nuanced picture. Derek's problem, this point of view suggests, is not a lack of appropriate reactions but a lack of adult emotional development. No new pattern of reaction, no matter how constructive or ingenious, will change the fact that he does not possess the emotional architecture to support appropriate behavior. Only by mastering more advanced levels of development—by learning to understand and think about and with his feelings—will Derek attain adult self-control.

As things now stand, however, he cannot work toward a result beyond his present ability to conceptualize. If he should seek treatment, he will almost certainly choose a form that deals with his problem as he understands it—that makes sense to him. He will most likely look for an approach that tackles his actions at a concrete level, possibly through a behavioral modification program that aims to alter his self-destructive habits, or by consulting a religious leader who lays out strict rules to manage his daily life.

But though these approaches make more sense to Derek than one requiring him to wrestle with feelings he cannot even dimly make out, they remove both the need and the opportunity for him to undergo the challenging but ultimately far more productive experiences that would help him advance to a higher level of mental development. Only that sort of progress can afford a true solution to Derek's struggle for impulse control.

THE LIMITS OF PILLS AND BEHAVIORAL APPROACHES

A similar contradiction plagues a number of the treatments that are popular today. These approaches may deal with an individual's problems in terms that she can understand at her current developmental level. However, because they do not provide the experiences that allow a person to move into new levels of mental development, they leave the fundamental problem unchanged.

The real issue bedeviling someone who cannot distinguish fantasy from reality or rein in destructive impulses or control emotional reactions is not just a troublesome idiosyncrasy but something far more basic. Such a person lacks the ability to perceive connections among emotions or to think reflectively about them. Therapies that treat only the immediate symptoms leave development where it is. Thus, though besetting problems may appear to pass—the individual learns to talk herself out of gloomy moods through positive thinking or overcomes the habit of striking those who don't agree with him— the patient misses the chance to grow in areas that have been stunted or blocked.

Another kind of problem often dealt with only on the level of symptoms rather than emotional growth is a psychosomatic one. Emotional reactions are expressed through physical symptoms such as heartburn, headaches, dizziness, insomnia, or a stiff neck. Doctors never find any physical cause for these ills, and the sufferer never relates them to emotions, such as anxiety, tension, sadness, or anger. Her consciousness is so closely bound up with her body that she conceptualizes both her problem and its solution in terms of purely physical complaints.

Patients with these problems tend to be drawn to medication rather than therapy based on either exploring emotions or behavior modification. They go on antidepressants or tranquilizers and immediately feel better. Neck pains ease, digestion improves, sleep comes more easily. The immediate concern disappears, but so does the opportunity to reach a more advanced developmental level.

When used wisely, modern psychoactive medications may vastly enhance some individuals' chances of making therapeutic progress. By allowing a depressed or overly emotional person to gain some control over her moods, or giving a person with disordered thinking some mental clarity, they may bring quite ill patients to the point at which they can participate in psychotherapy. They are as such a valuable element in an overall treatment program. Used without therapeutic support, however, they can produce changes in behavior, brain function, and even self-image and consciousness that the individual may not be able to absorb and that may in certain circumstances further destabilize an already troubled personality structure.

It is interesting to speculate about why individuals may find some medications more helpful than others or, in other circumstances, select different drugs to medicate themselves. Perhaps the mood created by the biological agent is similar to one experienced early in life. Perhaps the sought-after response seems to recreate an earlier state of well-being (e.g., an energized, alert state, a subdued, relaxed state) or harmony found in a relationship with a caregiver.[1]

The growing use of medications on their own is a worrisome trend. While more and more people on Prozac or Ritalin are becoming bolder or less distractible, at the same time, more and more people are altering their moods without understanding what is happening to them or how it relates to their core personalities. For example, Matthew, an articulate high school student, has been taking Ritalin for over four years to help improve his ability to concentrate. He is glad to be able to focus his attention in class, but when he's out with friends or on the basketball court he prefers to feel mentally looser, more spontaneous, less "straightjacketed," so he doesn't take the drug again when his lunchtime dose wears off. During finals, however, he takes an extra dose at dinnertime to help him study efficiently all evening.

At other times he uses other chemicals—all easily available in and around his suburban school—to help him feel the way he wants to, a process he likens to adjusting the dials on a television to select the "program" that suits him at that moment. Marijuana relaxes him and gives him a sense of euphoria. Cocaine heightens an encounter with a girlfriend. Indeed, he's beginning to worry a bit about how much he's using cocaine and thinks he ought to try to get off it. But a friend is coming to stay with him over winter break, and doing a bit of coke will enhance the visit. He'll stop, he confides to a counselor, after the holidays. The counselor sees that Matthew is heading for serious trouble and arranges for him to get help for his growing dependence on cocaine.

But possible addiction is not the only troubling aspect of Matthew's penchant for "tuning" his mind, which he has essentially been doing since he began taking Ritalin. At a time of life when he should be building a unified self, he has found a way to choose from a wardrobe of selves according to the occasion.

During adolescence, the child is trying to put the pieces of his personality together. Paradoxically, he is drawn to experiences that do the opposite and fragment his emerging sense of self. While sometimes these experiences provide an illusion of identity or integration, they rarely provide cohesion at the deeper levels of the mind. It is therefore an especially sensitive time to be taking medications that change mood or thought processes, which may undermine the adolescent's long-term goal of forming a unified sense of self. If such a medication is strongly indicated, it must be combined with therapy that can foster self-understanding.

Psychological therapies themselves can lead to unintegrated personality changes. For example, therapies that attempt to alter thinking patterns in a particular direction may foster polarized rather than more subtle types of thinking. A therapist may try to teach a person to overcome depression or anxiety by seeing himself favorably rather than unfavorably: as powerful or lovable or competent rather than weak, lonely, and afraid; or as bound for success rather than doomed to failure. This approach often appeals to individuals with highly structured, even rigid personalities who deal with life by following rules and formulas rather than by meeting problems with flexibility and creativity. It also appeals to individuals who feel emotionally overwhelmed and fragmented and seek positive message around which to organize themselves.

Some of these approaches do effectively arrest the slide into depression by training people to stop and consider the rationality of their thoughts. Patients learn to ask whether it is reasonable to base their emotional reactions on beliefs such as that their situation is hopeless or they are bad people. Is it reasonable for some to expect that no one will ever want to marry him or that he's sure to fail the test no matter how hard he studies? In many cases, of course, such beliefs misrepresent the objective truth. But more to the point, they represent extremely polarized viewpoints. Thus, merely substituting a positive but equally polarized notion ("I'm a good person and everything will be fine") for a negative one does not help the person move beyond a narrow emotional viewpoint to a broader and more flexible one that includes a range of grays.

Such a person may not distinguish among feelings such as anger, disappointment, sorrow, regret, and loss but instead experiences a kind of global "downer." Failing to get a job after an interview, for example, doesn't make him feel disappointed, or frustrated, or chagrined at flubbing a crucial question, or irritated at the unsympathetic attitude of the interviewer, or determined to do better next time. Instead he feels a generalized depression and the certainty that he's a completely incompetent person. Substituting the thought "I'm a good person" may change his immediate affect but will not help him see the event in a more differentiated and thoughtful manner, assessing what actually happened and expressing particular feelings of sadness or frustration. Approaches that aim to rework internal images rather than simply substitute one polarized belief for another can, however, in the hands of sophisticated therapists, enable patients to explore loss, disappointment, and gray-area thinking.

In some people, rigidity expresses itself in idealized pictures of those important in their lives. A boss or teacher or best friend appear not as a many-dimensional person with both virtues and foibles but as a cartoon image, an all-good or all-bad caricature of a human being. This can lead to interpersonal difficulties and disillusionment. Such an individual needs therapeutic help in perceiving a mixture of positive and negative qualities in others—warmth, intelligence, and thoughtfulness, for example, along with laziness, bossiness, or a short temper. Possessing any of these qualities does not, as someone with a rigid personality erroneously believes, prevent a person from possessing any or all of the others. Having undesirable qualities rarely negates people's admirable ones or makes them all bad.

An emotionally inflexible individual needs a therapist who can help her harmonize apparently clashing feelings. In seeking guidance, however, someone prone to idealizing others can, through unrealistic admiration for the therapist, lure her away from the difficult task at hand. A therapist inclined toward grandiosity herself may collude in helping the patient feel better for the moment without directing her in the emotional work necessary for developmental growth.

Talking therapies that delve into deeper symbolic levels do not in and of themselves guarantee developmental progress. Some very articulate patients merely wallow in the verbal satisfactions of introspection. Julian, for example, talks easily and fluently during his therapy sessions, relating the minutiae of his grievances against those who have wronged him at length. His therapist encourages his free associations and collaborates in his emotional dissections as Julian describes his hurt, anger, and annoyance, while his lack of compassion and concern for others' needs and wishes are never addressed. Having built his life around his skill at manipulating words, Julian assumes that the solutions to his problems lie in hitting on just the right verbal construction, concocting the perfect theoretical explanation. Meanwhile he continues to see no further than his own skin, and his therapist does not challenge him to do otherwise.

A strictly verbal approach, with its emphasis on examining connections and musing over underlying motives, suits the tastes and talents of someone like Julian and allows him to do lots more of what he would do anyway. But it does not serve his true needs. Given his already rich emotional vocabulary, his practiced ability to convert his experience into words, such treatment may put him in closer touch with facets of his feelings. But unless he is pressed to extend his focus, a talking therapy may not lead him to develop empathy for the feelings of others. Julian may well continue on, relishing the elaboration of his own already exquisitely represented feelings.

A therapist guided by the developmental understanding, noticing what Julian is not talking about and not doing, would see that he rarely considers other people's feelings, and that he needs experience in discerning and relating to such feelings. With the therapist's direction, Julian could explore the roots of his difficulties in being aware of others' emotions and intentions, perhaps reaching back to the early stages of mental development. The therapeutic relationship might then be a training ground to awaken his ability to engage others, correct distortions of their intentions, and empathize with their feelings.

GURUS

People given to idealization often gravitate toward an apparently all-wise guru or spiritual guide, a leader who offers clear-cut rules for daily living, perhaps in public audiences, workshops, or seminars. This paragon of insight might instruct devotees to recite or meditate on one-size-fits-all teachings derived from various spiritual traditions. Though potentially valuable as components of a genuine spiritual discipline, these usually unobjectionable messages promoting harmony and oneness can also become, in the hands of some teachers, oversimplified solutions to complex problems. A person may come to believe that her thoughts and feelings, regardless of their content, reflect an essential harmony with others, whereas in reality she has simply become less aware of what those around her actually think and feel. The guru's false assurances have rendered her less rather than more able to truly sense or empathize with others' intentions and emotions except in a contrived manner.

Also in this category are programs offering group experiences that, though they have no genuine therapeutic effect, produce an illusion of self-confidence, serenity, and well-being. What actually happens, however, is that the group leader exploits an intense, protracted situation designed to break down the boundaries of participants' personalities. The often rhythmic presentation of the program's ideas and agenda can feel exhilarating to the individual member of a large crowd in a packed room, which itself exerts a powerful dynamic that begins to erode self-definition. The person may blend into the group, becoming part of it and adopting its intentions as her own. This boundary loss causes regression to more primitive, less differentiated levels of emotional functioning. It may also increase susceptibility to hypnotic effects. These well-known results of extended mass gatherings have long been taken advantage of by promoters and demagogues, who then channel this sea of coalescing selves to serve their own ends.

Presenting himself as intensely certain of the beliefs he promulgates, the leader promises to solve the problems that trouble his hearers. His certainty offers an illusion of security that many find extremely appealing, especially those with a weak sense of their own identities. The weaker the individual's sense of self, the stronger the almost hypnotic appeal of such a ready-made guide to life. Indeed, those who emerge from group sessions like this compulsively eager to repeat the message and proselytize others to join the sect may be operating in a kind of posthypnotic trance.

A strongly defined sense of self developed in the early years of life is the best shield against the seductiveness of group experiences under a charismatic leader. Some people, however, cannot tolerate such experiences. It is not uncommon for these individuals to fragment under the strain, losing their sense of reality, becoming suspicious or depressed and uncertain about their psychological and bodily boundaries. Not infrequently they cannot carry on their regular activities.

Other participants in these sessions have personalities stable enough to take from the experience and the guru's message the elements that fit, integrate them, and discard the rest. The limitations of weekend workshops do not prevent a deep and reciprocal relationship with a spiritual guide or teacher from contributing to genuine emotional growth. But no relationship that lacks intimacy and reciprocity can take a person beyond the realm of polarized emotions or build a more defined sense of self. Such a change requires that new ideas and emotional experiences be tested against and then integrated into one's existing store of ideas and relationships. That takes time and true emotional engagement such as can generally occur only in a long-standing connection with a friend, mate, counselor, therapist, or spiritual mentor.

THE ESSENCE OF A THERAPEUTIC EXPERIENCE

The goal of mental health treatment is to help the individual move toward the level of development appropriate to his or her age. This requires guiding him as he learns to negotiate emotional experiences: engaging more deeply with others, understanding others' intentions, representing his feelings rather than crudely acting them out, or connecting certain emotional themes with the others composing a well-integrated personality. Even if the limitations of individual makeup or other circumstances keep a person from achieving this aim, any progress that is made toward mastery of the levels of development brings him that much closer to mental health.

Mental disorders are not simply random collections of symptoms. Therapies that stress changing surface behavior or that set forth rigid rules usually do not help a person move toward a higher level of mental health. To the degree that they may allow him to take part in satisfying long-term emotional relationships, however, they may support overall growth.

In clinical work with both children and adults and in observing friendships and marriages, I have seen that the mind grows from certain types of experiences. Insights, advice, and behavioral modification strategies do not provide these experiences.[2]

The therapeutic relationship presents a paradox. The goal of therapy is to bring an individual to a higher developmental level, to teach her capacities that she may not even know exist. But how can someone who does not feel anger or loss or dependency yet acts these emotions out realize that she needs to learn to be aware of them? The would-be client cannot go looking for something she does not know the value of. She can, however, avoid the appeal of simplistic solutions and endeavor to construct a therapeutic relationship with a practitioner able to lead her toward knowing the unknowable.

The case of Fred illustrates this point. Fred told his therapist that he was thinking of breaking up with his girlfriend, Jane, who had gone on vacation at a time when Fred could not get away instead of waiting for his vacation to come around. One clinical approach might be to empathize with Fred's apparent disappointment; the therapist might say, for example, "That seems to make you feel angry." "I guess so," Fred would answer with a shrug, going on to relate that he planned to attend a singles dance and find someone else to practice his new found assertiveness with before Jane returned. Another approach might be to suggest that Fred try to tolerate his anger and not act precipitously, as he generally did in such situations: "Why don't you just wait and see what Jane has to say?" the therapist could ask. "After all, you care about her and you've been going together a long time."

A therapist advocating the developmental approach, by contrast, would recognize Fred's reaction as typical of his mental level. The problem was not Jane's solo vacation but Fred's inability to tolerate the emotions of loneliness, abandonment, and jealousy and deal with the accompanying feelings of loss and sadness. The therapist would help him recognize and negotiate these emotions. Indeed, all therapeutic relationships, whether with therapists, good friends, or family members, involve such collaborations and offer support through experiences that foster the development of the different levels of the mind.

In a session in which Fred was speaking of his current independence, the therapist could ask, "What do you think Jane is doing now?" He would then help Fred construct as vivid a picture as possible of Jane at that moment. Was she walking on the beach? Swimming? Having a glass of wine on the hotel terrace? Was she thinking about Fred or enjoying someone else's company? By creating such images, Fred would begin gradually to construct feelings: thinking of Jane having fun without him, imagining her dancing with some other man, doing things that they had always done together, like playing tennis or going to the movies. He might see her missing him. From a vague sense of numbness and false independence would grow the awareness of his true emotions. These emotional representations, which he had never achieved before, would allow him to tolerate previously unrepresented feelings rather than acting on them impetuously. This approach would therefore not only help get Fred through the crisis of Jane's departure but also broaden his emotional capacities.

Effective therapy, in short, has as its goal mastery of the different developmental levels of the mind. The therapist aims to support the levels that the patient has already attained while fostering growth through the ones he hasn't yet mastered. Doing so, however, involves more than simply encouraging someone to be more assertive or showing him how to stick up for his rights, important though these abilities are. It requires nurturing much more basic processes through helping the patient explore new levels of feeling and relating. Therapists with a developmental orientation tend to be able to establish a warm and trusting rapport with patients, to empathize with their feelings and intentions as well as ideas, and to help them gradually elaborate on these and become more reflective. Therapists who practice only one technique or who are too quick to try this or that technique are often not using a developmental orientation.[3]

Creating such therapeutic relationships is not easy. As we will see in Chapter 12, personal relationships that support the growth of the mind also pose a difficult challenge. They have much in common, however. Stable relationships that allow opportunities for emotional interaction and elaboration are a critical foundation for such growth. Mastering new levels of the mind is like traveling toward a place you have never been to. Though no one can fully anticipate the experience of a canyon or a cathedral, a glacier or a rainforest before actually seeing it, all of us can understand the idea of making such a trip.

CHAPTER TEN

The Emotional Foundations
of Learning

UNDERMINING THE EFFECTIVENESS OF OUR EDUCATIONAL system is the dichotomy between the emotions and the intellect that underlies many of its principles. The separation between emotional and intellectual growth ignores developmental levels and individual differences, thus hindering many children's potential.

As semiskilled and unskilled jobs that pay a living wage continue to vanish, the ability to succeed in the classroom now determines many children's destinies in our technologically sophisticated society. Unfortunately, by the time caps and gowns are distributed after twelve or thirteen years of school, a large percentage will already have dropped out and many who receive diplomas will barely be able to read them.

Richard Lodish, a distinguished early childhood educator and collaborator in many of the ideas in this chapter, has pointed out that the great majority of such disastrous outcomes—misfortunes that will darken young lives forever—need not happen.[1] It is our belief that flaws in the educational system, not deficiencies in the children, account for most of these failures. We cannot afford to base our education on counterproductive notions of human development.

DANGEROUS ASSUMPTIONS

As it is now structured, American education largely ignores the emotional origins of intellectual development. Individual differences in the way children take in information are not taken into account unless they are large enough that children are labeled learning disabled, cognitively impaired, emotionally disturbed, or autistic. While paying lip service to children's developmental timetables, few schools tailor interventions to their actual level. Differences in family patterns and early experience get little attention unless a child is designated emotionally disturbed, even though her affective life forms the basis of her ability to learn. Gifted teachers, of course, have always been aware of this connection. It is time, however, for the schools to recognize it formally. Schools also tend to pay relatively less attention to the emotionally based generative aspects of thinking—the ability to create ideas—and instead focus relatively more on the ability to organize and sequence ideas. Unless we begin to build awareness of neurological and emotional development into our educational programs, we will continue to fail to educate large numbers of children even after holding them for thousands of hours in the classroom.

Some critics, however, have recently insisted that our educational system is erring in quite the opposite direction, catering to each child's idiosyncrasies in an overindulgent effort to build self-esteem by rewarding children for whatever they happen to do. Only by returning to traditional methods and demanding higher standards, they maintain, will the schools guide children toward academic mastery.

While there may be instances of programs such as those the critics describe, this criticism misrepresents what is actually happening in most of the nation's classrooms. Programs boosting "self-esteem" are largely limited to preschool, kindergarten, and the very early primary grades. By first or second grade, most schools have moved solidly into academics. From first grade on, children are sorted into fast and slow groups for reading, math, and other subjects, and the cheerful, cuddly titles teachers give to these units don't keep children from knowing exactly which is which and where they stand. "As any child can tell you," writes the physician and anthropologist Melvin Konner, consistently losing does not promote self-esteem, no matter how impervious to reality you may be. So every educational program needs to make a choice. You can get short-term gains in self-esteem and continue to lose ground; or you can try this theory: that self-esteem can also come from making a great effort, from facing uncertainty and overcoming obstacles that we were not sure we could meet, from doing our level best. You may have to struggle with a child from time to time to get her to overcome her doubts about herself, to dig in and really try. It's a risk. But only by taking it do you get to see that smile—no, it's a grin, really, and the face is open in a hint of astonishment—that breaks over the child's face as she slams the pencil down on the page and says in a thrilled, surprised voice, "I did it!"[2]

Real self-esteem, of course, can grow only from such mastery of genuine challenges. But this does not mean that children can all be taught according to a single set of standards. No human being—or indeed, any animal—can master material presented in a form that its nervous system cannot handle. Children given tasks beyond their capacities lose confidence, enthusiasm, and very shortly, interest in succeeding at school. But given a task broken down in a way that is appropriate to her capabilities, and taking into account strengths and weaknesses that often stem from differences in the way the nervous system works, every child can learn and experience the thrill of mastery. A child's success is not accurately measured by how quickly she learns, or whether her method resembles that of others, but by how well she learns when taught in a manner suited to her needs. Our schools' failure to educate masses of children fully capable of learning is not the result of overemphasis on unearned self-esteem or touchy-feely frills but from reliance on a model that ignores the nature of the learning process.[3]

Perhaps the best example of current misconceptions of how children learn is the overemphasis on group testing, which some say we should do more of, and underemphasis on individually oriented teaching. The old saying applies here: "You can't fatten a goat by weighing it." Letting children know how dumb they are won't make them smart. We are far better at documenting what children do not know than we are at figuring out ways to help them know. If a child is behind in math, for instance, but has no obvious learning disabilities, we mark his home-work wrong, test him, and kick him out of the faster math group. Rarely will someone sit down with him to figure out the source of his difficulties. Perhaps he is not picturing different quantities in his mind as he performs arithmetical operations. Trying to memorize a list of facts, he gets lost and confused. Helping him advance from objects he can manipulate to seeing them in his mind as he adds, subtracts, or multiplies might get him over the hurdle. But typically, instead of making this critical step, he will absorb the message that he's stupid or he's no good at math or he's not trying hard enough.

There is no need to choose between rigor and structure in edu-cation on the one hand and self-discovery, autonomy, and flexibility on the other. Rather, the focus should be on how to create a learning experience for each child. Criticism and testing aren't bad in them-selves. They undermine confidence only if they aren't immediately coupled with helping children figure out how to succeed at learning.

The issue is not how hard children work, either. Most children like work if it is productive and if they are learning. We must take a lesson from outstanding athletic coaches as well as outstanding teach-ers. Although they are often quite demanding and have more than a little bit of toughness, they tune into their students' strengths and weaknesses. They teach or coach actively, adjusting their programs to students' needs. A basketball player who misses a few passes is not labeled as having "bad hands." A good coach throws him balls that are high and low, fast and slow, from close by and from far away, while he's running and standing still, until he can catch balls in his sleep. The gifted teacher doesn't label a child a weak math student but diagnoses the missing step in his computations and develops exer-cises, whether in the curriculum or not, to enable him to master it. If not pushed two steps ahead of itself, the human mind is a veritable mastery machine.

At this point, the argument that we cannot afford the types of individualized instruction that would help almost all children master the basics is certain to arise. As will be discussed later in this chapter, our ignoring of potential resources creates the illusion that only an assembly-line model of learning is practical. Doing things the convenient way is often more expensive than doing them the effective way.

With our present understanding of how the mind grows, all children, with the exception of certain youngsters with very severe neurological difficulties, should be able to master the essentials of learning. But between what we could achieve and what the educational system actually does achieve a great gap yawns.

MRS. JACKSON'S CLASSROOM

Mrs. Jackson's first grade, in a school in an unexceptional middle-class neighborhood, resembles countless classes in schools across the country.[4] Energetic, experienced, and sincere, Mrs. Jackson works hard every day to introduce the twenty-five six-year-olds in her charge to the fundamentals of learning. But she must teach so many youngsters and spend so much time on paperwork that she has no choice but to present nearly all lessons to groups of students, sometimes as small as half a dozen or so, but usually a good deal larger. And because she has no assistance in the classroom, she must assign desk work to occupy those not being taught at any given moment.

Just now, for example, the Blue Birds, her top reading group, are doing work sheets in which they are to draw lines between pictures of animals and the first letters of the animals' names. In the second row, Magda is proceeding confidently down the page, connecting the letter *L* with the picture of a lion and *G* with the giraffe. She pauses to consider if a primate swinging from a tree is a monkey or an ape, but rejects the latter possibility because the sheet also contains an antelope. She can't quite decipher the directions printed at the top of her sheet, but she has figured out what Mrs. Jackson wants from her words, gestures, and body language.

The dozen members of the slower group, the Robins, are meanwhile grouped around Mrs. Jackson, taking turns reading aloud from their primers. Progress through the adventures of a pet dog and cat has been slow and disjointed as one narrator after another struggles through a sentence or two. Mrs. Jackson tries to keep up interest in the rather thin plot line by making comments and asking questions. Henry has not yet had his turn, but he isn't paying much attention to either his classmates' voices or the words on the page before him. He has only a vague notion of how far the group has gotten in the story, which strikes him as stupid, because he can't make the printed letters combine very easily into words.

Wriggling in his seat, he spots something that is far more engrossing: the toy car sticking out of Walter's side pants pocket. Just as Mrs. Jackson is thanking Sara for her efforts and is turning to ask Henry to pick up the reading, he makes his move, deftly plucking the little red car from his neighbor's pants. Walter sits up straight, pats his pocket, and punches Henry, who drops his book but keeps hold of the car.

Mrs. Jackson sighs. Another Robin reading lesson interrupted by children who lack the motivation to learn to read. Henry's test scores indicate cognitive ability equal to the task. She's convinced that he could learn if only he'd sit still and try. Walter, however, seems unable to control the impulse to hit anyone who annoys him. Both boys need work on reading, but for now she has no choice but to separate Walter from Henry and both from the remaining Robins, who have broken into giggles. She reprimands Henry, who responds with a cocky grin not lost on his appreciative audience. Once again, he realizes with relief, he has avoided reading aloud altogether, and thus the humiliation of not knowing where he should be or how to form many of the words. Instead of feeling embarrassed, he has managed to come off as bold and defiant. Banished to a "time out" seat at one end of the room, Henry glares tauntingly at Walter, exiled at the room's opposite end.

After a while the Blue Birds and Robins change places so that Mrs. Jackson can work in a more advanced book with Magda and a dozen other able readers. The Robins are assigned a work sheet. Mrs. Jackson explains the instructions slowly and carefully and asks if anyone has any questions. Henry fails to get the gist of what is expected but says nothing. As he usually does on such occasions, he spends a few minutes looking around at his classmates, trying to divine if the others know what they're supposed to be doing. Giving up, he then takes a crack at coloring in some of the pictures on the work sheet. Lolling about in his seat, he manages to spill his crayons on the floor. When Mrs. Jackson glances over to check on the Robins, she spies Henry on his knees under his desk, ostensibly retrieving the crayons but actually delighted to have escaped from the mystifying assignment.

Mrs. Jackson, considered a skillful, caring teacher, feels deep disappointment at the results of her efforts with students like Henry. He seems bright and spunky in conversation, but he doesn't respond to her attempts to engage him in his schoolwork and has steadily fallen further and further behind his fellow Robins—so far behind, in fact, that Mrs. Jackson is now seriously considering referring him to the school's "resource teacher." She hesitates, however, because her experience has been that boys of his rebellious disposition often become more rebellious when pulled out of class for stigmatizing special instruction. She's baffled at why he can't progress normally, like the other children, and about what she can do to help him.

UNFOUNDED ASSUMPTIONS

For all their hard work and dedication, Mrs. Jackson and her legions of equally frustrated colleagues cannot succeed with a child like Henry because of two unfounded assumptions behind our system of education. The first is the notion that children of the same age can generally be taught as a homogeneous group by standardized methods. Any child who cannot is regarded as "exceptional," either because of a disability or deficiency or because of unusual gifts.

According to the developmental model, however, each child is unique both in experience and inborn endowment. As we saw in Chapter 6, children enter the world with widely varied potentials and predilections. They diverge neurologically and physiologically, in their musculature and the way their senses function, and in many other ways. And they confront a multiplicity of disparate experiences. Each child therefore proceeds through the developmental stages at his or her own pace, finding some tasks more and others less difficult. Our educational system, however, assumes that twenty-five or thirty children born in the same year are sufficiently similar in developmental attainment, intellectual capacities, physical prowess, and level of visual, verbal, and manual skill to be taught in the same way. We therefore put them together under a single teacher and in a single room to learn together, in public, at roughly the same rate. Magda and Henry, for example, happen to have been born in the same hospital in the same week. But in readiness for formal learning and in practical academic skills they are already, at age six, several years apart, though neither falls outside the "normal" range for his or her age. Although there have been many attempts in recent decades to apply a developmental approach in the early grades, the underlying assumptions have not changed. The British primary school approach, for instance, has been adopted in some schools, but usually these are private or small experimental programs.

The second misguided assumption is that children can learn effectively through one-directional presentation of material in lectures, textbook reading, drill, and rote memory. As our postindustrial, information-based society moves out of the 1990s, it continues to try to educate children according to an antiquated model more appropriate to the 1930s and before. Our current mode of schooling, once proudly called the "factory system," in fact dates back to observations that the educator Horace Mann made in Prussia over 150 years ago.

In those early days of industrialization, the factory, with its implementation of scientific innovations for the purpose of boosting efficiency, enjoyed all the cachet that the computer does now. Forward-looking, progressive people wanted to organize life in accord with the new technology that was remaking and in countless ways improving daily life. Applying the principles of uniformity and standardization that were the basis for the production of the flood of new industrial goods, Mann designed a system of education built around standardized, even interchangeable, units. Teachers would provide uniform instruction, usually in the form of lectures, to homogeneous classes of students of the same age.

Students would also do standardized learning exercises involving memorizing, reciting, and completing work sheets. Teachers would evaluate their work according to a standardized numerical scale. Periods would be of standard length, and cohorts of same-age classmates would advance through the curriculum together at the same pace. Completion of a given grade or a given course of study would have a standard meaning. Schools would be efficient, productive, progressive, and modern.

However well this model may have served a society that offered ample employment opportunities for those who could not adapt to its rigid methods, it does not meet the needs of society today. In the era of the computer, nearly all gainful work, even in manual trades, involves a substantial level of verbal and mathematical literacy. Now that we have a far more accurate idea of how the human mind develops, we must base our educational methods not on tradition but on the best current insights into how children learn.

We must base it, in short, on a developmental model and on its key tenet: *intellectual learning shares common origins with emotional learning*. Both stem from early affective interactions. Both are influenced by individual differences, and both must proceed in a step-wise fashion, from one developmental level to another. The sort of learning a child acquires in kindergarten and the early grades is not the true foundation of her education. In fact, early schoolwork cannot proceed without previous mastery of various mental tasks. The "three R's" and all that follows, symbolic and increasingly abstract academic knowledge, cannot be understood by a person who has not grasped the sequence of skills that make learning possible.

THE REAL BASICS

Magda clearly possesses these skills. She arrived in kindergarten already experienced in sitting still; in looking at pictures and letters; at deciphering the words, intonations, and body language of an adult reading aloud; at following a story line; at describing the action depicted in an illustration; and at imagining the results that might follow when the clock at the ball strikes twelve or when Red Riding Hood visits poor Grandma. Magda also has a pretty good idea of when she doesn't understand a story and how to get Mom or Dad to go back and reread or explain the confusing part.

Magda's expertise at these skills makes listening to the teacher, grasping the point of lessons and assignments, asking questions, and working at her desk easy for her. She gets almost visceral enjoyment from knowing the right answer, completing her work sheet, sounding out words in her primer. She can monitor her own progress and compare it to her teacher's expectations. With the praise of Mrs. Jackson and her parents, doing well in school is one of her most easily obtainable pleasures.

Henry's experience could hardly be more different. He has trouble attending, doesn't see the point of memorizing apparently meaningless symbols, mixes them up when he tries, and misses about half of what the teacher is saying. He can't make his hand copy the shapes in his workbook or, even more maddening, on the blackboard—in fact, he often feels as though he were trying to draw them in a mirror. Though bright, curious, and a native speaker of English, he can't get the hang of certain unfamiliar expressions that the teacher insists on using and lots of the other kids, especially the girls in the top reading group, seem to understand with ease. So he generally finds himself in the lower ability groups. His work sheets are always a mess. His stabs at giving the teacher what she wants usually fail. For Henry, school is a scene of constant humiliation. To cover his continuing hurt, he may begin to "forget" lessons, books, and assignments, act up in class, and retreat into his own world of fantasy. Whatever his strategy, he will convince himself that school is "dumb" and, eventually, that he is too.

The skills that Henry needs to learn in school, and that would make it possible for him to reach his true intellectual potential, are not innate characteristics but proficiencies that can be taught. Indeed, they are nothing more than the skills acquired at the developmental levels explored in Part One. First, a child must be able to regulate his attention. Whether he learns this easily or with difficulty depends, of course, on the particular endowment he arrived with as well as the early nurturing he received. Second, he must be able to relate to others with warmth and trust. Those who lack adequate nurturing may not have learned to engage fully with other human beings. No teacher can then marshal this basic sense of connectedness. The child will not be motivated to please her, and ultimately himself, by doing well at schoolwork. Finally, he must be able to communicate through both gestures and symbols, to handle complex ideas, and to make connections among them. Those who have not mastered these early levels obviously cannot succeed at more advanced ones. The real ABCs come down to attention, strong relationships, and communication, all of which children must learn through interaction with adults. Learning will also be smoother if a youngster arrives at school able to reflect on his own behavior, so that, for example, he can tell whether he understands a lesson or assignment and if not, know which part he finds confusing.

Despite the utter indispensability of these skills, however, current classroom methods generally make it difficult for those lacking them to catch up once they have begun school. In most schools there is an assumption that children are normally ready to learn, and curricula are designed on that assumption—a misapprehension that has brought countless children to grief.

Typical classrooms like Mrs. Jackson's cater to a very narrow range of perceptual and learning styles, primarily verbally oriented ones like Magda's. Teachers dealing with twenty-five children at a time (in secondary schools, sometimes well over a hundred) cannot possibly establish a trusting relationship with all or even most of them. Children who are or have become withdrawn, angry, suspicious, or humiliated—that is, those who most need emotional support—are least likely to get it.

Throughout the school day, furthermore, the great bulk of communication goes in only one direction, from teacher to student. Because twenty or more people cannot speak or move about at will without producing chaos, most of the youngsters' spontaneous expressions are labeled disruption or disobedience. Very few who are not already adept at communication have much chance to build their skills. Since most teachers are too overworked to assign and correct many substantial writing assignments, few children get much practice in articulating, presenting, and linking ideas of their own. Finally, those who don't know they're lost—those who can't frame questions to pinpoint their areas of confusion, or even imagine what's expected of them—generally end up being reprimanded or punished instead of receiving the step-by-step guidance that would help them get their bearings.

For children to acquire these indispensable abilities, early education must follow developmental principles. (Not coincidentally, these are also the essential principles of good parenting.) First, effective teaching must tune in to the child's own developmental level. A teacher must have the time and resources to know each child as an individual and determine which developmental skills she has mastered and which need work. This means observing and assessing abilities such as reading nonverbal signals and reflecting on her own and others' ideas in addition to fine motor and language skills.

Second, effective teaching presents children not with information to assimilate but with problems to solve through active initiative and

participation. Such an approach could include hands-on tasks and experiments, field trips, writing projects, debates, and any other techniques that get the child to engage with others and with the material.
Given the emotional origins of learning, which give the child the capacity to digest and organize ideas, good teaching must involve the child's
feelings, fuel her curiosity, and harness her energy. In an autobiograph-
ical section of *Mindstorms,* his book on learning, Seymour Papert of
MIT writes of "falling in love with gears" as the key moment in early
childhood when his interest in learning began.[5] Such a passion, of
course, rests on the foundations we have described. Children at every
level of ability, from those lacking preparation for learning to the intellectually gifted, benefit from exploring, dissecting, classifying, arguing,
and other emotionally engaging aspects of hands-on schooling.

Third, effective teaching takes seriously the child's natural inclinations and perspective and uses them as a means of broadening her
understanding and experience. This implies far more than providing
examples from the child's daily life. It means seeing the material
through the eyes of the child, at her particular developmental level
and in the terms in which she understands it. Henry, for example, has
not yet made the connection between the names of animals and written letters. To reach him, the teacher must keep this very literal perspective in mind. She must help him build bridges between realms
that appear very separate to him. And she can do so only by recognizing his perception that the connections that teachers keep insisting do
exist between an object and the symbols representing it are totally
arbitrary and capricious. Starting from where Henry is, his teacher
would challenge this perception with carefully graduated experiences
in manipulating symbols. Many of these techniques, such as connecting the sounds represented by letters to the sounds in animal names,
are of course already used in classrooms. But helping the individual
child make this connection while taking into account the developmental stumbling blocks he may need to surmount makes all the
difference in the child's grasping a piece of knowledge essential for
learning to read.

The fourth principle of effective education follows from the one
before: a teacher must present material in steps and at a pace appropriate to the child's cognitive abilities and learning style. Only very

small steps taken gradually will get Henry to the goal of being ready to read, whereas Magda can sprint through much of this material, vaulting over several of the hurdles he faces. Were Magda forced to dally at his pace, she too would lose the pleasure of learning. When adults help children master a skill in steps that match their own strengths and tendencies, youngsters experience the exhilaration at doing something well that is intrinsic in the human nervous system.

The "unmotivated" child, therefore, often simply exemplifies the fact that the teaching she has received has failed to call forth these natural feelings of positive reinforcement. Preventing a child from learning takes real effort: learning is what the young nervous system is designed for, and what children do best. "If children grew up according to early indications," observed Goethe, "we should have nothing but geniuses." Except for those with serious neurological problems, any child—including those with common attentional and behavioral difficulties—can master the skills taught in the ordinary elementary and secondary curriculum.

If a task is within a person's ability and congruent with his natural abilities, he will feel enjoyment in accomplishing it. The pleasure is not simply one of mastery. The activity itself feels good, like making a perfect golf or tennis shot or effortlessly remembering the definition of an uncommon word. Someone with excellent physical coordination feels rewarded when he moves with grace and skill; a person with fine verbal gifts enjoys subtly manipulating words and meanings; the individual with outstanding visual abilities delights in devising new combinations of graphic images. These persons will gain less pleasurable reinforcement in the realms in which they don't naturally do as well. The activity itself may feel aversive, even painful, like trying to shoot a basket with your nondominant hand or draw a path within the lines of a maze while looking in a mirror. The inevitable response is to avoid this type of pain.

As they are now set up, most schools reward certain abilities at certain grade levels. The elementary years stress memory and eye-hand coordination; the child who can write clearly and remember details does well. In high school, analytical skills are more in demand, and the excellent third-grade reader who is not an equally excellent analytical thinker may find that his pleasure in learning as well as his academic standing has slipped considerably. What has changed, however, is not the student's intelligence or ability to be motivated by success but the skills and capacities the educational system values at her age level.

Finally, the fifth principle of effective teaching involves structure and limits. To feel successful, children must have standards to measure themselves against. To feel secure, they must believe that adults will help them keep their anger, greed, frustration, and other negative emotions in check. This must be done, however, through positive means that impose rigor yet protect the child's self-esteem. Rules must be clear, reasonable, and carry essentially automatic sanctions. When a child transgresses, he must pay the required penalty but not be humiliated by it. Limits must therefore be accompanied by support so that the child can understand and do better next time. By helping him to anticipate future temptations or problems, to picture specific situations, to recall the reaction that got him in trouble, and to devise more desirable alternatives, an adult can prepare the child to deal with limits constructively and creatively. The more he finds accepting rules and structure difficult, the more he needs such encouragement and support.

EFFECTIVE REFORM

How we can best help more children to succeed at school is a question so central to the welfare of our nation that it has been the subject of fervent debate for decades. Proposals of all sorts fill the airwaves, news columns, and agendas of school board meetings and legislative chambers. Stricter standards, back-to-basics curricula, a longer school year, tuition vouchers, privatization, national tests for teachers—each of these or a dozen other reforms will, proponents promise, do the trick. However, the developmental model suggests that these approaches will produce only the same disappointing results, and in a number of cases, at higher cost.

To be effective, educational reform must reflect the insights revealed by new research on how the mind develops. Three points must be paramount in this effort. First and foremost is the fact that affect and interaction, rather than the acquisition of specific information and skills, are the foundation of learning of every kind. For most students, the best kind of learning is experiential, involving interacting with others: for example, through small-group or one-on-one work with a teacher or tutor or in, say, a seminar format, in which students discuss their individual work under the guidance of a teacher. Another model is the study partnership of the traditional Jewish yeshiva, in which a pair of students, usually but not always under a teacher's supervision, closely examine and debate the interpretation of texts. "The student who doesn't ask doesn't learn," the Talmudic sages observed. The corollary is that the teacher who doesn't get students actively immersed in the material doesn't truly teach. In the Socratic dialogue, still the model of instruction at the finest law schools, the teacher does not present information to students but rather asks them questions that, by leading them through steps of reasoning, draws ideas from them. In effect, the student discovers ideas and information for herself and, in doing so, acquires the method of learning on her own.

Many innovative programs that follow one or more of these models permit committed interchanges among students or between students and teacher. However, this kind of personal instruction is usually offered only in honors programs full of able or gifted students. If it were made available to those performing at the average or sub-average level, such opportunities would do a lot of good. Indeed, when children from stressed families who are diagnosed as having poor attention and poor organizational skills are exposed to this sort of dynamic instruction, they do exceedingly well. Observers have generally attributed improvements to the novelty of unaccustomed attention and concern from those in charge. But their greater achievement in fact reflects something deeper than increased motivation: it indicates changes in the learning process itself.

The second essential of educational reform that is consonant with the latest research is as familiar as the proverb: "A stitch in time saves nine." By waiting until a child has reached preschool or even school age before starting to prepare her for academic work, we waste the prime learning years of an entire lifetime. By the time she shows up for nursery school at three years of age, her brain has already reached two-thirds to three-quarters of its adult size. By age five, when she enters kindergarten, so much of the brain is developed that a child

who has not been working for years on the "real ABCs" is drasti
cally—though not irremediably—behind. Any effective program c
reform must therefore have as a primary goal ensuring that everyon
who enrolls in elementary school has the necessary skills of attentioı
and communication as well as the ability to participate in relation
ships. For children from dysfunctional families, this principle implie:
intensive early intervention and support. For those facing significanː
perceptual or processing challenges, it means expert evaluation anc
therapy.

This brings us to the third requirement for effective reform: the
recognition that individual differences are real and that they matter.
This does not mean that some children are normal whereas others are
learning disabled. Rather, it means that each child has an individual
way of integrating sensation and information that is characteristic of
her particular developmental level. As we have seen, children vary in
their sensitivities, temperaments, and attitudes in ways that will certainly affect their approach to school. The overly sensitive child, the
self-absorbed child, the defiant child, and others each face obstacles in
meeting the demands of the classroom. Children also begin school at
quite different levels in the developmental process. Some enter able to
monitor their actions and even reflect on their thoughts and feelings.
Others do not attain these capacities until years later, if at all. To make
the greatest progress, each child needs teaching that takes this level
into account.

If children who have been deprived of needed developmental
experiences are to have a chance to grow emotionally and intellectually, we must find ways of furnishing them with these experiences.
Keeping a small group of children together with the same teacher for a
number of years—an approach now used in some private schools—is
one such way of building intimacy between children and caring
adults. Athletic coaches who work closely with youngsters over an
extended period develop similar relationships. Formal mentoring
programs, in which adults are paired with individual children or small
groups of children whom they see at least several times a week, preferably daily, have also been successful in this regard.[6] By staying abreast
of youngsters' lives, helping them talk through and solve everyday
problems, keeping tabs on school progress, introducing them to

wholesome new experiences and useful community resources, and generally showing empathy and encouragement, such mentors have helped support developmental growth.

Relationships like these can grow out of any number of organizational formats, including after-school homework-cum-recreation programs, Big Brother or Big Sister networks, and church youth groups. Some schools that specialize in working with at-risk children assign each student to a teacher or staff member who then spends time with the youngster daily. Schools are in fact best equipped for conducting effective mentoring programs since they are so central an aspect of children's lives.

Mentoring relationships work best if they are established on formal commitments that adults knowingly accept. Basing them solely on voluntary good will permits the mentor to bow out too readily if the child gets into serious trouble. As in any nurturing relationship, the mentor must tune in to the child's developmental level, follow the child's lead, involve him in issues and activities of interest, and perhaps most important, persevere even when the child becomes hostile or withdraws.

Children in special education programs also need such intensive long-term relationships with adults. Of all areas of the teaching profession, special education has historically shown the greatest awareness of the reality and importance of individual differences. As we have seen, skillful attention from teachers trained to work around these differences can often allow even youngsters facing challenges as severe as autism to succeed academically. Despite this devotion to meeting each child's particular needs, however, the field of special education still underemphasizes the significance of affective relationships in learning. Programs must be redesigned to incorporate the developmental approach, affording a great deal of interaction within very small groups. I describe such a program in great detail in a forthcoming book.[7]

Other current policies need to be questioned. In today's special education programs, children with similar challenges are often grouped together, either within their own class or across grades in their school. Though this is an efficient way to make specialized services available, it may cut children off from the most crucial ingredient of intellectual growth: interaction with a diversity of people.

Successful mainstream integration of children with special needs requires more rather than less money, smaller rather than larger classes, and expert help for the classroom teacher who must deal with an even wider range of abilities, skills, and sensitivities. Using integration merely as a means of saving money on special education makes a mockery of this worthwhile goal. Rather than bringing children of diverse potentials and experiences closer together, it pits their parents against one another as they struggle to make sure that their own children get what they need from an inadequate pot of funds.

If these reforms were to be carried out, schools would be very different places. But after all, what would lead a sensible person to conclude that a human child—the descendant of tens of thousands of generations of people who spent their days actively working to secure their subsistence—would find it congenial to sit in a room with one adult and twenty-five or more other children for six hours a day over twelve or sixteen or eighteen years? Our ancestors learned by doing, by taking on tasks under the intimate guidance of more experienced persons who could impart concepts, knowledge, and skills.

A school structured on the developmental understanding would arrange for children to work closely with adults throughout the day— with teachers during academic classes and with mentors at other times. In many cases, teachers would work with children individually or in twos or threes. At present the system often labels children who cannot learn in groups incapable of being educated.

But how are our financially strapped school systems to get the platoons of caring adults that the developmental approach to education calls for? If every child who needs one is to have a mentor, if every child who needs it is to work in a small group with a teacher, then the ratio between youngsters and grown-ups must change radically. As many successful programs have shown, however, many of these adults need not be trained educational specialists. Schools can recruit parents, grandparents, neighbors, retired persons, or other members of the community who are able to contribute some time as volunteers serving as mentors and classroom aides.

Nevertheless, even with a huge influx of volunteers, large public school systems might not be able to offer all children a full day of intense small-group or personal instruction like that generally available at the best private schools. But even hard-pressed schools could arrange for each child to receive the full attention of an adult—an aide or perhaps even a trained volunteer if not a teacher—for an hour or so of instruction each day. Under these circumstances, even a child like Henry would figure out how to read, to calculate, to write, and most important, to learn.

Well-supervised group projects could fill the rest of the time. An array of constructive but inexpensive activities would provide each child a chance to succeed at something (or several things) every day. Singing, drama, sports, chess, art, debate, conversation in foreign languages, creative writing, community service, running a small business—any number of endeavors would give children experiences that would help them master the basic skills of learning. At the end of six years in such a setting, unlike the failure so common today, almost all children would be able to read, many of them quite well. All would have explored stimulating new fields. None would have tasted the unrelieved bitterness and humiliation that now drive so many away. Though such a school, based on principles derived from the developmental model, would violate all the notions of standardized normality that currently hold both teachers and students in thrall, it would liberate them for true learning.

We thus face a straightforward choice. We can either begin to develop all of our children's potential or continue to throw much of it away. We can offer education that respects and enhances children's gifts or that rejects them, and the youngsters with them. Faulty notions of how the mind develops have previously supported us in the latter course. Given the results of new research into human capacities, however, we no longer have any excuse to allow this waste to continue.

In order to create change we must offer more than a model program here and there, though many of these innovative ventures, particularly in preschools and the early grades, have been admirable. The writings of Reuven Feuerstein, Howard Gardner, and Jim Comer as well as the developmentally based curriculum guidelines of the National Association for the Education of Young Children are a few examples of well-regarded approaches.[8] But these kinds of dynamic approaches have not been exploited by the great majority of schools at the different grade levels.

Part of the imperviousness of the status quo is owing to administrative, bureaucratic, political, and financial obstacles. Underlying these potentially solvable problems, however, is the long-standing but mistaken belief that intelligence and affect form two separate realms of experience. Although researchers have been amassing evidence about the adaptive nature of feelings for more than a century, the dualistic split between reason and emotion that goes back almost to the roots of our civilization will likely continue to prevail until the developmental perspective is fully understood and accepted.

An educational system that serves the needs of our society is compelled to recognize children's developmental levels, deal with individual differences, and foster dynamic affective interactions. We do not need to justify such interactions as part of training in social skills or other desirable goals that some argue should be left within the purview of the family. Rather, their importance is demonstrated by the fact that they are inextricably interwoven with the process of learning.

CHAPTER ELEVEN

Conflict Resolution and the Levels of the Mind

CHILDREN CAN TEACH US A LOT ABOUT HOW NOT TO SETTLE disputes. While conflict resolution provides ongoing employment for police, lawyers, judges, marriage counselors, and diplomats, most people first witness it in the playroom and the school yard. Forever after, many disputants, whether members of rival gangs, law firms, ethnic groups, or nations, continue to behave like the children they once were. Two grown men coming close to blows over who first spied the only empty bar stool resemble nothing so much as a pair of preschoolers shoving each other over possession of a toy car. A professional athlete refusing to don his uniform unless his salary tops a teammate's acts as enviously as a seven-year-old complaining that another child got more time at his turn in the game they are playing. A young thug punching a passerby whose expression he deems disrespectful acts on perceived humiliation in the same way as a kindergartner tripping the classmate who calls him a nasty name. Though other emotions fuel discord, this triad—greed, envy, and humiliation—gives rise to most conflict, whether sandbox squabbles or wars.

LEVELS OF DISCORD

Not only the emotions involved but ways of handling conflict have roots in childhood. When conflicts remain unresolved, we often label the adversaries' petty, intransigent behavior childish. Perhaps the characteristic that most strikingly separates the approach of children—and of persons of all ages who have difficulty dealing with conflict—from the kind of approach that we consider mature is the resort to impulsive or what we call "concrete" action rather than reflection.

Concrete behavior is motivated by feelings translated immediately into action. When a person operating in this mode wants something, she senses her desire as a reality in its own right that compels her to act. She craves a gooey brownie, so she takes one. A friend or her husband angers her, so she lashes out. An associate's promotion makes her jealous, so she repeats a malicious story about the rival. For a person stuck at this level, strong emotions permit no alternative to seeking immediate gratification.

A person operating in a reflective mode, by contrast, recognizes that her emotional reactions have no independent existence outside her head. In themselves, her feelings have no power to force any particular action. She may want a brownie but, knowing that she has to control her cholesterol, she reflects on her desire, moderates it, and chooses an apple instead. A friend or her husband angers her, so she makes her feelings known in an unthreatening manner and restores amity. Her envy surges when she sees another's success, so she discusses with her boss how she can qualify for advancement. The reflective person's feelings, rather than triggering action, signal the need to recognize a situation and change it. She doesn't deny her emotions but uses them as clues to make judgments. Rather than driving immediate action, feelings switch on the mental processes that lead to consideration of how to act. When two people who are seriously at odds lash out, they damage the possibility of mending their relationship. This possibility exists only when the disputants can react reflectively rather than impulsively, appreciate one another's needs and desires, and weigh the most sensible course of action.

People who do badly at resolving conflicts resemble small children in other respects as well. For example, their tendency to polarize issues leads them to distort experiences and express their views through unyielding demands, slogans, and rituals. They see themselves as the good guys, stalwart supporters of positions that are just. Their adversaries, by definition self-serving villains, must therefore support evil ones. All right resides on one side, all wrong on the other. This approach can be seen in children as young as three, the age at which they begin shifting blame to others. "He hit me first!" a youngster whines, conveniently forgetting the teasing that precipitated the first punch. Younger siblings expertly goad older ones—out of parents' sight, of course. While the innocent victim bawls, the older brother or sister is punished for striking first.

Once combatants of any age polarize a situation, positions harden and overwhelm any perception that the other person may also have a legitimate grievance. Each overlooks his own role in fomenting dissension and believes his self-righteous version of events. The interpretation of the causes of World War II heard in Japan, for example, astounds Americans with its claims of victimhood and complete discounting of Pearl Harbor. The conflict in the Middle East derives from the same kind of passion on both sides, the conviction of each that it holds the moral high ground. Battling spouses routinely forget their own roles as instigators. Parents, furious with rebellious, ungrateful children, often lose sight of their own contributions to family discord.

Polarization not only encourages but in fact requires such distortions. Otherwise how could anyone who fairly weighed all sides fail to see the multiple causes of conflicts? How could anyone with any experience of life believe that a given rule or principle holds true in every possible situation? Or that anyone's motives are ever entirely pure? Or that whole categories of people regarded with disdain always act in particular loathsome ways? Distortions and stereotypes of this kind are supported by simplistic slogans, like the line "better dead than red" of the McCarthyites, and can produce ugly acts of ritualistic terror, such as anonymous men in white hoods burning a cross on a lawn at midnight.

Polarized thinking thus goes hand in hand with every hatred born of in-group membership, whether racial, national, or religious. Teen gangs and ideologues both divide the universe into "us" and "them." Such thinking fosters ironclad beliefs impervious to scrutiny.

"All girls are dumb," chant third-grade boys as they heave water balloons across the school yard. Slogans and epithets abound: "Yankee go
home," the notion of a "yellow peril," the idea that police are "pigs"—
the list is endless. Slogans erase all the gray tones required in any
accurate appraisal of an individual or situation. Ritual responses keep
people from noticing that they see everything in black and white.

Polarization also feeds the need to win unconditionally. The
only satisfactory solution becomes total realization of one's maximum
demands. Group A, for example, must possess all the territory promised to them by God or won for them by their legendary hero or
traditionally inhabited by their people. Group B must completely
control the government, denying their adversaries any chance to exercise power.

Sometimes during negotiations parties are able to rank their
objectives in order of priority and discover that both sides can attain
their most important ones. More often, however, conflict resolution
involves compromise, with each party letting go of some objective
previously deemed critical. In negotiations between Israel and its
Arab neighbors, for example, Israel may be prepared to give up land
captured in prior wars for a peace treaty and assurances of security.
Each party gets something and each party gives something up. Such a
resolution can occur only when people can move beyond impulsive
action and polarization. Individuals negotiating a contract or neighbors with different ideas about how high the hedge separating their
property should be or what type of fertilizer to use on their lawns
must pause long enough to grasp what each of them is actually trying
to achieve.

Conflict resolution, however, is not a purely cognitive enterprise
or a rational weighing of options. It involves other capacities as well:
the ability to empathize and a moral sensibility, both of which stem
from mastery of the different levels of emotional development. In
many ways, a person's ability to deal with conflict is a natural extension of her ethical or moral awareness. Successful conflict resolution
requires the ability to put yourself in another's shoes, to acknowledge
and empathically experience the other's objectives. It's difficult to give
up any of your own goals if you can't intuitively understand the reasons the other person feels so strongly about his own.

To be able to empathize with others, however, and to compare their position with your own and then consider various trade-offs requires more than perceptiveness. Many people size up others and their intentions in order to try to outsmart them. Such manipulations will perpetuate rather than resolve conflict. A child vying with another for a certain present under the school Christmas tree might put an empty box with fancy ribbons on the pile. Bargaining with the other child, he might emphasize the huge size of the box he contributed and its flamboyant red ribbons. He might even convince the other child that no one is allowed to open his present until later. Needless to say, when the other child opens his box and sees only tissue paper, the temporary resolution of the conflict will break down. Preposterous as this example sounds, the child's brazen approach is not unlike that taken in some business and labor-management negotiations.

Lasting resolution of conflicts demands a high level of moral development. It involves equitable, empathic negotiation of the true needs of both parties. A resolution by which both parties give up a little and gain a little requires maturity on both sides. Immature but streetwise individuals, for their part, may negotiate merely to gain further advantages, not necessarily to resolve conflicts. Such "resolutions" are rarely stable. The conflict is temporarily smoothed over until one party discovers that the box is empty.

Another common error in conflict resolution results from assuming that those involved have the ability to represent their own desires as well as the desires of others symbolically. Individuals who lack this ability can only act out their intentions and wishes. A child who believes she can get whatever she wants simply by taking it often can hardly imagine her own needs and wishes in terms of an abstract feeling state, an urge, yearning, or desire. She simply pictures what she wants. Her approach to conflict resolution is to increase the immediate likelihood of getting what she wants, not to reflect and identify with the needs of others, which might lead to a long-term resolution.

Part of the tendency to polarize, the inability to deal with shades of gray and ambivalent or nuanced emotions, creates a further obstacle to resolving conflicts. Feelings of sadness or loss often accompany relief and satisfaction at the completion of successful negotiations.

Those who operate with polarized, all-or-nothing views have a hard time accepting these gray areas—that, say, the settlement of a conflict gives both parties at least some of what they wanted, but at the same time leaves them both a little disappointed. The fact that each of them is better off than if the conflict continued is entirely overlooked. The ability to tolerate loss and disappointment without disintegrating into tantrums or depression is an advanced mental capacity. This ability has its roots in the first five years of life, but it isn't well developed, even under the best circumstances, much before the age of nine or ten, or even twelve. Many people struggle to develop it throughout their lives.

TEACHING CONFLICT RESOLUTION

The teaching of conflict resolution skills in schools often assumes that most children will be capable of settling disputes if they know some of the steps to take, such as not hitting or hurting, talking rather than acting, and trying to compromise. While these steps are very important, many adults as well as children do not have the underlying emotional foundations necessary to follow them in more than a rote manner.

When empathy and an ability to tolerate disappointment are missing, people fall back on polarized thinking and unreflective action. A person who cannot hold in mind several different feelings, label them, and see the connections among them will not be able to evaluate the balance of feelings that motivate her adversary or imagine the incentives that might encourage him to negotiate. She cannot select the strategies that would let her deal simultaneously with her own and her adversary's wishes in order to sort out competing goals and desires.

To say that a person does not have such powers of reflection, however, is not to say that she is completely helpless before emotional ambiguity. Even if she can label only some of her feelings ("I'm really angry about that remark") but not sets of opposing feelings ("I'm really angry about that remark but don't want to start a feud in the family"), she can in effect "count to ten" before taking action, and her course will be less impulsive.

Game theory is often used in teaching conflict resolution. Whether applied to nuclear disarmament or to arguments over who got more candy, game theory shows that when contending parties try to achieve their aims in an all-or-nothing way, they often end up losing what they already have—spilling the candy or destroying the world. By contrast, when there is give-and-take and both parties are able to operate in the gray area, they each maximize their gains. The ability to put up with various shades of gray, however, requires a higher level of emotional thinking than is possible for many adversaries.

Underlying the ability to resolve conflicts are three fundamental skills developed over many years: the ability to engage empathically with others and imagine oneself in their situation; the ability to picture symbolically one's own and others' intentions; and the ability to tolerate disappointment, which allows gray-area thinking. Learning methods of conflict resolution, in short, requires maturity in the student; otherwise this knowledge is built on sand.

In teaching conflict resolution, therefore, we must support the emotional skills that go along with it. This may mean that we have to take several steps backward before we can go one forward. Children who have been deprived of warm, consistent relationships must learn to trust others in intimate interactions and to develop compassion. If there is no nurturing adult in a child's home, such a relationship must be found at school, on a sports team, in a mentoring program or church youth group, or in some other long-term setting. Children who tend to act out their feelings need to be helped to learn to picture their emotions and desires, and those whose thinking easily becomes polarized need to learn to tolerate ambivalence in the linking of feelings of disappointment and loss with satisfaction and achievement.

Whether aimed at children or adults, effective programs for teaching conflict resolution must begin at a much more basic level than outlining bargaining skills. They must help build the emotional structures that support the high-level capacities needed to negotiate mutually satisfactory settlements. These emotional foundations, it goes without saying, are not established through weekly classes or crash courses or retreats alone. However helpful these efforts might be to people whose thinking is mature, the essentials of conflict resolution are learned only from day-to-day experiences that let individuals advance through the stages of emotional development. A child who is angry or emotionally needy or who lacks friendships or other close ties cannot be expected to grow into a person who can reach agreement with an adversary. Fear of conflict may sometimes impose an apparent ceasefire, but the true capacity for resolving differences grows from within.

CHAPTER TWELVE

Marriage

THE EFFECTS OF STUNTED EMOTIONAL GROWTH AND IMMATURE mental levels are nowhere so vivid as in marriage. Half of all husbands and wives are unable to work out their differences and maintain stable families. Although many appear to marry for what seem to be the "right" reasons and complement each other personally, they eventually drift apart or become adversaries. The ability to deal with changes such as the birth of children, financial stress, and job shifts while remaining close and committed seems beyond most couples.

George and Alice, for example, seemed perfectly matched; everyone said so. Her warmth and solicitude recalled the emotional bolstering he had enjoyed from his devoted mother. His quiet, easygoing competence buffered her from many problems—balky electrical appliances, mysterious automotive malfunctions, the threat of burglars—that confused, frightened, or unnerved her. From the start, his good looks and obvious ardor promised the considerate, reliable sexual partner she needed.

They shared a romance that allowed them to give and receive what each loved most. She had always favored men who both craved attentive care and admired women who supplied it. His serious relationships had consistently involved very nurturing women. Their delighted families and friends came to the wedding without the trepidation that so often accompanies nuptials in these uneasy times. No one imagined that George and Alice could be destined for anything but a blissful golden anniversary surrounded by numerous happy offspring.

To the surprise of everyone, including themselves, only ten years and two children later George and Alice found themselves not at the altar renewing their vows but in court dissolving them. The loving union of the early days had degenerated into continual bickering and resentment intermittently punctuated by rancorous quarrels. She was "controlling and intrusive," George averred. He was "withdrawn, overcritical, and neglectful," Alice countered. Her "incessant and unnecessary nagging" and his "coldness and rejection" had made their life together impossible. "Irreconcilable differences," the judge agreed.

What changed the marriage of this devoted, compatible pair into yet another acrimonious failure? Americans ask this question millions of times a year as couples every bit as committed, every bit as sincere, every bit as hopeful as George and Alice watch their marriages disintegrate. Most of them, captivated by the romantic ideal of our culture, married for love. But all too soon, many find themselves inexplicably separated by bitterness they can neither bridge nor fathom. Observers offer many reasons for this all too common pattern of breakdown, blaming increasingly unclear gender roles, growing economic pressures, ever more lax sexual norms, shifting moral values, lesser degrees of commitment, and societal stress. But however valid, such vague cultural generalities do not completely clarify why so many marriages collapse.

Our developmental perspective helps to pinpoint the processes that lead to the deterioration of relationships. In particular it suggests a basic though insufficiently appreciated cause: many intelligent, successful people lack the emotional capacities needed to handle the predictable conflicts that arise during the course of any marriage.

THE HIDDEN CONTRACT

Like any partnership lasting an extended period of time, a married couple faces unexpected challenges and thus the potential for discord as circumstances change. To preserve their relationship, mates must possess the high-level reflective skills needed to readjust their roles and expectations repeatedly to fit the situation at hand. Indeed, an absolutely basic requirement of any alliance with a hope of succeeding, let alone prospering, over the long term—whether a marriage, a business partnership, a sports team, or a club—is that members possess the means and ability to make changes and settle conflict. They must, in other words, be able as the need arises to renegotiate the contract that defines their relationship.

Business partners usually set out the terms of their collaboration in detailed written contracts prepared by lawyers knowledgeable about the difficulties that may arise. Sports teams operate under practices standard in their game as interpreted by coaches, managers, and referees. Organizations follow written bylaws and *Robert's Rules of Order.*

Marriages also operate according to the terms of an agreement between the parties that establishes a division of labor and satisfactions to which both partners assent. But unlike the contracts of corporations, teams, or clubs, the agreements reached when couples marry are usually unspoken. While newlyweds might explicitly decide who will prepare dinner and who the tax returns, whether they want to have children, where they will live, and what silver pattern they will choose, more basic issues are left unaddressed: who has the role of comforting, or of bossing, or of depending on, or of worrying about whom. Each partner, moreover, brings to the marriage a whole bundle of unspoken assumptions about these issues, largely modeled on the relations between his or her parents.

Lovers rarely bargain openly about their emotional relationship. Indeed, central to the mystique of falling in love is precisely the certainty that the beloved understands one's profoundest desires and beliefs without being told. Instead, guided partly by personal and cultural expectations and partly by conscious and unconscious needs, during their courtship couples tacitly negotiate how to get along. Through these initial negotiations, they often arrive at a close and mutually very satisfying fit—satisfying because, mythology notwithstanding, people don't pick romantic partners at random. Quite apart from the ineffable qualities of love, one individual becomes committed to another because of that thrilling sense of being truly understood; put another way, because the beloved's qualities mesh with deep-seated needs within one's own psyche.

George and Alice complemented each other in very important respects. Her need to gain satisfaction, identity, and esteem by giving care fit his intense but unstated need to be cared for. He gained a sense of power and efficacy, meanwhile, by mastering the practical difficulties from which she craved protection. Each admired and enjoyed the other and treasured the relationship because of the sense of security and acceptance each felt in the other's presence. They fell in love basking in mutual appreciation and fulfillment. Both, in other words, supposed that they had at last found the stable, deeply gratifying relationship that we Americans believe to be everyone's birthright.

Unfortunately, several obstacles stood in the way of their realizing these dreams over a lifetime. Our romanticized notions about "falling" in love themselves create dangerous expectations. By emphasizing the individual's passivity before an inexorable force, they encourage people to believe that sound, enduring relationships are something that happen to people rather than something they create. Nothing a person actively *does,* the myth goes, causes the intractable "chemistry" to take hold. Nothing need or can be done, it therefore seems to many, to maintain the magic.

These assumptions bring in train a whole tangle of other, equally unrealistic expectations. In their first exhilaration, many lovers believe that the new partner will provide everything they ever vainly sought in previous relationships. Such high hopes, held by both partners, in turn burden them both. Laboring under the responsibility of fulfilling unspoken expectations, they must meet standards and play roles not only to which they have not agreed, but of which they may not even have heard. Should either partner fail to meet the requirements of this hidden contract, the hurt and anger felt by the disappointed spouse may gradually build into rage and accusation, with each spouse blaming the other for the squabbles and irritations that inevitably arise.

THE SURPRISE PACKAGE

The tie that holds couples together in the early stages of romance is usually a sense of well-being and security that each feels in the presence of the other—a sense that harks back to feelings the partners may have known as small children and that they consciously or unconsciously wish to recapture. Moving through courtship toward marriage, the couple codifies this exchange of satisfaction and gratification in an undeclared contract. The reasons that brought them together in the first place become implicit expectations inscribed in the psyche of each.

Like many other couples, George and Alice in their dating days unknowingly reached just such a balance between his need for nurturing and hers for protection. Living together after the wedding, however, they underwent a subtle shift. Both became aware of the strings attached to the exchange. He wanted her to provide warmth and caring without what he considered emotional intrusion. She wanted security and appreciation for her efforts, but not a relationship in which nurturing went only in one direction.

Every human being has traits apart from those that captivate a romantic partner. We are all complex packages of attributes and qualities—desires, beliefs, habits, memories—some of which will be compatible with those of the partner, others not. Along with the traits that mesh nicely, individuals bring to a relationship some that fit together less perfectly or even clash.

It is absurd for someone to expect that another human being should embody only those characteristics that he or she wants or needs. And yet, under the sway of the mythos of romantic love, that is just what many of us do. Piggybacked on George's desire for emotional support was his resentment of the controlling intrusiveness that went along with it. Coupled with Alice's pleasure in showing thoughtful concern was her feeling that she sometimes deserved to be looked after herself. But neither George nor Alice was willing to take the bad along with the good. Living together day by day made them ever more aware of the less desirable elements of the total package that they had initially ignored. Squabbles began. Why did she have to know every place he went? Why couldn't he show her more warmth? Forgetting the good qualities that had drawn them together, each began taking these for granted and complaining of the other's supposed faults—which were not serious character flaws but merely aspects of personality that fell outside the original contract. Irritation began to build.

When first one son and then a second entered the family, friction became even more pronounced. Children and their demands alter the nature and equilibrium of any marriage. So major a change requires a thoroughgoing renegotiation of roles and responsibilities. George and Alice, however, stumbled toward a new balance completely unawares. Raising the boys richly satisfied Alice's essentially maternal nature but exhausted her both physically and emotionally, so that little of her supply of caring remained for George. Meanwhile, when one of the boys, hungry or frightened by a nightmare, would bawl at three in the morning and Alice would go and comfort him, she found herself wanting to be tended too.

George also found the original contract inhibiting. His performance in the troubleshooting and fix-it role became less dependable as he coped with new responsibilities, including working extra hours to pay the family's higher expenses and to make up for the drop in income when Alice went part-time at her job. Lightbulbs stayed unchanged and the car unserviced longer than Alice had grown to expect. Busier and more tired, and getting less emotional support and more demands from Alice, he desired her less and resented her more. Their lovemaking dwindled as he withdrew emotionally from his wife and began to meet some of his need for intimacy through spending time with his sons.

Couples who successfully manage the transition to parenthood arrive at a new balance of needs and satisfactions. Unable to give or receive as much spousal attention as before, the partners often satisfy some of their need for comfort, admiration, and fulfillment by watching one another love and care for the child or by basking in the glow of the child's well-being. The new equilibrium broadens their roles and self-definitions from simply being spouses to being parental partners.

George and Alice, for their part, did not arrive at a satisfactory new contract. Instead, each privately nursed accumulating grievances. Rather than realizing that their mutual discomfort arose from the changes inherent in the progression from courting pair first to married couple and then to a family, each blamed his or her personal pain on the shortcomings of the other. Alice felt deprived not only of the sense of protection she needed to feel safe but of occasions for sexual intimacy as well. George felt unconsoled, even abandoned. Disgruntlement and chronic irritation grew. Each assumed that, since the original, blissful feelings had vanished, the partner's affection and concern must have as well. Cold war ensued, interspersed with increasingly frequent pitched battles.

George and Alice's sad downward trajectory is traced in countless homes across America every year. Millions of couples find themselves similarly locked in conflict as their circumstances shift and their initial unspoken contracts become obsolete. If fate adds to these normal stresses other, more severe, ones—a child with a significant physical or developmental disability, serious illness or death in the family, financial reverses, natural disaster, a transfer away from friends and family, or any of the multitude of other difficulties and misfortunes that befall people—then the possibility of misunderstanding and conflict becomes greater still. The likelihood that a couple already at odds can successfully redraft the original tacit agreement declines commensurately.

Why should sincere and caring people fail to achieve this revision of roles and expectations? In the previous chapter we had a preview of the reasons disputes go unresolved. Successful settlement of conflicts requires an ability on both sides to understand one's own and the other person's needs, to express these needs, and to tolerate feelings of loss and disappointment. Very few resolutions of disagreements meet all of each side's demands. Lasting ones, however, meet enough of both parties' wants and needs that they see what they give up versus what they get as an equitable trade-off. Working out such a bargain, especially within the charged emotional atmosphere of marriage, requires that both partners be able to empathize and to reflect on their feelings, skills that many may not have.

When a new understanding on which to base the marriage is not reached, the kind of polarized conflict that developed between George and Alice is the result. In their marriage stress and hostility mounted. Alice would lose her temper, screaming at George when he disappointed her. He would respond by withdrawing, sometimes literally walking away from conversations. Neither could tolerate venturing onto any middle ground. Each blamed the other for the breakdown of communication.

In light of the developmental model, the sad puzzle of George and Alice becomes much less mysterious. They could not manage the renegotiation necessary to maintaining their marriage because they could not manage the emotional level necessary to resolve their conflicts. Like many people locked in rancorous disputes, neither considered an obvious possibility: that the infuriating, inflexible partner lacked not the desire but the means to act in a manner that would foster conciliation.

When adversaries cannot reach agreement, observers often assume that simple orneriness bars the way. Clearly, they believe, at least one of the parties (if not both) doesn't want to agree; at least one lacks the interest or motivation or good will needed to find common ground. For the participants, each certain of his or her own desire to salvage the situation, it seems only natural to conclude that the other is being purposefully stubborn or unreasonable. But such suspicions only deepened George's and Alice's distress. Each knew that the other had grown up in a "good" home. Each knew that the other had had the benefit of responsible and loving care. What George and Alice did not know is that they each lacked not decency or concern for their family but the high-level reflective skills needed to handle the renegotiating they faced. While growing up, neither had experienced the kind of interactions that would enable them to acquire these skills. Both came from families held together not by continually working out a new balance but by strong social and religious sanctions against divorce. Both, in fact, had grown up among adults who, though they were good, loving people, had not reached much beyond the level of polarized emotional thinking. In the context of today's shifting gender roles, the restructuring that George and Alice's partnership needed required a genuine ability to accept compromise and consequently the shades of gray in their marriage.

As frustrations pile up, so do the outward signs of a situation fraught with unresolved tensions. Fights and arguments multiply. Passivity and withdrawal increase, as do self-absorption and negativism. Partners may grow fearful or distracted and even experience physical ailments like sore throats or bellyaches. Each does everything possible to advance his or her own position and almost nothing that would advance the couple toward concord.

George and Alice, for all the intensity of their early love, for all the comfort their relationship gave them, for all the good intentions that each brought to the marriage, could not survive as a couple because they were struck at a level of emotional development that precluded a mature approach to conflict. Neither could represent or tolerate feelings of hurt, loss, or disappointment, so both acted on them without thinking. Neither could see the other's good qualities and failings at the same time. As their images of one another became polarized, each accused the other of malice and betrayal. Neither perceived that the other's grievances had any reasonable basis or hurt as much as his or her own. Though adults, emotionally both functioned more like children.

THE MARRIAGE OF LIKE MINDS

The troubles of George and Alice, so common among couples today, rest on another curious fact: people tend to choose mates at their own developmental level. Once marital troubles set in, they often feel themselves superior to their spouses, complaining that he is boorish and insensitive, that she is unbearably emotional and intrusive. Clinical experience suggests, however, that couples generally interact at a developmental level common to both partners.

Imagine the situation in one household where the husband arrives home from work to find dinner late and his wife engrossed on the phone. He snaps at her; she hangs up, then bursts into tears. Weary and wary of an argument, he retreats to the family room, turns on the television, and parks himself before it, ignoring her pleas to listen. She returns to the kitchen and eventually calls the family for the tardy meal. He begins to eat, but partway through he attempts to break the painful silence. "Good meat loaf," he says.

Encouraged, his wife says, "Thanks," and goes on to tell him that she was delayed by a call from a close friend who was extremely upset because she had just learned she might have breast cancer.

"That's too bad," he says.

"I know," she answers. "I feel really sorry for her. What if it happened to me?"

They then abandon this uncomfortable subject and talk about more mundane matters.

Next door, the husband also gets home to find his wife on the phone and dinner not started. She sees his look of annoyance as he enters the kitchen and slips her hand over the mouthpiece. "I'm sorry things are disorganized tonight. I know you're hungry, but this is important. Why don't you take some cheese and crackers and go watch the news?"

Catching the seriousness in her voice, the husband nods and heads for the cupboard. Later, over dinner, she explains. "Betty just found out she might have breast cancer. She's terribly upset—I was on the phone with her for close to an hour. It's really scary. She's just about my age, and it seems to be happening to so many people. I just sort of lost track of dinner."

"No wonder you're upset. I hate hearing those things, too. Betty is awfully young for something like that. I can wash up if you want to go see her." The issue, her husband realizes, is not just her concern for her friend but her anxiety because she too may be vulnerable.

The first couple obviously shares life at the level of concrete action, the second at one of reflective emotional reasoning. It's hard to imagine a member of either couple living for very long with a member of the other: their extremely different styles of reacting would give them little common ground on which to build emotional understanding of one another. The reflective individual's thoughtful and empathic responses would baffle someone used to behavioral responses, while the latter's concrete, impulsive actions would infuriate a person used to reasoning out emotional situations.

People tend to sort themselves by levels of emotional development for many purposes, not just marriage, because those functioning at different levels are practically speaking different languages. Much has been made in recent years of emotional and communicative differences between the sexes, but the effects of differences in developmental levels are vastly greater. People widely separated developmentally in fact have very little to talk about. A person at the level of concrete behavior thinks not in terms of how he feels but of what he does. An upset spouse or a delayed dinner does not lead him to put into words feelings of disappointment or discouragement or anger; instead he pouts, or counterattacks, or withdraws affection. A person at the level of emotional ideas, for his part, can pick up cues and imagine what the upset spouse may be feeling.

There are many reasons people gravitate to others at the same level of emotional development. Encountering someone at one's own level often sparks a sense of connectedness and deep understanding that contributes to friendship or romantic love. The other person intuitively understands your signals and references. Your partner considers your tendency to swing into action or to search for meanings and connections among motives and ideas the most natural thing in the world. In the early days of their relationship, George and Alice each found deep comfort in the other's orientation toward action and polarized thinking—ironically, the very qualities that ultimately doomed their marriage.

This tendency of spouses to share a similar emotional level does not mean that they have similar personalities. In fact, quite the opposite is true. The great majority of us choose partners whose personalities complement our own. Warm, nurturing Alice and self-contained, competent George each had emotional features that the other lacked. Two shy people, or two highly gregarious people, or two passive or very competitive people often find it difficult to continue courtship long enough to consider marriage. A pair of vivacious, outgoing chatterboxes would constantly compete for the floor, and each would miss the appreciative audience that makes talking fun. Neither one of two silent, contemplative types might make the social and emotional overtures needed to sustain a relationship. Two very neat, precise partners might drive themselves into a frenzy of perfectionism. A couple both given to mess and disorganization would find the details of their lives dissolving in confusion.

Indeed, happiness at finding someone who complements one's own way of being, who supplies a piece missing in one's own life and personality and thus bestows new enjoyment and security, is an element in the "chemistry" of romantic love. The new relationship frequently echoes an earlier one with a parent who also provided emotional features that the individual lacked, thus recreating a familiar interactive style. Only rarely does a romantic attachment long endure between partners very much like each other; they cannot each give the other that beguiling sense of emotional completeness. Alice's emotionality made George feel alive; George's stolidity made her feel protected. But the fact that two people's personalities are differently structured doesn't imply that they also function on different emotional levels. George and Alice, as we saw, both organized their minds mostly around action patterns and polarized thinking, not around abstract ideas or the habit of reflecting on their feelings.

TO LOVE, HONOR, AND REFLECT

In the past, society did much more to stabilize marriages between those who operated reactively or in terms of polarized extremes. Communities were smaller and had more rituals and routines that drew their members together. More clearly defined norms meant that people understood what constituted acceptable behavior and what they could expect of others. The contract between husband and wife depended less on unspoken emotional agreements and more on external, usually explicit, notions of proper behavior. Religious teachings offered precise guidelines on what matrimony entailed. Individual couples did not have to negotiate who would nurture and who protect, who had which rights and which responsibilities, or when they could separate.

All around them they saw their friends and neighbors holding to much the same agreements they did, as had generations of ancestors before them. Such tradition made for more stable families and less open discord, safeguarding the basic unit of society, the mechanism for rearing the next generation, from the failings of ordinary people.

In recent years, however, both men and women have faced increasingly complex demands as society has moved away from traditional sex roles and generally accepted moral values. Shifting roles force people to look more closely at their own desires and aspirations. By leaving more options open to individual choice, our society makes it much harder for people to depend on a specific code of action to structure their lives.

This new uncertainty and freedom compounds the need for couples to be able to think reflectively about their feelings rather than simply react to emotionally charged experiences. Spouses must constantly be in touch with both their own and their partners' viewpoints and continually renegotiate their personal contracts in a spirit of compromise. People who have these reflective capacities can use them to work out new and mutually acceptable agreements. In marriages like George and Alice's, however, neither partner is able to reason about his or her own needs well enough to go beyond them and consider those of the other. Neither can see that the hurt feelings and hostile behavior on one side arise from equally disappointed expectations on the other. Neither understands that, to stay together, both have to surrender some of their preferences and expectations.

Though the old system of defined rules might have helped many couples like George and Alice stay together, it bought that advantage at a stiff price. Our much less rigid society permits far more personal liberty, but the opportunities are sometimes more than a couple can handle. Ideally, of course, people find a balance between freedom and responsibility that sacrifices neither individual expression nor social stability. Creating a society that combines flexibility and order, marriages that permit individuality and harmony, and families that nurture growth as well as provide security is an ambitious goal. It requires that the majority of men and women be able to develop the higher levels of mental organization that allow reasoning and reflection about emotions.

Although some social critics would like to go back to the days of prescribed roles, fixed norms, and unbreakable marriage contracts, most of us would feel confined. To do without, however, we must find ways to raise children with the ability to understand their own feelings and appreciate the validity of those of others, to see the common interests of opponents in a dispute, and to weigh the consequences of actions for others as well as themselves. Individuals of all ages need continuing experiences that foster such capabilities. The effects of neglecting these foundations of mature intelligence go far beyond broken marriages.

CHAPTER THIRTEEN

Violence and Deprivation

OF ALL THE ISSUES FACING US TODAY, NONE MORE GRAVELY threatens our domestic tranquillity than the cluster of sorrows afflicting the poorest families of our inner cities. Americans know this nagging problem by a number of labels, all familiar from years of headlines and news broadcasts and from the fear city dwellers experience in their daily lives. We see it in statistics on violence, crime, drug addiction, school dropout rates, chronic unemployment, inner-city decay, the welfare crisis, teen pregnancy, family disintegration. At bottom, all these troubles stem from a single festering woe: the large number of families utterly incapable of equipping their children emotionally and intellectually to function as productive members of society.

Severe dysfunction is seen at every socioeconomic level. However, in a small proportion of our nation's poorest families, disadvantages linked to poverty can combine with other challenges to produce an environment in which children have little hope of gaining the emotional as well as intellectual skills necessary for success in life. The results are staggeringly lopsided: from perhaps only 5 percent of poor families come most of the young people who leave school incapable of holding a steady job; the remorseless thugs who terrorize our streets; the hard-core drug users who support, often through crime or prostitution, a vast and bloody industry; the unmarried teenage girls who bear babies they are completely unequipped to rear; the abused and neglected children making repeated circuits among chaotic families, public institutions, and foster homes; the parents who torment these pitiful youngsters; the inmates of our prisons and mental hospitals.

The large majority of families struggling against poverty, whether on or off welfare, do manage to impart good values through loving care. But a tiny slice continues, generation after generation, to inflict on their children lives of deprivation and pain and on society yet another wave of amoral, disruptive young people doomed to populate a self-perpetuating underclass.

Ending this cycle of desolation and despair, and the terrible consequences it carries, has become a central political issue of our time. The fear of crime distorts life in many neighborhoods, turning honest people, especially the elderly, into prisoners behind multilocked doors and barred windows. More and more ordinary citizens seek the right to carry concealed weapons. A relatively small number of antisocial young men responsible for gang mayhem, drive-by homicides, fatal face-offs over jackets or basketball shoes, carjackings, and muggings have effectively robbed others of the freedom and sense of safety that makes urban life possible.

Since this has not always been true in our towns and cities, and since a similar level of violence does not prevail in most European and even Canadian cities, we must assume that there are solutions. Indeed, from all points of the political spectrum pour proposals guaranteed to succeed: stricter rules, work requirements, orphanages, job training, labor camps, welfare, time limits, subsidized day care. It is unlikely, however, that any government program can cure so deep and intractable a pathology. The violently antisocial individual does not occur in a vacuum but is merely the most sensational symptom of the severe social deprivation that is to blame for a whole array of other problems: young people who cannot learn and cannot work; who are depressed, passive, suicidal, or otherwise mentally ill; or who destroy themselves and their futures with alcohol or drugs. Only an understanding of what lies at the root of this complicated pathology can guide us toward remedies. There is of course a considerable literature on developmental, family, and community factors associated with violence and crime.[1] To this, the developmental perspective adds a clarifying view.

It used to be thought that parents' educational level rather than emotional competence best predicted a child's intelligence. Studies could not tease apart whether IQ scores reflected genetic endowment, habits of reading and conversation in the home, degree of economic stress on family members, access to educational or cultural resources, ability to meet emotional needs, or some combination of all of these. However, research that Arnold Sameroff of the University of Michigan and I took part in along with others concluded that emotional risk factors, independent of social class or parents' education, correlated with cognitive outcomes during childhood. Furthermore, when emotional risk factors were added to social and economic ones, we found that children who came from families with four or more adverse factors, such as depressed or addicted parents, a harsh emotional climate, poor education, low income, and low occupational or social standing, were twenty-four times likelier than children from homes with no more than one adverse factor to score below 85 in IQ. Kids from more fortunate families scored overwhelmingly in the normal to superior range. In addition, as expected, children from families plagued by difficulties suffered more behavioral problems. Follow-up studies of these children at age thirteen confirmed these findings.[2]

In a study aiming to isolate those aspects of caregivers' or families' actions and attitudes that underlie the difference, the way adults respond to their child's emotional and social cues emerged as decisive.[3] Adults who become partners in shared explorations and good readers of the child's intentions and wishes rather than those who are passive or overly directive are most able to nourish intelligence. Following the child's lead and reading and responding to her emotional cues rather than ignoring them or responding negatively also correlated with intelligence.[4]

Let me emphasize again that poverty alone does not account for the human wreckage of the underclass; countless people raised in impoverished circumstances live good and responsible lives. Nor does single parenthood or social upheaval or racism or any of the multitude of other factors commonly blamed. Victims of these mis-fortunes have managed to function as upright, productive citizens.

The severely damaged children who are now causing so much turmoil are from families caught in a complicated tangle of troubles. In these multirisk households, parents fail to fulfill even their most elementary obligations. The daily realities children in such families face include very young and incompetent mothers, often addicted to drugs or alcohol, severely depressed, or both; violent, abusive, and inconsistent treatment; material want; emotional deprivation; absent fathers or strife-ridden unions; and social instability and physical danger.

The combination of these conditions greatly multiplies a child's chance of growing up incapable of mastering the complexities of our increasingly technological society, finding and holding a job, or com-petently raising his own children. In the troubled fraction of the pop-ulation that we have described, many families suffer from several of these deficiencies. Half of all incarcerated women, for example, are not the sole members of their families behind bars. A third have parents who abused drugs or alcohol. A multiyear study of high-risk mothers and their children revealed that two-thirds of the women had experienced physical or sexual abuse or significant neglect during their own childhood; for fully half, abuse by family members or sexual partners continued into adulthood.[5]

Children from such backgrounds quite naturally show deficits at every stage and in every realm of development that render them un-suited to take advantage of the opportunities that are afforded by society. As we saw in Chapter 10, such youngsters fail early at book learning and drop out of school. They never learn the most rudimen-tary skills—punctuality, delaying gratification, conventional cour-tesy—needed to get jobs. As they move toward adulthood, they lack the credentials to enter legitimate channels of upward mobility such as the military or post–high school training. With normal paths to-ward independent adult status foreclosed, they fall back on the scanty resources of their beleaguered neighborhoods: crime, the drug trade, prostitution, welfare dependency.

All these later defeats grow out of early deficits, which in turn arise from the emotional deprivation and desolation of their early years. Because no competent adult ever cared enough or was in a position to nurture them, these children never mastered the developmental levels of mental organization. They often can't regulate their attention. They feel no trust and attach only shakily to other people. They convey their feelings and wishes poorly, with or without words, and act impulsively. They live barren inner lives devoid of fantasy. They don't know how to read the emotional cues of others and have no ability to tolerate loss or frustration.

These children, in short, have been shortchanged of the lessons that early emotional intimacy can teach. Their chaotic families have failed at even the most fundamental duties: to provide physical protection, emotional stability, and consistent warmth and care. Without drastic intervention, the kind of nurturing that would meet their emerging developmental needs is an unattainable, even unimaginable, luxury.

BREEDING VIOLENCE

As an example of such a childhood, consider the case of a young delinquent named Frank. For all of his nineteen years, Frank has lived a life that, though the result of cruel happenstance, could scarcely have been better designed to produce a violent, antisocial young man. At every stage in his development, the adults around him failed first to provide the nurturing he needed to progress through the normal developmental levels and then, through maintaining caring and intimate relationships, to begin to repair the damage already done. The environment in which this unfortunate youngster grew up was almost guaranteed to transform a naturally high activity level, low sensitivity to touch and sound, high tolerance for pain, and low threshold of frustration into anger, aggression, and unfeeling brutality.

Frank's natural constitution fits the active, aggressive pattern profiled in Chapter 6. He was a large, strong, very energetic infant who slept little and constantly reached, moved, and fidgeted in his search for stimulation. When he did fall asleep, only quite loud noises would arouse him. His mother, Trina, a single teenager, already had an eighteen-month-old boy when Frank arrived, and a third baby, a girl, was born seventeen months later, just before her nineteenth birthday.

Trina had dropped out of high school at the birth of her first son and since then had depended on welfare to support herself and her family in a small, dingy apartment in a squalid housing project.

Caring for even one child as challenging as Frank was beyond Trina's resources, and the demands of three babies under three utterly defeated her. Always disorganized and usually depressed, she became increasingly withdrawn, passive, and dependent on drugs and therefore was less emotionally available to her children as her family grew. Frank was the most frustrating of her babies. His underreactivity made him unresponsive to Trina's sporadic attempts at affection, while his physical strength and high activity level made him a whirling dervish whenever she let him out of his crib or playpen. Trina's solution was to park him in front of a television set, turned up loud to catch his attention. For extended periods she put little effort into wooing and cuddling or even changing and bathing him. Indeed, she frequently failed to meet even his needs for food and clean clothing.

Most of her emotional energy went into appeasing the string of boyfriends who kept her supplied with drugs and extra money and, incidentally, fathered her various children. Unemployed and themselves involved in drugs or heavy drinking, these men tended to be given to violent outbursts and were often abusive toward the children. None of them stuck around for very long. During the months when Frank should have been developing a sense of security, acquiring the ability to calm himself and regulate his attention, and intensely engaging with a devoted adult, Frank knew only fear, anger, and deprivation.

Shortly before Trina gave birth to her fourth child, her mother, Delilah, prevailed on the local social service agency to intervene. At just over two, Frank went with his brother and sister to live with their grandmother while their mother entered the first of several unsuccessful drug treatment programs. A kindly, churchgoing widow appalled at her daughter's way of life, Delilah struggled to give her three neglected grandchildren a good home. The small pension from her years as a hospital food service worker allowed her to devote herself to the children full-time. Her experience rearing her own brood of six— the other five of whom were more responsible and successful than Trina—equipped her to provide the warmth, emotional nurturing, and firm but gentle limits that Frank so desperately needed. Delilah's already failing health, however, deteriorated sharply under the strain of her new responsibilities.

By the time Frank had spent eight months in Delilah's care, he was on the road to positive development. After trusting no one in his short lifetime, he had begun to form a genuinely affectionate attachment to Delilah and was accumulating a repertoire of gestures that he used in interacting with her. Suddenly, however, her high blood pressure, which had troubled her for years and grown worse under the stress of looking after the children, erupted in a stroke that left Delilah partially paralyzed and incapable of caring for herself, let alone three active youngsters.

Trina's three sisters now divided her children among themselves. Frank went to Marie, who added the agitated three-year-old to a household that already included her own three children, one of whom had moderate cerebral palsy. Whereas Delilah had been affectionate and tender, Marie, though genuinely concerned about her nephew, had a less overtly emotional, more authoritarian style. Unable to continue using the gestures that had served him well with Delilah, the baffled toddler now found himself hard pressed to understand Marie's more subdued emotional range and signals. For her part, Marie was so highly stressed by the care of her disabled seven-year-old daughter, Natasha, as well as her job as a day-care center worker, that she lacked the insight or energy to meet Frank's urgent need to be wooed into another close and loving relationship. As she tried to integrate Frank into her household, Marie found herself increasingly locked into power struggles with a hostile, furious boy who refused to follow rules or respond to punishments that rapidly escalated into severe spankings.

Frank, meanwhile, let his anger out in ever more violent tantrums and soon in attacks on Marie's children. Finally, in a rage he kicked the defenseless Natasha off her bed and onto the floor. This was the last straw for Marie. Convinced that she could not harbor Frank and protect Natasha, she sought help from a social services agency. Frank was then placed in what proved to be the first of a series of foster homes. At the point when he should have been consolidating his ability to experience and feel security and love, read and respond to emotional gestures, create inner images of warmth, and use ideas to make plans and solve problems, Frank was sent to live in his fourth household, that of a married couple who had taken in almost a dozen children over a period of two decades.

Although friendly, competent, cheerful, responsible, and respectful of her charges' feelings, Mrs. Porter, Frank's new foster mother, had learned from bitter experience not to permit herself to form too close an attachment to any of them. Some years before a mother had unexpectedly reclaimed a child the Porters planned to adopt. Though she provided a warm, orderly, supportive home, Mrs. Porter always retained a certain reserve to protect herself from possible heartbreak.

She tried to encourage and gently discipline Frank, but neither she nor her husband engaged with him at a level deep enough to convince the increasingly angry and alienated boy that anyone truly cared for him. As for the emotional foundations of his growth, Frank had regressed to the problems he faced at the earliest levels. Like Marie, the Porters failed to enfold Frank in the human community. Though they saw that he got extra services at the local public school, where he was already falling behind, they did not succeed in having him transferred to a smaller, more personal class that might have met some of his needs for both intimacy and behavioral limits. Running their household more like a friendly dormitory than a genuine home for the children, they found Frank's aggressive behavior increasingly difficult to contain.

Just as they were considering talking with Frank's social worker about finding him a different placement, Trina reappeared in his life. Now recovering from her addictions, outfitted with a high school equivalency diploma, and determined to reconstitute her shattered family, she demanded and won custody of her four children and brought them to live with her in an apartment far from any of her relatives. Her current boyfriend, however, adjusted badly to the demands of the children. Before long he left the household, leaving Trina to cope with and support four youngsters who were essentially strangers to her and to each other. Although she struggled for a number of months to keep a job in a factory, her resolve gradually collapsed and she slipped back into drug abuse.

Frank was now old enough to fend for himself in matters of day-to-day survival, like grabbing food and putting on clothes, but he was falling further and further behind in both school and social development and was responding to the resulting humiliations with escalating aggression. Shortly after he pushed a schoolmate down a flight of stairs during an argument over a collision in the corridor, he was removed from Trina's custody and placed in another foster home and then a third. By the time he stopped going to high school at fifteen, Frank had moved to yet a fourth foster placement.

By now, the personal connectedness he had missed ever since he lost Delilah came mostly from the leader of a local drug gang who recruited neighborhood toughs with promises of wealth, status, and most important, attention. Frank eventually became one of his most effective "enforcers," moving up from fists to guns as he rose in the organization.

A boy whose boldness, energy, and dynamism might have been assets in a test pilot, a surgeon, a quarterback, or an entrepreneur thus became a brutal, remorseless thug. The difference between Frank and the kind of boy who might pursue such careers lies not in temperament or innate ability but in the fact that someone who aims to achieve in this way has "bought into" the human community and resolved to use his zest and courage for good. Frank, deprived of the chance for a deep and lasting human bond, never made the essential emotional connections that would have let him recognize the humanity he held in common with others. He never experienced the necessary intimacy that would have opened the human world to him. Because of this, he did not have the ability to read the nonverbal cues that communicate caring and support and instead misread threats into most social interactions. He developed neither empathy nor the capacity to represent his feelings nor the ability to restrain them—qualities needed to move beyond his primitive, emotion-driven reactive mode to the realm of self-reflection.

Frank was not genetically destined for his sorry fate. His constitutional characteristics expressed themselves in a tendency to low sensory sensitivity and high activity, but not in any particular behavioral traits. Children like Frank do especially well when they are provided with stable, nurturing relationships, extra practice at moderating behavior, special support for using words and exercising their imaginations, consistent and firm but gentle limits, and opportunities to learn self-reflection.

Not all at-risk children are like Frank. Some show the effects of their lost opportunities in quieter, more hidden ways. One such child, Tony, was born robust in body and mind. No deficits, either physical or cognitive, clouded the innate possibilities of this bright, well-coordinated, sociable infant. Early on he looked directly at people, followed sounds with bright, eager eyes, and seemed to be trying to reach out and even babble—all of which suggested precocious cognitive and motor skills. Barely into his second year he was running, making lots of sounds, using several words and short phrases, and hunting for hidden objects. Unlike Frank, he was easygoing and slow-moving; when frustrated, he was remarkable in his independence and self-reliance, often looking at picture books or playing on his own.

Gradually, however, Tony began to fall behind in the progress expected for a healthy, well-developing boy of his age. As he reached his second birthday, he put less and less effort into relating to those around him and very little into using the handful of words he had learned to utter. He became ever more self-absorbed. He seemed to misread others' intentions, often turning away as though he expected little pleasure from interaction.

By the time he reached preschool at age four, though he had begun to speak more fluently, he found it difficult to attend to the lessons his teachers presented. Easily bored, he would daydream or gaze about him at objects around the room. He used toys more as barriers to others than as vehicles for shared imagination and collaborative play. He ignored the cues and needs of others and tried to comfort himself in self-talk. He often nodded yes to requests but quickly seemed to forget or ignore what was asked. He made a slow start at learning his letters and numbers and consistently lagged behind in preparation for reading and math.

From the very start, Tony found school and peer relationships a constant and demoralizing struggle. Humiliated by his inability to keep up with either the other pupils or his teachers' expectations, he began avoiding other children to a greater and greater degree. Whereas as a toddler he had placed in the bright range on tests of

language and cognition, his scores now slid toward the lower end of
the curve. By age ten, he was spiraling downward into failure and
despair. He read at only a rudimentary level, showed an increasing
tendency toward depression, and before he was thirteen started using
various types of drugs.

Tony's family was characteristic of the multiproblem families
who are unable to support healthy emotional and intellectual growth.
Although his parents were well educated, his mother's severe substance abuse, beginning during Tony's second year of life, and his
father's abruptly leaving the family led to a series of unstable foster
placements. His undemanding, independent tendencies encouraged
his overstressed caregivers to let him fend for himself. Children like
Tony are especially sensitive to loss, however, and require exceptionally
wooing types of nurture to pull them into relationships and help them
learn to use their considerable skills assertively and confidently.

At any of a number of points in Frank's and Tony's sad histories, a
caring adult could have intervened to help them make the emotional
connections that would have let them feel a part of the human community. An intense relationship with a relative, foster parent, teacher, cler-
gyman, coach, or mentor could have done much to help either of these
children. But because of the multiple failures of the people and institutions charged with their care, no such relationship ever developed.

The restorative influence of just one caring adult, even when a
child is already well along in his development, is well established. A
long-term study by Milton Shore and Joseph Massimo in Massachusetts, for example, recruited a group of male high school dropouts to
participate in intensive mentoring relationships with male counselors.
A control group received no such opportunity. The counselor was
available to help teach his charge math at his job at the gas station,
argue on his behalf with the local police, help him figure out what to
say to a girlfriend—in short, to meet the teenager at his developmental level, on his turf. Through this unusually nurturing relationship, the mentor helped the youngster begin to learn how to relate
and trust—to read help, not just hostility, in others' overtures—
and to create images of warmth and support to guide his inner life
and problem-solving efforts.

More than twenty years later, 80 percent of those who had received mentoring were functioning well on the job, in their families, and in the world at large, whereas 80 percent of those in the control group were embroiled in the criminal justice or mental health system. More important, psychological testing revealed substantial differences in the inner lives of those who had been mentored. They were significantly more likely to find comfort in closeness with others, and were able to anticipate, plan, and reflect.[6] Although similar mentoring of such a severely deprived boy as Frank might well take years, he was not genetically or otherwise doomed. Regardless of age, youngsters can begin working on developmental levels they have been unable to master, but they can do so only in the context of a close, personal relationship with a devoted adult.

Ideally, intervention should begin early in life. There is now considerable evidence that a variety of early interventions can be effective. Sally Provence and Audrey Naylor found that work with families helped children do better in school and have fewer difficulties as they grew up.[7] Alice Honig and Ronald Lally showed that family support and early opportunities for socialization and cognitive enrichment improved academic and social functioning.[8] David Olds demonstrated a correlation between early family support and decreased teenage pregnancy and delinquent behavior.[9]

Two studies that followed children into adulthood, the Perry Preschool project and the Carolina Abecedarian program, have shown enduring social and intellectual gains.[10] In addition, the multicentered Infant Health and Development Program, modeled after the Abecedarian project, has demonstrated positive gains, as does analysis of the effects of Head Start programs.[11] Other ongoing undertakings are the well-known Parents as Teachers program, in effect in a number of states; Chicago's Ounce of Prevention Fund; and the work of the South End Community Health Center in Boston. There is wisdom from the past, such as the model developed by the historically important Peckham project, begun in London in 1935. Establishing a health center to serve as a social, recreational, and psychological as well as medical resource for disadvantaged families, it illustrated the usefulness of an integrated approach to the support of human development.[12] Lisbeth Schorr, in her book *Within Our Reach*, provides an excellent overview of programs that have worked and guidelines that would make them more effective in addressing all aspects of the challenge.[13] Studies of intervention efforts, including those that work and those that do not, support the efficacy of early preventive measures for a variety of emotional and developmental problems. They also point out that most intervention efforts are not comprehensive enough, in particular in the way they involve parents and families.[14]

Most difficult is intervention in families facing multiple challenges. Such families are often so distrustful of services that they will not ask for help or participate in support programs. We have tended to give up on just those families that are most at risk. Though we have ample evidence of the importance of emotional interaction in the healthy development of intellectual and social skills, as a society we have not yet agreed on the core needs of children and the best ways to make sure these are met.

THE SEVEN IRREDUCIBLE NEEDS OF CHILDHOOD

The requirements for healthy development are neither mysterious nor complicated. In 1993 I had the privilege of chairing a discussion among a group of leading clinicians and researchers to see if, despite our varying theoretical orientations and interests, we could agree on a set of basic principles to guide support efforts for at-risk children in the 1990s and beyond.[15] Participants were Kathryn Barnard, T. Berry Brazelton, Urie Bronfenbrenner, Eugene Garcia, Irving Harris, Asa Hilliard, Sheila Walker, and Barry Zuckerman. To our considerable surprise, we concurred relatively expeditiously on seven principles that echo the requirements for sound mastery of the developmental stages described in Part One.

First, every child needs a safe, secure environment that includes at least one stable, predictable, comforting, and protective relationship with an adult, not necessarily a biological parent, who has made a long-term, personal commitment to the child's daily welfare and who has the means, time, and personal qualities needed to carry it out. Wealth and a high level of education are not among these qualities; what is essential are maturity, responsibility, responsiveness, understanding, and dedication.

Second, consistent, nurturing relationships with the same caregivers, including the primary one, early in life and throughout childhood are the cornerstones of both emotional and intellectual competence, allowing a child to form the deep connectedness that grows into a sense of shared humanity and, ultimately, empathy and compassion. Relationships with both parents and day-care staff must have this stability and consistency. If these ties are cut off at arbitrary points, such as at the ends of fiscal years or semesters or when a child has reached a specific age, new losses are inflicted on youngsters who may already be scarred by loss and upheaval. Home visiting programs, for example, often stop at the first birthday; supports for teenage mothers end when her child turns two, just as a toddler is building and cementing relationships with adults. Day-care facilities often experience high staff turnover, in part because of poor pay and working conditions. For bureaucratic ease, many exacerbate the problem by assigning children to new caregivers each year, both rupturing the child's ties and discouraging the caregiver from investing deeply in any given youngster. Foster parents generally receive too little support and too few incentives to make their charges permanent members of their families rather than temporary visitors. Without the assurance that ties to a particular child will be lasting, child-care workers quite understandably try to insulate themselves from the pain of repeatedly "falling in love" with youngsters they know they will have to leave. But without that spark of spontaneous adoration that almost any baby can, given time, strike in some willing adult, the child cannot enjoy full and healthy development.

Third is the need for rich, ongoing interaction. Love and nurturing, though essential, don't suffice. During the first five years of life, children learn about the world through their own actions and their caregivers' reactions. They cannot develop a sense of their own intentionality or of the boundaries between their inner and outer worlds except through extended exchanges with people they know well and trust deeply. As their development advances, their interactions with others should also gain in complexity and in subtlety. This assumes the caregiver's ability to read a child's individual signals and to respond flexibly and appropriately. Such a relationship, of course, is especially crucial in infancy, when the child's initiatives are at their most rudimentary. A recent study faults day-care centers generally for providing mediocre levels of interaction and finds infant nurseries most deficient of all.[16] Many programs purporting to help vulnerable children involve far too many group activities and static, formal curricula.

Fourth, each child and family needs an environment that allows them to progress through the developmental stages in their own style and their own good time. Only in this way can children cultivate a sense of themselves both as distinct individuals and as members of particular groups. Effective intervention programs must tolerate and take advantage of individual differences. Far too many, however, emphasize the common features of many or most families rather than the personal uniqueness that distinguishes each one. Without speaking a household's special "language," the professionals involved can all too easily misdiagnose children's abilities, creating self-fulfilling prophecies of difficulty and failure. Later, respect for individuality will afford older children and adolescents a chance to develop strong identities while exploring or potential identities.

Fifth, children must have opportunities to experiment, to find solutions, to take risks, and even to fail at attempted tasks. From trying different approaches, seeking out allies, and assessing all options emerge the perseverance and self-confidence needed to succeed at any serious endeavor. A child's self-worth and positive self-esteem are rooted in relationships that support her initiative and ability to solve problems. The lived experience of engaging with and overcoming challenges makes real her belief in her own powers. Many programs subscribe to these values in theory while in practice following procedures that encourage passivity and helplessness by removing decision making from the individual child's hands.

Sixth, children need structure and clear boundaries. They derive security from knowing both what to expect and what others expect of them. They learn to build bridges among their thoughts and feelings when their world is predictable and responsive. Firm yet reasonable limits, set within an atmosphere of warmth and empathy, constitute a crucial element of any relationship that truly nurtures a youngster's growth and allows him to learn self-discipline and responsibility. Many people erroneously see a conflict between structure and spontaneity, between love and limits. Although every child needs both affection and kindly but unambiguous expectations—and the child from a chaotic background needs them most of all—few programs integrate them into a consistent and constructive approach.

Seventh, to achieve these goals, families need stable neighborhoods and communities. The appropriate, consistent, and deeply committed care that a child needs to master the developmental levels requires adults who are themselves mature, empathic, and emotionally accessible. Even without severe stresses, very few parents have the personal and material resources to nurture children entirely on their own. Effective programs to help at-risk youngsters must therefore help maintain whatever ties to friends, kin networks, and religious fellowships and cultural traditions a family may possess. Family members need to find the time and commitment for caring. Neighbors need to know one another, socialize together, and be available to help each other out. Neighborhoods need residents who share a stake in the community and churches, schools, businesses, and organizations willing to collaborate for the common good. Communities need citizens and institutions dedicated to their progress and survival.

Clearly, the areas where our poorest families cluster and the programs on which they rely for help rarely meet any of these standards. Their neighborhoods often lack even basic services such as adequate policing, fire protection, and medical care, let alone amenities like libraries, parks and playgrounds, community centers, and retail stores. Distant, impersonal bureaucracies rather than local groups and institutions make crucial decisions concerning children's welfare. Many programs ignore or undermine essential family, community, and cultural networks.

CONFLICTING TRADITIONS OF SOCIAL SERVICE

Although generations of social service professionals and officials at every level of government have struggled to help needy families, many would agree that the system we have evolved has often worsened matters rather than improved them. Despite what we know about the roots of violence, delinquency, helplessness, and self-absorption, our efforts to assist deprived and neglected children have rarely been successful beyond outstanding model projects. Huge bureaucracies sort, track, and account for our most disadvantaged youngsters and the money allotted for services for them. As the chaotic web of welfare offices, juvenile justice organizations, and child protective agencies is now constituted, it advances its own political agenda more assiduously than it does that of vulnerable children. Once a child's plight comes to official attention, often through brushes with the law, failure at school, or flagrant abuse by adults—once, in other words, years of deprivation and misery are transformed into a "case"—various agencies, often at cross-purposes, begin imposing their procedures.

The history of social services for families and children in this country reflects a continuing clash between two deeply divergent traditions. Cases of deprivation, abuse, and neglect have been approached by exponents of two very different ideas of human nature, family ties, and the social good. Each view has enjoyed its periods of political and cultural ascendancy, leaving its legacy in our laws, policies, agencies, and institutions. But advocates of neither approach have fully grasped the challenges facing severely troubled families or the steps needed to help them. Because of their own values and assumptions, they have ignored certain crucial elements of the problem.

One tradition focuses more on the child than on the family, emphasizing protecting youngsters from the influence of unsuitable and incompetent parents, whom its supporters hold responsible for children's difficulties. Though lacking influence in government for many years, it returned to prominence with the conservative ascendancy in Congress. At an extreme, proponents argue that kids should be removed from inadequate homes and placed in more "wholesome" environments—work camps, group homes, even orphanages. They maintain a high standard of what renders a home suitable for children and accept relatively lenient criteria for separating them from their birth families.

In placing the child's welfare above the parents' rights or the family's integrity, however, advocates of this view generally underestimate the emotional ties that bind a child to her parents, even abusive and negligent ones, and the harm that severing these ties can cause the child. They also overestimate the ability of an institution such as an orphanage to fulfill the needs of damaged children. Although the best institutions do provide safe and healthful care that far surpasses that in a severely dysfunctional home, few can offer the consistent, intimate emotional relationships children need. Keeping excellent staff over the long term, for example, is very difficult, requiring high salaries, training opportunities, and career ladders. The most effective ratio of adults to children is rarely affordable. Far more usual is a mediocre facility that cannot supply the love, warmth, security, and individual attention so central to healthy development. Some of the poorer ones inflict their own abuse and neglect. Most day-care centers, for example, do not furnish emotional closeness and individual concern.[17]

Nor does foster care provide the intended breathing space, in part because foster parents rarely receive the help they need to take on the challenge of an uprooted child. Even if a foster placement surpasses a child's original home by any number of objective standards, the move rips him from the only emotional anchor he knows. Youngsters who are challenging in their own families only become more so in foster homes, where untrained adults have to cope with both the child's original deficits and his increased sense of pain and disorientation.

The second tradition, dominant for most of the last two generations, focuses more on the family. Its supporters place ultimate responsibility for impaired children on the inequities of society and tend to view families as essentially warm, nurturing, and sympathetic, if often beleaguered by forces beyond their control. Families, in their view, are the only acceptable setting in which to raise children. With proper economic, therapeutic, and social support, they can succeed in bringing up healthy children. An array of social services to prop up failing family structures, including temporary foster care to give fractured families time to regroup, often figures in plans derived from this approach.

Whereas the first tradition errs in idealizing institutional care, this second one often does the same in idealizing families, even those whose troubles stretch back for generations. In the multirisk families my colleagues and I have studied, many of the parents, grandparents, and even great-grandparents of those responsible for today's children did a poor job raising their own broods. Neglect and abuse, addiction, and psychiatric disorders form patterns passed from parent to child. Such a heritage makes it extremely difficult for any individual to make a success of parenthood without major help. Never having experienced adequate care, those who grew up in such homes frequently have no idea how to provide it. Never having taken part in a satisfying mutual relationship, they have no idea how to establish one with their children.

Preservation of family ties, though generally a laudable principle, has nonetheless at times been seriously misapplied, even to the point of returning injured youngsters to the custody of unreformed drug addicts or violent aggressors. Rather than moving expeditiously to sever legal bonds to such demonstrably harmful adults and find the child a permanent safe harbor, practices based rigidly on this principle encourage attempts to return children to their original families or park them provisionally but often for years on end in a series of temporary foster placements that offer little possibility of enduring attachment.

Proponents of neither approach, therefore, hold all of the answers for children and families at risk. To have any chance of succeeding, intervention programs must combine the insights of both traditions, building on their strengths and mitigating their weaknesses. They must give due attention to the crucial bond between parent and child, preserving it if at all advisable. However, they must also safeguard children from the harm that a poisonous home environment can do, replacing it if necessary and as soon as possible with another permanent relationship. They must thus avoid the weaknesses of both the foster care and institutional care systems, offering both ongoing intimacy and the chance for competent care—in short, supporting both the family and the child.

THE BEST INTERESTS OF BOTH FAMILY AND CHILD

To protect children from the risks that breed violence, a successful program must itself be an unfailing constant in a family's life. It must involve the members with people willing to stand by them for years on end, not just months or weeks, and it must ensure that personal relationships built up between staff and clients endure and deepen.

The program's influence cannot stop with the individual household, furthermore, but must extend beyond it into the community of which it is a part. Without dire circumstances and much preparation, it will not uproot children from their neighborhoods or native cultures. The goal must be to galvanize the child's own developmental potential, breaking the chain of dysfunction by training a competent, responsible member of the greater society. Many of these elements have been incorporated into existing programs, but it has been difficult to combine them in a way that will reach the most challenging families.

One approach to a truly integrated program derives from the traditional village or neighborhood in which neighbors watched out for one another's kids and each adult took a sympathetic interest in everyone's child. Without neighbors, friends, and relations to serve as parents' surrogate eyes and ears and to help in times of trouble, without a safe area in which the child is known and cherished, without an array of grown-ups who embody admirable qualities and who support recognized community values, even the best, most devoted mothers and fathers find themselves hard pressed to do right by their children.

Of course, it is easy to romanticize a Norman Rockwell–style small-town life, but the ingredients of that ideal nevertheless represent the basic needs of every child. What form could the village ideal take today? My experience working with high-risk families and their children persuades me that realizing such a paradigm is feasible with the resources we already have.

A traditional village is a self-contained residential district of families linked by ties of common interest and long acquaintance. The new village community would also need geographical unity within the larger context of the urban metropolis. Rather than a cluster of houses around a country crossroads, for example, a sizable apartment building could serve as its physical frame. Like the traditional village—but unlike many of the devastated slums where our poorest families live—this vertical "village" would house a range of residents: some very dysfunctional households; some other families, both working and on welfare, who cope more competently with their lives; some older, perhaps retired, persons, living either alone or with relatives; some adults without children.

Apart from the support such a complex could offer struggling parents, services aimed at both children and their parents would be available within the building itself. A well-equipped, well-staffed infant and child center, for example, would welcome youngsters essentially from birth. Both children and adults would come here daily, the youngsters spending their time in play and learning activities, the parents availing themselves of education and guidance suited to their needs. Knowledgeable staffers would work at forming lasting, personal ties with each member, helping adults develop parenting skills while providing children with familiar, dependable care to backstop their often overstressed parents. For each high-risk family, one staffer would assume the role of surrogate "relative" along the lines of a sympathetic, capable aunt or grandmother. This trained caregiver would establish a permanent bond with the family, seeing that parents can manage the personal problems that stand in the way of caring for their babies and that children get the nurturing they need at each developmental stage, regardless of their parents' ability to provide it.

Coming to the center regularly, working with the same trusted helper over a period of four or five years, the child would gain a center of stability that endured despite upheavals that might occur at home. A mother too depressed to respond to her baby appropriately would thus not totally deprive her of the support and interaction she needs to build relationships or master communication. A drug binge or episode of inpatient addiction treatment would not throw a child's world into turmoil and the child into the uncertainty of foster care. A child could sleep in her own apartment or in the center itself, depending on day-to-day circumstances. Staffed around-the-clock, the center would be a safe haven at any time and for as long as needed, cutting drastically the chaos in youngsters' lives.

Such a reliable, nearby resource would also bring order and responsibility to parents' lives, offering, in addition to instruction in parenting skills, opportunities for personal counseling, drug treatment, health and family planning education, courses toward high school equivalency completion, and work training or job search assistance. Parents would be eligible to participate as long as they abided by clearly stated and reasonable rules—no drug use, for example— and were willing to pursue education and seek work. Many mothers and fathers could thus achieve the stability and direction in their own lives that would allow them to become more positive influences in their children's. With the center's backing, they could work on their own development without jeopardizing that of their children.

A child might spend all his time at the children's center, or he might return to his family's own apartment in the evening. The night staff would consist of familiar and trusted persons as well, removing from parents the pressure to care for children when they cannot. A parent in crisis would always have a place to turn for help, and in turn, center staff would demand that the parent meet a minimum level of maturity before family life could fully resume, thus enforcing standards of responsible care.

To make this system work, each troubled family would belong to a cohesive community, most of whose members functioned pretty well. The other families living in the building, some on welfare, some not, would also belong to the center, with children attending the nursery and adults taking part in classes, groups, and activities that suited their circumstances. Adults seeking job opportunities, for example, could be trained as child-care workers in preparation for taking paid positions in the center. Other adults, especially older or retired persons with backgrounds in child care and education, could work in the center either as volunteers or paid staffers. A variety of financial incentives—low rents, reduced child-care fees, educational opportunities—would attract residents to this diverse yet balanced "neighborhood."

Such an urban village would draw strength and support from the culture and institutions of the surrounding community. Churches, community centers, civic groups, and local charities, preferably associated with residents' cultural or ethnic heritage, would provide social, spiritual, recreational, and educational resources. Instead of being a ghetto for the most disadvantaged, like present-day public housing, the community would offer benefits not only to the very poor, but to households with other options. As the Israeli kibbutzim have demonstrated after more than a century of existence, unrelated families devoted to the ideal of working together to improve their lives can build strong communities and raise competent children. Even without the kibbutzniks' ideology and tradition of communal ownership, residents could be similarly committed to building an institution.

Ideally, a child at risk would be part of the village network from before birth. Rather than waiting to intervene until after a child has begun to have difficulties, staff would make help available early to maximize each baby's developmental chances. An impoverished young girl pregnant for the first time, a depressed woman expecting yet another infant, a mother whose older children have already become family service or foster care regulars would come under the wing of a support worker, either a social work professional or a trained and experienced volunteer. If necessary, a mother-to-be and her family would move into the building before the child was born.

From the moment of birth, therefore, the baby would belong both to her troubled biological family and to an extended community family providing a second tier of caring support. The key to success, however, would be that the program aim to serve both parent and child equally. A mother who in many cases is herself a needy child in an adult body can otherwise sabotage the entire undertaking.

Though highly cost effective in the long run, a program like this is far from cheap. Lack of staff available twenty-four hours a day has sunk such efforts in the past. When families encounter crises, sufficient numbers of trained staff must be ready to step in and maintain children's development.

Such a program obviously surpasses most current intervention measures in benefits to all concerned. It respects every child's need for continuity and the troubled parent's need for support and personal growth. It also rallies society's interest in guaranteeing every child a good upbringing. It neither uproots the child from the only family he knows nor abandons him to the mercy of a deficient parent. It neither segregates chaotic families from the community at large nor condones their dysfunctional behavior. Indeed, it creates through community structures the support that many families naturally get from their relatives.

A dysfunctional household usually lacks a kin network that can deliver solid help. It takes generations of incompetent parenting, generations of unmet needs, generations of neglect and abuse to produce the deep social pathologies that afflict such families and that have defeated many programs aiming to help them. A parent's painful past might inspire understandable resentment, anger, and suspicion of others' motives and have taught him destructive coping strategies.

Once such troubled adults do form bonds of trust, their own enormous dependency needs emerge, possibly overwhelming helpers' resources. To deal with these problems, village staff would need to consult experienced outside professionals and would require ongoing in-service training, supervision, and support.

Although much about the kind of program I have outlined is idealistic, it has been shown that long-term comprehensive intervention is entirely possible. In the late 1970s and early 1980s I had the opportunity, together with colleagues Serena Wider, the late Reginald Lourie, Robert Nover, Alicia Lieberman, Mary Robinson, and a very gifted group of clinicians and researchers to develop the Clinical Infant Development Program (CIDP), a collaborative project of the National Institute of Mental Health and Family Service of Prince Georges County, Maryland. We undertook to serve four dozen multirisk families.[18] Typical of such households, these women and their children had long histories of turmoil and trauma. Half of the mothers had experienced nine or more problems such as childhood neglect, sexual or physical abuse, witnessing abuse of other family members, family psychiatric disorders, personal psychiatric hospitalization, school failure or expulsion, inability to hold a job, juvenile delinquency, and rejection by peers. Even the more fortunate among the women lived lives of chaos and despair.

Through its intervention, the Clinical Infant Development Program succeeded in guiding even severely troubled mothers toward competent nurturing. Babies at acute risk for abuse, neglect, and concomitant emotional and intellectual problems were thus saved from the fate that initially threatened them. Parents and children attended daily the project's infant center, which was staffed by experienced child-care and family service workers. Limits on staffing, however, precluded the nighttime services that I believe are central to enduring success. As a time-limited research project rather than an ongoing service agency, the program ended after a period of several years. However, long-term follow-up revealed that, even offering less than continuous coverage, the program markedly improved outcomes for both adults and their vulnerable children.

Three examples of CIDP cases give an idea of how such an approach might work. Louise, an unmarried woman in her mid-twenties who had experienced continual rejection as a child, had none of the skills or resilience needed to nurture even an "easy" baby. Her son Robbie's inherent difficulties in calming himself and orienting his attention would have challenged the most competent mother. Louise, however, had already failed once at motherhood; she had several years before sent her six-year-old daughter, Terry, to live with a relative. Now, deeply depressed and unable to cope with her own problems, Louise was overwhelmed by her overreactive second child.

The unwanted product of an adulterous union, Louise had spent almost her entire childhood living apart from her mother, her mother's other children, whom she had long believed to be her full siblings, and her mother's husband. Only as an adult did she learn of her true origins. Her early years were spent in the care of a cold, punitive aunt who died when Louise was eight. The aunt's boyfriend, though he never actually molested Louise, nonetheless conveyed a sense of sexual threat to the young girl. A warm, empathic aunt next took over Louise's care, becoming her "only true mother." When this kindly woman also died prematurely, Louise was left emotionally bereft. She had intense fears and nightmares. Her sense of rejection was so pronounced that a psychiatric evaluation suggested a diagnosis of schizoid personality. Long, exploitative relationships ultimately led to Louise's two pregnancies.

The first weeks of Robbie's life presented the intervention team with the frightening prospect of a mother and child whose individual challenges fed on one another's. Robbie's inability to connect with other people had felt to Louise like rejection, exacerbating her own sharp need to be cared for and driving her away from this child who could not satisfy it. As her efforts to relate had repeatedly failed, her depression deepened. Louise's own flat, wooden affect, the product of her despondency, had led Robbie to disengage further from the human world and from any chance of connecting with this mother. Over the next weeks and months, he steadily deteriorated, losing what little responsiveness, cuddliness, and ability to focus that he had originally shown. His ability to master even the first stage of development seemed to dwindle rapidly. Louise, meanwhile, became increasingly agitated and withdrawn as the child drifted from her.

A team attached to the CIDP center worked with both mother and child to restore them to each other and to a chance at life. Therapy helped Louise begin to deal with her long-suppressed demons. While she struggled toward greater balance, center staff intervened to pull Robbie from his isolation.

This dual-pronged approach succeeded only because staffers knew both mother and child very well as individuals. A clinician noticed, for example, that Robbie attended to inanimate objects much more closely than to human faces. Trying to use his own strengths to engage him, she obtained several masks and would don one whenever she dealt with him, hiding behind one of the lifeless "things" that Robbie seemed to enjoy following with his eyes. Gradually she succeeded in making eye contact with him through slits in the false face and then, over time, in wooing the child into relating to her own and other human faces.

By the time Robbie reached eight months, he was eagerly seeking out his mother, but Louise needed longer to cope with her depression and rage. During this time, the baby's nourishing relationship with infant center staff maintained his developmental momentum. By the time Robbie celebrated his first birthday, Louise began to emerge from her troubles and to learn the basics of caring for and relating to him. When he was eighteen months old, though both were still somewhat vulnerable, mother and son were able to interact warmly and easily in joyful, increasingly complicated activities. Louise particularly loved a giggling game of hide-and-seek in which she apparently worked out in fantasy the issues of availability and loss that had once been stark reality. She had learned how to stimulate and connect with Robbie, who had reached each of the developmental milestones appropriate to his age. By this time, Louise was well on the way to caring for him in a manner that would sustain his continued growth. His progress heightened her enthusiasm to continue.

Even far more complex cases yielded to this approach. When the team first encountered Mary and her three-month-old daughter, Amy, the mother was a substance abuser given to self-destructiveness and magical thinking and the frail, unresponsive baby was rapidly losing ground through failure to thrive. Care of Amy and her two-year-old brother, Harold, was so negligent, in fact, that center staff seriously considered foster placements. Mary regarded her children mainly as bait for getting the attention of their father, who had left her. She also sought out other men and often ended up drinking or taking drugs with them. Her intoxication and short-lived relationships precipitated many crises, including "losing" Harold on several occasions.

Through intensive work, the infant center staff gradually estab-lished a relationship with Amy and over a period of years helped Mary to deal with her feelings about the abuse and abandonment that lay at the bottom of her impulsive, self-destructive behavior. In coming to terms with her complicated emotions toward a father she had never known, she was able to address her own severe ambiguity about sexu-ality and parenthood. Eventually she succeeded in establishing a more lasting relationship with a new man and in becoming far more emo-tionally available to her children. Three years later, when Mary gave birth to a robust boy, Amy was relating warmly and trustingly, if still somewhat timidly. While she functioned intellectually nearly at age level, her development was a bit delayed. With the emotional support of center staff, however, she made considerable progress in her ability both to relate to people and to recognize her feelings. Mary, mean-while, had taken significant steps toward understanding and rebuild-ing her own life. The new infant was less challenging than the more self-absorbed, lackadaisical Amy had been, and he offered much more obvious rewards to his caregivers. Now in charge of an active, respon-sive baby and strengthened by the infant center's guidance and con-cern, Mary proved herself able to respond to him appropriately and provide adequate care.

A third example showing the need for a flexible approach is that of Madeline, whose chaotic life at first caused the CIDP team almost to despair. The mother of four children under four, each already clearly on the road to emotional disturbance, twenty-year-old Madeline had emerged from a neglected childhood as one of twelve children full of fear and rage and unable to sustain any lasting relationship. A long and complicated intervention included many crises spurred by her intense depression and frequent inability to function at other than an ex-tremely reactive level, oblivious to past and future. Desperate and emo-tionally needy, she had almost no capacity to connect her actions to the continual disasters befalling herself and her children. When trouble struck, she either lashed out impulsively or retreated into despair.

The staff helped Madeline place her children in foster homes in an organized, well-thought-out manner rather than under the dire conditions that too often prevail. When offered the chance to visit them, however, Madeline fled and eventually relinquished them to adoption. This outcome permitted them to gain the stable nurturing they needed to progress in their stalled development. The center continued to work with Madeline over a period of years. Eventually she found some relief from her depression and was able to develop a degree of insight into her background and behavior, giving her greater control over her life. By the time she bore another daughter, several years into the program, she had the maturity to care for her responsibly.

These three mothers, like 80 percent of those enrolled in the CIDP study, increased their ability to cope with the terrible burden of their past. They learned new ways of interacting that led to better care of their children. With sympathetic support, mothers whose backgrounds and present situations imposed severe limits on their ability to nurture became more capable and empathic caregivers. Even very challenging children born to troubled parents were able to master the critical stages of development. At each point in a child's growth, as needs changed and demands grew more complex, the center staff stood ready both to guide the mother and to support and nurture the child. After several years, children initially headed for lives of difficulty, failure, and pain were well on their way to the most hopeful future anyone in their families had looked forward to in generations.

Every child deserves the opportunity that these children had, that of growing up in families able to nurture them appropriately. Unless we offer such ambitious care to all children who are at risk, however, the numbers of dysfunctional families and of the disturbed or violent youngsters they produce will only increase. A small yet immensely disruptive segment of our society has grown up unable to contribute or even to cope. Through no fault of their own, these young people have acquired none of the skills needed for success in life or, perhaps more important, for creating new families that can enjoy any semblance of equal opportunity.

The children of dysfunctional families will continue to cost billions of dollars in foster care, special education, crime control, prisons, and mental hospitals. It can be no more expensive to provide high-risk children and their families the support they need. The problems of such families have long been recognized. D. W. Winnicott in 1957 pointed out society's risk and responsibility.

> The more we think of these things the more we understand why infants and little children absolutely need the background of their own family, and, if possible, a stability of physical surroundings as well; and from such considerations we see that children deprived of home life must either be provided with something personal and stable when they are yet young enough to make use of it to some extent, or else they must force us later to provide stability in the shape of an approved school or, in the last resort, four walls in the shape of a prison cell.[19]

In this chapter we have tried to identify that "something personal and stable" and to show that we have, within our reach, new solutions to the problems of these troubled families.

CHAPTER FOURTEEN

Toward a Reflective Society

THE DANGERS OF IMMATURE OR STUNTED LEVELS OF development extend beyond the damage to individual minds and the small groups that mold our individuality, such as the family and the classroom. They can be seen in the behavior of large groups as well, from political parties to ethnic groups to nation-states.

Concern over international conflict has shifted from the two-way standoff that dominated world affairs for almost two generations after World War II to smaller but vicious ethnic struggles like those in Somalia, Rwanda, Chechnya, and especially the former Yugoslavia. The former great-power rivals now sometimes cooperate. But basic causes of warfare, such as territorial ambition and racial hatred, seem no more amenable to diplomacy and reason and no less capable of drawing others into armed strife than they ever were.

Explaining how large groups behave is quite distinct from interpreting the actions of individuals. Over a century ago, for example, social scientists observed that numbers of people massed together often act much more crudely and unthinkingly than the men and women composing the crowd might do on their own. A large literature documents the seeming irrationality and loss of personal boundaries of people in large groups.[1] In such settings, individuals not infrequently attribute their own feelings to others as well as adopt the feelings of others. Soccer matches turn into riots; whole societies dissolve into chaos and brutality, as among the clans of Somalia. An understanding of the developmental levels of the mind affords insights into how and why societies cohere or crumble. It also helps explain how each society indelibly stamps its common experience on the varied individuals that compose it.

These considerations may seem a long way from an infant reaching for a rattle or a small child acting out feelings of joy or envy. Analyzing the behavior of large groups has long been the purview of disciplines including political science, sociology, and anthropology, each of which brings to bear its own concepts and methods and has its own large literature of results. These observations are intended to complement rather than replace the perspectives of other fields. They provide another way of thinking about the often perplexing behavior of large groups.

GROUP DEVELOPMENT

Both as individuals and in families, human beings behave in ways that indicate the developmental levels that they have reached and the emotional tasks that they have mastered. In a similar fashion, group behavior too reflects developmental stages. A crowd of sports fans angered at a referee's call and storming violently onto the field is clearly acting at the level of immediate behavioral discharge. Political demonstrators denouncing a leader and then burning him in effigy are symbolizing ideas rather than acting directly, but they are doing so in a highly polarized manner. The fact that, despite shock and horror at a crime as hideous as the Oklahoma City bombing, Americans still recognized that the accused have the right to competent defense and a fair trial is evidence of widespread ability to reflect on abstract values and an agreement to use them in making decisions for the common good.

Social institutions that deal with disputes and make decisions also have a developmental aspect. For example, societies having institutions that encourage debate and reflection, such as those that divide judicial, executive, legislative, and other powers in such a way as to build in checks and balances, are organized at a different developmental level from those whose institutions allow unilateral decisions to be made without accountability. No matter how much citizens balk at the inefficiencies and absurdities of modern democracies, they essentially require that all important and controversial national decisions—whether to commit troops to a military operation, how to reduce the national debt, whether to permit abortion—eventually come before the bar of public opinion and legal review. The complicated U.S. system of governmental branches that can stymie one another and of lengthy and staggered election campaigns for the presidency and the two houses of Congress is specifically designed to ensure that significant issues are decided only after ample discussion and consideration. With all its flaws, such a reflective apparatus seems more evolved than one that allows a dictator to make decisions and to resort to polarized images and stereotypes to defend them, or violence and terror to enforce them. Institutions that require reflective thought and behavior thus help rein in primitive behavior within society and organize decision making at more symbolic levels: discussion, negotiation, and compromise. Even structures that appear to support reflection, however, can occasionally be misused in the service of highly polarized ideas. During the nineteenth century, for example, the Supreme Court justified racial segregation in *Plessy* v. *Ferguson.* In wartime the reflective process can be short-circuited by such irrational government decisions as the internment of Japanese Americans in California.

In addition to differences in the maturity of institutions, societies also vary in how they handle emotional themes. We have seen how individuals differ in their ability to reflect and respond across a range of emotions—how one, for example, may have delicately nuanced images and feelings involving love and dependency but only a crude set of reactions to anger, while another may distinguish among degrees of disgruntlement, irritation, and rage but deal in an either-or way with affection. Similarly, members of a society may suppress expressions of anger, say, seeing them as uncouth or threatening, while other societies indiscriminately approve of and glorify aggression and anger or reject notions of limits on behavior. In either case, when an expression of anger is either entirely censured or entirely acceptable, it is difficult to make distinctions, even to differentiate justified assertions of personal dignity from needless brutality.

Societies that regard any slight or affront as justifying revenge will find violent confrontation appropriate in resolving many issues. By contrast, a society that discriminates subtly along a spectrum of response offers more than a choice between meek surrender and mayhem. It is also more capable of dealing in a reflective and nuanced fashion with ancillary issues such as the right to self-defense and to bear arms.

In the United States, where self-reliance is a core value, the theme of obligation is far less developed than in a society like that of Japan, where there are more expectations concerning loyalty and conformity to the group, whether the family, the school class, or the industrial firm. These commonly held assumptions in turn support the expectation that organizations have the duty of taking care of those who play the assigned roles.

In addition to institutional arrangements, a society's visual and verbal symbols also reveal how it deals with certain themes. How rich and varied is its vocabulary, and therefore its ideas, for dealing with love, anger, competitiveness, obligation? How do its literature, art, music, movies, theater, television shows, and news coverage deal with these themes? If a group has a large number of words or symbolic images for representing and discussing an area of experience, clearly it can deal more precisely and possibly more reflectively with that array of feelings than a society able to avail itself of only a few roughly differentiated symbols. For example, in a group that conceptualizes "masculinity" as embodying the qualities of physical strength, aggressive competitiveness, and daring, relations between the sexes will be stereotyped and rigid, whereas a group that represents this idea more flexibly in words and symbols allows both men and women a greater range of interests, personalities, and modes of relating to one another.

A group's capacity to deal with and symbolize emotional themes is especially important in its child-rearing and educational practices. I have observed differences between various American subcultures in whether or not children are encouraged to express certain themes.[2] For instance, a toddler playing with dolls may be joined enthusiastically by his mother when the dolls are hugging or enjoying tea parties. The mother adopts the identity of one of the dolls, talking in a "doll voice" and participating in the unfolding story. But when the dolls begin to fight, the mother immediately exits the fantasy and in her own adult voice—and her adult character—criticizes the way her son is holding the dolls or complains that he will break them. Similarly, if his doll criticizes hers, she exits the imaginary scene and argues with her son as though the criticism concerned her and not the doll. In the fantasy interchange, the child is attempting to bring aggression into the world of shaded meanings. Instead, his mother inadvertently insists on keeping this theme at a concrete, literal level. When this is the pattern of interaction between parent and child, the child tends to remain concrete in those areas in which the caregiver is unable to support the use of ideas.

Some people can engage their children in play, discussions, and even debates about a number of emotional themes, such as love, dependency, separation, loss, anger, assertiveness, curiosity, and fears, while others may be able to deal with only one or two themes. Children who are thus shut out of learning to conceptualize act out their feelings instead. Often they are passive, negative, or impulsive. Their thinking doesn't progress to abstract levels. These difficulties can be mistakenly attributed to genetic factors rather than to variations in how parents or caregivers communicate with their children. Schools can reinforce these trends by the way different emotional themes are handled in the classroom. Is debate encouraged, or is the emphasis on rigid rules and rote learning?

LEVELS OF SOCIAL MATURITY

The idea that large groups operate in ways corresponding to the levels of mental organization observed in individual human development is a provocative one. This isn't to suggest, of course, that societies actually develop along lines that duplicate the human life course, or that everyone in a given society has attained more or less the same level. But the parallel does offer a new way of analyzing the behavior of large groups and the mental activity that underlies it.

Clearly, thinking and feeling take place at an individual level. Just as clearly, in order to support behavior consonant with a particular stage of development, a society must contain substantial numbers of people who have reached that stage. Every society may well include persons at every level of mental organization, from the most primitive to the most reflective; our own certainly does. Individual members of a society are more differentiated around certain emotional themes than around others.

Still, each society appears to organize itself in characteristic ways. The structures a society uses to organize itself, including its political, educational, and economic systems, determine to a large degree how individuals within that society use its resources and the energy and ingenuity they can put into its art, literature, science, and technology. Some structures are more likely than others to support the accomplishments that advance civilization.

The developmental level of a society, however, may have antithetical consequences. The society organized around reflection may provide a refined, humane environment in which many kinds of people can freely express their thoughts and values, but at the same time it may have a hard time responding quickly to an emergency. The action-oriented society, by contrast, can act and react with dynamism and unity. In *A History of Western Philosophy*, Bertrand Russell posed this reality as a historical dilemma. He argued that societies held together by simple, absolute truths, whether religious doctrines like those that led to the Crusades or superstitions and primitive beliefs like the notion of Aryan supremacy that animated the Nazi war machine, can maintain a level of homogeneity and morale that gives them a decided advantage over competing groups. As societies mature, however, they become more relativistic, more open to individual perceptions of truth and expressions of experience. In such an atmosphere, any endeavor requiring mental sophistication and subtlety can flourish. This certainly happened in the Muslim realms from Morocco to India and beyond after their military triumphs of the seventh and eighth centuries. Poetry, mathematics, philosophy, astronomy, painting, medicine—all the arts of civilization flowered in the wealthy, cosmopolitan cities and courts of the Islamic world. But such relativistic societies are harder to organize for action than are those holding to a more simplistic understanding of reality.

The contrast between these two social models presented for Russell a troubling paradox: an increasingly relativistic, tolerant society can make tremendous strides in culture but in the long run loses its ability to maintain itself against the aggression of less deliberative, hesitant societies. He did not see how a society could remain both cultured and secure at the same time. In theory, he proposed, liberalism—what we know as democracy—might do the trick. A society in which individuals fashion the institutions that govern them ought to succeed at affording cohesion and protection while also allowing a reasonable amount of freedom. In practice, however, he was skeptical that there was a solution.

Perhaps it is the case that some societies cohere at a relatively low level of development that depends on direct action and polarized thinking. In these societies, concrete ideas govern and direct relatively unreflective actions. Others cohere at a much higher developmental level that involves nuance and reflection. Here more intricate processes guide decision making, processes that can encompass a variety of points of view as well as manage conflict and change. Most societies obviously occupy the middle range between these two extremes.

The disciplines that traditionally study societies consider the behavior of large groups in the light of culture, class, structure, function, economic systems, and so on. The developmental understanding illuminates yet another aspect of social organization, allowing us to evaluate how well a given society supports a progression of emotional and intellectual abilities. Noting roughly where a society's institutions and practices fall along developmental dimensions translates into a measure, however impressionistic, of its collective mental traits. Although, as I said earlier, human groups do not have uniform memberships, this kind of analysis offers an indication of the mental levels at which the larger group may operate.

GROUP SECURITY

Providing physical protection from violent attack is perhaps the most basic of all social functions. Without this provision, other forms of social and cultural development become difficult if not impossible, just as an infant who does not acquire a sense of security through attaining the ability to regulate her attention at the first level of development is impeded at subsequent levels. Along this dimension, societies range from the chaos of Somalia, wracked by total civil war, to tidy states like Switzerland and Singapore. Somewhere between we find various scantily governed Third World nations as well as assorted police states where citizens vanish without a trace for indeterminate reasons; the United States, with rates of murder and violent crime exceptionally high for the industrial West; Canada, like our own country in many ways but substantially safer; and Japan, with a minuscule incidence of homicide despite what might seem to be an overwhelmingly dense population. Some societies, in other words, do a far better job than others of providing the sense of security and internal regulation that permits members to attend to the tasks and opportunities of their world.

SHARED ALLEGIANCE

The task at the second developmental level is to connect and engage with others, forming bonds of common humanity. In some nations, citizens feel a strong sense of mutual obligation; aware of themselves as a people, they recognize a shared destiny and the duty of each individual to contribute to and, if necessary, sacrifice for it. In other countries, however, people feel no such sense of national unity and commitment. They either owe their allegiance to some region or subculture, which may well be at odds with others or with the nation at large, or they may function as atomized individuals looking out for themselves and perhaps a small number of close relatives or friends.

A strong feeling of social commonality does not require uniformity of ethnic identity or even language. As the oldest democracy on earth, Switzerland has for 750 years maintained a peaceful multilingual state defended by a citizen army recruited through universal conscription. Speakers of French, German, Italian, or Romansh all regard themselves as equally Swiss, and their linguistic fellows across the border not as countrymen but as members of foreign nations who happen to speak the same language, much as Americans regard English-speaking Canadians or Swedes regard Swedish-speaking Finns. By contrast, people of essentially similar ethnic background who speak the same language can, like the Irish of the north and south, or North and South Koreans, regard each other as bitter enemies for generations.

In countries that are periodically washed by waves of immigration, as in much of the so-called New World, the concept of allegiance to the larger group must continually be stretched. Until the twentieth century, most settlers in North America originated from northern and western European countries, including the British Isles, the Scandinavian kingdoms, the Low Countries, various German statelets, and France. Over time, immigrants came to include eastern and southern Europeans, Iberians, Asians, and Latin Americans. Other groups intentionally excluded from full participation for much of our history, such as African Americans and Native Americans, did not develop such a sense until recently. This immense expansion of the notion of nationhood—the very word for which arises from the Latin root *natio*, meaning birth or race as well as nation—clearly calls into play forms of connectedness having nothing to do with inherited identity, blood, or ethnicity. For bonds of connectedness to endure among the increasingly varied kinds of "hyphenated" Americans, our people must experience and maintain a sense of commonality broader than ever before in the human experience.

SHARED ASSUMPTIONS

The next dimension for evaluating national entities corresponds to two developmental levels, simple and then intentional presymbolic communication, and concerns the affective messages conveyed by the nonverbal interactions within a society. As we saw, at these stages a child picks up on facial gestures, body postures, and tones of voice and through them becomes aware of the unspoken attitudes, values, beliefs, and feelings of those around him, forming the basis of the social "supersense" that he will forever after use both to judge his own intentions, affects, and actions and to maneuver among his fellow human beings.

Around the world, parents' behavior repeatedly conveys to children tacit cultural messages. An American parent greets a child's dressing herself with an eager and encouraging smile: "We are Americans, and we rely on ourselves." An English mother shakes her head reprovingly at a child's complaints about a late bus or an uncomfortable seat: "The English do not grumble." A Spanish father, witnessing his son swallow an insult, scowls derisively: "We Spaniards defend our personal and family honor." A Japanese mother ignores a youngster who brags about how he outdid a classmate: "In Japan we do not call attention to ourselves."

Each society regards life's many important emotional themes— love, longing, obligation, anger, passivity, sexuality, and the rest—in quite distinctive ways. At this stage of preverbal, intentional communication it conveys to the rising generation a strong and lasting sense of which approaches are "correct," thereby transmitting the most fundamental features of its culture and beliefs to its youngest members. The learning at this stage is so profound, in fact, that it results in something very close to what we think of as "values." To an important extent, it also structures an individual's sense of self. We are or are not, for example, people who show emotions openly, or who maintain a "stiff upper lip" or decorous demeanor for the sake of propriety. We are or are not people who ask questions about why things are the way they are, or who permit sexual innuendo, or who place filial obligation above personal fulfillment. People who do these things differently are—well—different from us.

When a child sticks her finger in her food or runs around the room or interrupts a conversation or cries or stamps her foot or laughs or tries to cuddle, a parent might respond with a warm smile, a raised eyebrow, a cold stare, a wink, a shake of the head, a pointing index finger, a pat on the bottom, a slap across the wrist. Each of these responses, of course, carries an emotional charge. Through thousands of such interchanges, the child learns what is and is not acceptable, what is and is not right, what is and is not done and felt and said. Adults do not devise these gestural interactions randomly. Rather, they base their behavior on their own values and sense of rightness and correctness—on what the smiles, scowls, hugs, shrugs, nods, and angrily turned backs taught them in their own experience.

Gestural communication imparts basic information about how a society functions. For example, are actions judged by fixed and rigid criteria, or are they assessed according to context? In one group, any and all assertiveness or disobedience by a child rates frowns and shaking heads, whereas in another, parents who generally expect to be obeyed will still shower smiles on a child who invents an imaginative way to circumvent an order, such as the toddler who finds a stool to help him get to the cookie jar. In the one society, the child may absorb the lesson that the right to assert one's individuality belongs only to elders, and that young people must defer to their parents and teachers in the answers they give on exams, the careers they follow, even the choice of whom they marry. In the other society, the youngster may learn that criteria are somewhat flexible and judgments depend to a considerable degree on context.

Societies convey to their members particular attributes that become part of individual personality. An American parent generally responds differently to a baby's helplessness than does a Japanese parent. Clinginess, timid behavior, automatic obedience make many American parents uncomfortable; through his developing affective understanding, the child will sense that such conduct results in dissatisfaction. Displaying initiative, curiosity, and assertiveness, by contrast—behavior that would make many American mothers, and especially fathers, proud—would discomfit the average Japanese parent, who finds individualism threatening. In the United States, the many facets of asserting one's individuality and standing on one's own two feet are elaborated in detail not only in the crib but in the classroom, on the playground, around the dinner table, and in the workplace. In Japan the finer points of reciprocal dependency and obligation are played out in the same kinds of surroundings.

Communication at the gestural level also indicates which cultural themes are open to further probing and which are not. When, for example, an American child eagerly inquires about the birds that visit the backyard trees or what goes on in a beehive seen on a farm or who were the greatest home-run pitchers or how to get on the Internet, the parental nods and smiles encourage further curiosity about nature or sports or technology, which in turn elicits more smiles and gestures. If, however, the same child asks pointed questions about "the birds and the bees," a tensed body, an embarrassed laugh or a pained frown, even a flash of irritation may indicate that sexuality is not an appropriate field for childish exploration, and any further questions will result only in more disapproving expressions and gestures.

Throughout life the gestures and expressions of others in response to our behavior impart with a power greater than any words could have what areas are acceptable to discuss and what are not. Societies and subcultures lavishly embroider certain themes and pay only scant attention to others. The Yiddish-speaking communities of Eastern Europe developed a vast gestural and verbal vocabulary for complaint and disparagement that allowed an oppressed people to release their anger, anxiety, and disappointment through humor rather than action. Densely populated, socially stratified, and relatively homogeneous, the island nations of Britain and Japan instead evolved a finely graduated system of courtesy and protocol to lubricate social life. African Americans may express a gamut of emotions, from bitter sadness to spiritual exaltation, in their rich and exquisitely nuanced tradition of vocal and instrumental music.

SYMBOLIC EXPRESSION

The themes that are elaborated by a particular society in nonverbal expression also predominate at the next, verbal, level. Verbal symbols express a concept or feeling that is already there, an intent, pattern, or affect present in presymbolic form. For the child just entering the symbolic stage, "Mama" thus refers to a loved and known person; "batti," for "bottle," to the familiar ritual of feeding; "out" to the experiences connected with playing in the yard. At the societal level as well, symbols stand for notions that are abroad in the population at the more basic level of gestural understanding.

A society's developmental level is reflected in the relationship of its symbols to its deeper values. Are symbolic objects perceived to carry power in and of themselves or as representations of important abstract values? Is the nation's flag, for example, sacred in itself, or as a symbol of "the republic for which it stands"? The difference is clearly seen in the contrast between the Nazi regime's burning books to suppress ideas it found objectionable and the decision of the U.S. Supreme Court that burning the American flag constitutes an act of protected symbolic speech. Though desecration of so dear an emblem deeply offends many Americans, the Court nonetheless insisted on separating the physical object itself from the ideas it represents. By honoring the flag, we honor not a piece of cloth but the principles it symbolizes. Permitting an act that many consider outrageous and repugnant proclaims the abstract principle of free expression.

Symbols are used at many levels of development. They can be extremely concrete, barely separated from a direct, bodily reaction to a situation or stimulus. Thus an individual might mutter "When he said that, I could have hit him" in place of actually taking the swing, or "My stomach feels tight" instead of taking flight. Shouting curses at an abortion doctor may take the place of shooting him. Such uses of symbols, however, are so close to behavioral discharge and so polarized that they cannot support any subtlety.

Only slightly more conducive to abstract thinking are symbols that are fragmented, inconsistent, idiosyncratic, and discordant with the reality they purportedly represent. Such symbols do not fit any coherent system of significance but exist as islands of meaning separate from people's understanding of the world. Communist regimes, like others, literally rewrote history—including the references made in official speeches and documents and the textbooks used in schools—to match current ideology rather than the common memory of those who had lived through the events in question, clearly violating citizens' shared sense of reality. Such societies often deal harshly with those who will not acquiesce in the malleability of the truth. Because families continue to transmit to their children a more basic nonverbal, presymbolic emotional "truth," these symbolic fabrications vanish immediately upon the collapse of the dictatorships that enforce them. After three generations of Soviet rule, traditional elements in Russian culture supposedly extirpated decades ago—the church, for example, and nationalism—reemerged as if by magic. Older and more fundamental emotional verities survived beneath all the symbolic manipulation and showed themselves again as soon as it had ceased. As a former Russian citizen recently explained to me, "The breakdown of communism should have come as no surprise in the West. My father, who ran a factory (like all those in similar middle-management positions), produced 50 percent of his goods for the black market. In the last ten to fifteen years, perhaps fewer than 2 percent of my fellow students believed in the communist economic philosophy. The system broke down because it was inconsistent with our nature as people. We are competitive, individualistic, and striving."

This sort of fragmentation and splitting contrasts with a far more integrated system of symbols that are consistent with an earlier

294 The Endangered Mind

pattern of values as well as with one another. In societies whose symbols cohere in this way, a rational approach to even controversial incidents becomes possible. For example, the Israeli government instituted an investigation into its military's handling of the massacres of Palestinians at the Sabra and Shatila refugee camps. Although the killings were perpetrated by Lebanese fighters, the Israeli military was in effective control of the large settlements of refugees. Israeli investigators came to the politically inconvenient conclusion that Israel bore responsibility, if not direct blame, for the bloodshed because the officers in charge did not exercise due caution and discipline to ensure the safety of the civilians under their authority.

The maturity of a society's symbolic system, like that of an individual, can also be assessed according to its degree of polarization and rigidity on the one hand or flexibility and integration on the other. Southern slave society, for example, viewed people with any degree of African ancestry as inherently inferior to those of purely European ancestry. Such polarized thinking dissociates one's own group from certain undesirable qualities and projects these traits on the other, rendering its members frightening, loathsome, or both. All forms of prejudice against groups of people perceived as undifferentiated masses defined by a single characteristic exemplify this kind of thinking. A more evolved society perceives human beings as individuals, each to be judged and appreciated as a unique mixture of strengths and weaknesses. The formal inclusion of such groups as women and African Americans in the circle of citizens protected by the Bill of Rights represents a significant step away from polarized attitudes. To the extent that actual practice falls short of official rhetoric, however, polarization continues to hold sway.

Slightly more advanced than polarized symbol systems are those that allow a few strictly defined categories of thought and behavior. The American electorate's sharp swings in presidential preference reflect such constricted thinking. Candidates are perceived by voters as exemplars of particular ideas, ideologies, and character traits rather than as fully rounded human beings. However, few chief executives— and none in recent history—can fulfill the expectations raised by their campaigns. Voters then tend to overreact to a president's perceived failings and to choose his opposite as a successor, setting themselves up for yet another disappointment. After the canny and shrewd but not always truthful Nixon (and a brief period of the down-to-earth Ford), voters turned to the scrupulously ethical but at times indecisive Carter. Reagan's single-minded, confident leadership, along with his uncritical and overly polarized sense of purpose, in turn contrasted with Carter's irresolution, without his judgment and appreciation of complexity. Bush adopted his predecessor's paternal stance, but though in 1992 he promised a continuation of the Reagan style, he was swept away by Clinton's purported ability to deal with political complexity as well as his touch of maternal warmth. People's dissatisfaction with their leaders often arises less from the imperfections of individuals than from the public's insistence on idealizing these leaders, much as a small child idealizes a parent. Rather than judiciously weighing the good and bad qualities of the human beings who lead us, we tend to bounce from one overblown and then discredited incumbent to his apparent opposite.

The mass media reinforce such polarized notions by covering politics and government as a contest between rivals rather than as a set of problems that require solutions.[3] The national debate of a pressing issue is often reported in terms of who wins or loses crucial votes. In the culture of competitive news gathering, in which organizations compete to "break" a story and broadcasters vie for audience share, either-or questions fill the news rather than a discerning examination of challenges facing the nation and the best approaches for meeting them.

INSTITUTIONS THAT ENCOURAGE REFLECTION

Just as for individuals, symbolic expression permits groups to reflect on problems and decisions. Some societies discourage self-critical evaluations, branding them, depending on the context, as unpatriotic, traitorous, heretical, or counterrevolutionary. As we saw, others have elaborate procedures for weighing issues of importance to the society at large—consider, for example, the Koerner Commission report that examined the causes of American racial unrest in the 1970s, or the searching self-examination by which the West German state has worked to rid itself of the remnants of Nazism.

Indeed, the legislative apparatus in democratic states exists for exactly the purpose of making decisions by deliberation rather than by fiat. The process prescribed by certain European parliaments or the U.S. Constitution is explicitly designed to force reflection, to make it essentially impossible for a nation to make any important decision without discussion and compromise among the various power centers of society.

Functioning consistently at this level is not easy in large groups because it demands considerable social maturity. But stable reflective structures lead to a far more balanced and judicious approach to issues, as is obvious from the fact that democracies, which require a majority vote before they can take action, almost never go to war with one another. Voters agree only with great reluctance to send their young people into harm's way, insisting that their leaders exhaust all other possibilities before they commit forces to combat. Aggressor nations tend to be dictatorships for the precise reason that they lack mechanisms that allow those who bear the heaviest costs of war to evaluate the decisions of the ruling group. Our future, however, depends on the ability of nations with stable reflective structures to mobilize their collective will.

Even economic trends may be influenced by these patterns. Reflective innovators create economic opportunities and carefully weigh investment decisions. Followers, however, if concrete and less reflective may make less "intelligent" investment decisions, swayed by impulse and poorly thought out expectations. Perhaps business cycles reflect the gradual entry of this second group, each member marginally less efficient than the one before. An atmosphere of economic success may further encourage this second group into the market, leading eventually to a downturn in the cycle. If a society becomes overly characterized by a lack of reflection, economic instability may well increase.

STABILITY THROUGH CHANGE

The final dimension is in a sense a measure of social maturity at its highest level, the societal counterpart of the individual's capacity to maintain a secure sense of self and identity through the changes of adulthood. A society functioning at this level corresponds to the healthy, flexible adult who uses reflection to chart a desired course through growth, loss, achievement, and change.

Sustainable societies have mechanisms that permit them to change while retaining core values. The United States and many European nations have gone several times from peace to war while preserving democratic institutions and practices—for example, holding elections in wartime and, in the most extreme case, in the midst of civil war. In a country that lacks such central values, however, leadership changes only with the overthrow of the ruling clique. New policies arise not from electoral landslides but from upheavals that can result in a new constitution, flag, and sometimes even name. At least one Latin American official expressed amazement that the U.S. government continued to function and to command its people's allegiance after the murder of President Kennedy, an event that in much of the world would have signaled armed uprising and civil strife. In still other countries, such as czarist Russia, core values are preserved but at the expense of any possibility of change.

THE EMOTIONAL CONSENT OF THE GOVERNED

The developmental view of social organizations highlights the tremendous importance of the type of "glue" that holds a group together. A society built on its people's ability to manipulate complex symbols attains cohesion at a much higher developmental level than one built on primitive urges like fear and hatred or crude polarized concepts of "us" against "them." In the first type of society, people are encouraged to invest their energies in the structures and processes by which they are governed rather than personal or absolutist beliefs. Certain institutions in turn produce citizens capable of weighing alternatives and agreeing on a course of action. Once children in elementary school have learned to conduct themselves according to *Robert's Rules of Order*—the protocol of motions, seconds, propositions, and rebuttals that structures congressional action—such an approach to group decisions becomes second nature. Individuals who have all their lives organized every group from sandlot teams to college councils by the familiar ritual of electing a leader and voting on contentious questions become readily able to serve on juries or corporate boards or city councils. Once people acquire the habit of ensuring a forum for the expression of a range of views, then taking a vote and, more crucial, accepting the result of that vote as binding, reflective decision making appears to be the only alternative for group regulation.

It is in this way that strong democracies provide the answer to Russell's dilemma: they command sufficient discipline to forge powerful fighting forces while still maintaining a sense of internal freedom and individualism. In World War II, individuals of the Allied nations, roused to the defense of their institutions, freely and even enthusiastically subordinated their personal desires for the several years it took to defeat the Axis.

On the early morning of D-Day, for example, American forces faced catastrophe on Omaha Beach. Invasion plans had gone seriously awry, and losses of men and equipment were so severe that commanders considered pulling the surviving forces off the beach and abandoning the effort, which would have seriously compromised the entire Normandy strategy and, presumably, the possibility of opening the Western front against the Germans. The military historian Stephen Ambrose has described in several documentary films how the remnants of shattered units arduously made their way under withering fire to the base of the bluffs, at the top of which sat the first line of the Nazi defense. There, under the ad hoc leadership of officers and noncoms who happened to survive, small, informal groups of men determined that, rather than dying helplessly on the sand, they would prefer to die trying to make a break inland, and perhaps taking some of the enemy with them. These random clusters of soldiers, equipped with whatever they had managed to salvage or scavenge, began to push off the beach in the direction of their originally assigned objectives. In so doing, they managed to fight their way through enemy lines and establish the beachhead that the strategic planners had envisaged. German officers, meanwhile, trained to act only on orders, lost time waiting for instructions while the Americans improvised.

What accounted for the ability of these men to coalesce into impromptu but effective fighting units was their reflection on the intolerable situation on the beach. It was each individual's ability to harness his sense of duty and self-reliance—indeed, his very sense of himself—to the objective problem that confronted the group. It was the ability of each man to find personal meaning in the common necessity to get off the beach by whatever means possible.

The strategic challenge that faced American forces on Omaha Beach is one example of many such situations in our lives. All our social institutions and the cultural symbols that surround them—the IRS, the infield fly rule, wedding anniversaries, the Catholic Church, Memorial Day, and countless others—are creations of the human mind. Yet they also acquire objective existence. They are something like a legal fiction such as a corporation, which has power and standing in court but no existence apart from the legal concepts that define it. What gives reality to such abstractions is the meaning, the emotional content, invested in them by the people whom they touch. Rather like Peter Pan's Tinkerbell, they exist because we believe they do. Were we all to agree to disregard them, they would cease to have any power over us. This is true even for so apparently august and mighty an entity as the IRS. Laws that are not enforced quickly become meaningless dead letters.

Paradoxically, it is therefore our inner affects that invest our outer reality with meaning. Our emotional attachment to the customs and institutions of our social world gives them their very being. Emotions form the bridge between the subjectivity of the individual and the objectivity of the larger world. Just as they connect individual physiology with physical reality, they animate symbolic outer reality. Only individuals who have evolved through the stages described in Part One can channel emotions to animate the abstract ideals of their society and the structures that embody them.

If a society consists largely of individuals able to function at the level of self-reflection, and if it possesses institutions in which its people lodge their trust, then that very trust—their collective emotional response, in other words—makes those institutions real. Social cohesion results from what Thomas Jefferson referred to as the "consent of the governed." It is a product of the affects widely held within a group rather than of compulsion and regimentation.

Unlike societies held together by blood loyalty or xenophobia or force, those whose cohesion arises from freely given emotional assent run two particular risks of fragmenting. If an institution violates the people's trust, only two choices exist: to remake it in a form that the people support, or to cease to give it their trust. But repairs require a large number of citizens reflective enough to see the need for change, flexible enough to accept it when it comes, and committed enough to make the great effort that the process demands. If the people lack that level of maturity, needed changes may never happen or may occur only through violence. To maintain a society that is both stable and creative, both cohesive and flexible, therefore requires institutional structures and processes strong enough to sustain themselves during change and a population that includes a substantial number of people able to think reflectively.

Such higher-level mental processes support another essential aspect of the modern world. Within this century, science has become our culture's model for truth. Though it appears independent of feelings, the scientific method and the reality it describes also depend on freely given assent. Scientific reality, like all human knowledge, evolves. Existing tools and paradigms impose limits on what we perceive, measure, and know. Thus, for example, Einstein's physics superseded Newton's to account for accumulating observations that did not fit Newtonian mechanics. Thomas Kuhn's notion of the paradigm shift— the replacement of one overarching conception of reality by another— is now almost commonplace.

Still, within the confines of accepted scientific formulations, results can be remarkably reliable and reproducible. Newton's calculations still hold for the circumstances in which he made them; Einstein's contribution was to expand the boundaries of physics and the phenomena it describes. It is the apparent "hardness" of scientific data and results, their seeming absoluteness and utter objectivity, that inspires the subjective trust that invests them with authority. The astonishing technological achievements that scientists have been able to produce of course play an important role in the confidence that we as a society bestow on the scientific endeavor, including its symbols and trappings. Even so, vast numbers of people who have never seen a virus or a gene, let alone an electron, believe implicitly in the powers attributed to these mysterious entities by recognized experts, as deeply as their ancestors believed in such invisible entities as evil spirits or bodily humors.

Indeed, the fact that certain segments of our society still adhere to older paradigms that conflict with the discoveries of science— Biblical inerrancy, for example, or astrology or numerology—underscores the role that common assent plays in the authority accorded to the apparently objective scientific world view. Adherents of such systems, some of whom are highly intelligent and articulate and, within

their own frames of reference, quite well educated and skilled in reasoning, believe as strongly in their ideas as do researchers who investigate black holes and DNA. Our ability to coexist depends not on the
ideas to which we give allegiance but to an ability to reflect, negotiate,
and give assent. Should larger and larger segments of our society one
day become completely polarized and believe in one absolute truth,
the stability of the reflective process could be lost.

HOW NATIONS COME OF AGE

The often puzzling relationships among nations can also be seen as
corresponding to the behavior of individuals at various developmental levels. In using this metaphor, I do not mean to imply that governmental policy decisions arise from the same motivations as individual
actions. However, the level at which nations deal with each other has
interesting parallels with the levels of individual development. Do
countries squabble over property like three-year-olds who want to
play with the same toy truck? Or do they take each other's needs into
account in negotiating issues, like two reflective adults attempting to
work out a mutual misunderstanding? Do they respond to one another with immediate actions or with well-considered replies? Do
they act on the basis of primitive feelrings and polarized concepts, or
do they discuss the merits of different positions?

   Most children advance through the various stages to reasonably
rational and constructive forms of communication, although probably not to the highest levels of reflectiveness. But that sort of maturity is often less apparent in international affairs, where adversaries
can remain trapped in cycles of self-defeating behavior. This can have
potentially catastrophic results in a world where weapons of mass
destruction are increasingly available and humanity's ability to comprehend and modulate its behavior remains stagnant.

   In recent decades numerous studies, including a report on ethnicity and nationalism by the Group for the Advancement of Psychiatry, have described how nations tend to distort each other's intentions
and to mistakenly ascribe to others their own motives and beliefs.[4] At
times their behavior is like that of a child at the level of early emo-
ional engagement: for example, disputants may simply withdraw

recognition from their adversaries. After the bombing of the Pan Am plane over Lockerbie, Scotland, in 1988, the United States determined to break relations with Libya and encouraged its allies to do likewise. The United States continues to try to penalize nations who trade with Cuba. In the complex tangle of attraction, envy, respect, and resentment binding the United States and Japan, our nation has shown a recurrent tendency to polarized characterization. Although our economy has benefited from infusions of Japanese capital, we have also objected to Japanese firms "buying up" some of our country's more symbolically charged assets.

Diplomats view such actions simply as moves on a chess board. A U.S. embargo on Libya or Serbia or South Africa forms part of an attempt to change the behavior of adversaries, preferably by internal overthrow of the offending government. In reality, however, the chief effect of ostracism is to block communication and make resolution impossible. A short period of isolation and resultant economic stress might weaken leaders hostile to U.S. interests, but decades of blacklisting may well have the opposite effect, strengthening our enemies in both their resolve to defy us and their prestige among their own people for having the gumption to do so. In the 1950s, rather than confront the very real problems that wracked the nation, the American political elite engaged in a bitter, damaging, and ultimately preposterous debate over exactly who was responsible for "losing" China to communism. Not until a generation later did President Nixon, who in an earlier phase of his career had helped lead the attack on the purported "disloyalty" of the State Department's corps of China experts, succeed in reestablishing open communication. In the interim, of course, U.S. and Chinese miscalculations of one another's intentions led to both the Korean and the Vietnam wars.

Accurate perception of what an adversary needs, can accept, and will do if frustrated is vital to negotiating any agreement. Recognition of the gestures that convey intentions and values is essential here. Such recognition can be undermined in five ways. First, people often prematurely substitute words for experience, as when the United States tried repeatedly to force Israel and the PLO to negotiate substantive issues before they had each developed enough common experience to comprehend one another's real intentions or trust one another's word.

Second, leaders may rely overly on mere verbal assurances and pay too little attention to actual behavior, as in the late 1930s when British prime minister Neville Chamberlain wishfully misinterpreted Hitler's annexation of Austria and designs on the Sudetenland as merely a reaction to the situation of ethnic Germans there rather than proof of his aggrandizing ambitions.

Third, when people try to force or manufacture accord when it doesn't exist, their interactions with others prevent nonverbal cues from betraying their true feelings. Servants keep smiling no matter how outrageously their employers behave; children tacitly forbidden to express anger or hostility toward their parents show a deceptively bland exterior. The Soviet Union supervised and orchestrated every aspect of Americans' visits so closely that the visitors were able to discern few of the internal signs of political and economic collapse that preceded the fall of the communist system.

Fourth, as tensions rise, both individuals and nations tend to minimize contact and thus the possibility of nonverbal communication. Kennedy and Khrushchev, for example, miscalculated each other's reactions during a difficult meeting in Vienna in 1962. The Cuban missile crisis arose not through direct contact between the leaders but through military gestures with warships and warheads. As the peril mounted, so did dangerous mutual confusion about what the other side would do.

Finally, individuals and nations often, and usually futilely, try to set limits for others' behavior without the benefit of a broader relationship within which to mediate disputes and accurately gauge the results of various actions. The United States has tried unavailingly to bring the isolated Libya to heel, for example, and struggled for decades to come to some accommodation with North Vietnam.

Sustained interaction and an understanding of symbols as well as emotional cues help nations resolve conflict but still leave room for misunderstanding. The lack of a structured identity and the sophisticated emotional thinking that allows reality testing can introduce considerable distortions into attempts at communication. Yasser Arafat executed skillful verbal gymnastics when he first attempted to acknowledge Israel's right to exist because he also needed simultaneously to assure his Palestinian colleagues that he was not a turncoat.

These formulations only roused the Israelis' suspicion that he, like others who had betrayed the Jewish people in the past, was up to a murderous trick. Russia's repeated experiences of mass invasion forced Soviet leaders to try to appear invulnerable at all times and thus markedly increased their intransigence at the negotiating table, far disproportionate to the situation.

It is sensitive collaboration and recognition of one another's needs that permits nations, like individuals, to settle the issues separating them. Only by evaluating nuances and subtleties as well as relative costs and benefits can countries determine the course likeliest to attain their goals without fomenting conflict. Polarized thinking—whether labeling opponents "godless communists" or "capitalist imperialists"—obviously makes such differentiated judgment impossible. It also prevents adversaries from perceiving each other's real intentions, strengths and weaknesses, and the areas in which some agreement is possible. In some instances true understanding leads to compassion and support. In others it allows limits to be set early rather than too late.

Looking at international affairs in terms of developmental stages offers guidelines for evaluating different approaches. Constructive communication means (1) maintaining unthreatening engagement through international organizations, (2) increasing interactions between both leaders and citizens through such avenues as diplomacy and exchange programs, (3) using sanctions and interventions only to set limits rather than to isolate an adversary from the world community, (4) offering respect and autonomy to other nations, (5) tolerating the distortions others make of facts or situations and analyzing these distortions for insights into the aims of others, and (6) negotiating differences using accurate information and realistic assessments of the other party.

The historical tendency of the United States to disengage from adversaries like Libya, China, and Cuba has not succeeded in forcing them to accept our will. Rather, it has kept us ill informed about their motivations and intentions, leading to such calamities as the Lockerbie bombing, the Korean War, and the Bay of Pigs fiasco. Retaining contact would at the very least permit us to gain more accurate information and at best allow us some influence over their actions.

Yielding to the temptation to regard the views and motives of others as all good or all bad has further prevented us from obtaining realistic information or devising profitable strategies. For well into five decades, both sides in the cold war were drawn into devastating military spending and two actual wars. The relations of the superpowers with countries around the world were distorted by categorizing them as allies or adversaries. This prevented efforts to understand each side's motivations and act on that understanding. Thus we might have understood the Soviet objection to U.S. missiles in Turkey to Russia's bitter memories of foreign invasion. Had we acknowledged and in some way tried to assuage this well-founded terror, it is possible that the Cuban missile crisis might have been settled without escalating to the brink of nuclear war.

Like many nations, the United States has repeatedly projected overly simplified notions onto others and has repeatedly discovered—in Vietnam, in Lebanon, in Iraq, in the former Yugoslavia—that foreign plans and aspirations are more complicated than was thought. Oversimplification has the deleterious effect of weakening internal institutions. If leaders give the public pat answers and polarized choices that do not represent the full complexities of challenges, they undermine both people's confidence and their ability to think reflectively about world affairs.

When political leaders use the mass media to feed the public misleading, polarized information, a danger exemplified during the McCarthy period in the 1950s, we lose the capacity to make careful distinctions in our national discourse. The question becomes "Who lost China?" rather than "How can we build more effective relations with nations in the communist bloc?" The goal becomes rooting out supposed traitors in the government rather than examining the views of experts who disagree with present policy. Misinformation may serve the short-term political advantage of some individuals, but in the long run it cripples our ability to govern ourselves.

Current polling techniques exacerbate this situation. After public figures have framed issues in a polarized way, pollsters conduct surveys to determine which positions are popular. Leaders then justify their policies and actions by referring to public opinion polls that were initially shaped by their own misinformation. A cycle of escalating misinformation and polarization replaces informed debate.

Our Constitution, like most documents on which democracies rest, assumes a body politic capable of reflective thinking. Originally the drafters tried to guarantee the needed qualities of moderation and reflection by limiting the franchise to men of position and property. Over the last two centuries, however, in keeping with the Constitution's true intent, the United States has broadened the electorate to include a number of formerly excluded classes. The survival of our democracy therefore depends on the ability of all our citizens to show the qualities of reflective thinking the Founders so cherished.

In the realm of foreign policy, today's and tomorrow's technologies leave us little alternative. The systems and devices that now allow instantaneous communication and stunningly detailed spying, not to mention worldwide mass destruction, have made such emotionally fueled policies as nonrecognition, posturing, and devious misrepresentation counterproductive. These may have served a purpose in the days when nations were not yet intertwined by the forces of global economics and technology. But today, when the entire world can simultaneously watch an incident live on television; when instant communications can cause stock markets to surge or plummet on every continent; when economies are ever more tightly interdependent; and when nuclear, biological, and ecological weapons threaten the entire planet, only a far more reflective approach to international relations provides any measure of national security.

Societies organized at a fairly high developmental level obviously offer their citizens a far better chance of living lives of freedom and themselves attaining a high level of consciousness than do those organized at low levels. Reflective societies tend overwhelmingly to be democracies, with or without a vestigial, ceremonial monarchy. Autocracies may offer a kind of security based on force and belonging based on uniformity, but personal freedom and a sense of meaning in individual lives are inhibited. Higher-level reflective thinking or expression, which might unmask the cruelties, pretenses, and inconsistencies of the society, are discouraged or prohibited. By burning books, jamming airwaves, forbidding citizens access to personal faxes, copiers, or computers, tapping telephones, censoring newspapers, monopolizing the media, prescribing curricula, eavesdropping on private conversations, monitoring public meetings, and punishing dissent, such societies crush all efforts to foster a free exchange of ideas.

Democracies not only encourage but require high-level mental abilities. They cannot survive without citizens who are able to weigh issues and draw their own conclusions. In the United States, all adult citizens are expected to be able to formulate and express opinions on the worthiness of candidates for office and the merits of various public issues. Our legal system assumes that any twelve citizens chosen at random will succeed in understanding both the facts and the legal principles involved in even the most complicated criminal trial. It does not require that jurors possess certain academic qualifications or that voters fulfill any intellectual requirements. It simply takes for granted that ordinary Americans can understand nuance, weigh alternatives, and come to fair and reasonable judgments. As long as a critical mass of people retain these abilities, our free institutions will endure.

CHAPTER FIFTEEN
Our Human Imperative

THE ASSUMPTION THAT THERE WILL BE ENOUGH REFLECTIVE
adults to maintain a free society is not to be taken for granted. If the
supposition I have set forth in this book is true—if emotional experience is in fact the basis of the mind's growth—then the spreading
impersonality and family stress that pervade our society may well be
threatening mental development in a significant number of individuals.

We can expect that persons who in childhood lacked opportunities to develop higher, more reflective mental qualities will act impulsively, think in rigid and polarized terms, fall short in nuance and
subtlety, and ignore the rights, needs, and dignity of others. Should
the numbers of such people grow, we would expect society to become
more unpredictable and dangerous, with rising violence and antisocial behavior and less self-restraint and negotiation. People would
show ever more extremism and self-absorption. In the long run there
would be less generative, creative thought. Rote cognitive skills would
supplant true innovation.

These trends are in fact already so well established that they have
begun to worry many thoughtful citizens. Seemingly aimless violence
and crime have risen sharply over the past generation. Assaults that
only two or three decades ago would have rated banner headlines now
fill the inside pages of the Metro section.[1] Ever younger children now

kill, and kill remorselessly, often over trivial points of precedence or possession of property that a generation or two ago would have resulted in no more than a fistfight. Any sense that all members of society bear mutual responsibility for the welfare of the weakest among us has been badly fractured as the more fortunate increasingly retreat into gated residential enclaves, shopping malls, and private schools.

Substantial numbers of citizens show the signs of operating well below the highest developmental levels, either because they failed to master important stages of mental growth or because something in their lives has made them regress to earlier levels. A frightening number of young people act as if their emotional development lagged years, even a decade or more, behind their chronological age.

Concerned citizens everywhere realize that innovative action is needed to stem the forces now undermining our society's ability to foster the qualities we most value. However, the steps that must be taken are less clear. In this book I have suggested avenues for change based on the developmental perspective. Some of these steps may entail material and professional sacrifice. Competitiveness, the drive for efficiency, and the expansion of bureaucracy, which all contribute to increasing depersonalization, have become powerful forces. Putting the care of children, relationships, and the quality of emotional experience first in families, education, psychotherapy, marriage, and the institutions of social welfare is, I believe, our human imperative.

This does not mean a return to the hierarchical household of the past. Genuine "family values," which center on the primacy of intimate interactions, demand not conformity to rigid roles but rather entail an understanding that emotional life is the foundation of intellect and of the judgment and moral sensibility needed in a democratic society.

Parents struggling to raise children in the hectic, pressured world of dual-career couples, single-parent households, around-the-clock shift work, nonexistent extended families, and financial insecurity often find themselves too busy, tired, or preoccupied to give their children the time and attention that intimate relationships require. A culture that regarded parenthood not as a private concern and a distraction from work but as the gravest, most challenging, and most socially useful task an adult could undertake would encourage and support far greater parental involvement than many of today's children now experience. For the long-term good of each child, and of society as a whole, the demanding project of raising a member of the next generation of adults needs recognition not merely as a family's privately chosen responsibility but as work done for our common benefit. Creative, contributing, compassionate citizens have always been our nation's most vital resource. Those who labor to produce them need recognition and support.

Long-proposed reforms like more flexible work schedules, greater availability of day care, and more liberal family leave, though useful, are only tiny steps toward making a society truly committed to the centrality of affective interchange in development. The real reform must take place in the values that guide our decisions—that is, in the conception of human nature that we use to frame the discussion. The false dichotomy between emotion and intellect, between education and interaction, underlies our neglect to provide social and financial supports for families.

If the split between, on the one hand, subjective, spiritual, and emotional and, on the other, objective, rational, and materialistic conceptions of human nature continues to divide us as it has long done in Western thought, we may well continue on our present course. We may look to mechanistic and materialistic solutions, such as tougher social policies and more prisons, instead of attempting to meet emotional needs in a framework of appropriate structures and discipline.

From the proposition that affective experience constitutes the foundation of the human mind and that providing it is the essence of the demanding but infinitely valuable task of raising children, it follows that child rearing and family life deserve the highest priority among the many conflicting demands made on individuals. Our highly competitive culture defines the successful person as one who excels on the job (preferably at a high-paying, high-prestige position), privately (with an equally successful spouse and high-achieving children), and personally (through self-improvement programs and fitness regimes). Indeed, it sometimes fosters a desire for achievement and self-fulfillment that resembles greed in its intensity and insatiability.

When satisfying all aspects of this hunger proves impossible, as it almost inevitably must, ambitious, well-meaning, conscientious individuals often feel cheated and disappointed. The desire not to miss out on anything can poison the taste of what a person does have. Striving for complete satisfaction or success in everything—work, family life, social life, recreation, community activities, relationships with colleagues—ironically steals away the time needed for the intimate emotional relationships that provide true satisfaction. In a society obsessed with work, adult self-expression, and social status, making time for a rich emotional life and the close relationships that support it often means fighting against conventional wisdom. It can mean asserting an individual set of values in the face of prevailing beliefs. Many people's circumstances make this very difficult to do.

At present, society does not fully acknowledge the extent of children's need for intimate interaction, nor does it instill in prospective parents a realistic sense that raising children must take priority in decisions regarding work schedules and career aspirations. A dualistic view of mental development obscures the fact that parents' most important gift to their child is not a good education, elaborate educational toys, or summer camp, but time—regular, substantial chunks of it spent together doing things that are naturally appealing to the child.

This fact conflicts not only with many parents' intellectual beliefs. It violates the years of training they received at school and on the job. Much of a person's early experience—getting through school and establishing herself at work—teaches that striving for an A+ brings copious rewards, whether in the classroom, on the playing field, or in a career. The teacher, the coach, the college admissions committee, the boss rarely point out that excelling in one area of life—especially one that offers public recognition such as academic honors and degrees, athletic prizes, or high pay—may mean a mediocre or even failing grade in other spheres of life. The product of such an upbringing may not realize that an A+ at work may carry the price of a D− in family life and child rearing. Moreover, since no authority figure records that terrible grade in life's most important undertaking, many parents don't even know that they received it.

The illusion that intellect develops independently of affect allows people to ignore the importance of intimate interaction. Only through such interaction can parents appreciate each child's physiological and temperamental makeup, empathize with his feelings through the happenings of daily life, design tasks and goals to meet his unique combination of strengths and weaknesses, establish and enforce limits and incentives based on warmth, firmness, consistency, and love, and provide, in short, emotional experiences essential for developing the highest qualities of the mind.

This is not to say that children need A+ parenting to grow up well, any more than most families need A+ finances to maintain a reasonable standard of living. Parents with high aspirations may face a difficult and unfamiliar choice—choosing to achieve less than they might in one area in order to do what needs to be done in another. Those who can arrange their activities to get solid Bs in both areas— who combine a serious commitment to intimate family relationships with a view of the moderate importance of career success—can ordinarily provide what their children really need for healthy development.

At present, youngsters learn to be parents in the imperfect training schools of their own original families. This training may perpetuate the neglect of early emotional experience and its separation from intellectual development. A new understanding of mental growth is needed in schools and in the media as well as in the home. Teaching the subject of human development from kindergarten to college as an integral part of the school curriculum like math or English, and affording students hands-on experiences with little children—sixth graders helping first graders with homework, for example, or high schoolers and college students working in day-care centers or discussing the challenges of marriage and family life—would do much to give future parents greater understanding of the needs of children. Because much of core subjects like literature and history are about human behavior, such an understanding of human development would undoubtedly also enhance a child's appreciation of these subjects as well. Insights related to emotions and families could be brought from home into the school. If emotional and intellectual life are one and the same, there is no conflict. If we keep these spheres separate, we set limits on both education and intelligence.

We can no longer afford to view the rearing of the next generation as parents' private concern. The work of conscientious parents struggling to provide love and care and to impart values deserves recognition as a contribution to the common good. New incentives in the tax code, the workplace, and the community are needed to make family life as important as earning a living or pursuing a career. Such incentives would help many parents set up their lives in a way that would better meet both their children's and their own affective needs.

This shift in priorities does not mean restricting one parent to staying home during the years that children are growing up. The point is rather that children's needs must be the chief concern in both parents' career and financial decisions. One compromise that I call the "four-thirds solution" can permit both parental care for children and professional opportunities for parents. If two parents were each to work two-thirds rather than full-time, a child could receive care from her own parents for two-thirds of the work week. This plan does require sacrifices in early career achievement, not to mention the reeducation of employers, but it can pay extraordinarily rich benefits in family life and child development.

In families in which a single parent must work full-time to meet basic needs, the four-thirds solution is of course not possible. If a long-term, intimate, nurturing relationship with a live-in grandmother or other caregiver is also impossible, it is critical for such families to realize that the attention provided in day care will not be adequate to meet a child's developmental needs. Institutional care and institutional love are inherently limited, even in the very best day-care centers, and the child will thus need additional intimate interactions. A single parent could consider leaving the television or computer off and recruiting a little interactive partner or partners in daily routines of cleaning, cooking, and shopping. Also, at dinner, in the bath, or while cuddling in bed, a caregiver can give the child "floor time" by following the child's lead and helping her elaborate her natural inclinations.[2]

For children in the first three years of life, institutional day care requires major changes to meet emotional needs. In-service training for day-care providers in the tactics that support interaction at each developmental level, greater involvement with parents as a sort of extended family, and administrative procedures that permit caregivers to stay with a group of children from the first through the fourth year so that emotional continuity is maintained and strengthened for both children and caregivers—such changes can heighten the quality of children's relationships with caregivers. Beyond this, greater regard, enhanced career opportunities, and improved wage scales are also needed for caregivers.

Changes in our educational system are also required. The outdated factory model must give way to one based on the way the mind develops. Curricula, school organization, and teaching methods should recognize the variety of children's developmental profiles and tailor instruction to particular strengths. Those who do not learn well in groups need at least an hour or two each day of individual work with teachers. Those who need an extra dose of emotional stability should stay with the same teacher or mentor at least throughout the elementary school years, and sometimes even beyond. Involvement with not only the subject matter but also teachers and other students allows children to master material and gives them experience of how to learn as well. All but very severely challenged youngsters can learn the content taught in elementary and junior high school. If a child attends school without learning the basic skills needed for a productive life, including logical and creative thinking, the fault lies not with the youngster's ability or attitude but with the adults entrusted with providing education.

Another area in which developmental understanding forces us to rethink our basic categories is that of mental health care. Our conception must go beyond symptoms and syndromes toward a broader view of mental illness as a failure of development. Medications should be regarded not as cures for disorders but as a means to make the experiences that foster growth available. Unintegrated, piecemeal approaches, whether pep talks from popular gurus or the most powerful new pills, must not be seen as legitimate therapy. Rather, nourishing the developmental process, not simply normalizing a disturbed individual's behavior, should be the mark of genuinely effective treatment. Moreover, cost-reducing plans such as managed care cannot be allowed to set treatment standards. Together with consumers, health-care professionals organized at both national and local levels must issue guidelines for appropriate diagnoses and treatment that will enable patients to negotiate with plan administrators and, if necessary, to take legal action.

Turning to the problem of family breakdown, we see that half of all marriages now fail not primarily because partners are selfish or irresponsible but because they have not been either taught about the pressures that arise in marital relationships or helped to develop the capacity for self-reflection that would let them respond flexibly and constructively to these challenges. Prospective spouses learn about marriage in their own childhood homes, in families often ill equipped to foster much reflectiveness in emotional relationships. If half of all doctors or bus drivers or air traffic controllers eventually proved unable to perform their tasks, society would be in an uproar, demanding new methods of training and preparation. The emergency is far greater in a situation that exposes vast numbers of youngsters to the turmoil of divorce and the difficulties of time- and money-stressed single-parent homes.

No society that takes seriously the affective origin of mental faculties would tolerate the treatment meted out to the neediest and most vulnerable of our children by the institutions with responsibility for their welfare. Adoption and foster care agencies and the juvenile justice system make decisions that do not provide for the emotional continuity that can repair early deprivation. Every child's need for intimate affective interaction within stable relationships could be more adequately met by expediting adoptions, carefully screening and supervising foster homes, and providing training and incentives for foster or adoptive parents willing to undertake long-term commitments to challenging children. A corps of well-trained and well-compensated social and community workers, mentors, and the like would help ensure that each child formed continuing relationships with people who knew and cared for him personally.

While family preservation would not be the goal at all costs, those who might benefit would receive extensive services and support before being deemed incapable of their task. Ignoring the needs of challenging multiproblem families is perhaps a society's most dramatic form of denial. We must view every child, whether rich or poor, whether belonging to the majority or a minority race, whether born in the prosperous suburbs or the chaotic slums, as the embodiment of our common future.

Our approach to substance abuse and other high-risk behavior reveals most dramatically our lack of an integrated concept of human intelligence. We tend to provide some health and education leadership, but for the most part leave personal emotional concerns to the family. The cycle of poor coping leading to substance abuse and high-risk behavior, which leads to further poor judgment and impaired mental functioning, continues unabated. What would it take to make the prevention of such behavior, which undermines individuals, families, and entire societies, the top of our domestic agenda? Only a concept of human functioning that unites these personal concerns with family, community, and national goals has any chance of elevating these challenges to their proper place in the future.

Finally, our approach to international relations must place new emphasis on understanding our allies' and adversaries' intentions and values. There is a tendency for many to believe they are experts in human nature when they are projecting their own frame of reference on others. Robert McNamara, secretary of state during the Kennedy administration, recently acknowledged that he and his colleagues had badly misread the intentions of the North Vietnamese and warned that we are now equally ill informed about the emotional underpinnings of the present conflicts in Europe and the Middle East.[3] Understanding the intentions of large groups is a task sizable and significant enough to justify a special government department or agency charged with gaining a thorough understanding of other cultures on their own terms. Rather than the current practice of scrambling to find academics with area expertise when a crisis in some far-off and little-known place erupts into the news, the people who make and execute our foreign policy must cultivate a real sense of each country's standing in developmental terms and the themes and interests that animate it. The source of international power is knowledge about other peoples. Both at home and abroad, we must couple traditional economic programs that provide opportunities and hopefulness with an understanding and support of the factors that enable individuals, families, and societies to develop their full human capabilities.

At the bottom of these proposals is a philosophical shift in the conception of what human beings are. Nations implement policies consistent with their view of who and what they are. If society continues to see the intellect and the emotions—the objective and subjective aspects of mental organization—as distinct and even conflicting entities, we will not take seriously the central role that intimate interactions play in the development of the mind. If we do not come to see subjectivity as basic to both intellect and creativity, and thus fundamental to our ability to compete or cooperate with other nations both economically and in world affairs, we will not only hinder our progress and risk further conflict. We may also become victims of a more dangerous paradox. As we attempt to progress as a society, we may unwittingly erode the building blocks that are the origins of our highest mental abilities.

If early emotional experience is the basis of our intellectual capacities as well as of our moral sense and creativity, we must give it higher priority in our personal, community, and national planning. The challenges that face us—ecological, economic, and military—require collective action. Such challenges require the development of our individual minds and the opportunity for each and all of us to attain full humanity. Attention to subjective experience is then not purely a humanitarian or aesthetic activity, but one that is crucial to human survival.

Notes

INTRODUCTION: QUESTIONING A HISTORICAL DICHOTOMY

1. Piaget, investigating the interactions between the child and his environment, referred many times to the importance of emotions. His main interest, however, was how a child creates cognitive structures from his actions, and he never fully explored the role of inner affects (see, for example, J. Piaget, *The Origins of Intelligence in Children* [New York: International Universities Press, 1952]; idem, *The Construction of Reality in the Child* [New York: Basic Books, 1954]; idem, "The Stages of the Intellectual Development of the Child," in *Childhood Psychopathology*, ed. S. Harrison and J. McDermott [New York: International Universities Press, 1962], pp. 157–66. For further discussion of this topic see S. I. Greenspan, *Intelligence and Adaptation: An Integration of Psychoanalytic and Piagetian Developmental Psychology* [New York: International Universities Press, 1979]).

Even the Soviet psychologist L. S. Vygotsky, who focused explicitly on the importance of social interaction as well as culture and conflict in learning, did not fully deal with the central role of affect in learning (see L. S. Vygotsky, *Thought and Language* [Russian ed., 1934; Cambridge: MIT Press, 1962]; idem, *Mind in Society: The Development of Higher Psychological Processes* [Cambridge: Harvard University Press, 1978]; idem, "The Genesis of the Higher Mental Function," in *The Concept of Activity in Soviet Psychology*, ed. J. V. Wertsch [Armonk, N.Y.: M. E. Sharpe, 1981], pp. 144–88; idem, *The Collected Works of L. S. Vygotsky*, vol. 1: *Problems of General Psychology* [New York: Plenum, 1987]).

The importance of early emotional development became prominent in the 1940s, 1950s, and 1960s through the work of pioneers such as Erik

Erikson, Anna Freud, René Spitz, John Bowlby, J. McV. Hunt, Lois Murphy, and Sibylle Escalona. They showed that early deprivation could derail healthy development and that early emotional experiences were important contributors to the nature and character of subsequent personality functioning.

In the 1960s, 1970s, and 1980s, research on normal emotional development in infancy and early childhood blossomed. Many aspects of emotional development, ranging from early infant proclivities to complex social and emotional interactions, were described by investigators such as Sally Provence, Selma Fraiberg, Louis Sandler, Berry Brazelton, Mary Ainsworth, Stella Chess, Leon Yarrow, Allen Sroufe, Robert Emde, Dan Stern, as well as many others (this body of work is referenced in Further Sources, located at the back of the book. See also note 7 in this chapter.).

This impressive body of work, however, did not find its way into prevention, clinical practice, or educational policies. In part, this was because there were insufficient studies of psychopathology and clinical intervention in infancy and early childhood, as well as a lack of empirical and theoretical linkages between emotional and cognitive development.

With these challenges in mind, in the early 1970s my colleagues and I began our clinical and research efforts at the National Institute of Mental Health (NIMH). We worked on identifying the earliest stages of emotional development, the types of disorders that could occur, and the factors that could lead to either disorders or adaptation at either stage. We also worked to understand the relationship between affective and cognitive development that was a foundation for many adaptive and maladaptive capacities.

The Growth of the Mind is an attempt to integrate insights drawn from over twenty years of observation, clinical work, and research. Some of our observations have been described in these works: S. I. Greenspan, *A Consideration of Some Learning Variables in the Context of Psychoanalytic Theory: Toward a Psychoanalytic Learning Perspective* (New York: International Universities Press, 1975); idem, *Intelligence and Adaptation;* S. I. Greenspan and R. S. Lourie, "Developmental Structuralist Approach to the Classification of Adaptive and Pathologic Personality Organizations: Application to Infancy and Early Childhood," *American Journal of Psychiatry* 138 (June 1981): 6; S. I. Greenspan, *Psychopathology and Adaptation in Infancy and Early Childhood: Principles of Clinical Diagnosis and Preventive Intervention* (New York: International Universities Press, 1981); idem, *The Clinical Interview of the Child,* 2nd ed. (Washington, D.C.: American Psychiatric Press, 1981); S. I. Greenspan and N. T. Greenspan, *First Feelings: Milestones in the Emotional Development of Your Baby and Child from Birth to Age Four* (New York: Viking Penguin, 1985); S. I. Greenspan, S. Wieder, A. Lieberman, R. Nover,

R. Lourie, and M. Robinson, *Infants in Multirisk Families: Case Studies in Preventive Intervention* (New York: International Universities Press, 1987); S. I. Greenspan, *The Development of the Ego: Implications for Personality Theory, Psychopathology, and the Psychotherapeutic Process* (Madison, Conn.: International Universities Press, 1989); idem, *Infancy and Early Childhood: The Practice of Clinical Assessment and Intervention with Emotional and Developmental Challenges* (Madison, Conn.: International Universities Press, 1992); idem, *Playground Politics: Understanding the Emotional Life of Your School-Age Child* (Reading, Mass.: Addison-Wesley, 1993); idem, *The Challenging Child: Understanding, Raising, and Enjoying the Five "Difficult" Types of Children* (Reading, Mass.: Addison-Wesley, 1995); idem, *Developmentally Based Psychotherapy* (Madison, Conn.: International Universities Press, 1996); S. I. Greenspan and S. Wieder, *Facilitating Emotional and Intellectual Growth in Children with Special Needs: The Floor Time Approach* (forthcoming from Addison-Wesley).

2. For further discussion of this topic see S. I. Greenspan, *The Development of the Ego*.

3. I. Kant, *Critique of Pure Reason* (London: Macmillan, 1963).

4. See H. Hartmann, *Ego Psychology and the Problem of Adaptation* (New York: International Universities Press, 1939); S. Thomkins, *Affect, Imagery, Consciousness*, vol. 1 (New York: Springer, 1963); H. Kohut, *The Analysis of Self: A Systematic Approach to the Psychoanalytic Treatment of Narcissistic Personality Disorders* (New York: International Universities Press, 1971).

5. D. Goleman, *Emotional Intelligence* (New York: Bantam, 1995).

6. A. Damasio, *Descartes' Error: Emotion, Reason, and the Human Brain* (New York: Putnam, 1994).

7. Beginning nearly six decades ago, the importance of emotions for aspects of learning was documented by psychoanalytic observers such as René Spitz and John Bowlby, who described the effects of emotional deprivation, and Heinz Hartmann and David Rappaport, who explored clinical and theoretical relationships (see R. A. Spitz, "Hospitalism: An Inquiry into the Genesis of Psychiatric Conditions in Early Childhood," *The Psychoanalytic Study of the Child* 1 [1945]: 53–74; J. Bowlby, *Maternal Care and Mental Health* [Geneva: World Health Organization, 1951]; Hartmann, *Ego Psychology;* D. Rappaport, *The Structure of Psychoanalytic Theory: A Systematizing Attempt* [New York: International Universities Press, 1960]). Sibylle Escalona and Lois Murphy have described individual differences in infants and their relationship to psychopathology (S. Escalona, *The Roots of Individuality* [Chicago: Aldine, 1968]; L. Murphy, *The Individual Child*, Department of Health, Education, and Welfare, publication no. OCD 74-1032 [Washington,

D.C.: U.S. Government Printing Office, 1974]). The behavioral pediatrician T. Berry Brazelton has systematized an approach to observing and describing the different aspects of an infant's adaptive repertoire, including important social and emotional capacities (T. B. Brazelton and B. Cramer, *The Earliest Relationship: Parents, Infants, and the Drama of Early Attachment* [Reading, Mass.: Addison-Wesley, 1990]). In my own *Intelligence and Adaptation,* I attempt to integrate cognitive and affective aspects of the mind.

8. T. T. Young, *Emotions in Man and Animal* (New York: Wiley, 1943).

9. S. I. Greenspan, *The Development of the Ego;* idem, *Developmentally Based Psychotherapy;* idem, *Infancy and Early Childhood.*

10. There is growing evidence that the link between the brain and behavior works both ways: behavior and experience are not simply shaped by the brain but influence both the structure and the formation of the brain. Early in life there appears to be a genetically induced overproduction of neurons. Experience then takes over, however, and fine-tunes or "prunes" this emerging structure. Experience also leads to new dendrite growth (connections between neurons) and the biochemical changes that support this growth. Experience-induced nervous system growth involving many areas of the brain can take place not only during early sensitive times but throughout development. Occurring almost immediately in response to appropriate experiences, it can be associated with a range of capacities, from complex cognitive abilities to well-known phenomena like imprinting. It seems that evolution has designed important aspects of brain growth to be responsive to the environment to which the brain must adapt (see W. T. Greenough and J. E. Black, "Induction of Brain Structure by Experience: Substrates for Cognitive Development," *Developmental Behavioral Neuroscience* 24 [1992]: 155–299; I. J. Weiler, N. Hawrylak, and W. T. Greenough, "Morphogenesis in Memory Formation: Synaptic and Cellular Mechanisms," *Behavioural Brain Research* 66 [1995]: 1–6).

11. See R. L. Holloway, "Dendritic Branching: Some Preliminary Results of Training and Complexity in Rat Visual Cortex," *Brain Research* 2 (1966): 393–96; A. M. Turner and W. T. Greenough, "Synapses per Neuron and Synaptic Dimensions in Occipital Cortex of Rats Reared in Complex, Social, or Isolation Housing," *Acta Stereologica* 2, suppl. 1 (1983): 239–44; idem, "Differential Rearing Effects on Rat Visual Cortex Synapses, I: Synaptic and Neuronal Density and Synapses per Neuron," *Brain Research* 329 (1985): 195–203; C. Thinus-Blanc, "Volume Discrimination Learning in Golden Hamsters: Effects of the Structure of Complex Rearing Cages," *Developmental Psychobiology* 14 (1981): 397–403.

12. See T. N. Wiesel and D. H. Hubel, "Single-Cell Responses in Striate Cortex of Kittens Deprived of Vision in One Eye," *Journal of Neurophysiology* 26 (1963): 1003–17; W. Singer, "Neuronal Activity as a Shaping Factor in

Postnatal Development of Visual Cortex," in *Developmental Neuropsychobiology*, ed. W. T. Greenough and J. M. Juraska (Orlando: Academic Press, 1986): 271–93; A. Hein and R. M. Diamond, "Contribution of Eye Movement to the Representation of Space," in *Spatially Oriented Behavior*, ed. A. Hein and M. Jeannerod (New York: Springer, 1983), pp. 119–34.

13. See M. A. Bell and N. A. Fox, "Brain Development over the First Year of Life: Relations Between EEG Frequency and Coherence and Cognitive and Affective Behaviors," in *Human Behavior and the Developing Brain*, ed. G. Dawson and K. Fischer (New York: Guilford, 1994), pp. 314–45; H. T. Chugani and M. E. Phelps, "Maturational Changes in Cerebral Function in Infants Determined by 18FDG Positron Emission Tomography," *Science* 231 (1986): 840–43; H. T. Chugani, M. E. Phelps, and J. C. Mazziotta, "Positron Emission Tomography Study of Human Brain Functional Development," *Annals of Neurology* 22 (1994): 487–97.

14. Chugani, Phelps, and Mazziotta, "Positron Emission Tomography."

15. S. M. Schanberg and T. M. Field, "Sensory Deprivation Stress and Supplemental Stimulation in the Rat Pup and Preterm Human Neonate," *Child Development* 58 (1987): 1431–47.

16. See, for example, B. D. Perry, "Incubated in Terror: Neurodevelopmental Factors in the 'Cycle of Violence,'" in *Children, Youth and Violence: Searching for Solutions*, ed. J. Osofsky (New York: Guilford, 1995).

17. See, for example, M. A. Hofer, "On the Nature and Function of Prenatal Behavior," in *Behavior of the Fetus*, ed. W. Smotherman and S. Robinson (Caldwell, N.J.: Telford, 1988); idem, "Hidden Regulators: Implications for a New Understanding of Attachment, Separation, and Loss," in *Attachment Theory: Social, Developmental, and Clinical Perspectives*, ed. S. Goldberg, R. Muir, and J. Kerr (Hillsdale, N.J.: Analytic Press, 1995), pp. 203–30; P. Rakic, J. Bourgeois, and P. Goldman-Rakic, "Synaptic Development of the Cerebral Cortex: Implications for Learning, Memory, and Mental Illness," in *The Self-Organizing Brain: From Growth Cones to Functional Networks*, ed. J. van Pelt, M. A. Corner, H. B. M. Uylings, and F. H. Lopes da Silva (New York: Elsevier Science, 1994), pp. 227–43.

18. In an experiment, both an infant and a monkey looked longer at a trick box that had only one item in it, even though they had just observed two items being put in the box. Is the conclusion that infants (and monkeys) therefore understand arithmetic warranted by this research? Perhaps, rather than an understanding of math, these observations reveal that infants can distinguish certain spatial relationships as well as provide evidence of basic perceptual motor skills and growing memory capacity.

19. S. I. Greenspan and S. Meisels, "Toward a New Vision for the Developmental Assessment of Infants and Young Children," *ZERO TO*

THREE: Bulletin of the National Center for Clinical Infant Programs 14, no. 6 (1994): 1–8.

20. For more information see S. I. Greenspan, *Infancy and Early Childhood;* S. I. Greenspan and S. Wieder, *Facilitating Emotional and Intellectual Growth in Children with Special Needs;* S. I. Greenspan, "Reconsidering the Diagnosis and Treatment of Very Young Children with Autistic Spectrum or Pervasive Developmental Disorder," National Center for Clinical Infant Programs, *ZERO TO THREE: Bulletin of the National Center for Clinical Infant Programs* 13, no. 2 (1992): 1–9.

21. See, for example, Greenspan, *Intelligence and Adaptation;* idem, *Development of the Ego;* S. I. Greenspan and N. T. Greenspan, *First Feelings;* S. I. Greenspan, *Playground Politics.*

22. S. W. Porges, J. A. Doussard-Roosevelt, A. L. Portales, and S. I. Greenspan, "Infant Regulation of the Vagal 'Brake' Predicts Child Behavior Problems: A Psychobiological Model of Social Behavior," *Developmental Psychobiology* (in press).

23. See A. J. Sameroff, R. Seifer, R. Barocas, M. Zax, and S. I. Greenspan, "IQ Scores of Four-Year-Old Children: Social-Environmental Risk Factors," *Pediatrics* 79 (1986): 343–50.

24. S. I. Greenspan et al., *Infants in Multirisk Families;* Sameroff et al., "IQ Scores of Four-Year-Old Children"; A. J. Sameroff, R. Seifer, A. Baldwin, and C. Baldwin, "Stability of Intelligence from Preschool to Adolescence: The Influence of Social and Family Risk Factors," *Child Development* 64 (1993): 80–97.

25. For further information see S. Provence and A. Naylor, *Working with Disadvantaged Parents and Their Children: Scientific and Practical Issues* (New Haven: Yale University Press, 1983); A. S. Honig and J. R. Lally, *Infant Caregiving: A Design for Training* (Syracuse, N.Y.: Syracuse University Press, 1981); J. R. Berrueta-Clement, L. J. Schweinhart, W. S. Barnett, A. S. Epstein, and D. P. Weikart, *Changed Lives: The Effects of the Perry Preschool Program on Youths Through Age Nineteen* (Ypsilanti, Mich.: High/Scope, 1984); C. T. Ramey and F. A. Campbell, "Preventive Education for High-Risk Children: Cognitive Consequences of the Carolina Abecedarian Project," *American Journal of Mental Deficiency* 88 (1984): 515–23; Greenspan et al., *Infants in Multirisk Families.*

CHAPTER ONE: THE EMOTIONAL ARCHITECTURE OF THE MIND

1. See S. I. Greenspan, *Infancy and Early Childhood: The Practice of Clinical Assessment and Intervention with Emotional and Developmental Challenges* (Madison, Conn.: International Universities Press, 1992).

2. Ibid.

3. S. I. Greenspan and S. Wieder, *Facilitating Emotional and Intellectual Growth in Children with Special Needs: The Floor Time Approach* (forthcoming from Addison-Wesley); idem, "Developmental Patterns and Outcomes in Infants and Children with Disorders in Relating and Communicating: A Chart Review of 200 Cases of Children with Autism Spectrum Diagnoses," submitted for publication.

4. See, for example, S. I. Greenspan, *The Development of the Ego: Implications for Personality Theory, Psychopathology, and the Psychotherapeutic Process* (Madison, Conn.: International Universities Press, 1989).

5. A. Einstein, *Ideas and Opinions* (London: Alvin Redman, 1956), p. 25.

6. See Greenspan and Wieder, *Facilitating Emotional and Intellectual Growth*; Greenspan, *Infancy and Early Childhood.*

7. For more information see W. T. Greenough and J. E. Black, "Induction of Brain Structure by Experience: Substrates for Cognitive Development," *Developmental Behavioral Neuroscience* 24 (1992): 155–299; I. J. Weiler, N. Hawrylak, and W. T. Greenough, "Morphogenesis in Memory Formation: Synaptic and Cellular Mechanisms," *Behavioural Brain Research* 66 (1995): 1–6.

8. S. I. Greenspan, *Intelligence and Adaptation: An Integration of Psychoanalytic and Piagetian Developmental Psychology* (New York: International Universities Press, 1979).

9. Quoted in J. Flavell, *The Developmental Psychology of Jean Piaget* (Princeton, N.J.: Van Nostrand, 1963), p. 80. See also Greenspan, *Intelligence and Adaptation;* B. Inhelder and J. Piaget, *The Growth of Logical Thinking from Childhood to Adolescence* (New York: Basic Books, 1958), pp. 347–48.

10. R. W. Sperry, "Consciousness, Personal Identity, and the Divided Brain," in *The Dual Brain: Hemispheric Specialization in Humans,* ed. Frank Benson and Erin Zaidel (Los Angeles: Guilford, 1985), pp. 11–27; Frank Benson and Erin Zaidel, eds., *The Dual Brain: Hemispheric Specialization in Humans* (Los Angeles: Guilford, 1985).

CHAPTER THREE: FROM INTENT TO DIALOGUE

1. E. Tronick, "The Primacy of Social Skills in Infancy," *Exceptional Infant* 4 (1980): 144–58.

2. S. W. Porges, J. A. Doussard-Roosevelt, A. L. Portales, and S. I. Greenspan, "Infant Regulation of the Vagal 'Brake' Predicts Child Behavior Problems: A Psychobiological Model of Social Behavior," *Developmental Psychobiology* (in press).

3. The nineteenth-century philosopher Clemens Brentano brought the concept of intentionality into the center of philosophical definitions of consciousness.

4. S. I. Greenspan and S. Wieder, *Facilitating Emotional and Intellectual Growth in Children with Special Needs: The Floor Time Approach* (forthcoming from Addison-Wesley).

5. S. I. Greenspan, *Infancy and Early Childhood: The Practice of Clinical Assessment and Intervention with Emotional and Developmental Challenges* (Madison, Conn.: International Universities Press, 1992).

6. See, for example, R. W. Sperry, "Consciousness, Personal Identity, and the Divided Brain," in *The Dual Brain: Hemispheric Specialization in Humans,* ed. Frank Benson and Erin Zaidel (Los Angeles: Guilford, 1985), pp. 11–27.

7. See, for example, M. Campbell and J. Shay, "Pervasive Developmental Disorders," in *Comprehensive Textbook of Psychiatry,* 6th ed., vol. 2, ed. H. I. Kaplan and B. Saddock (Baltimore: Williams & Wilkins, 1995), pp. 2277–93; M. K. De Myer, J. N. Hingtgen, and R. K. Jackson, "Infantile Autism Reviewed: A Decade of Research," *Schizophrenia Bulletin* 7 (1981): 388–451.

8. M. S. Mahler, F. Pine, and A. Bergman, *The Psychological Birth of the Human Infant: Symbiosis and Individuation* (New York: Basic Books, 1975).

9. See S. I. Greenspan, *The Development of the Ego: Implications for Personality Theory, Psychopathology, and the Psychotherapeutic Process* (Madison, Conn.: International Universities Press, 1989).

CHAPTER FOUR: CREATING AN INTERNAL WORLD

1. See, for example, S. I. Greenspan, *Intelligence and Adaptation: An Integration of Psychoanalytic and Piagetian Developmental Psychology* (New York: International Universities Press, 1979); J. Piaget, *The Origins of Intelligence in Children* (New York: International Universities Press, 1952).

2. See S. I. Greenspan, *Developmentally Based Psychotherapy* (Madison, Conn.: International Universities Press, 1996).

3. See S. I. Greenspan, *The Development of the Ego: Implications for Personality Theory, Psychopathology, and the Psychotherapeutic Process* (Madison, Conn.: International Universities Press, 1989).

4. For further discussion of this topic see ibid.; also G. Bower, "Mood and Memory," *American Psychologist* 36 (1981): 129–48.

5. See S. I. Greenspan, *Playground Politics: Understanding the Emotional Life of Your School-Age Child* (Reading, Mass.: Addison-Wesley, 1993).

6. See S. I. Greenspan and G. H. Pollock, eds., *The Course of Life,* 2nd ed., vol. 5: *Adulthood and the Aging Process* (Madison, Conn.: International Universities Press, 1990).

CHAPTER FIVE: ORIGINS OF CONSCIOUSNESS, MORALITY,
AND INTELLIGENCE

1. See B. Russell, *A History of Western Philosophy* (New York: Simon & Schuster, 1945).

2. The attempts to explain the mind strictly in terms of physical phenomena (materialism) have been in sharp conflict with views that claim that physical explanations alone cannot comprehend this distinctly human capacity. The debate, which has occurred throughout history, was highlighted in Descartes's suggestion that the substance and functioning of the mind were different from those of the body. His "dualism" is a relatively weak voice among the various current positions that suggest different versions of a physical explanation for the workings of the mind.

These positions range from general assumptions that physical phenomena underlie all mental phenomena to theories that there are specific neurological mechanisms that eventually will explain each and every mental act. (See, for instance, D. C. Dennett, *The Intentional Stance* [Cambridge, Mass.: MIT Press, 1987]; W. Lyons, *Gilbert Ryle: An Introduction to His Philosophy* [Atlantic Highlands, N.J.: Humanities Press, 1980].) Perhaps the most widespread current position, functionalism, assumes that psychological phenomena such as perception and self-awareness serve as functional intermediaries between physical inputs and outputs. Physical phenomena, however, are thought by many to be responsible for these functional states. In contrast, the modern philosopher Searle focuses on psychological phenomena, such as intentionality, to explain consciousness (see, for instance, J. R. Searle, *The Rediscovery of the Mind* [Cambridge: Cambridge University Press, 1992].)

3. Some neuroscientists and current philosophers who have attempted to explain consciousness in terms of physical phenomena suggest that it is an "emergent property of high order brain activity" (R. W. Sperry, "Consciousness, Personal Identity, and the Divided Brain," in *The Dual Brain: Hemispheric Specialization in Humans*, ed. Frank Benson and Erin Zaidel [Los Angeles: Guilford, 1985], pp. 11–27). Humanistic and depth psychologies have created frameworks that operate at the level of understanding experience rather than material phenomena. Current scientific and philosophical debate, therefore, divides between wondering if phenomena such as emotions are simply epi-phenomena (like the afterglow from a light), direct transformations of biology, understandable only in psychological terms, or simply not comprehensible to the human mind.

The developmental model formulated in this work suggests that materialistic and experiential factors work together in a way that can't be reduced to either one alone. In this model, certain physical properties of the brain make it possible to organize emotional experiences, which in turn further organize additional experiences, and so forth. Neither the physical nor emotional experiences, however, can be completely reduced or explained by the other. For instance, the unique love a mother has for her child is the product of her unique experiences with that child. The emotional organization that embodies that experience is in some respects like no other and in part is explainable only in relationship to that pattern of experience. Hormones that facilitate bonding, for one, can only explain a general tendency common to many caregivers, not the specific, almost infinite variety and textures of a mother's experiences in an intimate relationship with her infant.

While physical aspects of the brain play an important role in storing memories and organizing experiences, the experiences themselves define irreducible aspects of these organizations. What may make the mind unique is its reliance on and emergence from a distinct set of physical operations that help organize an equally distinct set of emotional, developmental experiences—and vice versa.

4. See S. Thomkins, *Affect, Imagery, Consciousness,* vol. 1 (New York: Springer, 1963); C. Izard, "On the Development of Emotions and Emotion-Cognition Relationships in Infancy," in *The Development of Affect,* ed. M. Lewis and L. Rosenblum (New York: Plenum, 1978); P. Ekman, "Universals and Cultural Differences in Facial Expressions of Emotion," in *Nebraska Symposium on Motivation* (Lincoln: University of Nebraska Press, 1972).

5. See W. T. Greenough and J. E. Black, "Induction of Brain Structure by Experience: Substrates for Cognitive Development," *Developmental Behavioral Neuroscience* 24 [1992]: 155–299.

6. J. Field (pseud. Marion Milner), *On Not Being Able to Paint* (1957; rpt. New York: Putnam, 1983), p. 131.

7. For further discussion of these ideas see S. I. Greenspan, *Intelligence and Adaptation: An Integration of Psychoanalytic and Piagetian Developmental Psychology* (New York: International Universities Press, 1979); idem, *The Development of the Ego: Implications for Personality Theory, Psychopathology, and the Psychotherapeutic Process* (Madison, Conn.: International Universities Press, 1989); S. W. Porges, "Emotion: An Evolutionary By-Product of the Neural Regulation of the Autonomic Nervous System," in *The Integrative Neurobiology of Affiliation,* ed. C. S. Carter, B. Kirkpatrick, and I. I. Lederhandler (New York: New York Academy of Sciences, in press); S. W. Porges, J. A. Doussard-Roosevelt, A. L. Portales, and S. I. Greenspan, "Infant Regulation of the Vagal 'Brake' Predicts Child Behavior Problems: A Psychobiological Model of Social Behavior," *Developmental Psychobiology* (in press).

8. Porges et al., "Infant Regulation of the Vagal 'Brake.'"

9. W. B. Cannon, "The Mechanism of Emotional Disturbance of Bodily Functions," *New England Journal of Medicine* 198 (1928): 877–84; idem, "'Voodoo' death," *American Anthropologist* 44 [1957]: 169; S. W. Porges et al., "Infant Regulation of the Vagal 'Brake'"; S. W. Porges, "Emotion."

10. R. N. Emde, Z. Biringen, R. B. Clyman, and D. Oppenheim, "The Moral Self of Infancy: Affective Core and Procedural Knowledge," *Developmental Review* 11 (1991): 251–70.

11. L. Kohlberg, "Development of Moral Character and Moral Ideology," *Review of Child Development Research* 1 (1964): 383–433.

12. Greenspan, *Development of the Ego*; idem, *Infancy and Early Childhood: The Practice of Clinical Assessment and Intervention with Emotional and Developmental Challenges* (Madison, Conn.: International Universities Press, 1992); S. I. Greenspan, S. Wieder, A. Lieberman, R. Nover, R. Lourie, and M. Robinson, *Infants in Multirisk Families: Case Studies in Preventive Intervention* (New York: International Universities Press, 1987).

13. E. E. Werner and R. S. Smith, *Vulnerable but Invincible: A Longitudinal Study of Resilient Children and Youth* (New York: McGraw-Hill, 1982).

14. S. I. Greenspan and S. Wieder, *Facilitating Emotional and Intellectual Growth in Children with Special Needs: The Floor Time Approach* (forthcoming from Addison-Wesley).

15. H. Gardner, *Frames of Mind: The Theory of Multiple Intelligences* (New York: Basic Books, 1983); R. Sternberg, *The Triarchic Mind: A New Theory of Human Intelligence* (New York: Penguin, 1988).

CHAPTER SIX: FITTING NURTURE TO NATURE: THE LOCK
AND THE KEY

1. J. O. Davis, J. A. Phelps, and S. Bracha, "Prenatal Development of Monozygotic Twins and Concordance for Schizophrenia," *Schizophrenia Bulletin* 21 (1995): 357–66.

2. M. J. Raleigh, M. T. McGuire, G. L. Brammer, and A. Yuwiler, "Social and Environmental Influences on Blood Serotonin Concentrations in Monkeys," *Archives of General Psychiatry* 41 (1984): 405–10.

3. See the works of Robert P. Ebstein and his colleagues at Herzog Memorial Hospital in Jerusalem and Jonathan Benjamin and coworkers at the Laboratory of Clinical Science, National Institute of Mental Health, as reported in the January 1996 issue of *Nature Genetics.*

4. C. R. Cloninger, R. Adolfsson, N. M. Svrakic, "Mapping Genes for Human Personality," *Nature Genetics* 12 (1996): 3–4; C. R. Cloninger, N. M.

Svrakic, T. R. Drzybeck, "A Psychobiological Model of Temperament and Character," *Archives of General Psychiatry* 50 (1993): 975–90.

5. S. I. Greenspan, *Infancy and Early Childhood: The Practice of Clinical Assessment and Intervention with Emotional and Developmental Challenges* (Madison, Conn.: International Universities Press, 1992).

6. For the variety of points of view see, for example, E. Avital and E. Jablonka, "Social Learning and the Evolution of Behaviour," *Animal Behaviour* 48 (1994): 1195–99; S. P. R. Rose, "The Rise of Neurogenetic Determinism," *Nature* 373 (1995): 380–82; S. P. R. Rose, R. C. Lewontin, and L. J. Kamin, *Not in Our Genes: Biology, Ideology and Human Nature* (New York: Pantheon, 1984); J. M. R. Delgado, *Physical Control of the Mind: Towards a Psychocivilised Society* (New York: Harper & Row, 1971); E. O. Wilson, *Sociobiology: The New Synthesis* (Cambridge: Harvard University Press, 1975); R. Dawkins, *The Selfish Gene* (Oxford: Oxford University Press, 1976).

7. A. Thomas and S. Chess, "Temperament and Its Functional Significance," in *The Course of Life*, 2nd ed., vol. 2: *Early Childhood*, ed. S. I. Greenspan and G. H. Pollock (Madison, Conn.: International Universities Press, 1989), pp. 163–227.

8. J. Kagan, "Temperament," in *Handbook of Child and Adolescent Psychiatry*, ed. J. D. Noshpitz et al. (New York: Wiley, 1996), in press.

9. S. I. Greenspan, *The Challenging Child: Understanding, Raising, and Enjoying the Five "Difficult" Types of Children* (Reading, Mass.: Addison-Wesley, 1995); idem, *Infancy and Early Childhood: The Practice of Clinical Assessment and Intervention with Emotional and Developmental Challenges* (Madison, Conn.: International Universities Press, 1992); idem, *The Development of the Ego: Implications for Personality Theory, Psychopathology, and the Psychotherapeutic Process* (Madison, Conn.: International Universities Press, 1989); S. I. Greenspan and N. T. Greenspan, *First Feelings: Milestones in the Emotional Development of Your Baby and Child from Birth to Age Four* (New York: Viking Penguin, 1985).

10. See, for example, T. B. Brazelton, "Neonatal Assessment," in *The Course of Life*, 2nd ed., vol. 1: *Infancy*, ed. S. I. Greenspan and G. H. Pollock (Madison, Conn.: International Universities Press, 1989), pp. 393–431.

11. S. I. Greenspan, *Intelligence and Adaptation: An Integration of Psychoanalytic and Piagetian Developmental Psychology* (New York: International Universities Press, 1979); idem, *Infancy and Early Childhood*.

12. Greenspan, *Infancy and Early Childhood*.

13. Greenspan, *The Challenging Child*; idem, *Infancy and Early Childhood*. See also idem, *Development of the Ego*; idem, *Developmentally Based Psychotherapy* (Madison, Conn.: International Universities Press, 1996).

14. J. Bowlby, "Forty-four Juvenile Thieves: Their Characters and Home Life," *International Journal of Psycho-Analysis* 25 (1944): 19–52, 107–27.

15. R. A. Spitz, "Hospitalism: An Inquiry into the Genesis of Psychiatric Conditions in Early Childhood," *Psychoanalytic Study of the Child* 1 (1945): 53–74.

16. J. Bowlby, "Forty-four Juvenile Thieves: Their Characters and Home Life," *International Journal of Psycho-Analysis* 25 (1944): 19–52, 107–27; idem, *Maternal Care and Mental Health* (Geneva: World Health Organization, 1951); idem, *Attachment and Loss,* vols. 1, 3 (New York: Basic Books, 1969, 1979).

17. L. Wynne, S. Matthysse, and R. Cromwell, *The Nature of Schizophrenia: New Approaches to Research and Treatment* (New York: Wiley, 1978); D. D. Jackson, *Etiology of Schizophrenia* (New York: Basic Books, 1960); T. Lidz, *Origin and Treatment of Schizophrenic Disorders* (New York: Basic Books, 1973).

18. L. Wynne et al., *The Nature of Schizophrenia.*

19. W. T. Greenough and J. E. Black, "Induction of Brain Structure by Experience: Substrates for Cognitive Development," in M. Gunnar and C. Nelson (eds.) *Developmental Behavioral Neuroscience* 24 (1992): 155–299; Rose et al., *Not in Our Genes.*

20. Greenspan, *Development of the Ego.*

21. Greenspan, *The Challenging Child;* idem, *Infancy and Early Childhood.*

22. Rose et al., *Not in Our Genes.*

23. M. G. Allen, S. Cohen, W. Pollin, and S. I. Greenspan, "Affective Illness in the NAS-NRC Registry of 15,909 Veteran Twin Pairs," *American Journal of Psychiatry* 131 (1974): 1234–39.

24. The behavioral geneticist Douglas Wahlsten of the University of Alberta has criticized as statistically inadequate all studies of genetic effects on behavior that include fewer than three to four hundred subjects; many include only thirty or forty (meeting of the American Association for the Advancement of Science, Atlanta, Georgia, 1995). Peter Schoenmann, a statistician at Purdue, commented during the same panel that "most of the data on the heritability of behavior should be ignored."

CHAPTER SEVEN: THE DANGER AND THE PROMISE

1. "Infants, Families, and Child Care: Toward a Research Agenda," in *Zero to Three Child Care Anthology,* ed. S. Provence, J. Pawl, and E. Fenichel (Washington, D.C.: ZERO TO THREE: National Center for Infants, Toddlers, and Families, 1992), pp. 138–41; M. Whitebrook, C. Howes, and

D. Phillips, *Who Cares? Child Care Teachers and the Quality of Care in America*, report of the National Child Care Staffing Study (Oakland, Calif.: Child Care Employee Project, 1989); E. Galinsky, C. Howes, S. Kontos, and M. Shinn, *The Study of Children in Family Child Care and Relative Care: Highlights of Findings* (New York: Families and Work Institute, 1994).

2. *Cost, Quality, and Child Outcomes in Child Care Centers,* 2nd ed. (Denver: Department of Economics, University of Colorado at Denver, 1995).

3. Galinsky et al., *The Study of Children.*

4. National Institute of Child Health and Human Development, Early Childcare Network (paper presented at the International Symposium on Infant Studies, Providence, R.I., 1996).

5. B. Willer, S. L. Hofferth, E. Kisker, P. Divine-Hawkins, E. Farquhar, and F. B. Glantz, *The Demand and Supply of Child Care in 1990: Joint Findings from the National Child Care Survey, 1990, and a Profile of Child Care Settings* (Washington, D.C.: National Association for the Education of Young Children, 1991).

6. *Starting Points: Meeting the Needs of Our Youngest Children* (New York: Carnegie Corporation of New York, 1994).

7. J. R. Lally, "The Impact of Child Care Policies and Practices on Infant/Toddler Identity Formation," in *Young Children* (November 1995): 58–67.

CHAPTER EIGHT: MENTAL HEALTH: A DEVELOPMENTAL VIEW

1. D. Goleman, *Emotional Intelligence* (New York: Bantam, 1995).

2. Readers who wish to pursue this topic in greater detail will find technical discussions in S. I. Greenspan, *The Development of the Ego: Implications for Personality Theory, Psychopathology, and the Psychotherapeutic Process* (Madison, Conn.: International Universities Press, 1989); idem, *Developmentally Based Psychotherapy* (Madison, Conn.: International Universities Press, 1996).

3. The material in this chart is discussed in Greenspan, *Developmentally Based Psychotherapy.*

CHAPTER NINE: PEP PILLS, PEP TALKS, AND REAL THERAPEUTIC EXPERIENCES

1. See S. I. Greenspan, *The Development of the Ego: Implications for Personality Theory, Psychopathology, and the Psychotherapeutic Process* (Madison, Conn.: International Universities Press, 1989).

2. For the principles of the developmental approach to therapy, see S. I. Greenspan, *Developmentally Based Psychotherapy* (Madison, Conn.: International Universities Press, 1996).

3. Ibid.

CHAPTER TEN: THE EMOTIONAL FOUNDATIONS OF LEARNING

1. Personal communication with Richard Lodish.

2. M. Konner, *Childhood* (Boston: Little, Brown, 1991), 269–70.

3. R. Brown, *Schools of Thought: How the Politics of Literacy Shape Thinking in the Classroom* (San Francisco: Jossey-Bass, 1993).

4. Material in this and the following sections was presented in S. I. Greenspan and R. Lodish, "School Literacy: The Real ABCs," *Phi Delta Kappan,* December 1991.

5. S. Papert, *Mindstorms: Children, Computers, and Powerful Ideas* (New York: Basic Books, 1982).

6. See, for example, M. F. Shore and J. L. Massimo, "Contributions of an Innovative Psychoanalytic Therapeutic Program with Adolescent Delinquents to Developmental Psychology," in *The Course of Life,* 2nd ed., vol. 4: *Adolescence,* ed. S. I. Greenspan and G. H. Pollock (Madison, Conn.: International Universities Press, 1990), pp. 333–56; idem, "Comprehensive Vocationally Oriented Psychotherapy for Adolescent Delinquent Boys: A Follow-up Study," *American Journal of Orthopsychiatry* 36 (1966): 609–16.

7. Such a program is described in detail in S. I. Greenspan and S. Wieder, *Facilitating Emotional and Intellectual Growth in Children with Special Needs: The Floor Time Approach* (forthcoming from Addison-Wesley). See also S. I. Greenspan, *Infancy and Early Childhood: The Practice of Clinical Assessment and Intervention with Emotional and Developmental Challenges* (Madison, Conn.: International Universities Press, 1992).

8. See, for example, R. Feuerstein (with Y. Rand, M. Hoffman, and R. Miller), *Instrumental Enrichment: An Intervention Program for Cognitive Modifiability* (Baltimore: University Park Press, 1980); H. Gardner, *Frames of Mind: The Theory of Multiple Intelligences* (New York: Basic Books, 1983); J. Comer, *School Power: Implications of an Intervention Project* (New York: Free Press, 1980).

CHAPTER THIRTEEN: VIOLENCE AND DEPRIVATION

1. See, for example, S. Buka and F. Earls, "Early Determinants of Delinquency and Violence," *Health Affairs* 12, no. 4 (1993): 46–64; F. Earls, "A Developmental Approach to Understanding and Controlling Violence," in *Theory and Research in Behavioral Pediatrics,* vol. 5, ed. H. E. Fitzgerald, B. M. Lester, and M. W. Yogman (New York: Plenum, 1991); F. Earls and M. Carlson, "Promoting Human Capability as an Alternative to Early Crime Prevention," in *Integrating Crime Prevention Strategies: Propensity and Opportunity,* ed. P.-O. H. Wikstrom, R. V. Clarke, and J. McCord (Stockholm:

National Council for Crime Prevention, 1995), pp. 141–68; R. Gittelman, S. Mannuzza, R. Shenker, and N. Bonagura, "Hyperactive Boys Almost Grown Up," *Archives of General Psychiatry* 42 (1985): 937–47; B. Henry, T. Moffitt, L. Robins, F. Earls, and P. Silva, "Early Family Predictors of Child and Adolescent Antisocial Behavior: Who Are the Mothers of Delinquents?" *Criminal Behavior and Mental Health* 3 (1993): 97–118; R. Loeber and P.-O. H. Wikstrom, "Individual Pathways to Crime in Different Types of Neighborhood," in *Integrating Individual and Ecological Aspects of Crime,* ed. D. P. Farrington, R. J. Sampson, and P.-O. H. Wikstrom (Stockholm: National Council for Crime Prevention, 1993), pp. 169–204; R. Menzies and C. Webster, "Construction and Validation of Risk Assessments in a Six-Year Follow-up of Forensic Patients: A Tridimensional Analysis," *Journal of Consulting and Clinical Psychology* 63 (1995): 766–78; T. Moffitt, "Adolescence-Limited and Life-Course-Persistent Antisocial Behavior: A Developmental Taxonomy," *Psychological Review* 100 (1993): 674–701; A. Raine, P. Brennan, and S. Mednick, "Birth Complications Combined with Early Maternal Rejection at Age One Year Predispose to Violent Crime at Age Eighteen Years," *Archives of General Psychiatry* 51 (1994): 984–88; M. E. Rice and G. T. Harris, "Violent Recidivism: Assessing Predictive Validity," *Journal of Consulting and Clinical Psychology* 63 (1995): 737–48; R. J. Sampson, "Family and Community-Level Influences on Crime: A Contextual Theory and Strategies for Research Testing," in *Integrating Individual and Ecological Aspects of Crime;* J. L. White, T. Moffitt, F. Earls, and L. N. Robins, "How Early Can We Tell? Predictors of Childhood Conduct Disorder and Adolescent Delinquency," *Criminology* 28 (1990): 507–33.

2. A. J. Sameroff, R. Seifer, R. Barocas, M. Zax, and S. I. Greenspan, "IQ Scores of Four-Year-Old Children: Social-Environmental Risk Factors," *Pediatrics* 79 (1986): 343–50.

3. S. I. Greenspan, E. Greenspan, and S. W. Porges, "Infant/Caregiver Interactions and Cognitive Development in Multirisk Families" (unpublished paper).

4. Sameroff et al., "IQ Scores of Four-Year-Old Children."

5. S. I. Greenspan, S. Wieder, A. Lieberman, R. Nover, R. Lourie, and M. Robinson, *Infants in Multirisk Families: Case Studies in Preventive Intervention* (New York: International Universities Press, 1987).

6. M. F. Shore and J. L. Massimo, "Contributions of an Innovative Psychoanalytic Therapeutic Program with Adolescent Delinquents to Developmental Psychology," in *The Course of Life,* 2nd ed., vol. 4: *Adolescence,* ed. S. I. Greenspan and G. H. Pollock (Madison, Conn.: International Universities Press, 1990), pp. 333–56.

7. S. Provence and A. Naylor, *Working with Disadvantaged Parents and Their Children: Scientific and Practical Issues* (New Haven: Yale University Press, 1983).

8. A. S. Honig and J. R. Lally, *Infant Caregiving: A Design for Training* (Syracuse, N.Y.: Syracuse University Press, 1981).

9. D. L. Olds, "Case Studies of Factors Interfering with Nurse Home Visitors' Promotion of Positive Caregiving Methods in High-Risk Families," *Early Child Development and Care* 16 (1984): 149–66.

10. J. R. Berrueta-Clement, L. J. Schweinhart, W. S. Barnett, A. S. Epstein, and D. P. Weikart, *Changed Lives: The Effects of the Perry Preschool Program on Youths Through Age Nineteen* (Ypsilanti, Mich.: High/ Scope, 1984); C. T. Ramey and F. A. Campbell, "Preventive Education for High-Risk Children: Cognitive Consequences of the Carolina Abecedarian Project," *American Journal of Mental Deficiency* 88 (1984): 515–23.

11. See, for example, J. Brook-Gun, C. McCarton, P. Casey, M. Mc-Cormick, C. Bauer, J. Berbaum, J. Tyson, M. Swanson, F. Bennett, D. Scott, J. Tonascia, and C. Meinert, "Early Intervention in Low-Birth-Weight Premature Infants: Results Through Age Five Years from the Infant Health and Development Program," *Journal of the American Medical Association* 272 (1994): 1257–62; Infant Health and Development Program, "Enhancing the Outcomes of Low-Birth-Weight, Premature Infants," *Journal of the American Medical Association* 263, no. 22 (1990): 3035–42; C. T. Ramey and S. L. Ramey, "At Risk Does Not Mean Doomed," National Health/ Education Consortium, occasional paper no. 4 (1992): 1–16; L. J. Schweinhart and D. P. Weikart, "The Effects of the Perry Preschool Program on Youth Through Age Fifteen—A Summary," in *As the Twig Is Bent* . . . (Hillsdale, N.J.: Erlbaum, 1983); S. J. Styfco and E. Zigler, "Using Research and Theory to Justify and Inform Head Start Expansion," *Social Policy Report* 7, no. 2 (1993): 1–20.

12. A. Stallibrass, "Child Development and Education—The Contribution of the Peckham Experiment," *Nutrition and Health* 1 (1982): 45–52; idem, *The Peckham Experience: A Hope for a Healthier Future* (London: Pioneer Health Centre, Ltd., 1984); I. H. Pearse, *The Quality of Life: The Peckham Approach to Human Ethology* (Edinburgh: Scottish Academic Press, 1979); K. Barlow, *Recognizing Health* (London: Privately published, 1988).

13. L. Schorr, *Within Our Reach: Breaking the Cycle of Disadvantage* (New York: Anchor, 1988).

14. K. R. White and S. I. Greenspan, "An Overview of the Effectiveness of Preventive Early Intervention Programs," in *Basic Handbook of Child Psychiatry*, ed. J. D. Noshpitz et al. (New York: Basic Books, 1987); idem,

"Conducting Research with Preventive Early Intervention Programs," *Basic Handbook of Child Psychiatry.*

15. Participants besides myself were Kathryn E. Barnard, University of Washington; T. Berry Brazelton, Children's Hospital Medical Center, Boston; Urie Bronfenbrenner, Cornell University; Eugene Garcia, University of California, Santa Cruz; Irving B. Harris, Ounce of Prevention Fund, Chicago; Asa G. Hilliard, Georgia State University; Sheila Walker, University of Indiana; and Barry Zuckerman, Boston City Hospital. For more information about this 1993 conference organized by the author, please contact: Interdisciplinary Council for Developmental and Learning Disorders, c/o Laura Weber, 7607 Exeter Road, Bethesda, MD 20814.

16. *Cost, Quality, and Child Outcomes in Child Care Centers,* 2nd ed. (Denver: Economics Department, University of Colorado at Denver, 1995).

17. Ibid.

18. For background on the program see S. I. Greenspan, S. Wieder, A. Lieberman, R. Nover, R. Lourie, and M. Robinson, *Infants in Multirisk Families: Case Studies in Preventive Intervention* (New York: International Universities Press, 1987); S. Wieder, S. Poisson, R. Lourie, and S. Greenspan, "Enduring Gains: A Five-Year Follow-up Report on the Clinical Infant Development Program," *ZERO TO THREE: Bulletin of the National Center for Clinical Infant Programs* 8, no. 4 (1988): 6–12.

19. D. W. Winnicott, *The Child, the Family, and the Outside World* (Reading, Mass.: Addison-Wesley, 1987).

CHAPTER FOURTEEN: TOWARD A REFLECTIVE SOCIETY

1. See, for example, P. Turquet, "Threats to Identity in the Large Group: A Study in the Phenomenology of the Individual's Experiences of Changing Membership Status in a Large Group," in *The Large Group: Dynamics and Therapy,* ed. L. Kreeger (London: Constable, 1975), pp. 87–158.

2. S. I. Greenspan, *The Development of the Ego: Implications for Personality Theory, Psychopathology, and the Psychotherapeutic Process* (Madison, Conn.: International Universities Press, 1989).

3. J. Fallows, *Breaking the News: How the Media Undermines American Democracy* (New York: Pantheon, 1996).

4. Group for the Advancement of Psychiatry, *Us and Them: The Psychology of Ethnonationalism.* (New York: Brunner/Mazel, 1987).

CHAPTER FIFTEEN: OUR HUMAN IMPERATIVE

1. For further discussion of this subject see R. Loeber and P.-O. H. Wikstrom, "Individual Pathways to Crime in Different Types of Neigh-

borhood," in *Integrating Individual and Ecological Aspects of Crime,* ed. D. P. Farrington, R. J. Sampson, and P.-O. H. Wikstrom (Stockholm: National Council for Crime Prevention, 1993), pp. 169–204; T. Moffitt, "Adolescence-Limited and Life-Course-Persistent Antisocial Behavior: A Developmental Taxonomy," *Psychological Review* 100 (1993): 674–701; R. J. Sampson, "Family and Community-Level Influences on Crime: A Contextual Theory and Strategies for Research Testing," in *Integrating Individual and Ecological Aspects of Crime.*

2. For a description of the floor-time philosophy and tactics to foster interactive learning see S. I. Greenspan, *Infancy and Early Childhood: The Practice of Clinical Assessment and Intervention with Emotional and Developmental Challenges* (Madison, Conn.: International Universities Press, 1992); S. I. Greenspan and N. T. Greenspan, *First Feelings: Milestones in the Emotional Development of Your Baby and Child from Birth to Age Four* (New York: Viking Penguin, 1985); S. I. Greenspan, *Playground Politics: Understanding the Emotional Life of Your School-Age Child* (Reading, Mass.: Addison-Wesley, 1993); idem, *The Challenging Child: Understanding, Raising, and Enjoying the Five "Difficult" Types of Children* (Reading, Mass.: Addison-Wesley, 1995).

3. R. S. McNamara, *In Retrospect: The Tragedy and Lessons of Vietnam* (New York: Vintage, 1996).

Further Sources

DEVELOPMENTAL STAGES

Erikson, E. H. *Childhood and Society,* rev. ed. New York: W. W. Norton, 1963.

Freud, A. "Normality and Pathology in Childhood." In *The Writings.* Vol. 6. Madison, Conn.: International Universities Press, 1965.

Freud, S. *Formulations on the Two Principles of Mental Functioning.* London: Hogarth Press, 1958.

Greenspan, S. I. *Intelligence and Adaptation: An Integration of Psychoanalytic and Piagetian Developmental Psychology.* New York: International Universities Press, 1979.

———. *Development of the Ego: Implications for Personality Theory, Psychopathology, and the Psychotherapeutic Process.* Madison, Conn.: International Universities Press, 1989.

Mahler, M. S., F. Pine, and A. Bergman. *The Psychological Birth of the Human Infant: Symbiosis and Individuation.* New York: Basic Books, 1975.

Piaget, J. *The Origins of Intelligence in Children.* New York: International Universities Press, 1952.

SELF REGULATION AND INTEREST IN THE WORLD

Berlyne, D. E. *Conflict, Arousal, and Curiosity.* New York: McGraw-Hill, 1960.

Deci, E. *Intrinsic Motivation.* New York: Plenum, 1977.

DeGangi, G., and S. I. Greenspan. "The Development of Sensory Functioning in Infants." In *Journal of Physical and Occupational Therapy in Pediatrics* 3 (1988).

———. "The Assessment of Sensory Functioning in Infants." *Journal of Physical and Occupational Therapy in Pediatrics* 9 (1989): 21–33.

————. *Test of Sensory Functions in Infants.* Los Angeles: Western Psychology Services, 1989.

Gewirtz, J. L. "The Course of Infant Smiling in Four Child-Rearing Environments in Israel." In *Determinants of Infant Behavior,* vol. 1, edited by B. M. Boss. London: Methuen, 1965.

————. "Levels of Conceptual Analysis in Environment-Infant Interaction Research." *Merrill-Palmer Quarterly* 15 (1969): 9–47.

Greenspan, S. I. *Infancy and Early Childhood: The Practice of Clinical Assessment and Intervention with Emotional and Developmental Challenges.* Madison, Conn.: International Universities Press, 1992.

Harlow, H. F. "Motivation as a Factor in the Acquisition of New Responses." *Nebraska Symposium on Motivation* 1 (1953): 24–29.

Hendrick, I. *Facts and Theories of Psychoanalysis,* 2nd ed. New York: Knopf, 1939.

Hunt, J. McV. "Intrinsic Motivation and Its Role in Psychological Development." In *Nebraska Symposium on Motivation,* edited by D. Levine. Lincoln: University of Nebraska Press, 1965.

Klaus, M., J. Kennell, and P. H. Klaus. *Bonding.* Reading, Mass.: Addison-Wesley, 1995.

Lipsitt, L. "Learning Processes of Newborns." *Merrill-Palmer Quarterly* 12 (1966): 45–71.

Meltzoff, A., and K. Moore. "Imitation of Facial and Manual Gestures by Human Neonates." *Science* 198 (1977): 75–78.

Sander, L. "Issues in Early Mother-Child Interaction." *Journal of the American Academy of Child Psychiatry* 1 (1962): 141–66.

White, R. W. *Ego and Reality on Psychoanalytic Theory.* New York: International Universities Press, 1963.

ENGAGEMENT, RELATIONSHIPS, AND AFFECTS

Ainsworth, M., S. M. Bell, and D. Stayton. "Infant-Mother Attachment and Social Development: Socialization as a Product of Reciprocal Responsiveness to Signals." In *The Integration of the Child into a Social World,* edited by M. Richards. Cambridge: Cambridge University Press, 1974.

Bates, J. E., L. A. Maslin, and K. A. Frankel. "Attachment, Security, Mother-Child Interaction, and Temperament as Predictors of Problem Behavior Ratings at Age Three Years." *Growing Points in Attachment Theory and Research: Monographs of the Society for Research in Child Development* 50, no. 1–2 (1985): 167–93.

Belsky, J., M. Rovine, and D. G. Taylor. "The Pennsylvania Infant and Family Development Project, III: The Origins of Individual Differences in

Infant-Mother Attachment: Maternal and Infant Contributions." *Child Development* 55 (1984): 718–28.

Brazelton, T. B., B. Koslowski, and N. Main. "The Origins of Reciprocity: The Early Mother-Infant Interaction." In *The Effect of the Infant on Its Caregiver,* edited by M. Lewis and L. Rosenblum. New York: Wiley, 1974.

Butterworth, G., and N. Jarrett. "The Geometry of Preverbal Communication." Paper presented to the Annual Conference of the Developmental Psychology Section of the British Psychological Society, Edinburgh, September 1980.

Egeland, B., and E. A. Farber. "Infant-Mother Attachment: Factors Related to Its Development and Change over Time." *Child Development* 52 (1984): 857–65.

Emde, R. N., T. J. Gaensbauer, and R. J. Harmon. *Emotional Expression in Infancy: A Biobehavioral Study.* New York: International Universities Press, 1976.

Escalona, S. *The Roots of Individuality.* Chicago: Aldine, 1968.

Grossmann, K., K. E. Grossmann, G. Spangler, G. Suess, and L. Unzner. "Maternal Sensitivity and Newborns' Orientation Responses as Related to Quality of Attachment in Northern Germany." *Growing Points in Attachment Theory and Research: Monographs of the Society for Research in Child Development* 50, no. 1–2 (1985): 233–56.

Lewis, M., and M. Feiring. "Infant, Maternal and Mother-Infant Interaction Behavior and Subsequent Attachment." *Child Development* 60 (1987): 831–37.

Meltzoff, A. N. "The Roots of Social and Cognitive Development: Models of Man's Original Nature." In *Social Perception in Infants,* edited by T. M. Field and N. A. Fox. Norwood, N.J.: Ablex, 1985.

Miyake, K., S. Chen, and J. J. Campos. "Infant Temperament, Mother's Mode of Interaction, and Attachment in Japan: An Interim Report." *Growing Points in Attachment Theory and Research: Monographs of the Society for Research in Child Development* 50, no. 1–2 (1985): 276–97.

Murphy, L., and A. Moriarity. *Vulnerability, Coping, and Growth.* New Haven, Conn.: Yale University Press, 1976.

Papousek, H. "The Common in the Uncommon Child." In *The Uncommon Child,* edited by M. Lewis and L. Rosenblum. New York: Plenum, 1981.

Papousek, H., and M. Papousek. "Early Ontogeny of Human Social Interaction: Its Biological Roots and Social Dimensions." In *Human Ethnology: Claims and Limits of a New Discipline,* edited by K. Foppa, W. Lepenies, and D. Ploog. New York: Cambridge University Press, 1979.

Pederson, D. R., G. Moran, C. Sitko, K. Campbell, K. Ghesquire, and H. Acton. "Maternal Sensitivity and the Security of Infant-Mother Attachment: A Q-Sort Study." *Child Development* 61 (1990): 1974–83.

Sander, L. "Issues in Early Mother-Child Interaction." *Journal of the American Academy of Child Psychiatry* 1 (1962): 141–66.

Scaife, M., and J. S. Bruner. "The Capacity for Joint Visual Attention in the Infant." *Nature* 253 (1975): 265–66.

Sroufe, L. A., E. Waters, and L. Matas. "Contextual Determinants of Infant Affective Response." In *The Origins of Fear,* edited by M. Lewis and L. Rosenblum. New York: Wiley, 1974.

Stern, D. "Mother and Infant at Play: The Dyadic Interaction Involving Facial, Vocal, and Gaze Behaviors." In *The Effect of the Infant on Its Caregiver,* edited by M. Lewis and L. Rosenblum. New York: Wiley, 1974.

———. "The Goal and Structure of Mother-Infant Play." *Journal of the American Academy of Child Psychiatry* 13 (1974): 402–21.

———. *The Interpersonal World of the Infant: A View from Psychoanalysis and Developmental Psychology.* New York: Basic Books, 1985.

INTENTIONALITY AND SELF AND BOUNDARY FORMATION

Brazelton, T. B., and H. Als. "Four Early Stages in the Development of Mother-Infant Interaction." *Psychoanalytic Study of the Child* 34 (1979): 349–69.

Brazelton, T. B., and B. Cramer. *The Earliest Relationship: Parents, Infants, and the Drama of Early Attachment.* Reading, Mass.: Addison-Wesley, 1990.

Brazelton, T. B., B. Koslowski, and N. Main. "The Origins of Reciprocity: The Early Mother-Infant Interaction." In *The Effect of the Infant on Its Caregiver,* edited by M. Lewis and L. Rosenblum. New York: Wiley, 1974.

Bowlby, J. *Attachment and Loss.* Vol. 2, *Separation, Anxiety, and Anger.* New York: Basic Books, 1973.

Bruner, J. *Child's Talk: Learning to Use Language.* New York: W. W. Norton, 1982.

Campos, J. J., K. C. Barrett, M. E. Lamb, H. H. Goldsmith, and C. Stenberg. "Socioemotional Development." In *Handbook of Child Psychology.* Vol. 2, *Infancy and Developmental Psychobiology,* edited by M. M. Haith and J. J. Campos. New York: Wiley, 1983.

Charlesworth, W. R. "The Role of Surprise in Cognitive Development." In *Studies in Cognitive Development: Essays in Honor of Jean Piaget,* edited by D. Elkind and J. H. Flavell. London: Oxford University Press, 1969.

Darwin, C. *The Expression of Emotions in Man and Animals.* Chicago: University of Chicago Press, 1965. (Originally published London: Murray, 1872.)

Ekman, P., W. Freisen, and P. Ellsworth. *Emotion in the Human Face.* New York: Pergamon Press, 1972.

Feinman, S., and M. Lewis. "Social Referencing at Ten Months: A Second-Order Effect on Infant's Responses to Strangers." *Child Development* 54, no. 4 (1983): 878–87.

Izard, C. E. *The Face of Emotion.* New York: Meredith & Appleton-Century-Crofts, 1971.

Kaye, K. *The Mental and Social Life of Babies: How Parents Create Persons.* Chicago: University of Chicago Press, 1982.

Kimmert, M. D., J. J. Campos, F. J. Sorce, R. N. Emde, and M. J. Svejda. "Social Referencing: Emotional Expressions as Behavior Regulators." In *Emotion: Theory, Research, and Experience.* Vol. 2, *Emotions in Early Development,* edited by R. Plutchik and H. Kellerman. Orlando: Academic Press, 1983.

Kleinman, A. *Social Origins of Distress and Disease.* New Haven, Conn.: Yale University Press, 1986.

Mahler, M. S., F. Pine, and A. Bergman. *The Psychological Birth of the Human Infant: Symbiosis and Individuation.* New York: Basic Books, 1975.

Markus, H., and Kitayama, S. "Culture and the Self: Implications for Cognition, Emotion, and Motivation." Unpublished paper, 1990.

Osofsky, J. D., and A. Eberhart-Wright. "Affective Exchanges Between High Risk Mothers and Infants." *International Journal of Psychoanalysis* 69 (1988): 221–32.

Schweder, R., M. Mahapatra, and J. Miller. "Cultural and Moral Development." In *The Emergence of Morality in Young Children,* edited by J. Kagan and S. Lamb. Chicago: University of Chicago Press, 1987.

Spitz, R. A. *The First Year of Life: A Psychoanalytic Study of Normal and Deviant Development of Object Relations.* New York: International Universities Press, 1965.

Stern, D. "Mother and Infant at Play: The Dyadic Interaction Involving Facial, Vocal and Gaze Behaviors." In *The Effect of the Infant on Its Caregiver,* edited by M. Lewis and L. Rosenblum. New York: Wiley, 1974.

———. *The First Relationship: Mother and Infant.* Cambridge, Mass.: Harvard University Press, 1977.

———. *The Interpersonal World of the Infant: A View from Psychoanalysis and Developmental Psychology.* New York: Basic Books, 1985.

Tennes, K., R. Emde, A. Kisley, and D. Metcalf. "The Stimulus Barrier in Early Infancy: An Exploration of Some Formulations of John Benjamin." In *Psychoanalysis and Contemporary Science,* vol. 1, edited by R. Hold and E. Peterfreund. New York: Macmillan, 1972.

Trevarthen, C. "Communication and Cooperation in Early Infancy: A Description of Primary Intersubjectivity." In *Before Speech: The Beginning of Interpersonal Communication,* edited by M. Bullowa. Cambridge: Cambridge University Press, 1979.

Tronick, E. "The Primacy of Social Skills in Infancy." In *Exceptional Infant,* vol. 4, edited by D. B. Sawin, R. C. Hawkins, L. O. Walker, and J. H. Penticuff. New York: Brunner/Mazel, 1980.

Winnicott, D. O. "Ego Distortion in Terms of True and False Self." In *The Maturational Processes and the Facilitating Environment.* New York: International Universities Press, 1965.

BEHAVIORAL AND AFFECTIVE PATTERNS:
THE PRESYMBOLIC SELF

Ainsworth, M., S. M. Bell, and D. Stayton. "Infant-Mother Attachment and Social Development: Socialization as a Product of Reciprocal Responsiveness to Signals." In *The Integration of the Child into a Social World,* edited by M. Richards. Cambridge: Cambridge University Press, 1974.

Ainsworth, M. D. S., M. C. Blehar, E. Waters, and S. Wall. *Patterns of Attachment: A Psychological Study of the Strange Situation.* Hillsdale, N.J.: Erlbaum, 1978.

Bowlby, J. *Attachment and Loss.* Vol. 2, *Attachment.* New York: Basic Books, 1969.

Dunn, J. *The Beginnings of Social Understanding.* Cambridge, Mass.: Harvard University Press, 1988.

Emde, R. N., W. F. Johnson, and M. A. Easterbrooks. "The Do's and Don'ts of Early Moral Development: Psychoanalytic Tradition and Current Research." In *The Emergence of Morality,* edited by J. Kagan and S. Lamb. Chicago: University of Chicago Press, 1988.

Kagan, J. *The Second Year: The Emergence of Self-Awareness.* Cambridge, Mass.: Harvard University Press, 1981.

Mahler, M. S., F. Pine, and A. Bergman. *The Psychological Birth of the Human Infant: Symbiosis and Individuation.* New York: Basic Books, 1975.

Piaget, J. "The Stages of the Intellectual Development of the Child." In *Childhood Psychopathology,* edited by S. Harrison and J. McDermott. New York: International Universities Press, 1962.

Radke-Yarrow, M., C. Zahn-Waxler, and M. Chapman. "Children's Prosocial Dispositions and Behavior." In *Handbook of Child Psychology.* Vol. 4, *Socialization, Personality, and Social Development,* 4th ed., edited by E. M. Hetherington and P. H. Mussen. New York: Wiley, 1983.

Sroufe, L. A., and E. Waters. "Attachment as an Organizational Construct." *Child Development* 48 (1977): 1184–99.

Werner, H., and B. Kaplan. *Symbol Formation.* New York: Wiley, 1963.

Zahn-Waxler, C., and M. Radke-Yarrow. "The Development of Altruism: Alternative Research Strategies." In *The Development of Prosocial Behavior,* edited by N. Eisenberg. New York: Academic Press, 1982.

REPRESENTING EXPERIENCE AND SHARING MEANINGS

Aber, J. L., and A. J. Baker. "Security of Attachment in Toddlerhood: Modifying Assessment Procedures for Joint Clinical and Research Purposes." In *Attachment in the Preschool Years,* edited by M. T. Greenberg, D. Cicchetti, and E. M. Cummings. Chicago: University of Chicago Press, 1990.

Arend, R., F. Gove, and L. A. Sroufe. "Continuity of Individual Adaptation from Infancy to Kindergarten: A Predictive Study of Ego-Resiliency and Curiosity in Pre-Schoolers." *Child Development* 50 (1979): 950–59.

Bell, S. "The Development of the Concept of Object as Related to Infant-Mother Attachment." *Child Development* 41 (1970): 219–311.

Bretherton, I., and M. Beeghly. "Talking about Inner States: The Acquisition of an Explicit Theory of Mind." *Developmental Psychology* 18 (1982): 906–21.

Cassidy, J. "Theoretical and Methodological Considerations in the Study of Attachment and Self in Young Children." In *Attachment in the Preschool Years,* edited by M. T. Greenberg, D. Cicchetti, and E. M. Cummings. Chicago: University of Chicago Press, 1990.

Cassidy, J., and R. Marvin, with the Attachment Working Group of the John D. and Catherine T. MacArthur Network on the Transition from Infancy to Early Childhood. "A System for Coding the Organization of Attachment Behavior in Three- and Four-Year-Old Children." Paper presented at the International Conference on Infant Studies, Washington, D.C., April 1988.

Dore, J. "Monologue as Reenvoicement of Dialogue." In *Narratives from the Crib,* edited by K. Nelson. Cambridge, Mass.: Harvard University Press, 1989.

Dunn, J. *The Beginnings of Social Understanding.* Cambridge, Mass.: Harvard University Press, 1988.

Dunn, J., I. Bretherton, and P. Munn. "Conversations about Feelings States Between Mothers and Their Young Children." In *Symbolic Play: The Development of Social Understanding,* edited by I. Bretherton. New York: Academic Press, 1987.

Easterbrooks, M. A., and W. A. Goldberg. "Security of Toddler-Parent Attachment: Relation to Children's Sociopersonality Functioning During Kindergarten." In *Attachment in the Preschool Years,* edited by M. T. Greenberg, D. Cicchetti, and E. M. Cummings. Chicago: University of Chicago Press, 1990.

Egeland, B., and E. A. Farber. "Infant-Mother Attachment: Factors Related to Its Development and Change over Time." *Child Development* 52 (1984): 857–65.

Erikson, E. H. "Studies in Interpretation of Play: I. Clinical Observation of Child Disruption in Young Children." *Genetic Psychology, Monographs* 22 (1940): 557–671.

Fein, G. "A Transformational Analysis of Pretending." *Developmental Psychology* 11 (1975): 291–96.

Fein, G. G., and N. Apfel. "Some Preliminary Observations on Knowing and Pretending." In *Symbolic Functioning in Childhood,* edited by N. Smith and M. Franklin. Hillsdale, N.J.: Erlbaum, 1979.

Fenson, L., and D. Ramsay. "Decentration and Integration of Play in the Second Year of Life." *Child Development* 51 (1980): 171–78.

Fenson, L., J. Kagan, R. B. Kearsely, and P. R. Zelazo. "The Developmental Progression of Manipulative Play in the First Two Years." *Child Development* 47 (1976): 232–35.

Gourin-Decarie, T. *Intelligence and Affectivity in Early Childhood: An Experimental Study of Jean Piaget's Object Concept and Object Relations.* New York: International Universities Press, 1965.

Goldberg, W. A., and M. A. Easterbrooks. "Toddler Development in the Family: Impact of Father Involvement and Parenting Characteristics." *Developmental Psychology* 55 (1984): 740–52.

Inhelder, B., I. Lezine, H. Sinclair, and M. Stambak. "Le Debut de la Function Symbolique." *Archives de Psychologie* 41 (1972): 187–243. (As cited in K. H. Rubin, G. G. Fein, and B. Vandenberg, "Play," in *Handbook of Child Psychology.* Vol. 4, *Socialization, Personality, and Social Development,* 4th ed., edited by E. M. Hetherington and P. H. Mussen. New York: Wiley, 1983.)

Kraus, R., and S. Glucksberg. "The Development of Communication: Competence as a Function of Age." *Child Development* 40 (1969): 255–66.

Lowe, M. "Trends in the Development of Representational Play: An Observational Study." *Journal of Child Psychology and Psychiatry* 16 (1975): 33–47.

Main, M., N. Kaplan, and J. Cassidy. "Security in Infancy, Childhood, and Adulthood: A Move to the Level of Representation." *Monographs of the Society for Research in Child Development* 50 (1985): 66–104.

Marvin, R., and R. B. Stewart. "A Family Systems Framework for the Study of Attachment." In *Attachment in the Preschool Years,* edited by M. T. Greenberg, D. Cicchetti, and E. M. Cummings. Chicago: University of Chicago Press, 1990.

Maslin-Cole, C., and S. J. Spieker. "Attachment as a Basis of Independent Motivation: A View from Risk and Nonrisk Samples." In *Attachment in the Preschool Years,* edited by M. T. Greenberg, D. Cicchetti, and E. M. Cummings. Chicago: University of Chicago Press, 1990.

Matas, L., R. A. Arend, and L. A. Sroufe. "Continuity of Adaptation in the Second Year: The Relationship Between Quality of Attachment and Later Competence." *Child Development* 49 (1978): 547–56.

McCune-Nicholich, L. "Beyond Sensorimotor Intelligence: Measurement of Symbolic Sensitivity Through Analysis of Pretend Play." *Merrill-Palmer Quarterly* 23 (1977): 89–99.

Nelson, K. "Structure and Strategy in Learning to Talk." *Monographs of the Society for Research in Child Development* 38, no. 1–2 (1973).

———. "Monologue as Representation of Real-Life Experience." In *Narratives from the Crib,* edited by K. Nelson. Cambridge, Mass.: Harvard University Press, 1989.

Nelson, K., and J. M. Gruendel. "Generalized Even Representations: Basic Building Blocks of Cognitive Development." In *Advances in Developmental Psychology,* vol. 1, edited by A. Brown and M. Lamb. Hillsdale, N.J.: Erlbaum, 1981.

Pastor, D. "The Quality of Mother-Infant Attachment and Its Relationship to Toddlers' Initial Sociability with Peers." *Developmental Psychology* 23 (1981): 326–35.

Peller, L. "Libidinal Phases, Ego Development, and Play." *The Psychoanalytic Study of the Child* 9 (1954): 178–98.

Piaget, J. *The Origins of Intelligence in Children.* New York: International Universities Press, 1952.

Pipp, S., K. W. Fischer, and S. Jennings. "Acquisition of Self-and-Mother Knowledge in Infancy." *Developmental Psychology* 23, no. 1 (1987): 86–96.

Rubin, K. H., G. G. Fein, and B. Vandenberg. "Play." In *Handbook of Child Psychology.* Vol. 4, *Socialization, Personality, and Social Development,* 4th ed., edited by E. M. Hetherington and P. H. Mussen. New York: Wiley, 1983.

Schank, R. C., and R. P. Abelson. *Scripts, Plans, Goals, and Understanding.* Hillsdale, N.J.: Erlbaum, 1977.

Sinclair, H. "The Transition from Sensorimotor to Symbolic Activity." *Interchange* 1 (1970): 119–26.

Sroufe, L. A. "Infant-Caregiver Attachment and Patterns of Adaptation in Preschool: The Roots of Maladaptation and Competence." In *Minnesota Symposium on Child Psychology,* vol. 16, edited by M. Perlmutter. Hillsdale, N.J.: Erlbaum, 1983.

Sroufe, L. A., N. E. Fox, and V. Pancake. "Attachment and Dependency in Developmental Perspective." *Child Development* 54 (1983): 1615–27.

Waelder, R. "The Psychoanalytic Theory of Play." *Psychoanalysis Quarterly* 2 (1933): 208–24.

Waters, E., J. Wippman, and L. A. Sroufe. "Attachment, Positive Affect, and Competence in the Peer Group: Two Studies in Construct Validation." *Child Development* 50 (1979): 821–29.

EMOTIONAL THINKING

Bruner, J. *Actual Minds, Possible Worlds.* Cambridge, Mass.: Harvard University Press, 1986.

———. *Acts of Meaning.* Cambridge, Mass.: Harvard University Press, 1990.

Buchsbaum, H. K., and R. N. Emde. "Play Narratives in Thirty-Six-Month-Old Children." *Psychoanalytic Study of the Child* 45 (1990): 129–55.

Donaldson, S., and M. Westerman. "Development of Children's Understanding of Ambivalence and Causal Theories of Emotions." *Developmental Psychology* 22 (1986): 655–62.

Dunn, J., and C. Kendrick. *Siblings.* Cambridge, Mass.: Harvard University Press, 1982.

Emde, R. N., and H. Buchsbaum. "'Didn't You Hear My Mommy?': Autonomy with Connectedness in Moral Self-Emergence." In *The Self in Transition: Infancy to Childhood,* edited by D. Cicchetti and M. Beeghly. Chicago: University of Chicago Press, 1990.

Fivush, R., "Gender and Emotion in Mother-Child Conversations about the Past." *Journal of Narrative and Life History* 1, no. 4 (1991): 325–41.

Flavell, J. H., F. L. Green, and E. R. Flavell. "Development of Knowledge about the Appearance-Reality Distinction: With Commentaries by M. W. Watson and J. C. Campione." *Monographs of the Society for Research in Child Development* 51, no. 1 (1986).

Gilligan, C. *In a Different Voice: Psychological Theory and Women's Development.* Cambridge, Mass.: Harvard University Press, 1982.

Greenspan, S. I. *Intelligence and Adaptation: An Integration of Psychoanalytic and Piagetian Developmental Psychology.* New York: International Universities Press, 1979.

————. *Playground Politics: Understanding the Emotional Life of Your School-Age Child.* Reading, Mass.: Addison-Wesley, 1993.

Harris, P. L. *Children and Emotion.* Oxford: Basil Blackwell, 1989.

Harris, P. L., E. Brown, C. Marriott, S. Whittall, and S. Harmer. "Monsters, Ghosts, and Witches: Testing the Limits of the Fantasy-Reality Distinction in Young Children." *British Journal of Developmental Psychology* 9 (1991): 105–23.

Harris, P. L., and R. Kavanaugh. "Young Children's Understanding of Pretense." *Monographs of the Society for Research in Child Development* 58, no. 1 (1993).

Hendrick, I. *Facts and Theories of Psychoanalysis,* 2nd ed. New York: Knopf, 1939.

Harter, S., and N. Whitesell. "Developmental Changes in Children's Emotion Concepts." In *Children's Understanding of Emotion,* edited by C. Saarni and P. L. Harris. New York: Cambridge University Press, 1989.

Mahler, M. S., F. Pine, and A. Bergman. *The Psychological Birth of the Human Infant: Symbiosis and Individuation.* New York: Basic Books, 1975.

Nelson, K. *Even Knowledge: Structure and Function in Development.* Hillsdale, N.J.: Erlbaum, 1986.

Nelson, K. "Monologue as Representation of Real-Life Experience." In *Narratives from the Crib,* edited by K. Nelson. Cambridge, Mass.: Harvard University Press, 1989.

Reiss, D. "The Represented and Practicing Family: Contrasting Visions of Family Continuity." In *Relationship Disturbances in Early Childhood: A Developmental Approach,* edited by A. J. Sameroff and R. N. Emde. New York: Basic Books, 1989.

Singer, D. G., and J. L. Singer. *The House of Make-Believe: Children's Play and Developing Imagination.* Cambridge, Mass.: Harvard University Press, 1990.

Smetana, J. "Preschool Children's Conceptions of Transgressions: Effects of Varying Moral and Conventional Domain-Related Attributes." *Developmental Psychology* 21 (1985): 18–29.

Stewart, R. B., and R. S. Marvin. "Sibling Relations: The Role of Conceptual Perspective-Taking in the Ontogeny of Sibling Caregiving." *Child Development* 55 (1984): 1322–32.

Wolf, D. P. "Being of Several Minds." In *The Self in Transition: Infancy to Childhood,* edited by D. Cicchetti and M. Beeghly. Chicago: University of Chicago Press, 1990.

——. "Narrative Worlds: The Acts of Forming and Attending to Meaning." In *Affective Processes,* edited by D. Brown. Psychoanalytic Press, in press.

Wolf, D. P., J. Rygh, and J. Altshuler. "Agency and Experience: Actions and States in Play Narratives." In *Symbolic Play,* edited by I. Bretherton. Orlando: Academic Press, 1984.

Wooley, J. D., and H. M. Wellman. "Young Children's Understanding of Realities, Nonrealities, and Appearances." *Child Development* 61, no. 4 (1990): 946–61.

Zahn-Waxler, C., J. L. Robinson, and R. N. Emde. "The Development of Empathy in Twins." *Developmental Psychology* 28, no. 6 (1992): 1038–47.

Index

About the Authors

STANLEY I. GREENSPAN, M.D., is Clinical Professor of Psychiatry, Behavioral Sciences, and Pediatrics at the George Washington University Medical School and a practicing child psychiatrist. A supervising child psychoanalyst at the Washington Psychoanalytic Institute in Washington, D.C., he was previously chief of the Mental Health Study Center and director of the Clinical Infant Developmental Program at the National Institute of Mental Health. Among his many national honors and awards are the Edward A. Strecker Award for Outstanding Contributions to American Psychiatry, the American Psychiatric Association's Ittleson Prize for Outstanding Contributions to Child Psychiatry Research, and the Heinz Hartmann Prize for contributions to psychoanalysis.

A founder and former president of ZERO TO THREE: The National Center for Infants, Toddlers, and Families, Dr. Greenspan is the author of more than one hundred scholarly articles and chapters and is the author or editor of twenty-seven books for both scholarly and general audiences. These include *Infancy and Early Childhood, Developmentally Based Psychotherapy, Intelligence and Adaptation: An Integration of Psychoanalytic and Piagetian Developmental Psychology, The Development of the Ego, First Feelings* (with Nancy Thorndike Greenspan), and *Playground Politics* and *The Challenging Child* (both with Jacqueline Salmon).

BERYL LIEFF BENDERLY is the author of several books, including *Dancing Without Music: Deafness in America* and *The Myth of Two Minds: What Gender Means and Doesn't Mean*. She has been awarded the National Psychology Award for Excellence in Media and twice has been a Fellow of the Knight Center for Specialized Journalism. A frequent contributor to magazines and newspapers, she lives in Washington, D.C.